RAINY LAKE HOUSE

RAINY LAKE HOUSE

Twilight of Empire on the Northern Frontier

Theodore Catton

JOHNS HOPKINS UNIVERSITY PRESS   *Baltimore*

Johns Hopkins University Press
2715 North Charles Street
Baltimore, Maryland 21218-4363
www.press.jhu.edu

Library of Congress Cataloging-in-Publication Data

Names: Catton, Theodore, author.
Title: Rainy Lake House : Twilight of Empire on the Northern Frontier
    / Theodore Catton.
Description: Baltimore : Johns Hopkins University Press, 2017. |
    Includes bibliographical references and index.
Identifiers: LCCN 2016046989| ISBN 9781421422923 (hardcover : acid-
    free paper) | ISBN 9781421422930 (electronic) | ISBN 1421422921
    (hardcover : acid-free paper) | ISBN 142142293X (electronic)
Subjects: LCSH: Tanner, John, 1780?–1847. | McLoughlin, John,
    1784–1857. | Long, Stephen H. (Stephen Harriman), 1784–1864. |
    Frontier and pioneer life—Rainy River Region (Minn. and Ont.) |
    Pioneers—Family relationships—Rainy River Region (Minn. and
    Ont.)—History—19th century. | Missing children—Rainy River
    Region (Minn. and Ont.)—History—19th century. | Indians of North
    America—Rainy River Region (Minn. and Ont.)—History—19th
    century. | Fur trade—Rainy River Region (Minn. and Ont.)—
    History—19th century. | Hudson's Bay Company—History—19th
    century. | Rainy River Region (Minn. and Ont.)—Ethnic relations—
    History—19th century.
Classification: LCC F612.R18 C37 2017 | DDC 977.6/79—dc23
LC record available at https://lccn.loc.gov/2016046989

A catalog record for this book is available from the British Library.

*Special discounts are available for bulk purchases of this book. For more
information, please contact Special Sales at 410-516-6936 or
specialsales@press.jhu.edu.*

Johns Hopkins University Press uses environmentally friendly book
materials, including recycled text paper that is composed of at least 30
percent post-consumer waste, whenever possible.

To the memory of
ROBERT M. BASSETT,
1940–2016

CONTENTS

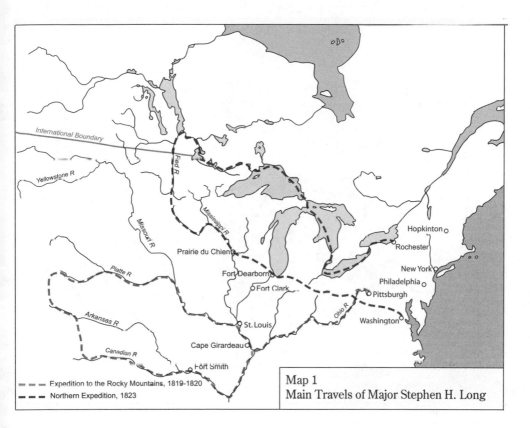

International Boundary

Yellowstone R

Red R

Missouri R

Mississippi R

Platte R

Arkansas R

Canadian R

Prairie du Chien

Fort Dearborn

Fort Clark

St. Louis

Cape Girardeau

Fort Smith

Ohio R

Hopkinton ○

Rochester ○

New York ○

Philadelphia ○

○ Pittsburgh

Washington ○

– – – Expedition to the Rocky Mountains, 1819–1820

▬ ▬ ▬ Northern Expedition, 1823

Map 1
Main Travels of Major Stephen H. Long

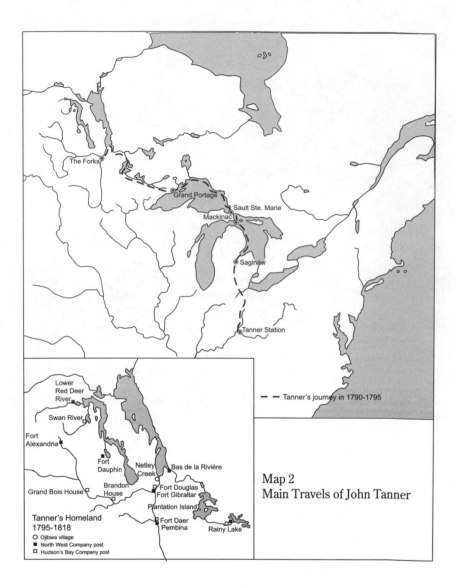

The Forks

Grand Portage

Sault Ste. Marie

Mackinac

Saginaw

Tanner Station

—— Tanner's journey in 1790-1795

Lower
Red Deer
River

Swan River

Fort
Alexandria

Fort
Dauphin

Netley
Creek

Bas de la Riviére

Grand Bois House

Brandon
House

Fort Douglas
Fort Gibraltar

Plantation Island

Tanner's Homeland
1795-1818

○ Ojibwa village
■ North West Company post
□ Hudson's Bay Company post

Fort Daer
Pembina

Rainy Lake

Map 2
Main Travels of John Tanner

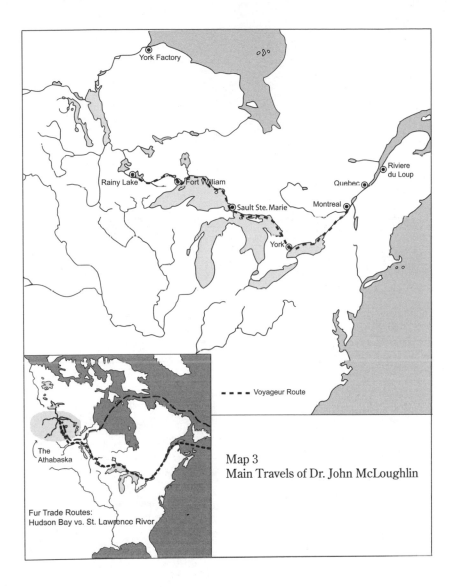

York Factory

Rainy Lake Fort William

Sault Ste. Marie

York

Quebec

Montreal

Riviere
du Loup

- - - - Voyageur Route

The
Athabaska

Fur Trade Routes:
Hudson Bay vs. St. Lawrence River

Map 3
Main Travels of Dr. John McLoughlin

TIMELINE

RAINY LAKE HOUSE

INTRODUCTION
Rainy Lake House, 1823

Under a brooding late-summer sky, two men made their way up a path toward the tall wooden gate of a Hudson's Bay Company trading post. One of the men walked with difficulty, clutching his right arm to his chest. We will call him John Tanner. To the fur traders he was known as the white Indian, for he had been taken captive by Indians as a child and had lived with them for nearly thirty years. British traders referred to him as the American, since he had been born in that territory and had made two journeys back in recent years. The Ojibwas knew him as Shaw-shaw-wa ne-ba-se, the Swallow, and more lately as Gichi-mookomaan, the white man. Now he hobbled slowly up the path to the trading post, for every jostle of his arm made him shiver with pain. Until that afternoon, he had lain in bed for more than a month, since the day of the shooting, when his arm had been shattered by a musket ball fired at close range.

Despite the wracking pain, Tanner's mind was focused on recovering his two young daughters. He believed the men in the fort were holding them against their will—bullying them, threatening them, and probably worse. He had heard the men's taunts and seen them leer. Once, a few weeks earlier, the trader in charge had trapped the two teenage girls inside the stockade and ordered them to sleep in the men's quarters. But the girls had slipped through the gate and fled to the nearby farmstead of Old Roy, a retired company servant and friend, with whom they found safety. Old Roy had brought the girls back to their father, even though Tanner, in his lame condition, was hardly able to come to their defense if they once again fell into the Hudson's Bay men's clutches. And now he perceived that just that had happened.

Tanner stood at the fort's gate and called out to his missing daughters. His companion rang the bell and bellowed for the men to let them in. Someone opened the tiny aperture in the picket wall next to the gate, a hole barely big enough for a man's hand, and peered through it. Other men's faces appeared through a narrow crack in the gate. Tanner fixed them with his cold, blue eyes and stated his business in Ojibwa while his companion translated. He wanted to search the servants' quarters for the two girls. If they were not there, then someone inside must know where they could be found.

The handful of French Canadian employees who gathered behind the gate insisted they had not seen the girls. Speaking through the narrow opening, they refused to let the two in. Tanner began to shout at them in a mix of French and Ojibwa, and they shot back a barrage of insults. Tanner's daughters had probably grown weary of tending his stinking wound, they jeered. Most likely they had deserted him and run away to their mother. *C'est la vie!* The girls were old enough to choose for themselves.

❄

Nearby on that same late-summer evening, Major Stephen H. Long sat at his field desk in his tent making notes by the light of a candle. An officer in the US Topographical Engineers, he was exploring the northern prairies from the upper Mississippi to the forty-ninth parallel as well as the wooded borderlands west of Lake Superior. The northern expedition was an encore to his famous expedition to the Rocky Mountains in 1820. He and his men had arrived at Rainy Lake House on the Rainy River, on the boundary between US and British territory, today's border between Minnesota and western Ontario.

In the waning light of the evening, two men appeared at the door of his tent: the expedition interpreter, Charles Brousse, and the American, John Tanner. It was the fourth time the wounded American had visited him that day. Only a short time ago, Long had finally agreed to take Tanner and his daughters to Mackinac in the expedition's canoes. He thought, *Now what could the matter be?*

Tanner began speaking to him in broken English, but he was so agitated his words came tumbling out, incomprehensible. Brousse broke in to explain that Tanner's daughters were missing—perhaps being abused by the men in the fort. The Hudson's Bay men had not only refused Tanner entry into the fort, they had provoked him with vile insults. Tanner wanted the American commander to intervene.

Long was skeptical. The girls had probably run off when Tanner told them they would be going with the American expedition. Still, with all the depravity Long had seen in other fur traders' establishments, he could not be too certain. In any case, he had made his decision: the expedition was going to help Tanner search for his missing daughters.

Long summoned the expedition's surgeon, Dr. Thomas Say, and the four men started back up the path to the fort. Night had fallen, and with low clouds hiding the moon and stars they fumbled along the path through inky darkness. Admitted through the gate, they made their way across the muddy courtyard to the officer's house, where a faint light from oil lamps shone dimly through moose-skin windowpanes—the only source of light in an ocean of darkness.

❄

That night, the proprietor of Rainy Lake House, Dr. John McLoughlin, arrived home at a late hour, having pushed his twenty canoemen to paddle the last few miles of their journey after dark. As a chief factor in the great Hudson's Bay Company, McLoughlin was in charge of the whole area of borderlands west of Lake Superior, tasked with opposing the petty traders who operated out of US territory. He was returning from his summer-long trip to Hudson Bay, where he had delivered twenty packs of furs, attended the Northern Department's annual meeting, and secured more trade goods for the resupply of his post. Now, leaving the men to unload the cargo, he hastened up the path to see his wife and children after a separation of more than ten weeks.

Going through the gate and approaching the house, he heard raised voices within the officers' quarters. He wondered, *What in the devil is all the commotion about?* He stooped through the door—at six feet, four inches, he was a head taller than most men in the fur trade—and burst in on a heated conference. The room fell silent. The tall, broad-shouldered doctor, with his stern visage and wild mane of hair, often had that effect on men.

McLoughlin did not need introductions. He recognized Major Long, having been informed that the famous US army explorer was in the neighborhood. He also recognized the man with the wounded arm, the one they called the American. Years ago he had doctored him through some broken ribs. *A good, honest, intelligent fellow,* he once jotted in the post's journal. McLoughlin made a mental note such as that for every Indian who ever traded at Rainy Lake House. But his interest in this man ran a bit deeper than it did for most Indians. *Might have made a fair interpreter had he been willing to serve the company. But he kept to himself and the Indians, devoted to the old Ottawa woman who raised him.* A few years ago, McLoughlin knew, the old Ottawa woman had died and the American had gone in search of his white kinfolk in the United States. Before leaving the country, Tanner had paid him a visit. All of this McLoughlin had recalled earlier that summer, when word passed around that Tanner had been shot and was recovering from his wounds at Rainy Lake House.

Now he learned that Tanner's daughters were missing—runaways, he was told by the fort's summer caretaker. The Hudson's Bay men stood accused by Tanner and the American officers of holding them captive in the men's quarters. Nonsense, the doctor insisted, siding with his own people.

The girls could be nowhere in the house; he gave the Americans his word on it. He would organize a search at daybreak. He would offer a reward to the local Indians for their safe return. Until then, everyone must get some rest.

❋

Stephen H. Long, John Tanner, and Dr. John McLoughlin each made his own record of the events that occurred at Rainy Lake House on the late afternoon and evening of September 1, 1823. McLoughlin made an entry in the trading post's journal, which was later preserved in the Hudson's Bay Company Archives. Long and his men wrote in their expedition journals, and the expedition journalist, William H. Keating, later compiled all their notes and produced the official narrative of the expedition, which was published in 1824. Tanner, for his part, recalled the events from memory when he related the story of his life to an ethnographer, Edwin James, some five years later in 1828. Tanner's autobiography was published in New York in 1830 under the title *Narrative of the Captivity and Adventures of John Tanner*. Long's, Tanner's, and McLoughlin's written records of what happened basically corroborate one another. Moreover, the journal entries, which recorded the events right after they had occurred, support Tanner's account pulled from memory. They help authenticate Tanner's remarkable narrative as a true and unembellished testament of a life lived among Indians in an oral culture without writing.

Yet there are subtle variances in the three men's accounts—differences not of fact but of perception. Each man had pressing questions on his mind to which the others were either indifferent or unaware. Long was perplexed by Tanner's character as much as he was moved by Tanner's circumstances. Long considered him to be an American citizen, or at least a former US citizen, yet in manner and speech he was more Indian than white. The onetime captive struck the American explorer as a tragic figure caught in a no-man's-land between drastically different cultures. Half-civilized and half-savage, Long thought, a hopeless misfit. Long wanted to help him, but he felt at a loss how to *save* him.

Those concerns contrast with Tanner's, who alone of the three men believed his daughters would be raped by the Hudson's Bay men. Tanner saw, as the others apparently did not, the lustful, plotting looks that followed his young teenage girls wherever they moved around the fort.

McLoughlin, meanwhile, had the interests of the Hudson's Bay Company in mind. As a doctor and a humanitarian, he was concerned about the welfare of the wounded American. Yet, his entry in the post journal reveals other concerns. Why had the Rainy Lake Indian called Little Clear Sky tried to kill Tanner earlier that summer? Would the attack put a damper on their trade in the coming winter? In the de facto law of the country, an Indian attack on a white man demanded blood for blood. Since the wounded American had been rescued by the Hudson's Bay men, would the Rainy Lake Indians stay away from the Hudson's Bay post, in fear of revenge? Would they go to the American trading posts instead?

Tanner, Long, and McLoughlin were not just witnesses to the events of 1823 but are sources on the wider world of the fur trade in the early nineteenth century. Their differences of perspective color many other mutual experiences beyond their encounter at Rainy Lake House. The three men all came together in the same place just once, but in their years of experience on the frontier before 1823, they saw many of the same things from different angles. All three were participants in the changing power dynamics between Europeans and Indians, Americans and British, Ojibwas and Sioux, and the rivalry of fur companies great and small. All three struggled with the meaning of race and culture in that place and time. Comparing their biographies side by side, and listening closely to their discordant voices, one finds a kind of frontier Rashomon tale.

In the 1950 film classic *Rashômon*, director Akira Kurosawa presents the rape of a woman and the murder of her samurai-warrior husband as told by four different witnesses to the crimes. Each faces the camera in turn, so that the audience takes on the role of a jury, measuring the truth of their stories. As each one starts to testify, the action shifts to the scene of the crimes so that the camera is now showing the audience what happened, in a flashback sequence, from that witness's point of view. First, a bandit, who is charged with the crimes, offers his version of events. Then the rape victim gives a contradictory story. This is followed by the dead samurai's account as told through a psychic medium, by which the audience learns that neither of the two previous accounts can be trusted. And finally, a woodcutter provides yet another version. It seems that as the woodcutter was merely passing by when the crimes were committed, the film audience has at last received a version that is detached and closer to the truth than the other three. Yet in a final twist, the audience learns that the woodcutter, too, had reason to shade the truth. *Rashômon* is about the subjectivity of perception and the challenge of constructing truth from multiple points of view.

By the time Tanner came to the Canadian prairie with his Indian family in 1795, the fur trade was already three centuries old. Gradually it had spread over much of the continent, taking form wherever Indians and Europeans exchanged animal hides for articles of European make. Indians mostly sought metal and cloth items to augment their material culture of bone, skin, wood, and stone. Europeans wanted furs to make into clothing products for Europe's upper classes—above all, they desired beaver skins with their exceptionally fine undercoats, which they turned into stylish felt hats. Both parties had something the other coveted, and both had ideas of how to drive a bargain. To bridge the enormous gulf between Indian and European cultures, the parties devised trade rituals, patterns of intermarriage, simplified language forms, and other symbolic behaviors that eased negotiations. And while their conventions largely succeeded in forming a functional context for trade relations, misapprehensions abounded, making a Rashomon-like tapestry of competing truths.

By Tanner's day, the fur trade was a far-flung but significant piece of a much larger trans-Atlantic economy. Insofar as the free-market law of supply and demand shaped the fur trade, Indian labor was often the item in short supply. Firms such as the Hudson's Bay Company depended on Indian men and women to hunt and trap animals and dress hides for them. Although Indian men and women did not work for company wages, they did function essentially like a factory labor force from the company's standpoint. They produced the original product for redistribution to distant markets. The fur companies found Indian labor to be indispensable because there was no other way they could obtain furs in large enough quantities for an affordable cost so far from home. Consequently, the companies' traders put much effort into recruiting more Indian labor into the fur trade—persuading subsistence hunters and their wives to become part-time market hunters and tanners, as it were. The economic relationship between traders living at trading posts and hunters living nearby brought them into close, sustained contact. This is the feature of the fur trade of most interest today: it formed the principal context for the encounter between Indian and European cultures almost from first contact until around the mid-nineteenth century. The encounter was sometimes intimate, sometimes violent, seldom straightforward, and often uneasy.

Early efforts to understand the nature of Indian-European relations in the fur trade were based almost entirely on printed sources on the European side of the relationship. European traders viewed their experience through a powerful set of cultural lenses. They took for granted, for example, that they belonged to a superior, "civilized" race of people while their Indian trading partners were "savages." They assumed, too, that trading soon drew Indians into a position of economic dependency as Indians incorporated items such as guns and metal pots into their material culture. Traders thought an Indian hunter with a gun was more advanced than one who used bow and arrows, even though the hunter now had to trade more furs in order to replenish his supply of ammunition or replace a worn-out gun. These two basic notions—that Indians were inferior to Europeans and that trade made the Indians dependent on European traders—pervaded everything the traders wrote about Indians in their record books and correspondence. The traders' observations had a powerful influence on state policy as European powers and then the United States passed laws to regulate Indian affairs. The traders' basic assumptions of Indian inferiority and dependency worked their way into congressional reports, parliamentary debates, and other contemporary records concerning the fur trade.

For a long time, histories of the North American fur trade followed more or less in the vein of the historical source material, taking for granted that the relationship between Europeans and Indians was an unequal one and that the fur trade drew Indian peoples into a state of dependency. Then, around the 1970s, historians began to reinterpret the Indian-European relationship from the Indian side in light of evidence offered by ethnohistorical and anthropological studies. These revisionist histories emphasized how some Indian tribes took more interest in the fur trade than others, how they held their own in this relationship at least through the mid-eighteenth century, and how Indian cultures adapted to their changing world rather than simply disintegrating under European influence. But in developing those new perspectives, historians still faced a major challenge in the fact that practically all of their primary sources were produced by non-Indians. The Indian experience in the fur trade had to be gleaned through a careful rereading of all the old material. Fur company records, which continued to form the core of primary source material, were not only distorted by cultural and racial prejudice, historians noted, but were tainted by the economic self-interest of the fur companies as well.

This book depicts the fur trade through the intertwined lives of three men, whose biographies are shaped around the notion of differing points of view. The reader is herein advised that much of the narrative to follow is constructed in a way to represent their three subjective realities, not necessarily objective fact. To take one stark example, the word "savage" will appear sometimes without quotes or other commentary. The idea is to approach these stories in a comparative framework in order to better appreciate why their values and motivations differed so. When one views these men's experiences in the fur trade in close comparison, one can glimpse their world from its various colliding vantage points: American, British, and Indian; imperial, capital, and labor; explorer, trader, and hunter.

McLoughlin, Long, and Tanner were all born within four years of each other in the early 1780s, but they came from varied backgrounds. McLoughlin was born to Irish Catholic and Scottish Presbyterian–French Catholic parents in Lower Canada. Long came from Puritan New England stock and grew up in New Hampshire. Tanner's parents were southern plainfolk who migrated across the Appalachian Mountains to the Ohio frontier when he was very young. Each man entered the fur trade at a different age. Tanner's Indian upbringing began at the age of nine, and by the age of twelve he was participating in the fur trade in northern Michigan, trapping marten for his Indian family to trade at Fort Mackinac. The year was 1793. McLoughlin completed an apprenticeship in medicine in Quebec and joined the North West Company as an apprentice clerk in the Lake Superior country at the age of eighteen, in 1803. Major Long was not exposed to the fur trade until his first military assignment in the West when he was thirty-one, in the year 1816. By the time the three converged at Rainy Lake House in 1823, Tanner was forty-two and McLoughlin and Long were each thirty-eight.

Their collective experiences in the fur trade spanned two crucial decades, roughly the twenty years surrounding the War of 1812. These years saw resolution of two epic confrontations. The first involved the struggle between the North West Company and the Hudson's Bay Company for control of the fur trade in British America (Canada). The bitter conflict finally ended with the merger of the two companies in 1821. The second involved the effort by the United States to "Americanize" the fur trade within US territory—to evict British traders operating in the Great Lakes, upper Mississippi, and upper Missouri, and supplant them with American traders. These were separate, parallel confrontations occurring on either side of the US-British border, but in a broader sense they were two sides of the same coin, being an effort to reorganize the North American fur trade in the face of rising American nationalism.

The early life stories of McLoughlin, Long, and Tanner provide three significant points of view on the fur trade experience during this pivotal time. John McLoughlin is known to history as the "Father of Oregon," for it was in the Pacific Northwest that the capable and principled administrator served the Hudson's Bay Company from 1824 to 1845, providing aid to a growing number of American emigrants who arrived in the Oregon country before it became part of the United States. In his less well-known early career, McLoughlin became deeply entwined in the struggle between the great fur companies in British America. Entering the North West Company in the capacity of apprentice clerk and physician, he spent nearly all the years from 1803 to 1823 either at Rainy Lake or Fort William, the company's entrepôt on the north shore of Lake Superior. At the latter place, he met and married his Métis wife, Marguerite McKay. Rising to partner in 1814, he was drawn into the escalating strife between the two companies. He took part in a plot that led to a deadly clash of Hudson's Bay and North West Company partisans, a skirmish known to history as the Battle of Seven Oaks. Taken prisoner by Hudson's Bay men, he eventually stood trial on charges of conspiracy to commit murder for his role in the one-sided battle. After his acquittal, he played a key role in fashioning a corporate merger, landing a good position in the reorganized Hudson's Bay Company when it swallowed his former company. McLoughlin experienced the fur trade as a trader, as a husband and father ensconced in fur-trade society, and as a player in the rise of one of the first great corporations of the industrializing world.

Stephen H. Long was a leading explorer of the American West, remembered most for his ill-famed characterization of the Great Plains as the "Great American Desert." A strong supporter of national expansion, he took a keen interest in how to advance the nation's strategic aim to Americanize the fur trade in the upper Mississippi and Missouri valleys. Taking an intellectual and nationalistic interest in the American Indian, Long came to view the fur trade as an instrument for raising Indian peoples from their "savage" state and assimilating them into the American nation.

Tanner's experience in the fur trade was mostly that of an Indian. Taken captive by a Shawnee-Ottawa war party at the age of nine, he was subsequently traded to an Ottawa chieftess. At thirteen, he migrated with his adoptive family from northern Michigan to the Canadian prairie and lived among the western Ottawas and Ojibwas for almost thirty years. Becoming a skilled hunter, he provided food for his family and frequented a dozen different trading posts from Lake Superior to present-day Saskatchewan. He joined war parties against the Sioux. He married twice and produced eleven children while living in Indian country. When Tanner eventually took steps to return to a white man's life, he worked one year for the American Fur Company—just prior to his ill-fated attempt to rescue his daughters in the summer of 1823.

The humble trading post below the outlet of Rainy Lake where the three men came together was a "house" in every sense of the word. A post for carrying on the business of the fur trade, it was also a dwelling, way station, and emergency shelter for the mixed population of English- and French-speaking traders, Ojibwa hunters, and former *engagés*, or freemen, who lived within its ambit. Under its roof, in the shadow of its picket walls, beside the Rainy River, and in the cold, misty veil of the nearby falls that gave the river its name, people from different worlds entered that space to form bonds. And as in every house, those bonds could be fraught.

❊{I}❊ LEAVE-TAKINGS

The Explorer

{ **1** } On all his western explorations, Major Stephen H. Long began each day's march before the crack of dawn. Morning reveille sounded before five o'clock, and the expedition got underway in almost complete darkness or by the light of the moon. Whether traveling by horse, foot, bateau, or canoe, he was exceedingly disciplined about making those early starts. For one thing, it was a defensive measure, since the Indians liked to attack a sleeping camp in the hour before sunrise. For another, it allowed his men to cover a lot of ground before the warmest part of the day. The predawn departure increased the overall speed of the expedition, and greater speed translated into more distance covered for the same government expense. Dollars-and-cents efficiency mattered a great deal to Long because he took up exploring in a decade of waning government support for army exploration of the West. At the end of his career he boasted that his five expeditions, which took place from 1816 to 1823, covered an aggregate distance of more than 26,000 miles—many more miles than either Lewis and Clark or Captain Zebulon M. Pike had traveled on their western explorations in the years 1804 to 1807. In Long's view, his expedition to the Rocky Mountains in 1820 and his treks through the upper Mississippi and upper Great Lakes regions produced as much cartographic and scientific information as the more celebrated expeditions of his predecessors.[1]

Four months and 3,000 miles into what would be his final expedition, Long and his men started from camp at the usual early hour, paddled up the Rainy River for five miles, and arrived at the falls known as Koochiching (the rain) well before sunrise on August 31, 1823. Dimly they could see the horizontal white streak of the falls blocking their way a half mile ahead, mist rising over the falls, and the British and American trading posts on opposite banks of the river below, facing off across the border. They landed at the small American Fur Company trading post first, but finding its solitary proprietor unable to help them, they crossed to the British side. There they learned that the Hudson's Bay chief factor, Dr. John McLoughlin, had not yet returned from Hudson Bay with his brigade of voyageurs and fresh supplies for the coming winter.

Long asked the Hudson's Bay trader in charge, Simon McGillivray, for permission to encamp for a few days while his canoemen repaired their canoes. One of their three canoes had taken considerable punishment coming through rapids on the Winnipeg River, and all three needed to be repitched. The expedition also needed supplies. McGillivray granted permission for the men to make camp beside the fort and use the canoe yard for as long as necessary. They could purchase supplies from him when they prepared to depart. Cordially, he invited Long and his officers and the expedition's scientific gentlemen to join him at his table for dinner that night.[2]

McGillivray then put in a request of his own. A man they called the American, John Tanner, lay in a tent outside the Hudson's Bay post recovering from gunshot wounds. For more than a month and a half he had barely stirred from his bed. Though the Hudson's Bay Company had taken him under its protection, McGillivray had not been able to provide him much medical care. In fact, he had mainly left that matter to Tanner's two daughters, about fourteen and sixteen years of age. The girls tended their father's fire, prepared his food, fetched his water, washed his clothes, gathered berries, snared rabbits, and performed other sundry tasks around their camp. But even after his long convalescence, Tanner still rarely came out of his tent. Would the expedition's surgeon please examine his wounds?

Long took Thomas Say, the surgeon and zoologist, and his interpreter, Charles Brousse, and proceeded to Tanner's tent. They found the invalid lying on a good, comfortable bed with his daughters beside him. Tanner showed the surgeon where the musket ball had entered his right arm above the elbow, shattering the bone and passing on into his breast. The ball had torn into his breast muscle, barely missing his right lung. There was an incision next to his breastbone where the ball had been extricated. The incision had mostly healed. The wound under the armpit had scarred over. The broken upper arm bone had set properly. The hole in the arm had not yet closed up, but it was clean and appeared to be improving. Though his injured arm still had no strength or movement, he could stand up and move about.[3]

That evening, Long, Say, and a handful of other officers and scientists joined the Hudson's Bay men in McGillivray's house for dinner. Their meal would have been simple—fish caught that day, peas and potatoes from the garden, perhaps a helping of scorched dumplings that McGillivray proudly styled as "damper," wine, coffee, and tea. McGillivray was a convivial host, and he would have set a fire in the fireplace or illuminated the table with an oil lamp to be certain that their little party continued into the night. From the expedition's journals it appears that following the meal the men talked at length about the fate of the wounded American. (It also seems apparent, from an account left by another traveler who dined with McGillivray a month prior to this evening, that McGillivray relished the opportunity to share Tanner's lurid story with them.)[4]

Tanner had been traveling through the country in his canoe with his two daughters and their mother when he was ambushed while paddling up a stretch of rapids. His attacker had shot him from a hiding place on the river bank. In McGillivray's recounting, Tanner was pitched out of the canoe, and clinging to a rock in the rapids, he called out to his wife to come rescue him. But the woman left him there, taking the girls with her. Tanner managed to drag himself out of the river and hide in the bushes, lying still as his attacker went up and down the riverbank in search of him. If he had yet had his knife, he would have jumped his adversary. Instead he stayed quiet till the man left the area. For three days he lay by the river, bleeding and delirious, suffering the torment of the biting flies. He was about to fling himself into the rapids to end his misery when a Hudson's Bay canoe happened along.

Tanner and his family had passed Rainy Lake House on their way to Mackinac just a few days before the ambush, the story continued. McGillivray was certain that Tanner's wife was accessory to his attempted murder. For many years, she and Tanner had been separated and the girls had lived with her. Early that summer, Tanner had gone to the girls' village, demanding to have his daughters back though he barely knew them after so long a time. The village chiefs had consented on the condition that he would take the girls' mother as well. So the long-estranged couple had reunited, and the reconstituted family of four was making its way to the States when Tanner was shot.

Somehow the woman had conspired with a young Indian man, who had joined them east of Rainy Lake, to kill her former husband. It was unknown how she had convinced this miscreant to commit murder for her, but McGillivray was sure she had done it. He knew because a few days later she had come to the trading house with her daughters and given herself up. And when Tanner had arrived a few hours after her in a Hudson's Bay canoe—not dead as she had presumed but still alive—she had panicked and attempted to flee to the woods.

Then McGillivray came to the part of the story that most intrigued his American guests. Although the Hudson's Bay men had immediately captured and detained the woman, Tanner would not be satisfied with her punishment alone. He had to have revenge on the man who had shot him.[5]

Listening to the trader present this story, Long and his men fixated on Tanner's demand for revenge. Dr. Say had challenged Tanner on that very point during his interview with him earlier in the day. *Why must he have revenge?* Tanner had resolutely answered him: "Why did he shoot me? If he wishes to kill me, it is my duty to kill him, for he is a bad man." Say later wrote in his notes, "This was uttered in a cold, decisive manner; it was not the result of passion, but of a conviction, founded upon a process of reasoning, to which he had been long accustomed."[6]

For Long and his men this was proof that the wounded American had reverted to a near state of savagery during his many years of living among the Indians. To most US citizens in their time, there was no more indelible mark of the savage mind than the hellish desire for revenge.

As devout Protestants, Long and his men were indoctrinated with Christianity's many injunctions against revenge. At home, these men read the Bible and attended church regularly. They were familiar, in a way that modern people generally are not, with the words of their sacred Scripture. *All who take the sword will perish by the sword . . . Blessed are the merciful, for they will be shown mercy . . . May the Lord judge between me and you, may the Lord avenge me against you, but my hand shall not be against you.* The Christian Bible taught that every act of revenge by one man against another was a wrongful act, for it violated the law of God and worked to perpetuate evil. Christ's message was that no person was free from sin; therefore, no person could take revenge with a pure heart. Only God could rightfully take revenge. For Long and his contemporaries, the Bible's many injunctions against revenge were well known and deeply felt. They found the "vengeful Indian" an affront to God. *Do not seek revenge or bear a grudge against one of your people, but love your neighbor as yourself. I am the LORD.*

As men of the American Enlightenment, Long, Say, and the other scientists on the expedition condemned Tanner's vow of revenge on grounds of civil law, too. Dividing all of humanity into "civilized" and "savage" peoples, they took for granted that virtually all Indians were in the latter category. They assumed that Indians were universally beholden to the revenge principle according to their tribal customs. Long's own thinking on this went roughly as follows. (1) Civilized peoples had the rule of law; savage peoples did not. In civil society, blood-for-blood revenge had no legitimate place except as meted out through a state-controlled criminal justice system. But when men lived in a primitive condition without the rule of law, by necessity the revenge principle stood in for the rule of law as the elemental rock of justice. (2) In a primitive society, a person who suffered a wrong by another person had both a right and a duty to avenge the wrongful act. Vengeance upon the perpetrator was the perpetrator's due punishment. Retaliation was the victim's rightful means of compensation. (3) The fear of revenge acted like a brutish deterrent on all members of the tribe, keeping tribal members' worst impulses in check.

Tribal law was far more complex than that in reality. But this crude caricature shaped white people's perceptions of what they heard and saw of Indians' pursuit of justice. When Tanner uttered his declaration of the revenge principle, the men on the expedition saw their stereotyped impression of a savage mind at work.

The conversations around Tanner's predicament led Long to ponder. Was Tanner an American citizen, or was he now essentially an Indian living beyond the pale of American civilization? His attachment to the revenge principle pointed to the latter. When Long wrote in his journal two days later, he observed that Tanner had "become completely a savage . . . in every respect but complexion." Only after his long-lost white family had located him and taken measures to "reclaim" him, some four years prior, had Tanner begun to reacquire civilized ways. At the present juncture, Long concluded, Tanner stood somewhere in between, half-savage and half-civilized.[7]

❋

Americans in Long's day called people like Tanner white Indians. Since colonial times thousands of individuals of white parentage had opted out of white society, preferring to live among Indians. A large percentage of those individuals were onetime captives who, upon being absorbed into Indian life, declined to return to their families when they had the opportunity. Americans found that troubling. Benjamin Franklin, among others, commented on how seldom it happened the other way around. Comparatively few Indian individuals chose to join white society. It was not right that a nation founded on ideals of equality, freedom, and the pursuit of happiness, a young nation claiming to be the light of the world, should find so many of its citizens defecting to Indian tribes.[8]

Long and his men had actually learned of the white Indian named John Tanner many days before they reached Rainy Lake House. Coming into the region, the exploring party began hearing reports of a "citizen of the United States" who had been taken captive as a child and who had lived for many years among the Indians, becoming one of them in language, dress, and manner. They learned that this man had recently returned to the region after an absence of a few years and that he had been attacked by an Indian while making his way back to Mackinac with his Indian children. Long and his men eventually connected this person with a captive whom they had read about some years before in the newspapers. Tanner's story had circulated in the nation's press around the time that he was finally reunited with his family. "A Captive Found," one of these stories was headlined. "Indian Captive Reclaimed," announced another. Nothing drew the attention of American readers like an Indian captivity story. Indeed, more than four years had passed since Long and his men had read those notices, so the fact that they remembered them shows what a strong impression they made.[9]

As a native of upper New England, Long had grown up with such captivity stories. One of the most popular literary genres in colonial America, captivity narratives retained their hold on the American consciousness for several decades into the nineteenth century. In their most basic, unembellished form they were an American equivalent to the Icelandic saga—narratives particularly suited for great storytellers and passed down by oral tradition. In the eighteenth century, as more captivity narratives were put in writing and published, they became the forerunner of the nineteenth-century dime novel—cheap, popular, sensational reading. But though they were often embellished they were never tales of complete fiction; the power of the genre was that the stories were authentic and dealt with firsthand experience.[10] The actual number of non-Indians taken captive by Indians can never be known, but it was a common enough experience that a large swath of the population could count a friend or relative a victim, making the nightmarish scenario not just strongly imagined but in some way personalized.[11]

Long's hometown of Hopkinton, New Hampshire, had a few captivity stories of its own. Dating back to Long's grandparents' generation and the time of the French and Indian War, these tales were passed down orally with spellbinding detail. One familiar account began with events on the morning of April 22, 1746, when a party of Abenakis slipped through an open gate in Woodwell's garrison, left unsecured while one of the inhabitants went out to feed the cattle. After a brief struggle inside the garrison, five men, one woman, and two children were taken captive, while a man escaped into the woods, and a woman eluded capture by dashing to the cellar and hiding under a barrel. The Abenakis marched their captives north to Quebec, a twelve-day journey through the wilderness of northern New Hampshire, on one scanty meal a day. The Abenakis had the intention of either trading them as slaves or selling them to the French, who paid a bounty on English captives. Two of the eight died of yellow fever in a Quebec prison, four others were ransomed from the French, and the remaining two—a boy and a girl, both in their teens—lived with the Abenakis for three years until their families finally secured their release.[12]

Another story told of two Hopkinton youths who were taken on the morning of April 13, 1753. The first captive, Abraham Kimball, was driving his father's cow over the road from Putney's fort to Kimball's fort when he was seized. The second was engaged in burning a brush pile outside the Putney farm. That night, while the Indians were trying to make off with yet more captives, they were attacked by a pack of dogs and the two boys escaped. As the Kimballs and the Longs were related by marriage, Stephen probably heard this story when he was a boy, possibly in repeated tellings.[13]

Both Long's father and maternal grandfather had fought in wars, so the young Stephen would also have heard stories about his elders' service in the military. His maternal grandfather, Captain Stephen Harriman, fought in the French and Indian War before becoming a tavern keeper in Hopkinton in the 1760s. Prominent afterwards in town government, he later served as a delegate to the Exeter convention in 1775, which was called to reform New Hampshire's colonial government on the eve of the American Revolution.[14] Stephen's father, Moses Long, served in the Continental army in the Revolutionary War. He endured hardships at Valley Forge in the winter of 1776–77, and witnessed the surrender of General John Burgoyne at Saratoga. Among the prized possessions in Stephen's boyhood home was his father's "queen's arm," a gun that he had traded for a captured Hessian musket before he left the army. After his military discharge in 1780, Moses Long became a farmer and cooper in Hopkinton. He and Long's mother, Lucy Harriman, married in 1783. Stephen Harriman Long was born on December 30, 1784. Stephen was the second of thirteen children, and the oldest of ten to survive infancy. Such a large family was not uncommon in New England in that era.[15]

The threat of Indian raids in northern New England had long since ended by Stephen's time. This relative security attracted a new wave of settlers around the year he was born. But the thousands of people who poured into New Hampshire and Vermont after the Revolution faced other challenges: a shortage of fertile farm land, limited access to markets, and high taxes. By the time Stephen was a boy, the tide of migration had reversed. Many young people, unable to take up farms near their parents' homes, left upper New England in search of better opportunities elsewhere.[16] Stephen himself and at least three of his eight brothers would eventually join that out-migration.

The Hopkinton of Stephen's boyhood stood at the threshold of this northern frontier. By the early 1800s, when he was in his upper teens, the town had a population of about 2,000 people. Cows and sheep dotted the hillsides, watermills stood on the banks of every major stream, and the village square bustled with artisans' shops and mercantile stores. A few years later the town would become a stop on a new stage route between Boston and Quebec.[17]

As in most New England towns, Hopkinton's religious life centered on the Calvinistic Congregational church. Both the Long and Harriman families were active in the church; Moses Long was a deacon. During the 1790s, when Stephen was a boy, a schism occurred in the congregation, which left the town with two places of worship, known henceforth as the east and west Congregational meeting houses. In the early 1800s, an evangelist Baptist meeting house appeared in the town, too, further dividing the faithful between New Light and Old Light denominations. The New Lights believed in the power of individual salvation through worship, while the Old Lights held to the sterner teachings of predestination. Long's family stuck with the Old Light faction in the community.[18]

Stephen Long's religious upbringing in Hopkinton laid the foundation for a devout Christian outlook in his adult life. On his expedition to the Rocky Mountains in 1820, he would make it a rule to rest the party on Sundays, directing everyone to attend to their health and cleanliness.[19] His Christian faith would also color his views on Indians.

Stephen Long's parents valued education as well as religion. Stephen's uncle, Enoch Long, owned a bookbindery and bookstore in Hopkinton, and his father later produced a local history for the New Hampshire Historical Society.[20] Stephen and at least three of his brothers pursued a college education. At the age of nineteen or twenty, Stephen entered Dartmouth College, New Hampshire's first school of higher learning. Dartmouth offered a liberal education, including philosophy, history, classical literature, mathematics, and engineering. He was a voracious reader: in his freshman year, he not only read his assigned texts of Homer, Virgil, and Cicero but devoured another twenty books from the college library, including Gibbon's *Decline and Fall of the Roman Empire* and Plutarch's *Lives*. He joined the school choir and served as vice president of the Handel Society, developing an active interest in music that continued well into his adult life. Years later, while on his way up the Rainy River, he would record in his journal in musical notation a few bars of Ojibwa music from what he described as a scalp dance.[21]

An unusual feature of Long's college experience was that he lived on campus with a handful of Indian students. Dartmouth College was founded for the purpose of acculturating and Christianizing young Indians as well as educating young whites. By the time Stephen matriculated, the missionary zeal of the college's founding years had diminished. Still, five Indian students appear in the records of Dartmouth College during the years when Long was a student.[22] One, a Mohawk from New York by the name of Eleazar Williams, boasted that he was descended from Eunice Williams, a white captive of the Iroquois raid on Deerfield, Massachusetts, in 1704. Eunice Williams became famous as "the unredeemed captive" for her refusal to rejoin white society.[23] Her great-grandson Eleazar led an unusual life in his own right, repeatedly reinventing himself. After leaving Dartmouth, Eleazar became an ordained minister and worked for the American Board of Missionaries among the Iroquois. During the War of 1812, he served American interests as a spy in Canada. In the 1820s, he became an Indian political leader, persuading Christianized New York Indians to seek a new home in Wisconsin. Late in life, in his most beguiling transformation of them all, Eleazar claimed to be the Dauphin, the long-lost heir of Louis XVI and Marie Antoinette, allegedly spirited away as an infant at the onset of the French Revolution, protected by anonymity in an Iroquois village in Quebec until the age of ten, and grown to manhood among Indians in the backwoods of upstate New York. More than a few European aristocrats were taken in by this story, and he lived on their charity until his death in 1858.[24] One wonders what impression Eleazar Williams made on Long when they were students together at Dartmouth. Though Williams's tenure at the college was brief, this fellow, so mercurial in later life, might even then have struck Long as a living legacy of Indian captivity.

Graduating from Dartmouth in 1809, Long spent the next four years as a school principal and teacher in Salisbury, New Hampshire, and in Germantown, Pennsylvania. Toward the end of the War of 1812, he applied for an officer's commission in the Corps of Engineers. Owing to his skills as an engineer and inventor, he was among a handful of officers appointed to the new US Topographical Engineers. He then taught mathematics for one year at West Point Military Academy while the Corps of Engineers went through a reorganization and the Topographical Engineers temporarily folded after the war.[25] On April 24, 1816, Congress reauthorized the Topographical Engineers for the purpose of surveying and mapping the western territories. Two days later, Long applied for a new commission. For some time, he had been nurturing a desire to travel and explore. At the age of thirty-one, he found the opportunity.

The Hunter

{ 2 } In the years after the American Revolutionary War the Ohio valley was the scene of much raiding and fighting between whites and Indians. Settlers pushed north out of Kentucky and west out of Pennsylvania into southern Ohio, encroaching on the hunting grounds of the Shawnee, Delaware, Wyandot, Ottawa, Ojibwa, and Kickapoo nations. Under pressure from the US military, all of the Indian nations met in council with the Americans at Fort Harmar save one, the Shawnees. Over the next year, as fighting between the Americans and the Shawnees intensified, US forces attacked and burned the principal Shawnee towns and drove the tribe northward. But even as the Shawnees regrouped on the Maumee River nearer to their British allies, they made frequent raids into southern Ohio in an effort to hold the line on white settlement at the Ohio River.[1] Shawnee war parties challenged the Americans all up and down the Ohio, attacking farms, killing settlers, and taking away captives. Into this cauldron of war in the early spring of 1790 came a Virginian named John Tanner with his wife and six children, including a nine-year-old boy by the same name.

The Tanner family traveled by wagon from Elkhorn, Kentucky, to the Ohio River. When they got to the Ohio, the senior John Tanner bought three flatboats for transporting his horses, cattle, household goods, few slaves, and family down the river. The nine-year-old John Tanner would later recall that the sides of these flatboats were bloodstained and bullet-holed and that previous passengers had been killed in an Indian attack. Tanner's childhood memory accords with the accounts of other emigrants who were setting out down the Ohio from western Pennsylvania during that same spring. Emigrants were advised to keep to the middle of the river and ignore all pleas for help from people on land, no matter how anguished, for the Indians were known to use white captives as decoys for luring victims to the riverbanks, where they would be ambushed and taken prisoner or slain.[2] The Tanner family saw no hostile Indians on their trip on the Ohio, but as they were passing Cincinnati (a small settlement of about 60 log cabins and 200 inhabitants in 1790) they had another close call. The flatboat carrying the family's livestock sank. John's father leaped aboard the sinking vessel and cut loose the horses and cattle, and although the animals went into the river they survived.[3]

The Tanner family took possession of a deserted farm on the Kentucky side of the Ohio River across from the mouth of the Big Miami. Squatters had recently cleared the land only to be driven away by Indian attacks. It seems that, in spite of the danger, the Tanners thought they could turn the squatters' misfortune into their own opportunity. In about two weeks' time they resurrected the farmstead's two partially destroyed log cabins, one for the family dwelling and the other for slave quarters, and built a defensive stockade around both buildings. But only a few weeks later they, too, experienced a heavy loss.[4]

One day at the end of April, all the men and older boys were outside the stockade replanting an old cornfield. The oldest son, Edward, and the slaves were dropping corn in the furrowed earth, while the senior John Tanner stood watch for Indians with his gun in hand. Nine-year-old John was playing in the shade of a walnut tree. Unbeknownst to any of them a Shawnee-Ottawa war party looked on from the edge of the woods. It was the last time the boy would ever see his father.[5]

Some days prior to this, about 250 miles to the north, an Ottawa named Manitoo-geezhik left the village of Saginaw with his grown son Kish kau ko and two other men and headed for the Ohio River to make war on the whites. Near Lake Erie they were joined by three Shawnees, making a war party of seven. Manitoo-geezhik's goal was to take a young boy captive to bring home for his wife, who was grieving the recent loss of their youngest son. It was a common practice among Indian peoples to replace a child who had died from sickness or a son who had been killed in war with a captive of about the same age. Often such captives came to be treated like adopted children and would remain with the family for years. Besides providing consolation for the bereaved parents, these young people often grew up to bolster the population of the tribe. Adopted males became warriors; adopted females bore children. Numerous whites and blacks and Indians of other nations were to be found among Indian groups in the late eighteenth century, all having come into the tribe by way of capture and adoption. When taking captives, the Indians did not discriminate on the basis of race.[6]

Manitoo-geezhik and his followers descended the Big Miami, crossed the Ohio under cover of night, and staked out the Tanner farmstead early in the morning. For hours they hid in the woods at the edge of the cornfield, watching the men and one grown boy in the field and waiting for an eligible child to emerge from the stockade. Several times Manitoo-geezhik had to counsel patience, as the younger men wanted to dispatch everyone in plain

sight and then search inside the stockade. Finally, about midday, they saw
nine-year-old John Tanner come through the gate and settle under a walnut
tree, where he began collecting walnuts in a straw hat. Manitoo-geezhik
and Kish-kau-ko crept up on the boy and seized him from behind, clapping
a hand over his mouth. Kish-kau-ko took the straw hat from the young
Tanner's hands, dumped the walnuts, and put it on the boy's head. Then,
with each one grasping an arm, they lifted him off his feet and whisked him
away.[7]

A mile from the farmstead the seven Ottawas and Shawnees had a canoe
and provisions stashed under some bushes on the bank of the Ohio. They
offered Tanner dry venison and bear fat, but he was too frightened to eat.
Thrusting him into the canoe, they crossed the Ohio and started up the Big
Miami. After a while they ditched the canoe and continued their journey
on land, Manitoo-geezhik and Kish-kau-ko once more flanking the boy and
gripping him by the wrists. Pushed along on his bare feet, Tanner tried to
make mental notes of their route so he could find his way back. He thought
about how he might get away when they all went to sleep for the night. But
when they finally stopped at the end of the day he was so exhausted that he
immediately fell deeply asleep and remained so until his captors rousted
him in the morning.[8]

They continued their journey the next day and the next, and mile by mile
Tanner lost hope of making his escape. Coming to a large stream, Manitoo-
geezhik put the boy on his shoulders and waded across. As the river was
wide and the water came up to Manitoo-geezhik's armpits, Tanner realized
that here was a barrier which would once and for all prevent him from returning home on his own two legs.[9]

When Tanner's captors reached the northward flowing Maumee River,
they built hickory bark canoes and continued their journey on water. Downstream, at the mouth of the Auglaize River, they came to the Shawnee village where Manitoo-geezhik had picked up three of his companions. As
they landed their canoes, residents of the village swarmed around them.
One young woman, giving a cry, walked up and struck Tanner on the head.
Having recently lost close kin in a skirmish with the Americans, she and
her relatives wanted to kill the young white captive for revenge. Manitoo-
geezhik and Kish-kau-ko had to talk them out of it. Their party, reduced to
four men and the boy after the other three men returned to their lodges, remained in the Shawnee village for two days. Surrounded as they were by so
many other Indians, whose language was incomprehensible to him, Tanner
was soon made to understand that he was under Manitoo-geezhik's protection. The old Indian knew a few words of English and began ordering him

to fetch water, collect firewood, and perform other tasks, treating him more like a slave than a captive. As a matter of self-preservation, the boy readily answered to his commands.[10]

Leaving the Shawnee village, they floated down the Maumee River toward Lake Erie and arrived the following day at a British trading post. When they approached the British traders, Manitoo-geezhik and his followers made no effort to conceal their captive. Nor did the traders betray any alarm at the sight of Tanner, despite his bloody feet and the obvious fact that he had been abducted. Calmly the traders offered to purchase the boy, but Manitoo-geezhik declined their offer, explaining that the boy was to take the place of his deceased son. The traders were already familiar with this Indian practice. They gave Tanner a meal and, after explaining to him what had just passed between them and the old Indian, told him that in ten days they would follow him to the Indians' village and rescue him. But Tanner sensed this was a lie and, when his captors prepared to leave, began to weep. He was surprised by his own tears, for until that point in his ordeal he had been too tired or frightened to cry.[11]

In a few more days they came to the frontier settlement of Detroit. The young boy's interest was piqued as the Indians paddled the canoe close to shore to exchange some words with a white woman walking along the riverbank, but their conversation was in French and after a brief exchange they continued on past the settlement. Once out of sight of the town, the Indians landed the canoe. After a short search in the woods they found what they were looking for, a hollow log in which to hide their captive and assorted valuables while they returned to town. Ordering Tanner to crawl into the log alongside their blankets and kettles, they placed another log against the opening, sealing him in. Tanner stayed imprisoned in there for many hours. When the Indians at last returned, night had fallen, but Tanner could see that they had acquired three horses. The Indians put Tanner on one horse, their baggage on another, and took turns riding the third. With horses they traveled much faster, and about three days later they arrived home at the village of Saginaw. Their mission complete, the small war party disbanded without hoopla.[12]

Manitoo-geezhik lived in a log cabin that did not look appreciably different from the log cabins Tanner knew in Kentucky. When they arrived in front of Manitoo-geezhik's home, his wife emerged and immediately began to cry tears of joy and smother the boy with hugs and kisses. Though unprepared for her emotional outburst, he would soon come to appreciate how it made sense in the context of her world. According to her belief system, the courage shown by her husband and son in going to the Ohio River and back had succeeded in "raising up the dead." She no longer had to grieve the loss of her son, for his spirit had arisen once more in the body of this little boy. Tanner had to accept that he himself was that boy.[13]

As was generally the case in this form of adoption, most of the Ottawas did not rush to form bonds of affection with the nine-year-old Tanner but waited to see how he would respond to this new phase of his life. Tanner participated at once in all the family's activities—planting corn in the spring, going with the whole village to its hunting grounds in the summer, gathering the corn and fishing for sturgeon when autumn came—but until he acquired their language he had to learn how to do things more by observation than by direct instruction. While his mother was mostly kind to him, his father and three brothers treated him badly, beating or knocking him down, as he would later recall, nearly every day. Manitoo-geezhik was particularly violent and cruel on occasion. Once that first summer, he tomahawked the boy in the head and left him bleeding and unconscious outside their camp, seemingly indifferent whether he lived or died. One day the following winter, he grabbed Tanner by the hair and rubbed his face in excrement, then threw him in a snowbank.[14]

The following spring, Manitoo-geezhik announced that he would lead another war party to the Ohio River. This time his plan was to return to the same farmstead and kill all of the white boy's relatives. Brutal as it was, his plan had a rational design. He wanted to expunge all thoughts Tanner might have of ever returning to his original family. As Tanner by this time had become conversant in Ottawa, Manitoo-geezhik boasted to his adopted son of what he planned to do. Then he left. A few weeks later he returned with an old white hat, which Tanner recognized from a mark in the crown as his older brother's hat. Manitoo-geezhik told him that his war party had killed everyone at the Tanner farm—the entire family, all of the slaves, and even the horses.

Many years passed before Tanner learned that this massacre never happened. Although the war party did indeed go back to the Tanner farm, they killed no one. They took Tanner's older brother Edward captive, but he escaped in the night from the Indians' first camp on the Big Miami. And yet the whole thing worked out according to Manitoo-geezhik's plan, for when he returned from the raid and told Tanner his horrible lie, it had exactly the psychological impact he had intended. Tanner was too young and naïve not to believe him, especially when presented with Edward's hat as evidence. Tanner would take to his new life as an Indian more readily with the belief that all his white kin were dead.[15]

After two years, the abusive Manitoo-geezhik finally did his adopted son one good turn: he sold him to another Indian, a woman. Her name was Net-no-kwa, and she was a village chief among the Ottawas. Her people lived on the northern shores of Lake Huron and on the upper and lower peninsulas of Michigan. She was related through kinship to Manitoo-geezhik. In the summer of 1792 she visited her kinsman who, notwithstanding his wife's lamentations, sold his adopted son for the price of some blankets, trinkets, and tobacco, and a ten-gallon keg of whiskey.[16]

When Net-no-kwa adopted Tanner, the boy once more replaced a child of similar age who had died. Although the trade made him a newcomer in a strange family all over again, Tanner quickly recognized that this second adoption was favorable for him, for Net-no-kwa treated him much better than Manitoo-geezhik ever did. Net-no-kwa gave him a mother's affection, something he had not really enjoyed since his original mother had died when he was two years old. His relationship with his Ottawa mother would grow into one of the strongest, most enduring bonds he would ever have. Though she was already older when she adopted him—she may have been forty years old—she still possessed great energy and a subtle command over her whole family. In the eyes of the eleven-year-old boy, she had a beautiful face as well.[17]

Tanner soon learned the makeup of his new extended family. Net-no-kwa was married to a much younger man, and her husband had two other wives who were about his own age. Net-no-kwa had one grown daughter and two adolescent sons from a past marriage. The daughter had a husband and two small children. That made eleven people in the family, counting Tanner. Net-no-kwa was the esteemed elder in this three-generation family. Tanner was the youngest family member other than the two small children, and as an adoptee he was the lowest in the family hierarchy. Although Net-no-kwa was tender hearted, she still treated him as the family drudge.[18]

Taw-ga-we-ninne, Net-no-kwa's husband, was seventeen years younger than she. Indeed, he was not much older than Net-no-kwa's daughter. Net-no-kwa's children addressed him as their father, and he addressed Net-no-kwa's children in speech as he would his own daughter and sons, but in actual manner he treated them more like equals. He had a gentle, affable way. Tanner saw that Taw-ga-we-ninne generally deferred to Net-no-kwa's decisions for the family and that Net-no-kwa owned everything. Net-no-kwa's superior age and Taw-ga-we-ninne's subordinate role were not the usual pattern in Ottawa families, but they were not that exceptional either.[19] In part, the young Tanner observed a family dynamic that contrasted sharply with the rigidly patriarchal family structure he had known in Kentucky.

Taw-ga-we-ninne was not Ottawa but Ojibwa. His tribe and Net-no-

kwa's tribe both belonged to a large group known as Algonquian for the
similarities of their languages and cultures. Algonquian tribes occupied an
expansive territory extending from the Atlantic Coast far into the interior of
North America, but they were most numerous around the Great Lakes. The
Algonquian peoples included the Shawnees, Potawatomis, and Kickapoos,
among many others. Besides being affiliated through language and culture,
the Algonquian peoples also encouraged intermarriage to strengthen their
place in the world. By way of marriage alliances, they recognized and hon-
ored elaborate kinship networks that not only extended beyond the family
and band but reached into other tribes as well. Thus, Net-no-kwa recognized Manitoo-geezhik as her relative, even though they lived in widely
separated villages and may not have ever met before. Through her marriage
to Taw-ga-we-ninne, she acquired relations among the Ojibwas who lived
many miles to the west.[20]

Net-no-kwa's band of Ottawas lived on the northern tip of Michigan's
lower peninsula, where the waters of Lake Michigan mingle with the waters
of Lake Huron through the five-mile-wide Straits of Mackinac separating
Michigan's upper and lower peninsulas. This junction of the upper Great
Lakes had been a center of the fur trade since the days of Jean Nicolet and
Père Marquette. Just east of the Straits lies Mackinac Island, where the British had built a fort in 1780, replacing one on the mainland that the French
had occupied since 1715. Net-no-kwa's village of Cheboygan stood on the
shore of Lake Huron about fifteen miles east of the Straits of Mackinac.
Another Ottawa village, called by the French L'Arbre Croche for a crooked
tree that the Indians held sacred, stood at the base of a sandy spit jutting
into Lake Michigan a few miles west of the Straits. Along with the two Ottawa villages there were small settlements of Ojibwas bordering the Straits
on Bois Blanc Island and Point St. Ignace, the latter village occupying the
site of an old Jesuit mission. Tanner came to know all of these places in the
course of his family's wanderings, and he took pride in the fact that Net-no-
kwa was a principal chief of the Ottawa. The traders at Fort Mackinac recognized her canoe by the Union Jack she flew in their honor, and they gave
her a salute with the fort's cannon every time they saw her approaching.[21]

Tanner had been with Net-no-kwa for about a year when she announced
one day that it was time for her son to learn how to hunt. Taw-ga-we-ninne
owned a cavalryman's pistol, which he at that moment loaded and handed
to Tanner, telling him that if he managed to kill anything with it then he
would be given his own gun and taught how to use it. The boy had been
among the Indians long enough now to know what a propitious offer this
was. Eagerly he rose, took the pistol, and went out. Only a little distance

from camp, a pigeon flew in and obligingly plumped down on a nearby bush. Carefully the boy cocked his piece, held it to his cheek, and pulled the trigger. The discharge seared his cheek and knocked him down, and the pistol flew from his grasp. But when he got to his feet he was delighted to find the pigeon lying dead beneath the bush. Taw-ga-we-ninne kept his promise, not only teaching him how to hunt with a gun, but also how to make traps and catch marten. Now in his twelfth year, Tanner found that by becoming a hunter he rose markedly in the Indians' esteem.[22]

The Trader

❋ 3 ❋ It was no coincidence that the adult John Tanner, after being ambushed and badly wounded in Canada that summer of 1823, ended up in the care of Dr. John McLoughlin. McLoughlin was then the only surgeon in all of the Hudson's Bay Company's vast domain. For two decades, he had provided medical services for sick and injured fur traders, who came for treatment often from hundreds of miles away. During his many years with the old North West Company from 1803 to 1821, he resided most summers at Fort William, the Nor' Westers' great gathering place on the north shore of Lake Superior. There he ran a hospital and apothecary, attending to the many cases of venereal disease, hernias, and broken bones incurred by the several hundred employees who congregated for the yearly rendezvous. Indians came to him for help as well. He had given medical aid to John Tanner on two prior occasions: once when Tanner suffered broken ribs after falling from a tree and another time when he fell sick after over-turning his canoe in an icy river. Not all of McLoughlin's patients came to see him at Fort William or Rainy Lake; sometimes he took his medical kit and traveled by canoe for days to visit a patient at some isolated outpost.[1]

But practicing medicine made up only a small part of McLoughlin's duties as a trader and administrator, and he often brooded about the twist of fate that had caused him to enter the fur trade instead of acquiring a comfortable medical practice in Quebec, as he had once imagined. At the end of his first five-year engagement with the North West Company in 1808, he looked back on the whole experience with regret and pronounced it a "sad experiment." After his second five-year hitch, he wrote plaintively to an uncle, "People talk of the desert of Siberia, but this is as bad." The harsh environment, the rough society—it was all "one Universal sameness." In another letter home, he wrote that he would rather be "living on potatoes and milk than in this country." These were not simply ill-humored remarks written on a gloomy day but markers of his growing disillusionment. Life was passing him by. "Removed so far as I am into the wilderness," he wrote to his uncle again, "it is not in my power to communicate any thing very new or agreeable to you." And in another missive, "When a man has been for any

time in this Country he is entirely unfit for any other." McLoughlin continued to characterize his life in the fur trade as one long, dreary, self-imposed
exile even after he gave up any thoughts of returning to his native Quebec.[2]

John McLoughlin was born October 19, 1784, in Rivière-du-Loup, an
agricultural village perched on the south bank of the wide St. Lawrence
River. His father was of Irish Catholic extraction, his mother a mix of Scottish Presbyterian and French Catholic. John was the third of seven children.
Through John's early childhood the family lived on a prosperous farm fronting
on the great waterway. When he was eight the family moved to Quebec, the
colony's fortress city with a population of about 10,000 inhabitants. It was
there, at the age of fourteen, that John decided to become a doctor and thus
began a three-and-a-half-year apprenticeship with one of Quebec's leading
physicians, Dr. James Fisher.[3]

John's maternal grandfather, Malcolm Fraser, was a towering figure in his
early life. He was owner of a *seigneury*, or large estate, at a place called Murray Bay about thirty miles upriver and on the opposite shore from Rivière-
du-Loup. Malcolm Fraser spoke English, Gaelic, and French, was an avid
reader of books on ancient and modern history, and loved to regale his
grandchildren with colorful stories about their Highland Scot forebears and
his own bygone days as a soldier. His father—John's great-grandfather—had
fallen at Culloden, the storied battle that finally brought to heel the rowdy
and independent clans of Highland Scotland. Malcolm, who like his father
was loyal to the English King, joined the 42nd Highland Scots Regiment in
the British army and came to North America during the French and Indian
War. His own day of valor came in the Battle of Quebec, when he and his
men scaled a cliff and subdued a French picket before dawn, permitting the
rest of the British troops to engage and defeat the main French forces on
the Plains of Abraham. After the conflict the Crown rewarded him with a
large land grant, the Mount Murray Seigneury, a 160-square-mile tract of
wilderness, which he transformed into a thriving country estate over the
next two decades. By the time he was a grandfather, Seigneur Fraser was a
person of considerable wealth. Proud and domineering, he gave his Catholic
daughter and son-in-law more land at Rivière-du-Loup on the condition
that they recant their Catholicism and raise their children as Presbyterians.[4]

John's uncles on the Fraser side—his mother's two younger brothers—
were also important influences on the young boy. The older of the two, Alexander Fraser, apprenticed to the North West Company when John was
still quite small. Although this took his uncle far away, stories of his exploits
probably formed John's earliest impressions of the fur trade. In 1801, when
John was sixteen, Alexander returned to Quebec on a one-year furlough.

Having risen to partner in the company, his next assignment was to the King's Post, a very old fur-trade establishment across the St. Lawrence from Rivière-du-Loup at the mouth of the Saguenay River. This assignment enabled Alexander to remain close to his property at Rivière-du-Loup, to which he retired in 1806.[5]

Simon Fraser, John's favorite uncle, studied medicine at the University of Edinburgh, returning to the colony to start a medical practice in Terrebonne near Montreal. In 1795 he became a surgeon in the British army. As John entered his teens and began his apprenticeship with Dr. Fisher, he heard occasional reports of his uncle Simon's exploits in the wars of the French Revolution. While fighting Napoleon's army in Egypt, Simon received a wound in the hand and was discharged from the army. Returning to Terrebonne in 1801, he somehow managed to resume his practice as a surgeon in spite of his maimed left hand.[6]

In the spring of 1803, John McLoughlin completed his apprenticeship and prepared to follow in his uncle Simon's footsteps, expecting to start his own medical practice. But just then he committed a misstep that forced him to abort this plan and follow his uncle Alexander into the fur trade instead.

According to family lore, his transgression was a gallant but foolish brush with the law. As recounted by a nephew long after McLoughlin's death, John was escorting a young lady over some planks laid in the mud of a Quebec street when a British military officer approached from the opposite direction and haughtily pushed the young lady aside. McLoughlin, who at age eighteen was already a big, strong fellow and possessed with a volcanic temper, lifted the British officer off his feet and threw him down in the mud. No sooner had he done this than he realized the gravity of his offense and fled in short order to the frontier to avoid punishment.[7]

The story sounds apocryphal, but McLoughlin once conceded in a letter to his uncle Simon that "it was entirely by my own want of conduct that I came up to this Country." In another lament he wrote, "I am sorry I ever came to it however this was perhaps not a matter of Choice but of Necessity on my part."[8]

Whatever the precipitating misstep was, McLoughlin barely had time to secure his medical credentials before fleeing to the frontier. It appears that he sought temporary refuge with his uncle Simon in nearby Terrebonne. There, on April 1, 1803, the young man prepared his petition for a medical license, hoping that the trouble would blow over, or at least not catch up to him, until he had obtained his license. In his anxious state he must have confided everything to his uncle, for Simon Fraser helped him plan his escape while they nervously awaited action on the petition. His uncle first proposed that he sail to the West Indies and then, on further reflection, that he go to the Indian frontier. Perhaps Alexander Fraser's connection with the North West Company made the latter escape seem preferable. At last, more than three weeks after submitting the petition, young McLoughlin was summoned before a board of commissioners in Montreal to take his medical examination. He passed the exam, but now he faced an excruciating wait for the government to issue his license. According to protocol, the petition together with the examiners' certificate would be forwarded to Dr. Fisher in Quebec with a request that the doctor attest to the apprentice's good conduct. Ultimately, Mr. Fisher's letter divulged nothing about any "want of conduct," and the lieutenant governor issued McLoughlin's license without more ado on May 3, 1803. But by then McLoughlin had already cast his lot with the fur trade.[9]

The day after sitting his exam, he went with his uncle to the office of McTavish, Frobisher & Co., Montreal agents for the North West Company. There, he signed the indenture that bound him for five years of service as a surgeon and apprentice clerk for the lowly sum of £100, or just £20 per year. That was hardly a good return on investment for the three-and-a-half-year apprenticeship he had just completed with Dr. Fisher. It was a contract entered under duress.[10]

The terms of the labor contract were harsh but no different from the terms set for most North West Company employees. The company would provide transport from Montreal to the Northwest and back to Montreal at the end of his five-year indenture. During that time he would obey all company officers' lawful commands and go wherever they chose to send him. (In this instance, "Northwest" referred to all of British America west of the St. Lawrence River valley, a vast, unmapped territory that the Nor' Westers themselves had just begun to explore.) The company would provide for all his needs, and he would receive no wages until his return to Montreal. Embezzlement of peltries or goods was strictly forbidden and was grounds for both dismissal and forfeiture of wages. In other words, the company did not allow its employees to engage in any trade with Indians except under its auspices. At £20 per year, McLoughlin's wages as apprentice clerk were marginally inferior to those of the North West Company's laboring class— the engagés who worked at the trading posts and who also manned the canoes—but unlike those men McLoughlin had the possibility to advance to the rank of clerk and ultimately to partner. This placed him in the upper echelons even though he first had to serve his apprenticeship.[11]

As for McLoughlin's credential as a licensed physician, it appears that he and his uncle incautiously bargained that away. The white-haired Simon

McTavish, the semilegendary figure who had largely created the North West Company more than two decades earlier, coolly informed Simon Fraser that the company already had one physician, Dr. Henry Munro, among its several hundred employees. This man was a clerk on the way to becoming a partner. Should the company eventually require young McLoughlin's services as a physician, then he would be compensated as Dr. Munro was; that is, he would be paid an additional £100 per year. Moreover, McTavish held out the prospect that the young McLoughlin, with his unusual training as a surgeon, might expect rapid advancement following his apprenticeship. At least that was how McLoughlin later remembered it. But McTavish's promise was not put in writing, and it appeared nowhere in McLoughlin's contract.[12]

Such were the seeds of his later disillusionment. To no one's surprise he began to practice medicine almost as soon as he took up his duties and, within a year or two, took over Dr. Munro's practice as well. McTavish died unexpectedly in 1804, which left McLoughlin with no other recourse than to ask his uncle Simon to bear witness to the agreement that they had made with the deceased concerning his early promotion and higher rate of pay. Simon Fraser procrastinated. He apparently concurred with McLoughlin that there had been some sort of gentleman's agreement but finally advised his nephew that "the promise dies with Mr. McTavish."[13]

McTavish's nephew William McGillivray succeeded him as head of the company. McGillivray's ascension to leadership not only demonstrated McTavish's skill in promoting the interests of his own clan, it also marked a shift in power from the Montreal agents to the younger men like McGillivray, who generally spent the entire year in the wilderness—the so-called "wintering partners." As a result, the administrative center of the company shifted from Montreal to Fort William on the northwest shore of Lake Superior, where the partners convened each summer to count their returns, bring in new partners to replace those who were retiring, and plan operations for the coming year.

McLoughlin could not let go of the idea that the North West Company owed him substantial back pay for his service as a doctor. It was an injustice that darkened his whole view of the enterprise. In the summer of 1808, as his five-year apprenticeship drew to a close, one of the wintering partners asked him confidentially if he would be "going down"—that is, did he intend to leave the business and take his passage back to Montreal? McLoughlin answered that he was undecided. The partner then advised him to *say* he was going down so that the partners would offer him better terms to stay. A few days later McGillivray sent for him and made him an offer: McLoughlin could take a promotion to physician and clerk for £150 per year. McLoughlin hesitated, then boldly asked what prospects he had for becoming a partner. McGillivray answered instantly, "those of other young men of character." His voice rising, McLoughlin told McGillivray that he had been led to expect more when he engaged with the company. Otherwise, "I would not have given five years of my time after studying a profession for the paltry sum of £100." Referring to McTavish's original promise, he stated flatly that he would not have served those five years had he not understood that his medical training assured him "a certain right" to rapid advancement. At this McGillivray shot back a withering reply: "No promise of the kind could be made *by any body.*"[14]

Three days later McGillivray raised his offer to £200 pounds, and McLoughlin accepted. But despite coming to a compromise, neither man would forget their earlier blunt exchange. They soon came to despise one another. McLoughlin resented the way McGillivray had ridden his uncle's coattails to the head of the company. Moreover, as McTavish was now dead, he had nobody to blame except McGillivray for swindling him out of his doctor's pay. McGillivray, for his part, found the tall, lean, young doctor insufferably uppity and irascible.[15]

❧{II}❧ LONG

"The English Make Them More Presents"

❊ **4** ❊ On his first assignment in the West in 1816, Brevet Major Stephen H. Long was eager to test his abilities as a surveyor, to show what the Topographical Engineers could do for westward expansion, and perhaps even position himself to inherit the mantle of Lewis and Clark. Before leaving New York for St. Louis, he wrote to Secretary of War William Crawford proposing that he take a small party of cadets from the West Point Military Academy under his command to assist with the topographical survey. Crawford denied the request; however, he gave Long permission to take some survey instruments from the academy, and he embellished Long's orders to the extent of saying, "Much useful information is expected from observations you will be able to make on the general face of the country, the navigable streams, and fertility of the soil." He expected "diligence but not haste."[1] That was all the encouragement Long needed to conceive of his task as a bit of exploration.

It was a modest beginning to his seven years of western exploration for the US government. The region of his first topographical survey contained no shining mountains. Spanning the northern half of the Illinois Territory, it was nothing but flat prairie. As an old man, he would recall that the country was "wild, solitary and dreary"—so different from the way it appeared some forty years later "occupied by a numerous and widespread population, and checkered with counties, towns, and villages."[2] Moreover, the topographical survey was not the main purpose of his first assignment in the West, but rather an add-on to a summer taken up with examining and reporting on forts. Still, this was his opportunity.

Bright and ambitious, Long aimed to make connections not only inside the officer corps but also in high places outside the military. He wanted to become known to the president and his cabinet as well as newspaper editors, publishers, scientists, and scholars.

He had been angling for social and political connections for half a decade already. Before joining the army, while living in Germantown, he made frequent trips to nearby Philadelphia to make friends among the elites in what was then the undisputed cultural capital of the nation. In a city where patronage controlled access to power, he had become a smooth operator, hobnobbing with members of the august American Philosophical Society, canvassing the booksellers and publishing houses to find the most up-to-date books and periodicals, and reading the most talked-about works of fiction and nonfiction, such as Mary Brunton's novel *Self-Control* and Edward Clarke's *Travels in Russia, Tartary and Turkey*.[3] Even after joining the army officer corps, he continued to use the patronage system to personal advantage. "I think patronage is a good word to be used by inferiors in relation to any countenance or support they may have received of their superiors," he once confided to a friend.[4] General Joseph Swift, the chief of engineers and Long's first mentor, described him as "an amiable & discreet gentleman."[5] Others spoke of him as intelligent, enterprising, energetic, and suave.[6]

Early in October, Long started up the Illinois River with two privates and a mixed-blood guide, François Leclair, who spoke French and Potawatomi. Leclair shared his knowledge of the river system as Long explored the low marshy divide between the headwaters of the Illinois and the Chicago, the latter stream meandering through wetlands for a few short miles before emptying into Lake Michigan. Leclair showed Long a three-mile portage where the French and Indians had made "a kind of canal" for getting their canoes across the height of land. If a ship canal were built there, Long observed, it would complete a waterway from the Mississippi to the Great Lakes. Where the city of Chicago stands today, the party encountered only a tiny, polyglot community of Potawatomi, British, and French traders, and two companies of American soldiers who had arrived on July 4 to rebuild Fort Dearborn. The old fort had been attacked and destroyed by Potawatomi allies of the British in 1812. Inspecting the natural harbor at the mouth of the river, Long became the first American to envision a great city rising there. From Fort Dearborn the party proceeded overland to Fort Wayne. There, Long sent his soldier escort and guide back to St. Louis while he proceeded onward through Ohio, Pennsylvania, and Maryland to the nation's capital, where he made his topographical report to the War Department.[7]

On his journey through northern Illinois and Indiana, Long had his first encounter with western Indians and the fur trade. In his topographical report he listed the principal tribes in the region as the Sacs, Foxes, Potawatomis, Kickapoos, Miamis, Delawares, Ojibwas, Shawnees, and Kaskaskias. Most of those nations, he wrote, had fought with the British against the United States in the recent war "and probably would do the same again upon a renewal of hostilities with Great Britain." Allied with the British ever since the Revolutionary War, they still had a stronger affinity for the English than for the Americans. As some Indians had directly informed him, "The

English make them more presents than the Americans. They furnish them with better articles, and at a cheaper rate. They are more punctual in fulfilling their engagements to the Indians. Those appointed to transact business with the Indians are not in the habit, like the Americans, of taking every advantage in their dealings with them."[8]

Though Long titled this section of his report "Indians," he was really talking about fur traders. Here in a nutshell was the army's interest in the fur trade. To secure the northern frontier against the British, the army needed to pacify the Indian tribes; to pacify the Indian tribes, it wanted to reorganize the fur trade so that the Indians would no longer depend on British traders. In short, the United States had to take control of the fur trade within its borders so that the tribes would finally abandon the British-Indian alliance of the Revolutionary War era.[9]

American military strategists had been driving at this problem for many years. President Washington sought to put American trade with Indians on a stronger footing by means of the Trade and Intercourse Acts. Under those laws, the federal government took responsibility for licensing traders and regulating intercourse between whites and Indians. The army was called upon to track the traders, removing violators while protecting legitimate traders against Indian attack. But enforcement of the Trade and Intercourse laws was weak. In fact, during the first three decades of American independence, licensed American traders played a relatively insignificant role in the fur trade. British traders vastly outnumbered them and operated within US territory with impunity. In Jay's Treaty of 1794, British traders were specifically guaranteed the right to maintain their trading posts on American soil. Americans' strong resentment of those terms formed one of the causes of the War of 1812. Following the war, American interest in the fur trade burgeoned. The army built forts along the Indian frontier and took other steps to control the Indians. Long was destined to play a significant role in those efforts, first as a surveyor of new forts and then as a western explorer. He would become a keen observer of the fur trade and advise the government on how it might better regulate it.[10]

The first major statement of US aims in the fur trade after the Treaty of Ghent came in a report to the Senate by Secretary of War Crawford in March 1816. Long's ideas paralleled Crawford's, and it is likely he familiarized himself with Crawford's report before preparing his own. The secretary's report was a major statement on federal Indian policy—according to Crawford's biographer, it was one of the signal accomplishments of his short stint at the War Department. Befitting the mood of national expansion, Crawford's main concern was to consider ways to Americanize the fur trade within the territorial limits of the United States.[11]

Crawford began with the widely held assumption that all Indian peoples were more or less dependent on the fur trade for some of their necessities —the more so wherever their hunting grounds were depleted of game. He stressed that the United States had to support the trade in one form or another or it would "alienate the affections" of the tribes. The British traders could not be evicted from US territory precipitously, because in many areas it would create a hardship for the Indians. Crawford pointed to such remote areas as the upper Mississippi and the upper Missouri, where the Americans had little knowledge about the tribes and could not simply move in as the North West Company and the Hudson's Bay Company vacated their trading posts. In such areas the British fur companies must be permitted to continue operations under US licenses for an interim period. As soon as the United States acquired more information on the Indians, then the British traders would be made to surrender their licenses so that American traders could take their place.[12]

Crawford wanted the government to increase its support of government-run trading houses, or "factories," but only as a stopgap until private enterprise was able to meet the demand. The unpopular factory system dated back to the 1790s. When the federal government began to regulate the fur trade, it did so through two parallel measures: licensing of independent traders and establishment of factories. The government-run factories were intended to have a beneficial effect on Indian-white relations by supplying the Indians with manufactured goods at fair price, placing honest men in charge of the government stores, and keeping the more rapacious independent traders in check. President Jefferson expanded the factory system, giving it the mantle of "civilizing" the Indians. It was his belief that more trade would eventually lead the Indians to adopt a more settled way of life. (He also argued that it would promote Indian indebtedness, giving the United States an upper hand in extracting land cessions.) Congress was wary of establishing a government monopoly in the fur trade, however, and provided only half-hearted support for the factory system. Chronically underfunded, the factory system never became the dominant force on the frontier that its champions wanted. The licensed traders hated the government trading houses, since the purpose of the government traders was to keep a watchful eye on them and undersell them when necessary. By the second decade of the nineteenth century most westerners shared the private traders' scorn for the government-subsidized trading houses, thinking that they discouraged capital investment on the frontier. Congress was increasingly inclined to heed western opinion and reduce funding for the factory system.[13]

If the factory system was a disappointment, the licensing system was even more fraught with problems. The law provided for the governors of the territories to issue licenses to anyone who could post bond. Ostensibly the bond was a guarantee that the licensed trader would abide by the government's regulations. But with practically no enforcement the regulations were largely ignored. There were many disreputable traders who cheated the Indians out of their furs by whatever means they could. Often they plied the Indians with liquor and then stole from them. Competition between traders only made the situation worse by contributing to the use of illegal liquor in manipulating the Indians. Viewing the independent traders with much skepticism, Crawford urged Congress to amend the Trade and Intercourse Acts so that governors would have authority to select traders on the basis of moral character. Traders bore a responsibility as the torchbearers of "civilization," and it was only reasonable to expect that they present a good face to the Indians.[14]

Crawford's main idea for Americanizing the fur trade was for a large, well-capitalized company to enter the field and establish a private monopoly. Such a company would be easier for the government to regulate, and by ending competition between traders it would eliminate some of the worst abuses of the fur trade. The problem was how to attract sufficient capital, which could only be found in the commercial cities of the Atlantic seaboard. Unfortunately, venture capitalists tended to view the fur trade as a bad risk. Crawford's solution was to establish a government factory at St. Louis that would serve as a forward supply base, furnishing goods, capital, and skilled persons to the trading houses located on the frontier. At first this factory would supply government trading houses. In time, when the desired company had arisen to take the place of the government, the whole operation could be sold to private enterprise.[15]

Crawford based his ideas on the conviction that the policy of an "enlightened nation" must be "to draw its savage neighbors within the pale of civilization." For if the federal government were simply to withdraw from regulation of the Indian trade, allowing land-hungry whites to strike their own deals with Indian peoples, the outcome would be "continual warfare, attended by the extermination or expulsion of the aboriginal inhabitants of the country to more distant and less hospitable regions." A civilized people must abhor such an outcome, Crawford declared. So, the Indian must be assimilated.

Crawford echoed the Jeffersonian idea that the fur trade was an incubator for raising the Indian from a "savage state." A growing dependency on trade goods would instill in the Indians the value of personal property, he believed. From a keener desire for personal property would come a desire for separate property in the form of land, and from this would come an inclination to farm. Once the Indian became a landowner and a tiller of the soil, he would acquire a respect for laws and be on the path to full American citizenship. It was a hopeful vision of universal human progress. But there remained the question of whether the Indian had sufficient time, given the pressure of white land hunger, to proceed unmolested along this path from savagery to civilization. Given that pressure, Crawford added his own recommendation to the Jeffersonian idea of civilizing the Indian, which many of his contemporaries found shocking. "When every effort to introduce among them the ideas of separate property . . . should fail," Crawford urged, "let intermarriages between them and the whites be encouraged by the government."[16]

Crawford was a southerner and a slaveholder, the owner of a small plantation in Georgia, and a co-founder and vice president of the American Colonization Society, an organization dedicated to ending slavery in the United States by colonizing freed slaves in Africa. Evidently he had higher hopes for assimilating Indians into white society than he had for blacks. His idea was not a new one; missionaries had been advocating intermarriage between whites and Cherokees for a number of years. But Crawford's proposal for the government to encourage interracial marriage caused dismay among some members of Congress. Three days after he submitted his report, the Republican Party caucus met to nominate a presidential candidate. With Crawford's name in contention alongside James Monroe's, several members who opposed him pilloried his report with its odious suggestion that the Indian and white races amalgamate. The caucus chose Monroe over Crawford by a vote of 65 to 54. Crawford never retracted his words about interracial marriage, but privately he allowed that the statement had been politically damaging.[17]

Long could not have known anything about what went on in the Republican Party caucus, but there is a good chance he was following Crawford's political star that spring and summer of 1816. While Long was en route from St. Louis back to Washington in the fall, Crawford left the War Department to become secretary of the treasury. Three weeks later, James Monroe was elected fifth president of the United States, the last of the Virginia Dynasty. That winter, as the president-elect assembled his cabinet, Long wrote his topographical report and prepared a large map of the Illinois country. He addressed his report to Acting Secretary of War George Graham, who headed the War Department in the last few months of the Madison administration. Graham apparently approved of Long's ardent recommendations for internal improvements and his nationalist tone. He gave the report to his friend, Joel Mead, editor of *The National Register,* with the suggestion that he publish an abstract of it in his weekly paper. Mead chose to print the entire report, presenting Major Long of the US Topographical Engineers to the American public for the first time.[18]

Encounters with the Sioux

❊ 5 ❊ Long obtained his second assignment in the West the following year. Reporting to General Thomas Smith at Fort Belle
Fontaine, near St. Louis, in May, he received his new orders. He was to
make a military and topographical reconnaissance of the upper Mississippi,
essentially completing the work he had begun in 1816. On his way up the
Mississippi River he would inspect frontier defenses: Forts Edwards, Madison, Armstrong, and Crawford, the last of these being situated at Prairie du
Chien at the confluence of the Wisconsin and Mississippi rivers. From Prairie du Chien, he was to make a side trip up the Wisconsin River to survey
the portage between that river and the Fox River flowing into Green Bay on
Lake Michigan and to recommend a site for a fort there. This was the main
route used by the French and British for supplying the fur trade west of the
Great Lakes. After returning to Prairie du Chien, he was to proceed north
to St. Anthony Falls, the farthest point of navigation on the Mississippi,
investigating possible sites for more forts in that direction. Long's reconnaissance of the upper Mississippi served the national aim of establishing
a cordon of forts between the Northwest Indian tribes and the British. A
subsidiary purpose was to meet with the Sioux Indians inhabiting the upper
Mississippi and learn if they were peaceably disposed to the United States.
For Long, the final leg of this expedition from Prairie du Chien to St. Anthony Falls was exactly the kind of exploration he was itching to do. What
little was known about the area came from the published accounts of two
previous explorers, the celebrated eighteenth-century fur trader and traveler,
Jonathan Carver, and the late Captain Zebulon M. Pike.[1]

Governor of Missouri William Clark, the veteran explorer of the Lewis
and Clark expedition, presented Long with a six-oared skiff for the voyage,
while General Smith assigned him six enlisted men, a corporal, and an interpreter. It was a larger command than on his previous expedition through
the Illinois country. In addition to this eight-man crew, the boat carried
provisions, cooking utensils, a single camp tent, and supplies of whiskey,
tobacco, and other items for making presents to the Indians. The expedition set sail from Fort Belle Fontaine on the first of June. Six weeks later it

arrived at Prairie du Chien, where it took on board fresh supplies and one additional soldier for exploration of the upper Mississippi.[2]

Prairie du Chien was not only the jumping-off point for Long's first major exploration, it was the center of the fur trade in Wisconsin in 1817. With a population that was predominantly French-speaking, substantially mixed-blood, and salted with a few British traders, it was typical of the Anglo-French-Indian milieu that persisted throughout most of the Old Northwest even after the War of 1812. Governor Clark had led a military expedition to this old French settlement in May 1814, establishing Fort Shelby as a defense against a British invasion from Canada, but the British had captured the fort just two months later and held it until the end of the war, blowing it up when they withdrew. Even with the return of peace, American traders were hardly welcome there. A report reached Washington after the war ended of Americans' scalps being bought and sold in the village of Prairie du Chien and strung on poles as a warning to American traders not to come into the area. In July 1816, General Smith arrived with a force of soldiers and built Fort Crawford on the site of the previous fort. When Long arrived in July 1817, the US Office of Indian Trade had recently established a government factory nearby under the supervision of John W. Johnson. This government trader informed Long that the Indians who lived on the Mississippi above Prairie du Chien would probably give him no trouble. But hostility toward Americans on the part of the village occupants and their Indian trading partners was still palpable; Johnson himself, despite being married to an Indian, said he could not wait to get away from "the cursed stinking Indians."[3]

Long's impression of this frontier settlement was no more favorable than Johnson's. Prairie du Chien was named for an elongated plain lying between the Mississippi River and a line of bluffs. The prairie was beautiful to behold, but as portions of it were swampy and periodically inundated by the river, he found the whole place pestilential. Fort Crawford was situated on an island where the river braided into many channels, and in times of low water— as when Long visited there in July—the fort was surrounded by stagnant pools. The settlement of Prairie du Chien, located on the mainland, was only marginally better off than the fort, as much of the surrounding plain was infiltrated by sloughs and marshes. A single village street, lined with stores, workshops, and stables, ran parallel to the river for about a half mile, while dwellings were scattered more widely about. Zebulon Pike had estimated the village population at around 500 or 600 people in 1805, but it appeared to Long to be much less; he counted a total of thirty-eight occupied family dwellings. About one mile in back of the settlement was the grand farm, which was enclosed against wandering livestock and cultivated by the inhabitants in common. Long, with a New Englander's eye for how to lay out a farm, thought the existing crops of corn, wheat, and potatoes showed a decided lack of initiative by the inhabitants. "They have never yet taken pains to seed the ground with any kind of grain except the summer wheat, which is never so productive as the fall or winter wheat." With proper care, he commented, the farm could yield much larger and more varied crops.[4]

Long took a disparaging view of the people of Prairie du Chien. Noting that most of them had "savage blood in their veins," he gave voice to a common perception of his era in which all of humanity existed on a continuum from savage to civilized. He thought the community was not only dwindling in size, it was also slipping backwards into a state of savagery after the disruption of peaceful trade for a number of years during the War of 1812. "If we compare the village and its inhabitants in their present state with what they were when Pike visited this part of the country, we shall find that instead of improving they have been degenerating," he wrote. "Their improvement has been checked by a diversion of the Indian trade into other channels and their degeneracy accelerated not only by a consequent impoverishment of the inhabitants, but in addition to natural decay, their unconquerable slothfulness and want of enterprise."[5] The idea of human degeneracy ran like a motif through American thought in Long's day, so the explorer was hardly alone in perceiving a community's economic decline in social and moral terms. In Long's mind, Prairie du Chien's degeneracy provided a window into the savage state of Indian peoples.

As Prairie du Chien stood on the border of Sioux territory, Long replaced his first interpreter with a second, a mixed race named Roque, who spoke the Sioux language. But as he found it difficult to communicate with Roque in French he took aboard yet another interpreter, a New Englander by the name of Hempstead, who had resided in Prairie du Chien for eight years and spoke fluent French. Thus, to communicate with the Sioux his speech would be translated from English into French and from French into Sioux. He also permitted two young Americans to join the party when they paddled up suddenly in their birchbark canoe. Grandsons of Jonathan Carver, with the names King and Gun, they had journeyed from New York to claim a tract of land that their grandfather had purchased from the Indians more than fifty years earlier.[6]

On the first day of the journey the expedition passed a village of the Winnebagos, deserted since 1814, and saw not a single Indian. On the second day, about forty miles above Prairie du Chien, the expedition passed a cluster of Sioux lodges on the left bank of the river. When the Sioux saw the skiff with its American flag, they hoisted an American flag in greeting. Long returned the greeting by discharging a blunderbuss, whereupon the Sioux fired two guns over the water ahead of the skiff. Since the skiff was under sail and making swift progress upstream, Long decided not to put ashore, but when six young men of the Sioux village jumped in a canoe he slackened sail so that their canoe could overtake them. As the canoe came alongside the skiff, he took the hand of the head man, exchanged a few words, and gave him some tobacco and a pint of whiskey, after which the Indians shoved off. [7]

The next day, the expedition came to a larger Sioux village, where a similar ritual greeting unfolded. This time Long put ashore. The Indians gathered around the boat landing, seating themselves on the ground in a manner that suggested they expected a speech. Talking through his two interpreters, Long inquired if their chief was at home and learned that he was not. He then stated that he would like to talk with their chief and hoped to see him on their return trip. He further stated that he had been sent by the Great Father, the new president, who wanted to learn more about his red children. After this brief speech the Indians showed their friendly disposition by inviting Long and the interpreters to go through their village. It was evident that the Indians had just broken off a ceremony. They described for him what they called a bear dance, which was occasioned when a young male had a powerful dream that signaled his coming into manhood. Long pumped them for more information, and although the leaders would not identify the young man at the center of the ceremony they did give the explorer considerable details, which he carefully recorded. Long's description of the bear dance ceremony, running to several pages in his journal, constituted his first effort at ethnography. It showed him to be an inquisitive and careful observer of native culture even though he assumed that it was inferior to his own. [8]

Long had few other encounters with the Sioux on this voyage. He made a brief stop at another village and passed still another that was deserted, the occupants being away hunting. The expedition reached St. Anthony Falls (the site of modern-day Minneapolis) after seven days of rowing from Prairie du Chien, camped one night on the shore just below the cataract, and then turned back. A few miles below the falls, Long inspected the bluff where the St. Peter's River (now named the Minnesota) flows into the Mississippi, and found it to be an admirable location for a fort. He determined that the St. Peter's was 200 yards wide at the mouth and navigable for Mackinaw boats, but he did not venture upstream to the three Sioux villages that he thought he would find about nine miles above. Going back down the Mississippi, he stopped at one more Sioux village at a wide section of the river known as Lake Pepin, but he spent only "a very few minutes" with the Indians there so as to take advantage of a strong wind blowing the skiff down that long stretch of slack water.[9]

Long's haste and cursory Indian diplomacy were necessitated by a shortage of supplies. Running out of food, Long had to stop early each day so the men could catch fish for their dinner. Long blamed the shortage of provisions on his corporal, to whom he had entrusted the task of issuing rations. When the corporal disclosed the shortage, he admitted to having no prior experience in managing an expedition's supplies. More troubling than the dwindling food supply, however, was the fact that the expedition ran out of whiskey soon after turning about at St. Anthony Falls, which meant that the commander had little to offer Indians by way of gifts. To shorten the return trip—and, perhaps also, to avoid Indians—Long ordered the expedition to run portions of the river at night, floating with the current and steering by the light of a fire, which burned on a raft towed behind the skiff. Even this arrangement presented problems, as the leading craft occasionally ran aground on the many sandbars. Notwithstanding those hazards and privations on the return, however, Long returned to Fort Belle Fontaine on August 15 with all men in good health. The expedition covered nearly 1,400 river miles in just seventy-five days, making an average distance of 18 miles per day, an excellent pace. With this journey Long proved his ability to lead men safely over great distances at relatively low cost to the government.[10]

Race and History

❋ 6 ❋ Working from his journals, Long wrote an account of his expedition in the following spring. He adopted a more literary style in this report than in his previous one on the Illinois country, evidently aiming to reach a wider readership.[1] Besides reporting on the lay of the land and recording his impressions of the Sioux, Long included some elaborate, almost flowery descriptions of the scenery and antiquities observed en route. Those rather lyrical passages provide valuable insights into Long's personal responses to the land and people he encountered.

Near the head of Lake Pepin, the explorer ascended a high hill to obtain a view of the surrounding country. Standing on the summit of this hill about 400 feet above the river, Long was enraptured by the view of forest-clad knobs and valleys spreading in all directions. To take it all in, he pictured the scene as it might have appeared in the remote past: inundated by a vast inland sea, a world totally given over to aquatic life until some great convulsion at the center of the earth caused most of the water to drain off, leaving the present landscape with its "rich and fertile alluvion, well adapted to vegetation of all kinds."[2] Long's sense of the earth's history reflected a mix of scientific and Biblical influences. The geological theory that a primitive ocean had once covered the whole surface of the globe, and that all landforms had been created by a cataclysmic lowering of the sea level, formed a kind of scientific orthodoxy until the 1820s. One of the strengths of this theory was that it explained how fossil remains of sea life could occur in the middle of continents. It also jibed with a short earth history and worldwide flood event as described in Genesis. An alternative theory held that the center of the earth was hot and molten and that most landforms resulted from the countervailing forces of mountain uplift and water erosion. The latter theory began to emerge in the late eighteenth century but was still considered a scientific heresy in Long's day, mainly because it posited that the earth must be billions of years old. Long's musings on the origins of the landforms along the Mississippi River were perhaps more romantic than scientific, but they nevertheless demonstrated that his mind was engaged with geologic theory.[3]

Perhaps nothing excited the explorer's imaginings more than the ancient mounds that he investigated by horseback on the day after returning to Prairie du Chien. These extensive earthworks, some linear and others in the form of circles or squares, were spread all over the uplands at a point over-looking the Wisconsin River about three miles above its junction with the Mississippi. He described the arrangement of the mounds in detail, surmis-ing that they had been constructed principally for defense, although at least a few evidently doubled as burial mounds. Some of the linear earthworks, which he called parapets, appeared to have been aimed at defending against cavalry attack. He took measurements, made computations, and marveled at the amount of labor required to build them. Long had seen smaller mounds on the Mississippi above the Illinois River and was aware that they existed in many other locations throughout the Mississippi valley. He presumed incorrectly that the mounds were the work of an extinct race of people un-related to nineteenth-century Indian peoples.[4] It is now well established that the widespread mounds were the works of a pre-Columbian Indian cul-ture called "Mississippian" by archaeologists, and that Mississippians were ancestral to numerous village plains tribes.

What little information about the mounds Long could glean from local informants reinforced his belief that the mound builders were a mysterious, ancient, bygone race. The Indians around Prairie du Chien, he was told, had no traditions that would point to the mound builders being their own ancestors. "They only suppose that the country was once inhabited by a race of white people like the present Americans, who have been completely exterminated by their forefathers," he wrote in his journal. One informant, a Mr. Brisbois of Prairie du Chien, told the explorer that while digging a cellar near his house he had unearthed eight enormous human skeletons lying side by side. Judging by the length of one shin bone, which he had held against his own leg for comparison, Brisbois thought these ancient people stood about eight feet tall. Long recorded this information in his journal with only a hint of skepticism, noting that the man said the bones crumbled to dust as soon as they were exposed to air and hence could not be preserved.[5]

Like his musings about the geologic origins of the landforms around Lake Pepin, Long's response to the mounds reflected the mainstream thought of his contemporaries. Americans had been debating the question of who built the mounds since the 1780s. Thomas Jefferson excavated a relatively small mound near his home in Virginia, revealed its stratigraphy, and deduced that it had received human burials over many generations. In his *Notes on the State of Virginia* he asserted that the mounds were the work of Indian peo-ples. But Jefferson was practically alone in that conclusion. Most others who wrote on the question believed that the race of people who now inhabited the Mississippi valley did not have the interest or the social organization to build such monuments. To their way of thinking, the sustained effort of building the mounds must have come from an ancient, vanished civilization originated in Europe or Asia. Various theories held the mound builders to be offshoots of ancient Egyptians, Phoenicians, Canaanites, Hebrews, Hindus, Celts, or some other wayfaring people of the Old World. One of the more influential theories held that the mounds were built by Vikings who then migrated to Mexico and became the Toltecs.[6]

The question of who built the mounds fanned interest in the origins of American Indians. Since the time of Columbus, American Indians had presented Western thought with an intellectual problem that was part of the larger question of how to account for the varieties of the human species found around the globe. Christian doctrine held that humankind originated when God made Adam and Eve, and that after the Great Flood all of humanity descended from Noah and his three sons. That the origins of American Indians were not explicit in Genesis was troubling and led to numerous interpretations as to which Old World people they were descended from and how they had come to be in the Americas. But what was clear to all Christian thinkers was that Indians had souls and were part of God's creation. The Christian worldview took for granted that American Indians had somehow migrated to the Americas, and it embraced Indian peoples as part of the unity of the human race.

How then to explain their different culture, their paganism, their savage state? Puritan thinkers favored the idea of *degeneration*, which they linked to Original Sin. Ever since the expulsion of Adam and Eve from the Garden of Eden, the human species had been prone to degenerate. As various peoples migrated around the globe after the Great Flood, local circumstances had resulted in some isolated peoples degenerating more than others. The diffusion of the human race accounted for the great contrasts between civilized and savage peoples. In short, American Indians had degenerated into savagery while European cultures had retained their grip on the civilization inherited from the ancients.[7] It is impossible to know if Long held similar beliefs, but traces of this persuasion are evident in his reporting on the "degeneration" he found in Prairie du Chien, and in his assumption that Indians could not have built the mounds.

Christian doctrine was not the only source of influence on these questions. Scientific discourse on the origins of the human species—what would eventually become anthropology—began to emerge around the turn of the nineteenth century. The seminal work of this kind in the United States was

Essay on the Causes of the Variety of Complexion and Figure in the Human Species by the Reverend Samuel Stanhope Smith, a professor at the College of New Jersey (later Princeton University). First published in 1787, Stanhope's treatise was republished in expanded form in 1810, the year that Long moved to Germantown. As the book was abstracted and reviewed by all the literary digests on its second printing, and as its author was prominent in the American Philosophical Society, to which Long himself aspired to belong, it is likely that Long was familiar with the book. Smith's thesis was that the variety of human races in the world had developed from a single origin. The human species had spread around the world because it was uniquely capable of adapting, both culturally and physiologically, to every type of environment. In other words, environment changed people and accounted for the variety of human characteristics. By insisting that humans were all of one species, Smith's treatise supported the Christian doctrine of the unity of humankind and, more important, it affirmed the American political doctrine that "all men are created equal." For that reason, it challenged those thinkers who had begun to argue that the several human races had formed separately and constituted different species.[8]

Another writer who had a wide influence on Americans' perception of Indians in Long's day was Scottish historian William Robertson, whose *History of America,* published in London in 1777, continued to have a strong readership in the United States forty years later. Robertson contended that American Indians had migrated from Asia to the Americas by way of ice formed across the Bering Strait. Isolated in the New World from the rest of the human race, American Indians had degenerated into a savage state owing to the harsh American environment. Robertson subscribed to the Enlightenment view of universal human progress, in which all peoples were on a path from savagery to civilization, and he found American Indians, because of their peculiar environmental adaptations, to be in the "rudest form" or most primitive state of any people in the world.[9]

The question of Indian origins continued to be of interest to white Americans in the years following the War of 1812. As historian Robert F. Berkhofer, Jr. has shown, theories about Indian origins helped to shape and justify white Americans' prejudices about Indian culture, and those prejudices in turn helped to shape and justify national policy and government actions designed to incorporate Indian peoples into the American nation.[10] In 1816, a new theory about the peopling of the New World appeared in a book entitled *Researches on America* by Dr. James Haines McCulloh, an officer in the US army. McCulloh debunked the idea of a Bering Strait crossing and argued that the continents of the two hemispheres had once been joined by land, facilitating the migration of humans and animal species to all parts of the globe. McCulloh reckoned that the land migration had occurred some 2,600 years before Christ, and that at some indistinct point in time after that a great convulsion of the earth had caused large portions of the earth to sink, forming the Atlantic, Pacific, and Indian oceans. Although the convulsive event would have destroyed many lives, the remaining continents and islands would have preserved many others. As a result, McCulloh supposed, "fragments of the human family" became separated for generations, forming distinct cultures, until "the spirit of navigation and modern enterprise once more united the links between them and their brother men." Concerning the origins of the mounds, McCulloh thought they were built by "ancient white aborigines of America" who had been driven out of the Mississippi valley, perhaps into Mexico, by a barbarian horde that then disintegrated into modern Indian tribes.[11]

Researches on America lurched back and forth between rambling expositions of various scientific works on earth history and the more familiar historical terrain of the Bible. Quirky though the book was, it appealed to Long's countrymen because it was authored by an American and it managed to sound both learned and pious. One reviewer lauded the book for its "common sense" theory. Certainly Long's ideas about earth history and the origins of the mound builders bear a similarity to McCulloh's. The book was published in August 1816, two months prior to Long's return from his first expedition through the Illinois country, and it is reasonable to imagine him reading it during the winter in anticipation of his second expedition in the West. But whether he did or not, what matters is that Long drew upon contemporary thought to fashion his own ideas about Indians and their place in American westward expansion.[12]

To Civilize the Osages

{ **7** } Soon after Long returned from the upper Mississippi, news of a war between the Osages and the Cherokees reached General Smith's headquarters at Fort Belle Fontaine. The conflict between the Osages and the Cherokees lay far to the south of Rainy Lake House and Long's eventual contact with John Tanner and John McLoughlin, but it is relevant to the story in the effect it had on Long's developing ideas about the Indian frontier. General Smith ordered Long to accompany a force of riflemen under the command of Major William Bradford so as to locate a site for a fort in Osage country (the location of today's Fort Smith, Arkansas). Bradford's force would proceed to the upper Arkansas River, build the fort according to Long's plan, and restore peace between the Osages and the Cherokees. Although Long's immediate task was to situate and design the fort, as usual he had broader objectives to explore the country and report on the Indians and the white settlements—the latter composed largely of squatters who were trespassing on Indian lands. Long's report on the Osages would stand as one of his most detailed commentaries on Indian peoples.

The expedition departed St. Louis in September and descended the Mississippi River to the mouth of the Arkansas. Long went with his own crew in his six-oared skiff, while Bradford took his men and supplies downriver in keelboats. From the mouth of the Arkansas, Long went ahead of the slower keelboats and located a site for the post, the future Fort Smith, which he called Belle Point. He also made observations of the river valley and continued on upstream to its head of navigation in present-day northeast Oklahoma.[1]

While exploring the upper Arkansas he encountered an Osage war party. He informed this party of the approach of US troops and invited them to a council one month hence for the purpose of making peace between themselves and the Cherokees. Long then returned to Belle Point and made a plan of construction for the fort. In early December he left with an escort of two soldiers and a guide and traveled over the Ouachita Mountains to the Red River of the South, where the guide left the party by prior agreement and Long and the two soldiers turned homeward.[2]

The first leg of their return trip was hellish. Reentering the Ouachita Mountains, Long soon found himself in a "wilderness country" of broken hills and numerous streams swollen by heavy winter rains. Each stream crossing presented the men with a perilous choice between wading and swimming or expending the time and energy to build a raft. Every forest opening presented another tough slog through head-high canebrakes. They spent over half a month covering a straight-line distance of about 100 miles, and finally fetched up at a large cluster of hot springs on the Ouachita River at dusk on New Year's Eve. It was one day past Long's thirty-third birthday, and he was grateful to have gotten himself and his escort through the mountains alive. On New Year's Day they rested and examined the springs, taking the temperature of the waters, which ranged from 64 to 151 degrees Fahrenheit.[3]

The remainder of their overland journey through present-day Arkansas was relatively easy. There were many farmsteads. A census the previous summer had counted nearly 2,000 white inhabitants, but Long met with so many new immigrants that he reckoned the population closer to 3,000. He thought the "rich & luxuriant soil" would be good for growing cotton, and the many small creeks well suited for watermills. Long's line of march took him past the White and St. Francis rivers to the Mississippi. Striking the Mississippi at the hamlet known as Herculaneum, he ascended the great river back to St. Louis.[4]

In his report of this, his third expedition, Long gave most of his attention to US Indian policy and the Osages. Long was already familiar with the Osages by reputation, for they were the most powerful Indian nation in the region and they held a dominant position in the fur trade south of the Missouri River. At the time of the Louisiana Purchase, the Osages numbered perhaps 5,000 and their territory covered a large part of the present states of Missouri, Arkansas, and Oklahoma. They had long been allied with the French and Spanish in the fur trade, and they had plentiful hunting grounds on the edge of the Great Plains. But in the years after the Louisiana Purchase the tribe had become beleaguered by enemies on all sides. The Americans pressed on the Osage territory from the east, while the Pawnees and other enemy tribes, armed with guns by the Spanish, encroached on their hunting grounds from the west. Most troublesome of all, waves of Cherokee emigrants, having acquiesced to American demands to leave their homes in the East and resettle on the Arkansas River, pushed into Osage territory in the Ozark Hills north of the Arkansas River. Warring between the Osages and the western Cherokees became incessant. In 1816, US Indian agent William Lovely brought the chiefs of the Osages and Cherokees together in council and offered to settle all US claims for Osage depredations in return for a cession of their territory that would serve as a buffer between the two tribes. But in spite of the so-called Lovely Purchase, the Osages continued to raid Cherokee farms. The western Cherokee chiefs decided to take matters into their own hands and mount a war of extermination against their Osage enemies. Raising an army of about 600 men, composed mainly of Cherokees, Shawnees, Delawares, and Quapaws, and including eleven white settlers, the Cherokee-led force advanced up the Arkansas and Grand rivers to attack the largest of the Osage villages. Accounts varied as to what happened next. Some accounts stated that the Osage men of warrior age were away hunting while the women, children, and old men were left in the village; others stated that the warriors fled to the hills and the women, children, and old men hid in a cave. The accounts agreed that the Cherokees and their allies slaughtered the defenseless Osages whom they found there and then burned the village. Reports of the conflict reached General Smith at Fort Belle Fontaine about the time that Long returned from his expedition to the upper Mississippi.[5]

The Osages were divided into three bands known as the Big Osages, the Little Osages, and an offshoot known as Clermont's band. The latter group had formed around the leader Clermont and had come to outnumber the other two divisions, and it was this group that bore the brunt of the conflict with the Cherokees. Long was aware of the internal divisions within the tribe, but in his view the United States had to treat with all the Osages as one people and he regarded Clermont as the tribe's principal chief.[6]

Long found that the Osages' grievances against the United States revolved around the Lovely Purchase. The agreement purportedly included more land than the tribe had intended to sell. Although Clermont had signed the agreement, he felt he had been deceived by the interpreter. Moreover, Lovely had acted on his own initiative without instructions from the US government. The tribe, so far as Long could discern, was unaware that the Lovely Purchase had no legal standing unless it was ratified by Congress.[7]

William Lovely had died the previous February, so it was necessary for Long to piece together information about the purchase from his parley with the Osages and interviews with white settlers. He definitely relied more on the latter, for his account of the Osage tribe's attitude toward local whites reflected the settlers' bias. He stated that the Osages had invited the Americans to settle on their lands, become their neighbors, and teach the tribesmen how to cultivate the ground and the women how to spin and weave. The Osages frequently expressed a desire "to change their mode of life," Long reported, and showed a "high regard for the attainments of Americans." They had observed how the Cherokees kept farms in imitation of the whites, and wanted to obtain those same advantages for themselves. Supposedly they saw the necessity of adopting the white people's ways so that they could survive when their hunting grounds were depleted. No other Indian nation in the Mississippi valley, Long reported, showed such a strong inclination to advance from savagery to civilization. No other Indians with whom he was acquainted were more deserving of the US government's "humane exertions" to help them assimilate. Unfortunately, it seemed that William Lovely had led the Osages to believe that the purchase would be opened exclusively to white settlers, not Cherokees. The Osages were upset to find that the Americans were allowing Cherokees to move in and hunt in the purchase area.[8]

Long's analysis of the triangular relationship between the Osages, the Cherokees, and the Americans was fairly accurate, but he revealed his bias in favor of the white settlers. The white population squatting on Indian lands on the upper Arkansas and upper White rivers at this time were hardly the culture bearers and teachers that Long imagined them to be. Although the white homesteaders might run a few head of livestock and raise a small amount of corn, their main object was to hunt and trap animals for their hides and furs. Some had tanneries in which they prepared buffalo hides for market, transporting the hides and tallow to New Orleans. One contemporary traveler said that these inhabitants were living off the country much like Indians; another claimed that a significant portion of them were renegades from justice. William Lovely, the former Indian agent, described the white population in 1813 in the most disparaging terms: "All the white folks, a few excepted, have made their escape to this country guilty of the most horrid crimes and are now depredating on the Osages and other tribes, taking off 30 horses at a time."[9] Long took a more charitable view of them, saying that they had not yet had time to put in crops. These people's reliance on hunting and trading was only temporary, as they wanted to "raise an honest livelihood from the cultivation of the soil."[10]

Long stated that the United States had three military objectives in the area. First, it must prevent further strife between the Osages and the Cherokees. Second, it needed to prevent whites from trespassing on the hunting grounds of the Indians. Third, it had to protect the white settlements from depredations by the Indians. He thought that the future Fort Smith would be adequate to keep peace on the upper Arkansas, but the remote hill country north of the Arkansas would require a chain of forts linked by a military road. Further, the United States should make another land cession treaty with the Osages in order to legitimize the Lovely Purchase. With these actions, white settlers would come into the area and develop an agriculture-based economy. By moving the frontier of settlement westward in this region, the United States would secure its control of the Mississippi River valley all the way from New Orleans to St. Louis.[11]

In Long's view, what was good for the United States was good for the Osages. As white farmers moved into their neighborhood, the Osages would adopt the whites' way of life and become civilized. As the new agricultural economy replaced the tribe's dependence on the hunt, the fur trade would quickly fade into insignificance.

When Long looked northward to the tribes on the upper Mississippi and upper Missouri, his outlook was less sanguine. The agricultural frontier would advance more slowly in the colder climate found at that higher latitude, denying tribes like the Sioux the opportunity to learn farming the way the Cherokees and Osages were doing. For those Northwest tribes, the fur trade would have to form some kind of a bridge as Indians negotiated the difficult road from savagery to civilization.

❖{III}❖ TANNER

Westward Migration

❄ { 8 } ❄ When Stephen Long thought about the westward expansion of the American nation, he focused on the westward movement of whites, not Indians. But he knew full well, as did a good many of his contemporaries, that white settlers were following on the heels of a westward migration of Indian tribes. The western Cherokees in Arkansas were just one example among many of Indians going west. Indian peoples went in search of new lands remote from white settlement. In doing so, they invaded the hunting grounds of other tribes. More often than not, tribes positioned nearer to the Atlantic seaboard were better armed with guns than tribes located farther west, giving the invaders an upper hand in warfare. This domino effect began virtually with the advent of European colonization. It accelerated as soon as the American colonies gained independence and white settlers began to pour over the Appalachian Mountains. Stephen Long was aware of this great Indian migration intellectually. John Tanner, on the other hand, experienced it personally.

In the spring of 1794, Tanner's new Ottawa mother, Net-no-kwa, decided to take her family to the prairies west of Lake Superior. Such was her influence among the Ottawas that a considerable number joined in the migration, including a principal chief of the village of L'Arbre Croche and six canoes of his followers, as well as others from Net-no-kwa's village of Cheboygan. Whether all of these emigrants traveled together is not known, but at least a portion of them did, for when they reached Sault Ste. Marie they loaded their baggage on board the North West Company's sloop as it was about to set sail for Grand Portage. They then continued in their canoes around the north shore of Lake Superior, making excellent time with their lightened loads. That the North West Company provided them this baggage service is significant, because it shows that the fur traders wanted to assist the Ottawas' migration. The traders were motivated to help the Indians emigrate, since they wanted additional hunters working in the more plentiful beaver grounds lying to the west.[1]

The Ottawas' migration formed part of a larger movement of Indian peoples from the Great Lakes region to the northern prairie country. The migration of Ottawas and Ojibwas took place around the end of the eighteenth and beginning of the nineteenth centuries. For many, the movement began as an extended hunting trip and ended with their relocating permanently in a new homeland. Many fur traders maintained that the westward movement of Indians was prompted by the depletion of beaver stocks in eastern areas and the promise of relatively untouched trapping grounds lying to the west. Some Hudson's Bay men believed that whole bands of Ojibwas accompanied the North West traders as they moved west. The Nor' Westers may have fostered that idea, since it implied Ojibwa attachment to their company.[2]

Although beaver populations were indeed nearly wiped out in some eastern areas, those conditions were hardly universal. Similarly, big game populations were knocked down in some areas more than others. Reading the fur traders' accounts of declining returns, historians used to accept the traders' view that Indians overhunted when they turned to hunting for the international market. More recently, historians have challenged that assumption. Discerning that declines in fur trade returns often stemmed from factors other than wildlife depletion, such as competition from rival traders or waning interest on the part of Indian fur hunters, historians now question whether overhunting of beaver was so ubiquitous after all.[3] Moreover, Tanner's own experience notwithstanding, historical records simply do not support the notion that fur traders aided and abetted Indian migrations on a significant scale. Although fur traders did encourage Indians to migrate westward, their influence was only peripheral.[4]

Studies of emigration refer to push factors and pull factors that motivate people to emigrate. Net-no-kwa's motivations for moving westward were a mix of both. Her declared purpose, as later recorded by Tanner, was to take advantage of the greater abundance of beaver and other fur bearers in the Red River country. This was a pull factor rather similar to the economic opportunities motivating migrant workers in recent times. Net-no-kwa and her family were also keen to reunite with relatives. Some of Taw-ga-we-ninne's relatives had already gone to the Red River and sent word of it back home. That was another pull factor. Emigration by people of literate cultures often would beget more emigration as early colonists or pioneers sent letters or published reports about their new circumstances back home. Emigration by people of oral cultures often followed the same pattern as information filtered back by word of mouth.

Health concerns may have contributed to Net-no-kwa's family's decision to emigrate, too, constituting a push factor. In the previous fall Net-no-kwa's people had suffered an outbreak of measles. The older among them remembered the devastating smallpox epidemic that had struck the tribe a dozen years before. Nothing was so terrifying for Indians in the eighteenth century as an epidemic. Though they did not know how diseases were spread, they had a general understanding about their relative susceptibility to European-borne diseases. To shield her family from the sickness that appeared in the previous fall, Net-no-kwa took the family farther up the Cheboygan River, well away from the rest of the band. Even so, everyone in the family except Tanner and her became ill. While all survived, it was a brush with disaster. Perhaps she thought that moving west would improve their chances of avoiding another epidemic.[5]

Though the westward migration could have been managed without serious mishap, Net-no-kwa's family had terrible luck. While they were camped with other Ottawas at Mackinac Island awaiting a favorable wind, the men obtained some liquor and got drunk. Taw-ga-we-ninne, the husband of Net-no-kwa, got into an altercation with some other young men. Walking beside two fellows, he stumbled and grabbed one of their sleeves, accidentally tearing the man's shirt as he fell down. The person took offense and threw a rock at Taw-ga-we-ninne as he lay on the ground, hitting him in the forehead and knocking him out cold. When Taw-ga-we-ninne came around, he was certain he was going to die. While he had been lying unconscious after receiving the blow he experienced his spirit leaving his body. "I am killed," he said to Tanner when the young boy saw him that night with the wound in his head. And to the whole family he said, "I have to leave you. I am sorry that I must leave you so poor." According to Ojibwa religion, a person's soul comprised two spirits, one that left the body and traveled about in the person's dream state and another that stayed with the body and piloted it until death. When a person died, the traveling spirit departed first, the bodily spirit following after a while. Taw-ga-we-ninne must have seen things when he was unconscious that convinced him his end had come.[6]

Taw-ga-we-ninne rallied and managed to accompany the expedition as far as Grand Portage, where he soon relapsed into a feverish state and announced a second time that he was dying. Once more expressing regret to his family that he was leaving them so poor, he took his gun and stepped out of their lodge, saying that he must go kill the man who had hit him with a rock, as that man must die with him. However, Net-no-kwa's eldest son stopped Taw-ga-we-ninne right outside their lodge, reminding him that the fellow had many friends in the place where they were going to live, and to kill this man now would only bring revenge upon their family at a later time. Taw-ga-we-ninne saw the truth in his son's words. He came back into the lodge and laid aside the gun, saying that he loved his son too much to refuse his request. He died later that evening. Net-no-kwa went to the Grand Portage traders for a coffin and the use of a wagon to transport the body, and the family buried him in the traders' burial ground near the trading house. The young man who had caused Taw-ga-we-ninne's death attended the burial ceremony as a token of reconciliation.[7]

The family's misfortunes were not over. When the North West Company's schooner arrived from Sault Ste. Marie and dropped anchor offshore, Tanner's two brothers, Ke-wa-tin and Wa-me-gon-a-biew, went out in a canoe to retrieve the family's possessions. Jumping into the ship's hold, Ke-wa-tin fell and struck his knee on a knot of rope tied around a bundle of goods, busting his kneecap. The family waited eight days for him to recover, but the swelling on the knee only got worse. So they put him on a litter and carried him on their shoulders across the Grand Portage, a distance of ten miles. Given the difficulty of carrying Ke-wa-tin, they left their canoes at the trader's house and stopped on the other side of the portage to make new ones. By now the season was advancing and most of the Ottawas who had set out with Net-no-kwa had gone ahead of them. Ke-wa-tin informed his mother that he could go no farther but must die there.[8]

At this point, Net-no-kwa's daughter and son-in-law and one of Taw-ga-we-ninne's young wives, anxious over the approach of winter and the safety of their small children, decided to continue on with the main group. All who remained were Net-no-kwa, her three sons, and Taw-ga-we-ninne's other young wife: two women and three boys with no capable hunter in the group. Their situation was precarious but not desperate, and Net-no-kwa clung to the hope that Ke-wa-tin's condition would improve and allow them to complete their journey before winter was upon them. As they were camped by a lake with fish and there were berries to eat, they stayed in that place for about six weeks. But as the nights turned cold and the lake began to freeze, Ke-wa-tin's knee injury still refused to heal. Anxious that they might become snowbound there, Net-no-kwa decided they must beat a retreat back over the Grand Portage and encamp near the trader's house. Ke-wa-tin lived for a few more months and died in the depths of winter. They buried him next to his father, placing Net-no-kwa's prized Union Jack over the two graves.[9]

❄

The deaths of Taw-ga-we-ninne and Ke-wa-tin drew Tanner closer to his Indian family. Although in the preceding three years he had been treated fairly well by them, there were also constant reminders of his status as an adopted child and cultural outsider, and so he had remained emotionally

distant. In the aftermath of these two deaths, that changed. The family's
dire circumstances stirred in the thirteen-year-old a new sense of interdependence. His role in the family suddenly was magnified. His grieving Indian mother showered him with affection, while his one remaining Indian
brother, Wa-me-gon-a-biew, treated him much as he had behaved toward
his blood brother, Ke-wa-tin. That winter, after the family set up camp near
the Grand Portage trading post, Wa-me-gon-a-biew took Tanner with him
whenever he went out hunting. Wa-me-gon-a-biew was seventeen, not
yet experienced or mature enough to wear the mantle of principal hunter.
Though the boys would be out several days at a time in their quest for
game, they often returned empty-handed. Despite their lack of success, it
was on these hunting forays that Tanner experienced the first glimmers of
manhood.

Ke-wa-tin's death also changed the family dynamics in another way.
As Wa-me-gon-a-biew and Tanner were now Net-no-kwa's only surviving sons, they developed an intense sibling rivalry that would continue into
their adult lives. Tanner began to compete with his Indian brother for their
mother's favor. In time, Tanner would displace Wa-me-gon-a-biew as principal hunter and form a remarkably tight bond with Net-no-kwa while the
natural son floundered and drifted in and out of their family group. The
brothers' competition for the mother's love propelled the young Tanner toward becoming Indian.

On one of their hunting trips that winter, the two boys attempted to cross
a river that did not freeze over as solidly as most because of its swift current.
As they had been hearing the trees crack in the severe cold, they thought
the river ice would be firm. But they broke through, Tanner going in up
to his knees and Wa-me-gon-a-biew getting completely wet in his frantic
efforts to squirm out of the hole and spread his weight before the rest of the
ice collapsed under him. When they reached the riverbank they knew they
must quickly get out of their wet clothes or face certain death. But with their
hands and fingers going numb, they could barely work the leather laces of
their snowshoes, moccasins, and leggings. After at last removing his freezing
things, Tanner was dismayed to see his half-naked brother seek out a place
on the riverbank where the wind had blown away the snow. There, Wa-me-
gon-a-biew quietly lay down to die. Tanner, determined not to perish that
way, walked in circles to get his blood flowing again. Then he searched out
a rotten tree stump under the snow and dug into it to get some dry punk to
tinder a fire. Once he accomplished it, his brother roused himself to assist
in gathering wood, and with the aid of a good blaze they were able to get
through the night. The episode left a deep impression on Tanner. Forever

after, he was unable to shake his disappointment with Wa-me-gon-a-biew for having resigned himself to death that day.[10]

As the brothers managed to kill very little game during the winter, it is likely that Net-no-kwa obtained at least some food for the family at the trading post. That would explain why they made their winter camp nearby, even though they knew game would be scarce in the area. They may have received food from the traders themselves or, more likely, from other Indians who came and went.[11]

Late in the winter an Ojibwa man came to their lodge and, being informed by the traders that they had very little to eat, he invited them to accompany him to his own lodge two days' journey to the west, where he would provide for them until spring. Generosity between perfect strangers was common among Algonquian peoples and formed a critical part of their adaptation to the harsh northern winters. Implicit in the man's offer was the understanding that if he or his kin were ever to encounter Net-no-kwa's people when they themselves were in need, then they might expect a like kindness in turn. Such reciprocity provided a social safety net that could spell the difference between life and death when a small subsistence group lost its principal hunter. Insofar as the fur trade drew Algonquian peoples from a subsistence economy into a money economy, it tended to erode that ethic. Many years later, Tanner would comment in his autobiography that this man's generous behavior was already, in the year 1795, something of a throwback; it was no longer typical of the Ottawas and Ojibwas living farther east, who were more attuned to the white man's philosophy of self-interest.[12] Net-no-kwa's family lived with this man for several weeks, returning to Grand Portage in the spring when he did.

After a few days back at Grand Portage, Net-no-kwa and her family accepted a similar invitation by another man of the same Ojibwa band. But this time the invitation was to travel in the other direction, out across the ice-cold waters of Lake Superior to Isle Royale. They soon began to address this man, like the other, as their brother-in-law. The familial title was an acknowledgment of their obligation to remember his kindness whenever they might see him again.

On reaching Isle Royale with their new provider, they immediately speared two large sturgeon. While the women set to cutting and drying the meat, their new brother-in-law showed the boys where they could find gulls' eggs along the island's rocky shore. The next day he went off by himself to hunt, returning in the evening having killed two caribou. After the gnawing hunger they had experienced over the winter, the island's bounty and the hunter's assuredness came as a welcome change. They stayed with him on

Isle Royale through the spring, enjoying an easy life of catching beaver, otter, and other game, which they found in plenty around a clear, shallow lake in the interior of the island.[13]

Near the start of summer their benefactor's band joined them on Isle Royale, arriving in eight canoes. They all camped together on the lakeshore, waiting for a windless day to make the hazardous passage back to the mainland. On the chosen day, they all started out together in ten canoes. When they had paddled just a few hundred yards out into Lake Superior, they paused to offer a prayer to the spirit of the deep. The chief, or principal man of the group, in the lead canoe, shouted in a loud voice for all to hear, praying that the waters should remain calm for their journey. Speaking in this vein for five or ten minutes, he threw a pinch of tobacco into the lake. Then he began a song, which everyone joined in singing.

Tanner was deeply moved by this occasion, observing how solemnly the Indians listened to the chief's prayer. He reflected that they must indeed be placing their trust in some sort of higher power to deliver them safely across the great lake. If Tanner did not fully accept the Indians' religion at this point in his life, he now realized that he did not remember anything about the whites' religion either. And not only had he forgotten the white man's religion, he had practically forgotten the white man's language, too. Indeed, he had almost forgotten the name of his white family—was it Tanner or Taylor? His first Ottawa family had renamed him Shaw-shaw-wa be-na-se (the Swallow) and he had gone by that name ever since. After the pleasant months on Isle Royale, he felt a warm attachment to his Indian relatives such as he had never felt before.[14]

Soon after the band landed safely at Grand Portage, the young Tanner experienced another epiphany. It was that time of year when the white fur traders gathered in great numbers and the place became a hive of activity. Yet, to his surprise, Net-no-kwa gave him complete freedom to go where he pleased. She had kept him under watch when they were there the previous summer. And before that, whenever they visited Mackinac, she had kept him well hidden from the traders. Now, he realized, she was allowing him to go over to the whites if that was what he chose to do. It seems that Tanner and Net-no-kwa never had a conversation about this; he simply had to work out the problem in his own mind. As he observed the French Canadian voyageurs going about their chores, following the commands of the British, their lot did not compare favorably with the easy times he had just experienced on Isle Royale. He remembered, too, what he had seen on the farms in Kentucky: it was a toilsome life compared to that of a hunter. He also reckoned that he would have to reenter the white man's world as a pauper, without relatives or friends or support of any kind, whereas among Indians a person who had nothing could find relatives or friends or even a perfect stranger who would give him shelter and food aplenty. Weighing all that in his mind, the fourteen-year-old boy came to his first adult decision: he would choose an Indian life.[15]

Net-no-kwa, meanwhile, deliberated over her family's next move. Thus far, the journey from Lake Huron had taken the lives of her husband and son; now she was aggrieved to learn from the traders that her son-in-law had died in a drunken brawl at far away Moose Lake the past winter. Her daughter, the traders said, awaited her at Rainy Lake. What ought to have been a journey of a few months had turned into an ordeal that was killing off the family. It was midsummer by the time Net-no-kwa made up her mind: they must go as far as Rainy Lake to reunite with her daughter. Once there, they would decide whether to return to Lake Huron or go on to the Red River.

At Rainy Lake they found her daughter in the care of other Indians, mourning her husband's death. Tanner and his brother listened and overheard as Net-no-kwa and their older sister argued over where the family should go—or which relatives they should seek out—before the onset of winter. Net-no-kwa recounted the family's heavy losses and urged that they stick to the original plan of going to the Red River to hunt beaver. There they would find the relatives of Taw-ga-we-ninne and inform them of his untimely death, expecting to rely on their support. At length Net-no-kwa prevailed (as she always did), and the westward journey was resumed.[16]

But Net-no-kwa could not go on forever being the family's pillar of strength. After passing through Lake of the Woods and canoeing down the Winnipeg River, the family arrived at Lake Winnipeg, where the traders had a fort called Bas de la Rivière. There, Net-no-kwa obtained some traders' rum and proceeded to get dead drunk. Her children had seldom seen her so intoxicated. Fearful of what might befall them if they lingered at the fort, they loaded their unconscious mother in their canoe in spite of it being a windy day for a lake crossing. The traders tried to talk them out of it, cautioning that the wind was too strong. Though the gale would be at their backs crossing the lake, it would likely run them into the rocks on the far shore. But Tanner and his brother and sister, thinking the traders were trying to deceive them for some underhanded reason, pushed off anyway. Soon it became apparent that the winds were indeed perilous and far too strong for them to turn around. When Net-no-kwa woke up she found herself and her children in the middle of the lake surrounded by whitecaps, the wind rising, night falling, and everyone on the verge of terror. Seizing a paddle, she prayed aloud to the Great Spirit and began paddling furiously while barking commands to her sons. Hours later, in starlight, they at last sighted land and by sheer good luck aimed the canoe into the only spot of sandy beach in miles of rocky shoreline. Once safely out of the water and sitting comfortably around a fire, they all suddenly burst into laughter. What seemed so funny was the thought of their mother awakening from her drunken stupor to find them all in such terrible peril. The brothers took turns lampooning her and laughing hilariously, even though her drinking bout had very nearly led to the whole family's demise.[17]

At the Forks they found Taw-ga-we-ninne's kin encamped with a few hundred other Ojibwas and Ottawas. Tanner had never seen such a large gathering of Indians. The western Ojibwas and Ottawas were closely allied, with many clans being united by marriage. In this, the family of Net-no-kwa and Taw-ga-we-ninne was typical. And all were immigrants as well, although many Ojibwas had immigrated before the Ottawas. Certainly the Ojibwas were the more established and numerous of the two peoples.[18] Net-no-kwa's family received a warm welcome. In a council, the chiefs indicated that they would not go wanting through the coming winter. Not long after this, a man approached Net-no-kwa with an offer to provide for her family, and she readily accepted.

As it was already the middle of autumn when they arrived at the Forks, the large encampment soon broke up. The mass of people dissolved into many smaller groups, although some of these, including Tanner's, still traveled together up the Assiniboine River en route to their various wintering grounds. As they traveled, Tanner saw the scattered patches of forest give way more and more to large expanses of prairie. Giant white oaks grew along the banks of the meandering Assiniboine River. There were frequent buffalo wallows and ubiquitous sign of elk, moose, bear, and other big game.

By this time Tanner aspired to the status of a full-fledged hunter. On the second day of their movement up the Assiniboine, the men invited him on a buffalo hunt. They found and killed four bulls—a most gratifying result for one morning's pursuit. It appeared to Tanner that he and his family had come upon a land of plenty. He reveled in the idea that he truly was becoming a hunter. Already he could feel himself rising in the Indians' esteem.[19]

At a place called Prairie Portage the Ojibwas and Ottawas dispersed into the hills to hunt beaver along the many small streams. The chief of their band assigned Tanner and Wa-me-gon-a-biew to a particular creek, one that the boys could treat as their own hunting territory for that season, and Net-no-kwa gave Tanner three steel traps that she obtained from a trader. Tanner learned how to set his traps and started hunting beaver by himself, though he was too small yet to carry more than a single trap and beaver on his back at one time. Their winter camp consisted of three lodges. Later they were joined by a group of Crees who numbered four more lodges. The Cree language was similar to their own, though less so than Ojibwa was to Ottawa.[20]

That winter a pivotal event in the sibling rivalry between Tanner and Wa-me-gon-a-biew occurred. Game had become scarce, and the band was preparing to move camp. On the eve of the group's departure, Net-no-kwa prayed aloud and chanted through the night in hopes of preparing her elder son for a medicine hunt. A medicine hunt was only performed in time of great need, for it involved calling on the Great Spirit to bring success to the hunter. In answer to her prayers Net-no-kwa had a vision, and in the morning she confided to Wa-me-gon-a-biew that he would kill a bear that day. She told him he must look for it in a round meadow with a path leading away, and when he found this place he would see steam rising where the bear lay in its den. Wa-me-gon-a-biew scoffed at his mother's vision in the presence of the other young men, but as he repeated her instructions Tanner listened and decided that he would go on this medicine hunt instead of his brother. That afternoon, while everyone was engaged in moving camp, Tanner was told to stay with the baggage where it was temporarily deposited along the trail to the next camp. Seeing his chance, he loaded his gun and backtracked down the trail in search of the round meadow of his mother's description. Off to one side of the trail he found a round clearing in the woods, and though the ground lay deep under snow he could tell that it had once been a pond that had since filled in with grass. That led him to surmise that the path in his mother's vision was actually the old outlet of the pond, and so he followed the perimeter of the clearing in search of this feature. Coming to a narrow gap in the underbrush, he crept along it expecting to see steam above where the bear lay in its den. Suddenly he stepped into a hole under the snow. After extricating his leg from this hole, he peered down into it and saw the head of a bear! Quickly he shot the bear before it woke up.[21]

For anyone to kill a bear in its winter den was big medicine. For a boy of fourteen, it was a coup. When Net-no-kwa learned what he had achieved, she hugged and kissed him profusely then proudly directed some of the men to go with the hunter and retrieve the carcass. As this was Tanner's first bear-kill, the whole animal was cooked at once in ceremonial fashion, providing a feast for the entire group, including the Crees. That same day one of the Cree hunters killed a moose and gave a large share of the meat to Net-no-kwa in gratitude for her good medicine.[22]

The incident is revealing on a number of fronts. It shows how fiercely the young Tanner competed with his brother for his mother's affection and how crucial each boy's hunting success was to the outcome of that struggle. From this point onward, it seems, Tanner was his mother's favorite. It also shows Tanner's growing acceptance of Indian religion. His astonishing feat, so wondrously predicated on his mother's dream, was a kind of religious experience. He sincerely believed he had been led to the bear by supernatural powers. Finally, the incident is suggestive of Tanner's developing skills as a hunter and primitive naturalist, for he was able to take abstract details in his mother's dream and relate them to patterns of vegetation and hydrology, which he had previously observed in a summertime environment, even when those same natural features now lay obscured beneath a deep blanket of snow.

Six Beaver Skins for a Quart
of Mixed Rum

❊{ 9 }❊ Tanner's mother and sister were ambivalent emigrants. They had not yet passed an entire winter on the prairie when they began to pine for their old homeland. At the conclusion of that year and each of the next two, Tanner's family started for Lake Huron, and each time the trip had to be aborted. Tanner seems to have been too young to form strong feelings about it one way or the other, but his older brother Wa-me-gon-a-biew, the skulking teenager, finally decided for himself that he was not going back. It was due to his obstinacy that Net-no-kwa finally abandoned the plan once and for all.[1]

As a result of Net-no-kwa's ambivalence, the family made several transits across what is now southern Manitoba and western Ontario during the closing years of the eighteenth century. To a degree, the family's long-distance roaming reflected a pattern common to all western Ojibwas and Ottawas as they adapted to their new prairie environment. Many Ojibwas and Ottawas traveled back and forth between the Red River area and their ancestral villages around Lake Superior and Lake Huron, in some cases repeating those long-distance trips annually.[2] However, Tanner's family roamed farther west than that, and probably covered even more miles in these years than was typical. Net-no-kwa had at least three reasons to lead her family on such long journeys. One was her on-again, off-again plan to take the family back to Lake Huron. Another was to seek out the most productive beaver grounds. The third was her new alliance with an old Ottawa war chief named Pe-shau-ba, who had a snug log hut far to the west.

Pe-shau-ba entered young Tanner's life during their first winter on the prairie. He appeared in their camp one day, announcing that he had come from afar on news that a powerful old Ottawa woman was living near Prairie Portage in a destitute condition after losing her husband and son-in-law on her westward journey. He recognized Net-no-kwa as a relative, and she him. Pe-shau-ba had three male companions, Waus-so, Sag-git-to, and Sa-ning-wub. In Ottawa culture, these followers were known as his "young men," although one of the three, Waus-so, was not so young, having more winters behind him than his leader did. Waus-so had once been a principal hunter himself but had long since retired from that position. Since Pe-shau-ba's subsistence group had no women or children and Tanner's family had no men, they were a good fit to come together as one unit. Pe-shau-ba proposed that they combine, and Net-no-kwa agreed.

Everyone in this new group took to their customary gender roles. The men and boys brought home wild game; the women dressed the skins, dried the meat, made moccasins, cooked, and performed sundry other camp chores. Tanner noted that Net-no-kwa soon began to address Pe-shau-ba as her son, though he was not many years younger than she was. Perhaps it signified that their relationship was not sexual, though the two did become fond of each other and vied for leadership over the others in an amicable sort of way. Net-no-kwa, seeking to reclaim some of the status she had possessed back home, established clear divisions within the group; she took care of Pe-shau-ba's needs and left it to her daughter and the young widow of Taw-ga-we-ninne to attend the needs of the other three men. Net-no-kwa also claimed responsibility for Tanner and Wa-me-gon-a-biew, while the younger women looked after the two small children in their group. At first their group had no young girls who were old enough to work, but Net-no-kwa corrected that circumstance by purchasing a ten-year-old female slave, one formerly of the Gros Ventre tribe, who had been captured by an Ojibwa war party.[3] Tanner and his brother, for their part, mostly followed the men in their activities. Net-no-kwa encouraged the boys to look up to Pe-shau-ba not as an older brother but as a new father figure. Tanner greatly admired him, later describing him as a large and very handsome man, a brave and principled war chief, and a great provider who taught him most of what he knew in the arts of hunting.[4]

Pe-shau-ba taught them how to utilize the prairie's greatest resource, bison. Even though they were in the depths of winter, he told them to discard the stiff reed *pukkwi* mats they used for covering their wigwams, insisting that they were too bulky to transport. Thenceforth, traveling the wintry prairie on snowshoes, they carried only their blankets and slept under the stars. Whenever they needed more protection from the cold, they killed bison and made a shelter with the hides. The fresh hides quickly froze in the wind, making a sturdy little tent. (Pe-shau-ba's device was a crude form of the buffalo-hide tepees that the western Ojibwas and Ottawas would soon adopt from other Plains Indians in place of their reed-mat wigwams.) Sometimes they huddled in their little buffalo-hide tents for a week or more, waiting for clear weather before resuming their journey. In this way they covered a distance of about 150 miles in 75 days to reach Pe-shau-ba's lodge.[5]

Pe-shau-ba's cabin stood on the shore of Clear Lake in what is now Riding Mountain National Park, Manitoba. In the preceding months he and his companions had taken a great many beaver in the surrounding hills, caching the skins in the woods near the cabin. When the new group arrived at the end of winter, they immediately broke into the cache and the women dressed the skins while the men and boys made canoe frames for transporting them out. As there was no birchbark for sheathing the canoes, they used green moose hides instead. The women carefully sewed the hides together, and the men stretched them over a wood frame to dry and harden in the sun. The technique made a serviceable watercraft capable of carrying a few hundred pounds of cargo apiece, although it did not last long in warm weather.[6]

In the spring, Pe-shau-ba's and Net-no-kwa's group took their several packs of skins to a trading house they called Mouse River Fort. The Mouse River is today's Souris River, and the fort was the Hudson's Bay Company's Brandon House located near the junction of the Souris and Assiniboine rivers. The country stretching from the Red River westward up the Assiniboine to the Souris and Qu'Appelle rivers was the scene of much competition between fur traders in this period. The Hudson's Bay Company had established Brandon House four years earlier in 1793, challenging the North West Company's monopoly in the area. Independent traders followed the next year, and soon a number of trading houses vied for the Indians' trade. Near the mouth of the Souris the Hudson's Bay Company and the North West Company each had a post; the two houses faced off across the Assiniboine River. The Indians welcomed the competition between traders, since it meant better prices for their peltries. The watershed of the Assiniboine River was known as the territory of the Assiniboine tribe; however, the Ojibwas and their Ottawa allies were fast moving into the country, for they were aggressive beaver hunters. Though the Ojibwas and Ottawas soon located the best beaver grounds, the Assiniboine nonetheless welcomed the newcomers as allies against their common enemy, the Sioux. The traders assumed that they were leading the Ojibwas and Ottawas into Assiniboine territory, but the Ojibwas and Ottawas saw it the other way around: the traders followed them there.[7]

At Brandon House, Pe-shau-ba and his companions proceeded to get drunk. The trader had a variety of goods for sale—blankets, ironware, articles of clothing—but all this went untouched, because the first "present" the trader gave them was a quantity of rum. When the men began drinking, the trader readily supplied them with more. Being too young to partake in the festivity, Tanner looked on with dismay as the adults drank the firewater and alternately brayed and blustered, loafed and passed out. As he later remembered it, Pe-shau-ba and his companions sold their entire stock of 100 beaver skins for four gallons of watered-down rum. Despite the obligatory ritual of treating the rum as a present, the trader effectively started a bar tab and took everything they had. The price, Tanner recalled, was six beaver skins for a quart of mixed rum. The drinking went on for days.[8]

Possibly the group received additional articles besides liquor that went unmentioned in Tanner's account. Indeed, the pattern of furs for rum is repeated in Tanner's *Narrative* with such regularity that one suspects it colored his memory, crowding out other items included in the exchange. Obviously, Tanner's group had acquired their guns and blankets through previous trade. If nothing else, they had to obtain more ammunition. The North West Company trading houses had a standard issue of "small equipment" for Indian hunters that included measures of shot and powder, 25 balls, 4 gunflints, 1 gunworm, 1 firesteel, 3 awls, 3 skeins of thread, and 2 needles, as well as 1 fathom of tobacco and 5 pints of rum.[9] The package suggests the variety of items required just to use and maintain guns. Still, the traders' records basically confirm what Tanner described. As often as not, the Indians exchanged furs for practically nothing but rum. As much as the traders disliked seeing the Indians engage in *boissons*, or drinking bouts, outside the trading houses, they encouraged it by their own practices. Sometimes this furs-for-rum exchange also wiped away "debt," or the value of "presents" that the trader had supplied to the Indian on an earlier visit.

For Tanner, the drinking party on this occasion led to a second disappointment. A large number of Assiniboines and Crees had gathered near the trading house at the same time Tanner's group was camped there. After a time, the Assiniboines and Crees formed a war party to go against the Hidatsas, who lived on the upper Missouri. Among Tanner's group, the elderly Waus-so decided to join the war party. Net-no-kwa had intended to take their group to Lake Huron, but now Pe-shau-ba demurred, for he did not like the thought of the old man going to war without him. As he and Net-no-kwa were at loggerheads, they at last agreed on a new plan: the four men would go to the upper Missouri while the women and children would go to Lake Winnipeg, where the boys would hunt beaver, and in the fall the men would rejoin them there. Just before the group divided, Wa-me-gon-a-biew decided to go with the men. Abruptly, Tanner received the mantle of hunter for Net-no-kwa's shrunken party.[10]

Young Tanner and the women and children set out down the Assiniboine River, the youth feeling anxious to prove himself in his new role as provider. They had not gone very far when they came upon a sturgeon stranded in a shoal behind a sandbar, its spiny back protruding out of the water. Tanner jumped out of the canoe and killed the great fish with a rock. As the sturgeon was the first one he had ever caught, Net-no-kwa insisted that they pause in their journey to celebrate the feast of Oskenetahgawin, or first fruits, even though they were alone in that country without any friends to join in the ceremony.[11]

As they proceeded down the Assiniboine to its junction with the Red River, Tanner soon realized he had no need to worry about finding enough game for them to eat. The abundance of animals on the prairie in those years was a thing to behold; no one could have imagined how fast they would disappear in the coming decades. Every spring, the swollen rivers carried thousands of dead bison downstream. These animals had perished along the river or fallen through the ice during the winter, and where their carcasses washed ashore the riverbanks were lined with wolves and bears feasting on carrion. There was also an abundance of smaller game such as otters, muskrats, foxes, and beavers. Near Lake Winnipeg the Red River branched into many channels. The islands in the middle of the river were thick with rushes and reeds, and the place teemed with waterfowl. Camping there through much of the summer, Tanner killed many geese, swans, and ducks, as well as beavers. Tanner also took his first elk, which provided occasion for another ceremonial feast.[12]

After reuniting with Pe-shau-ba and the others in the fall, they all went to Clear Lake to pass the winter. This was the best time of year for hunting beaver, since the beaver pelts carried a plush layer of underfur for insulation from the cold. When spring came Tanner went with the women and children to a place ten miles upstream from Brandon House to make sugar. Around Lake Huron, the Ottawas made sugar by tapping into maple trees when the sap began to flow in the spring. There being no maples on the prairie, the western Ojibwas and Ottawas found that box elders provided a good substitute. While the women made sugar, Tanner hunted bison to feed the camp. The bison were so numerous he was able to hunt them on foot with bow and arrow and the help of some hunting dogs. Tanner's older brother, meanwhile, went off with the men to hunt beaver. Late in the spring they came down the river with their beaver skins loaded in canoes; but once more they all went to Brandon House, where they sold practically the entire stock for rum so that the grownups could enjoy another round of riotous drinking.[13]

Here the members of the group decided to split up for the last time. Net-no-kwa wanted to travel to Lake Huron, but Waus-so and Sa-ning-wub declined to go. Pe-shau-ba chose to stay with these two, while Sag-git-to elected to accompany Net-no-kwa and her group. Sag-git-to was troubled by an abscess on his belly, and he had begun to think he might die soon.

Moreover, it seems he had fathered a child with Net-no-kwa's daughter, so he may have been reluctant to abandon them. Pe-shau-ba and Net-no-kwa parted on amicable terms, but the breakup placed Tanner's group in a difficult situation. Once more they were without a principal hunter. Tanner's brother, Wa-me-gon-a-biew, was not yet old enough to fill the role. Saggit-to was too sick to hunt, and in fact he did die that summer as he had predicted.[14]

Slowly Tanner's family migrated eastward, hunting beaver along the way. When winter came they tried to join a band of Ojibwas near Lake of the Woods. Rebuffed by these Indians, they backtracked to the Red River to the trading house of Alexander Henry, a clerk in the North West Company. Presumably they obtained provisions from him on credit, for they hunted beaver with his men through the rest of the winter. In the spring they set out again for Lake Huron. Along the way they recovered over 400 beaver skins, plus a like amount of other animal skins, which they had cached the previous year near Lake of the Woods. Altogether this amounted to twenty-one packs, or nearly one ton of product. Net-no-kwa intended to transport the whole lot all the way to Mackinac to get the best possible price.[15]

Around midsummer they arrived at the ten-mile-long Grand Portage between the Pigeon River and Grand Portage Bay on Lake Superior. The North West Company had established an outlying post on the Pigeon River side, and the clerk there eagerly offered to transport their twenty-one packs across the portage in the company's wagons. But Tanner's people, fearing they would be robbed, declined the offer. Instead, they carried the heavy loads on their backs, making several trips over the portage in the course of several days. In the meantime, as they began to accumulate their peltries on the other side, the traders in charge of the big trading house on Grand Portage Bay offered to stow them in one of the storerooms. The principal trader was William McGillivray, the future head of the North West Company, and his assistant was Charles Jean Baptiste Chaboillez. These two gave Net-no-kwa a present of rum and allowed her to stay in the room to safeguard the packs while her sons completed the portage. The traders then tried to persuade her to sell them the furs rather than take them to Mackinac. When Net-no-kwa refused, Chaboillez's son, a man in his midthirties, threatened to beat her until she would submit. But Net-no-kwa still did not budge, and the older Chaboillez called off his son before he laid any blows on the old woman. The furs were, for the moment, left in her possession.[16]

But at this juncture Wa-me-gon-a-biew unexpectedly thwarted Net-no-kwa's long-cherished plan to return to Lake Huron. At Grand Portage, Wa-me-gon-a-biew met an Ojibwa girl with whom he became instantly infatuated. Just as his own family was preparing to depart for Mackinac and Lake Huron, he eloped with the girl and her family to the other side of the portage. Frustrated though she was with her son, Net-no-kwa would not leave without him.

Unable to deliver the twenty-one packs to Mackinac herself, she divided them into two lots. The bigger lot she entrusted to the young widow of Taw-ga-we-ninne, who agreed to board the traders' schooner and dispose of them at Mackinac according to Net-no-kwa's wish. The smaller lot she traded for rum, which she shared with the other Indians encamped at Grand Portage. As Tanner saw it, when Net-no-kwa realized that she might never return to Lake Huron, she decided to drown her sorrow by throwing a party. Much to his chagrin, three packs of beaver skins plus a number of buffalo robes were squandered in a single day of drinking.[17]

Tanner was now seventeen years old. Already he had seen his Indian family wantonly dispose of its hard-earned wealth several times over. He had garnered hundreds of those furs by his own labors, contributing the whole lot to the family coffers, only to see them sunk again and again in a drinking spree. The Indians' penchant for such prodigality was one aspect of their culture he could not understand and had come to loathe. He himself did not take part in the drinking bouts. He disliked the white traders, and he associated the trading houses with his family's reversals of fortune. Yet he blamed his Indian kin, too. He felt sorry for Net-no-kwa who, despite her strength and determination, ultimately failed in her plans to take her family back to Lake Huron. In Tanner's mind, the group's zigzag pursuit of that goal and its senseless trading of furs for rum went hand in hand. Both epitomized elements of an Indian mindset that he still found foreign.

The Test of Winter

❋ 10 ❋ Winter in the north country was a brutal test of endurance and survival. Algonquian peoples had developed a way of life that was finely adapted for dealing with those hard months. Everything from their material culture to their diet and metabolism conformed to the rhythms of the northern winter. Their pared-down social structure was specifically tailored to get them through it. But, well adapted as Algonquian peoples were to the harsh conditions, individuals and families still had little leeway in the event of accidents. The line between survival and death was very fine. If a wigwam burned down and a family was left without shelter, it might perish in a single night. A hunter who got his clothes wet could succumb to hypothermia in a matter of minutes. The loss of a subsistence group's hunter might lead to starvation for the whole group.

The fur trade may have affected the Indians' odds of survival through the winter. The trading posts functioned as emergency shelters. They were fixed points where people could go for assistance when they found themselves in dire straits. Moreover, the fur trade introduced new goods and technology that made it easier for Indian peoples to feed, clothe, and shelter themselves. The contrary view is that the fur trade made winter survival more problematic, as the hunt for furs diverted energy away from the basic hunt for food. Moreover, as the decades passed, the commercialization of hunting led to overharvesting of various resources, including vital food resources. Thus, by disrupting aboriginal patterns, the fur trade weakened the Indians' safety net and left them more vulnerable to starvation, despite what the trading posts offered by way of emergency assistance.

The latter view presents something of a paradox, for it suggests that Indians, by participating in the fur trade, acted in ways that were counter to their own best interests. As historian Calvin Martin stated so provocatively more than thirty years ago in *Keepers of the Game: Indian-Animal Relationships and the Fur Trade,* "What we are confronting is a monumental case of improvidence. It is difficult to imagine how an individual whose subsistence economy was underpinned by a reliance upon fish, game, wild plant foods, and in some cases, cultivated plants could have been so oblivious to wildlife population dynamics as not to see that his present course of hunting was far too exploitative."[1] Martin goes on to suggest that Indians acted as they did because they somehow came to blame wildlife for the devastating epidemics that raged through the Indian population in the seventeenth and eighteenth centuries. When Indians took part in wildlife overkill, according to Martin, it was in retaliation for the animals' betrayal of the sacred trust relationship between humans and animals.

While Martin's thesis met with considerable skepticism, it served to heighten historians' debate about how Indians fared in the fur trade. Other studies have taken the same general view as Martin did—that Indian participation in the fur trade led to an overall decline in the Indians' well-being—but they explain this seeming paradox in more nuanced terms. Because of the fur trade, hunting territories became smaller and more localized as each hunter concentrated on killing fur-bearing animals and transporting the furs to the nearest trading post. As the hunter operated within a smaller geographic area, he was deprived of access to multiple ecological niches and a wide array of other food resources. This narrowing of the subsistence base carried serious risks. Instances of starvation became more common, not just as a result of overharvesting of certain animal species, but because hunting territories grew smaller. Changes in the spatial geography of hunting territories were accompanied by changes in the social geography of the various bands and even the Indian culture itself. When subsistence groups confined their movement to smaller territories, it had an atomizing effect for the culture, reducing the amount of sharing and mutual assistance between groups. Indians who specialized in hunting beaver for white traders had less incentive to engage in resource-sharing with their kinsmen. The fur trade tended to discourage reciprocity and to promote economic behavior based on Christian/capitalist ethics of productivity and the accumulation of wealth through trade.[2]

Tanner's experiences do not necessarily support one historical interpretation or the other. To ponder whether Tanner's family would have been better off in the absence of the fur trade does not really make sense, since the family had migrated to the northern prairie largely to hunt beaver and participate in the fur trade in the first place. What Tanner's experiences do reveal is how one Ottawa family became attached to the fur trade in ways both good and bad for its own welfare.

The winter of 1798–99 may have been the hardest in Tanner's life. At the start of the season, the family went to the North West Company house at Rainy Lake to obtain supplies. Having parted with all their furs at Grand Portage, they took credit from the trader to the amount of 120 beaver skins and purchased new clothes and blankets and other supplies for the winter.

The debt obligated them to remain in the Rainy Lake area, hunting for the company's trader to repay their debt. Rainy Lake was already known as a poor area in which to find game, and again they found themselves facing winter without an older hunter to provide for them. Although Wa-me-gon-a-biew had rejoined them (his ardor for his new girlfriend having quickly cooled), neither he nor Tanner could qualify as an experienced hunter. At the trader's house they picked up an older fellow named Waw-be-be-nais-sa and his wife and children, but he proved to be a poor provider.[3]

As the days grew bitter cold and snow lay deep on the ground, their situation soon became precarious. Net-no-kwa resorted to prayer and sent Waw-be-be-nais-sa and her elder son on a medicine hunt, from which they returned with the meat of one moose. But as the winter wore on, they were gradually reduced to a state of famine. Scouring the country for game, they became more and more desperate. Weary of moving camp day after day, they discarded some of their pukkwi mats and abandoned other possessions to consolidate loads. They ate their last dog when it became too weak to keep up. The children of Waw-be-be-nais-sa were told to eat their moccasins. At last, reduced to eating the inner bark of trees, several members of the group, including Tanner's older brother, were too weak to stand. They could not go on. In this desperate state, Net-no-kwa sent Tanner to seek help at a trader's house, which they knew to be about a two-day walk from their camp. It was unlikely Tanner could make it in his weakened condition, but this seems to have been their last hope for survival.[4]

Tanner had to cross a large frozen lake to get to the trader's house. The wind had risen as soon as he departed, and as he faced into it across the open expanse of lake, it lashed his flesh and sapped his remaining strength. When at last he reached the shelter of the trees on the other side, he sat down to rest. But in another instant he got back on his feet, realizing that the overwhelming urge to sleep meant almost certain death. He had to keep moving. Fortunately, the wind had died away. All through the still, moonlit night he walked, and in the morning he reached the trader's house. He did not have to tell the men inside the house that he and his people were starving, for they could see it in his face. The trader immediately directed one of the French Canadians to pack some supplies and go in search of the destitute family. Meanwhile, the trader invited Tanner to thaw out in front of a fire. If the trader noticed that the Indian boy with long dark hair was actually a white boy, he said nothing about it to Tanner.

Hearing the wind rise, Net-no-kwa had followed her son out of camp soon after he left, for she feared he would succumb to the wind's deadly chill. Losing his tracks in the drifting snow, she walked on through the night, not knowing if he was alive or dead. She reached the trader's house a few hours behind him. Tanner heard her desperate query outside the door: "Is my son here?" When the door was opened wider, she wept with relief: her little Swallow was alive! In a few days the others followed her in, the French Canadian having successfully delivered the aid package to their camp.[5]

After they had recuperated at the trading house, the family joined a band of Rainy Lake Ojibwas. This band numbered three lodges and included four capable hunters, and as long as Tanner's group remained with them they were well provided for. Much to Tanner's and Net-no-kwa's disgust and embarrassment, their erstwhile principal hunter, Waw-be-be-nais-sa, feigned illness and contributed nothing to the band's collective hunting efforts. However, the other hunters tolerated him well enough and through the rest of the winter gave his family a share of each moose or caribou they brought in.

As winter turned to spring, Tanner's family left the band and began hunting beaver near the trading house. Freed of the lazy Waw-be-be-nais-sa, they lived for a brief time in the company of another Ojibwa hunter. This man had several dogs that he used for hunting and tracking moose. He was such a fast runner that in certain terrain he could outrun his dogs. With them he could pursue a moose for hours. When the moose at last wearied and they closed in on it, one or two of the dogs would put on a final burst of speed and get around in front of it, holding it at bay while the man came up from behind and killed it.

Tanner, meanwhile, was improving his own skills as a hunter. He seems to have shown a fearless instinct. Once, while hunting ducks with buckshot, he startled a bear out of its den. Before the groggy bear could make its escape, he loaded a ball in his gun and pulled the trigger. As the ball had a load of buckshot behind it, the gun blew apart halfway down the muzzle. Without wasting a moment, he loaded a second ball into what was left of his gun and fired again. His second shot brought down the bear.[6]

Just above the inlet to Rainy Lake was a set of rapids where the Indians sometimes gathered to catch fish. The river dropped into Rainy Lake over a series of rock slabs and short waterfalls, and at the base of some of the falls the water eddied in deep round holes worn in the rock. Sometimes the fish were so dense in these whirlpools they could be scooped out of the water by hand. Tanner was fishing there one day with hook and line when a very large sturgeon came over the falls and got stuck in his fishing hole. Acting quickly, before the fish could thrash its way to safety, Tanner brained it with a rock. As it was the first sturgeon taken in that spot, it became the occasion for a feast with all the Ojibwas who were present.[7]

That summer, the younger widow of Taw-ga-we-ninne rejoined their group. She had traveled to Lake Huron and back to reclaim her five-year-old son, who had been living with relatives since he was an infant. She brought back a valuable piece of paper for Net-no-kwa: a promissory note made out by the fur trader at Mackinac for the value of the seven packs of furs she had delivered on Net-no-kwa's behalf. This transaction was a rare instance of the fur traders' credit system recording a debit in favor of the Indian, promising to redeem what the company owed to her at a later date. Whether the trader duly recorded the amount of the note in his ledger book is not known. Since Net-no-kwa would lose this check in a fire the following winter before she was able to cash it, the North West Company never had to make good on it.[8]

The next winter, Tanner went to work for the trader at Prairie Portage. This man the Indians called Aneeb, or Elm Tree. Tanner's role was to hunt elk and bison and provision the trading house with meat, for which Aneeb paid him in handsome metal ornaments. His arrangement with Aneeb was more along the lines of an employment agreement than the customary trading relationship. Although such an arrangement was not the norm between traders and Indians, it was not uncommon either. The trader at Brandon House also employed an Indian hunter that year. In time, numerous Métis worked for the traders under similar terms, and Tanner himself would return to this occupation at different points in his life.[9]

Working for Aneeb, Tanner hunted and tracked elk on foot, just as he had with the Ojibwa hunter and his dogs the previous year. Once, pursuing an elk for many hours on end, Tanner became so drenched in sweat that when he at last gave up the chase his clothes froze to his body. His leggings, which were made of cloth, turned into tubes of ice on his legs. Wet, cold, and exhausted, he fought the urge to lie down and sleep. Starting for his mother's lodge several miles distant, he knew that he must get there or die. If Tanner was sometimes slow to perceive danger, he always showed tremendous grit once the danger was upon him. As he trudged on, his fingers and toes ceased to ache—not because they had warmed up, he knew, but because they had grown numb with frostbite. Later, he fell into a trance. In his dream state, his traveling spirit wandered off, while his bodily spirit stayed put, telling his legs to keep walking, never to stop or allow the rest of him to lie down. Waking from his dream state, he realized that he had been walking in tight circles for what seemed like a long time. He set his course for camp again. He was delirious when he finally made it and crawled into the wigwam to collapse on his buffalo-robe bed next to a warm fire. The last thing he saw before falling into a deep slumber was large frost crystals clinging to the underside of the pukkwi mats. Reflecting the firelight, they twinkled overhead like stars.[10]

Tanner was a whole month recovering from that ordeal. His face, hands, and feet were frostbitten, and his bodily reserves were so spent that he could hardly get out of bed. Some weeks later, his older brother joined him in convalescence, having fallen into a campfire and burned himself during a drinking bout. With both sons incapacitated, their family would have been in deep trouble had it not been for the generosity of Waw-be-be-nais-sa, the usually lax hunter who had joined them the previous winter at Rainy Lake. Over the summer, Waw-be-be-nais-sa had divorced his wife and married Net-no-kwa's daughter. Net-no-kwa had tried to prevent the marriage, thinking that he would be nothing but a drag on her family, but she relented when she learned that his ex-wife had married someone else and taken the children with her. In the present emergency, with both her sons unable to hunt, her new son-in-law came to the family's aid. Waw-be-be-nais-sa placed his lodge about a day's walk from Net-no-kwa's lodge and every so often he brought her the present of an elk.[11]

Yet another calamity befell Tanner's family before the winter was out. The brothers had by this time recovered from their respective ailments and had both returned to hunting. Net-no-kwa departed on a two-day trip to visit her daughter and son-in-law, leaving the lodge in the care of her adopted daughter, the Gros Ventre girl. A onetime captive like Tanner, her name was Skwah-shish and she was now a runty youth of about thirteen. Somehow Skwah-shish allowed the wigwam to catch fire and burn to the ground. When Tanner returned to camp late that night, he found her crying and shivering under a blanket beside the pile of ashes where the wigwam had stood. All of the family's wealth was destroyed, including Net-no-kwa's promissory note from the traders at Mackinac and Tanner's metal ornaments from the trader Aneeb.[12]

Such a devastating loss in wintertime might have been not only demoralizing but fatal. Yet the family survived and bounced back. Taking stock of what had happened, Net-no-kwa decided that they must go to the trader's house and obtain new supplies. Aneeb, the trader, allowed them a credit of forty beaver skins, with which they purchased blankets and cloth. They then found temporary shelter at the lodge of Waw-be-be-nais-sa, where the whole family set to work making the pukkwi mats of woven cattail reeds that would give them a snug, new wigwam. While everyone worked long hours to get it done, no one worked harder than Skwah-shish. On the morning after the fire, Net-no-kwa had been so upset with her that she made the girl beg for her life. But now she teased her good-naturedly, and the family was restored to harmony.[13]

So it was that Tanner's family alternately skirted disaster and enjoyed a relative prosperity.

Red Sky of the Morning

✦ **{ 11 }** ✦ Because Tanner was dutiful and brave, he was Net-no-kwa's favorite son. She was a proud old woman, and Tanner learned how to prop her up when she most needed it. Having lost the large following she had had in the old homeland, Net-no-kwa hankered for recognition. She had pretensions of being a medicine woman. Wa-me-gon-a-biew belittled her whenever she put on such airs, but Tanner showed the old woman respect, even when he only half-believed in her spiritual powers himself. Sometimes he saw right through her artifices, as when she discovered a bear in its hiding place and the following day directed hunters to the spot as if she had seen it in a vision.[1] But he kept these observations to himself. He and his mother seldom quarreled. For the most part he adopted her values and formed opinions of people much as she did.

As Tanner rose in his mother's favor, his older brother grew more shiftless and detached from the group. When Tanner was nineteen years old, Wa-me-gon-a-biew went off and married an Ojibwa woman. Thus Tanner became the group's sole hunter. Net-no-kwa considered her older son irresponsible for having left the group to its own resources just as winter was coming on. When Wa-me-gon-a-biew and his in-laws came to them in distress at the end of the season, she was spiteful. Handing them ten beaver pelts to take to the trading house for provisions, she chided them for their want, declaring that those ten beavers were just a fraction of what her younger son, the Swallow, had killed over the winter.[2]

Net-no-kwa increasingly allowed Tanner to guide the group's movements, and it was probably at his urging that they purchased six horses in order to travel more than 200 miles to the Red Deer River, in what is now Saskatchewan, to hunt beaver during the coming winter. There is a good chance old Net-no-kwa and the others had never ridden a horse before. The western Ojibwas and Ottawas seldom used horses before migrating to the Canadian prairie, and it was only in the early 1800s that they began to acquire them.[3] As for Tanner, the last time he had been on a horse was when he was captured by the Ottawa-Shawnee war party eleven years earlier. Although he had grown up with horses on his father's farm in Kentucky, that experience was now a distant memory. Moreover, the horses they purchased were not draft animals like his father's, nor were they equipped with saddles and stirrups. They were probably a good bit wilder and fleeter than the horses in Kentucky. In all likelihood they were acquired from Assiniboines, who got them from Mandans, who obtained them in trade with Shoshonis on the upper Missouri.[4] While relearning how to ride, Tanner was thrown off his mount and, with one hand still tangled in the bridle rein, got trampled as well. He broke a rib in the accident, which failed to heal properly and pained him from time to time for the rest of his life.[5] Despite the mishap, Tanner had no regrets; he remained as enthusiastic as any of his tribesmen about the value of a good horse.[6]

With the six horses they traveled swiftly, west up the Assiniboine River past Riding Mountain, then northwest following the river through flat, verdant grasslands. Near the headwaters, about midway to the Red Deer River, they came to Fort Alexandria, a North West Company trading house. As it was summer, the post was occupied by just one clerk, two interpreters, and a handful of laborers, together with their six wives and thirteen children. The laborers were erecting two blockhouses on either side of the gate and making repairs on the fort's existing bastions. The Nor' Westers were bolstering their defenses in anticipation of an attack by the Gros Ventres, who were rumored to be upset with them for selling firearms to their enemies, the Assiniboines and Crees. Six lodges of Crees were presently encamped near the stockade in case of attack, the women and children being desirous of the fort's security while their men were off making war on the Gros Ventres.[7]

When Tanner's group arrived there, Net-no-kwa hung back and her adopted son stepped forward as the group's leader. This was Tanner's first time in that role. He spoke to the traders in Ojibwa, since that was the language used by one of the two interpreters. With his wealth of horses, his youth, and his white skin, he made a striking impression on the traders. The clerk in charge, one Daniel Harmon of Vermont, noted in his diary that a white Indian visited that day who was "regarded as a chief among his people."[8]

During Harmon's brief encounter with Tanner on July 9, 1801, he guessed Tanner's age correctly at twenty years, and he observed the close bond between him and Net-no-kwa. He got the gist of Tanner's background right, though he was wrong about specifics: he recorded that Tanner had been taken captive by Ojibwas and that he came from a farm in the Illinois country. As Tanner would not speak a word of English, Harmon conversed with him through the interpreter. Tanner was reticent on the subject of his white relations and fidgeted when the traders called attention to his race. Indeed, with his long hair falling over his shoulders and the whiskers on his chin plucked clean away, Tanner looked almost completely Indian except for the color of his skin.[9]

As Tanner emerged from his mother's shadow, fur traders sometimes questioned him about his race and background. The following spring, a Hudson's Bay Company officer offered to take him to England. The identity of this trader is not known, but it would appear his motive was partly exploitative and partly philanthropic; he suggested that Tanner might tour his country and then return with him to North America. Tanner declined the offer, but he did consider it long enough to weigh his alternatives. He felt strong attachments to both the hunting way of life and his Indian mother, and he was not prepared to abandon either one. Moreover, he harbored the thought of someday seeking out his white relatives, if any still survived. With his distrust of traders, he feared the fellow might abandon him in England. He had a good enough grasp of world geography to know how calamitous that would be.[10]

A few months after that encounter, Tanner received another offer. This one came from Hugh McGillis, a wintering partner in the North West Company. McGillis and Tanner became acquainted in the course of several visits the hunter made to the Red Deer River trading house in the winter of 1801–2. McGillis valued Tanner's productivity and inferred from his appearance that he was a white man who had lived among the Indians most of his life. Once, when Tanner came to the Red Deer River post without Net-no-kwa, McGillis took the opportunity to invite Tanner to live in the trading house and become an employee of the company. Knowing of Tanner's personal attachments, he urged him to leave the Indians and reclaim his white heritage. Again, Tanner was ambivalent. Joining McGillis could be just the first step on the road to repatriation. It would afford him a chance to recover his native tongue and prepare his return to the United States. But he did not think about it for long. Reckoning that he would find the drudgery and confinement of life in the fort intolerable, he decided that he preferred being a hunter.[11]

As Tanner confronted the choice of living either as Indian or white, his ambivalence was compounded by his dawning sexuality. At the age of twenty-one he was tall, handsome, and sexually reserved. By conscious choice, he put aside all thoughts of sex with Indian girls whom he met. In his understanding of Ottawa-Ojibwa culture, when two young people had sex they were bound to marry. Marriage was not necessarily a lifelong commitment, but sexual partners were nonetheless expected to form a stable union. Although there was no shame in two young people coming together by their own volition, the preferred pattern was for parents to select their children's first marriage partner. Whenever he did think about sex in these terms, he imagined that he would hold off and eventually marry a white woman.[12]

Net-no-kwa had other plans for him, however. One day she took him aside and said she had found him a match. Her candidate was the young daughter of an old Ottawa chief, Wa-ge-tote. They had already been living with Wa-ge-tote's band for two months, but until then Tanner had paid little attention to the girl. Net-no-kwa advised her son that she was getting old and it was time that he took a wife to make his moccasins, dress his skins, and attend to his lodge. Wa-ge-tote, she disclosed, had consented to the marriage. Wa-ge-tote was a strong, capable, virtuous man and would make a good ally for their family. When Tanner balked at her plan she was insistent, saying that she had already obtained Wa-ge-tote's assurance that his daughter was willing. When Tanner still declined, she announced that he really must agree to it, as she and Wa-ge-tote had already settled the matter; the girl would be brought to his lodge that evening. Tanner was obstinate: in that event, he would refuse to sleep with her. Grabbing his gun, he announced that he was going hunting. He stayed out all day and returned late in the evening with the meat of a bull elk. Taking his time to hang the meat outside his lodge, he strained to hear if the girl waited for him inside. He had already made up his mind to sleep somewhere else should he find her there. But his bed was empty.

The next day Wa-ge-tote's band prepared to depart for another hunting ground, as previously planned. Before they set out, Wa-ge-tote came to Tanner's lodge. Cheerfully making a little conversation, he made no mention of his daughter. For the record, it appeared, the old chief took no offense at Tanner's refusal of his daughter. Net-no-kwa, however, was disappointed and embarrassed for her son, and she stayed at a distance during the men's exchange.[13]

Wa-ge-tote's discretion in the matter was probably more apparent than real, for word soon got around among the western Ojibwas of Tanner's reluctance to take a wife. In the middle of winter, a solitary man walked into Tanner's camp. His name was Ozaw-wen-dib, and he was one the Ojibwas called an *agokwa*, a person with two spirits. He had the body and dress of a man, yet the posture, movement, and speech of a woman. The Ojibwas revered such people, perceiving them as conjoined male and female personalities sharing one body. Regarded as neither man nor woman, agokwas had the perspective of both genders and could see things men and women could not. They had more powerful dreams than ordinary people. They were noted, too, as hard workers, with skill-sets spanning both gender roles.

Ozaw-wen-dib exemplified the agokwa's exalted status and versatility. The son of a celebrated war chief, he was himself a renowned warrior as well as a valued homemaker. He had shown rare courage in fighting the Sioux and was known as the fastest runner among the western Ojibwas. Yet whenever he took a husband (and he had had many) he proved to be as proficient and industrious in the female arts as any wife. Soon after his arrival in Tanner's camp, Ozaw-wen-dib announced his purpose: he had traveled many days to find the young white chief in the hopes of joining his lodge.[14]

Tanner accepted Ozaw-wen-dib into his lodge; however, he stubbornly refused the agokwa's frequent sexual advances. Among the Ojibwas, as among many Indian tribes, sex between a man and an agokwa was accepted on the basis that the agokwa was deemed to be of a different gender, whereas sex between two men or between two agokwas was taboo. Nevertheless, whenever Ozaw-wen-dib offered himself, Tanner declined. In time he became so uncomfortable that he could barely speak to the agokwa. Net-no-kwa laughed at her son's squeamishness; she encouraged Ozaw-wen-dib to stay and persist in his sexual overtures. But Ozaw-wen-dib soon grew weary of this awkwardness and left. A few weeks later, Tanner and his group visited the camp of Wa-ge-tote, where they found Ozaw-wen-dib living with the old chief and his two wives. Tanner heard sniggering around the camp concerning Wa-ge-tote's new marital arrangements, but as was customary in Indian culture the gibes were directed at the man, not the agokwa. Tanner felt relieved that Ozaw-wen-dib had entered into a new marriage.[15]

A year later, an old medicine man came to Tanner with his fifteen-year-old granddaughter and the girl's parents. Tanner thought the girl was pretty, but before he had time to give their proposal much thought Net-no-kwa advised him against it. Divining that the girl had something fatally wrong with her, she urged her son to leave on a hunt and be gone for several days until the family wearied of waiting for him or accepted his absence as a sign of disinterest. This time, Tanner followed Net-no-kwa's advice. When the girl did indeed sicken and die later that year, he praised his mother's intuition.[16]

But Tanner had long since decided that in matters of the heart he would not necessarily conform to his mother's wishes.

One summer evening, standing by his lodge, he allowed his eyes to fall on a beautiful young woman who was idly wandering about smoking a pipe. To gaze so intently on a young person of the opposite sex was not customary, Tanner knew. Presently she sidled up to him and asked if he would like to share her smoke. He took her pipe and puffed a little, ruminating on his first taste of tobacco. They stood there talking for a long time. Tanner found he enjoyed everything about her—her cheekiness, her sensuality, the soft sound of her voice. Indeed, after they parted he could hardly get her out of his mind.

In the following days, he sought her out around the village. At first he kept their encounters brief to avoid arousing the village gossips. And he did not say a word to Net-no-kwa. But as the two became intimate, he could no longer contain himself. Wearing his ornaments and playing his flute as he sauntered about, he was as obvious as a dancing woodcock. If Net-no-kwa needed proof of what was happening, it came one night when her son crept into the lodge just before dawn. He had barely settled down to sleep when she woke him with a stern rapping on his feet. "Up, young man, you who are about to take yourself a wife," she exclaimed. Since he was about to marry, she announced, he must impress his bride by bringing home a large kill of fresh meat. Without answering, Tanner got dressed, took his gun, and shambled out. In spite of his ardor, he was still not inclined to marry. But his spirits rose after he found and killed a large moose. While he was away, Net-no-kwa met with the girl's parents. When he returned, he found his young lover sitting demurely inside his lodge, gazing at the floor. He stopped at the door, hesitating to enter, until Net-no-kwa barked at him to go on in.[17]

Her name was Mis-kwa-bun-o-kwa, or Red Sky of the Morning. It was an apt name for the young woman who finally overcame Tanner's shyness about sex. Unfortunately, little else is known about her. For when Tanner gave an account of his life some twenty-five years later he practically cut her out of his story, so hurtful was her memory. In their five years of marriage, she bore him one son and two daughters.

Warrior

✳ 12 ✳ In the summer of 1804, Tanner chose to join a war party against the Sioux. The Ojibwas and their Ottawa allies had been at war with the Sioux for upwards of three generations. After the British claimed sovereignty over the area from the French, British fur traders tried to get the Ojibwas and the Sioux to make peace, for the fur traders saw intertribal wars as a distraction from the business of hunting furs. Viewing Indian warfare from an economic perspective, the traders assumed that the Ojibwas and the Sioux fought over hunting territory and access to European trading posts. It was easy for the traders to conclude that the two Indian nations competed over land and resources much the way France and Britain did. The whole disputed area ran along the margin between eastern woodland and western prairie, where the unique blend of habitats produced an exceptional abundance and diversity of animals, including beaver, bison, and deer. If only the tribes would cease fighting, the traders believed, Indian hunters would be free to enter those rich beaver grounds that lay in the no-man's-land between their warring nations.[1]

The traders had little success in ending the conflict. The fact that the Ojibwas and the Sioux faced off where woodland met prairie may have had less to do with fur-trade interests than it did with the balance of forces between the two tribes. The Ojibwas were better supplied with guns from the north and east, the Sioux with horses from the south and west. In the woodland environment the Ojibwas prevailed with superior numbers and firepower, but wherever they pushed too far out on the prairie the superior mobility of the Sioux gave that nation the edge.[2]

Year after year, the Ojibwas and the Sioux formed war parties to harass and kill each other. The war parties might number a dozen, a few score, or more than a hundred men. On occasion they might be satisfied to shed the blood of just one or two of the enemy; or, conversely, they might fall upon a village and massacre men, women, and children. What the fur traders failed to understand about Indian warfare was that it answered cultural needs as well as economic objectives. It strengthened group identity, raised the status of chiefs, and gave men an opportunity to prove their mettle. For Tanner,

war was a profoundly socializing experience. Perhaps as much as hunting
or marriage, war formed a crucial part of his induction into tribal society.[3]

As this was Tanner's first war party, he went through various rites of ini-
tiation for a young warrior. Each morning, he had to paint his face black. At
night, he was required to sleep at one end of the camp with the other black-
faced young warriors. He had to lie on one side with his face to the east to
show the Great Spirit that he hoped to return home safely, and he had to
remain stock-still like that all night long. As they traveled, it was necessary
to walk his horse in the footsteps of a veteran. On the march he was not allowed
to eat or drink or stop for a rest; if compelled to stop for any reason, he must face
east and pray to the Great Spirit. He could not share his knife or drinking bowl
with anyone, nor could anyone even touch those items. He could not scratch
himself with bare fingers but must use a twig and then toss it away.[4]

After gathering in the Red River valley, the war party journeyed westward for several days through present-day North Dakota. On the hot, dry
prairie, a major concern was finding water. As Tanner had a horse, he was
selected to be among the scouts. One day they spotted a single Indian, who
fled as soon as he was seen, confirming in everyone's minds that he was an
enemy scout. But if there was an enemy war party in the neighborhood, they
failed to find it. After a few more days' march, the party became parched
with thirst. Wracked with dissension, it finally broke up. Tanner, with his
brother Wa-me-gon-a-biew and three other men, split off and found their
own way home.[5]

❄

The following summer, a war party of about 300 Sioux fell upon a small
band of Ojibwas encamped within a few miles of Alexander Henry's trading
post on the Red River. The first Ojibwa to fall in the attack was the chief,
who also happened to be Henry's father-in-law. Unaware that the Sioux had
sneaked up on the camp during the night, this man climbed a tree to look
for buffalo first thing in the morning and was struck by two arrows from
below. He shouted an alarm as he fell, and in the next moment his companions heard a thunder of hooves as the main body of the Sioux war party
charged the camp on their horses. The Ojibwas sprang from their tents, the
men shooting their guns as the women and children attempted to flee on
foot to the nearby woods. But the mounted Sioux quickly overran the camp
and caught up with all but a few of them. About a dozen men, women, and
children were slaughtered. One man and two women escaped into the thick
woods, where the horses could not pursue, while four children were taken
captive. One twelve-year-old boy survived by hiding in a patch of willows.[6]

The next day this young survivor made his way to Henry's trading house. Henry was not there, but the clerk in charge formed a burial detail. Accompanying the boy back to the site, they found a horrible scene. The corpses were pierced with arrows and hacked to pieces. The chief's head was severed from his body, the scalp lifted off, and the top of the skull removed. His arms and legs were cut off and his torso disemboweled. His severed penis was stuffed in his dead wife's mouth. The wife's body was also cut to pieces and her genitals mutilated. The bodies of her small children were dismembered and the limbs thrown in all directions. The other victims' bodies were found wherever they had fallen, and those, too, were horribly desecrated.[7]

Runners took the news of the massacre to several hundred Indians encamped at the Forks and up the Assiniboine River. Tanner and his group were drying a large quantity of buffalo meat on a *sunjegwun,* or scaffold, when a messenger arrived in their camp. Dropping their work, they hastened to Pembina, where they found many Ojibwa already gathered, mourning the deaths of their kinfolk and preparing for war. Such a mass display of grief was among the tribe's most effective ways of raising a war party. By tribal custom, relatives of the victims were required to mourn the dead for one year; however, the period of mourning might also be concluded by taking a relic of the deceased to war and smearing it with the blood of the enemy.[8]

Alexander Henry arrived with his outfit a month after the massacre, on August 2. On his arrival, the Indians broke into fresh lamentations. Henry gave them a nine-gallon keg of gun powder and 100 pounds of balls and encouraged them to revenge the death of his father-in-law and family. The chiefs approved of Henry's gift, telling him he showed almost as much sense as an Indian. If only he would open a few kegs of rum, they added, then he would be fully as wise as they were. Henry remained at Pembina for a week, then headed back to Lake Winnipeg. Meanwhile, the gathering of Indians continued to grow until finally, toward the end of summer, a war party of 400 started out on the trail of the enemy.[9]

It was a multinational force that went against the Sioux. Besides about 200 Ojibwas, there were perhaps 100 Assiniboines and a smaller number of Ottawas and Crees. The war party included many chiefs. The chief of the Ottawas was none other than Pe-shau-ba—the same man who had taken Tanner's family under his wing when they first came west. To keep such a large, composite force together was impossible. On the second day out, about half the Ojibwas deserted. The next night, most of the Assiniboines stole away with a large part of the horses. Four of those horses belonged to Tanner. Tanner appealed to Pe-shau-ba, asking permission to take some of his Ottawa friends and go in pursuit. But the old chief would not allow it, foreseeing that it would lead to more dissension and could break up the expedition. Desertions were rampant anyway. Bad omens abounded. The party came upon a dead man laid on a scaffold in a tree; the retreating Sioux had made a hasty burial. Some of the men pulled down the corpse and started to desecrate it, while others insisted it should be left alone; a scuffle broke out that left everyone feeling uneasy. By the time they reached Lake Traverse, they were reduced to 120 men.[10]

As they marched deeper into enemy country, the danger of interception grew. Two days west of Lake Traverse, when they knew they were just shy of the enemy's village, they halted in the cover of woods and waited for darkness. After nightfall, they crept forward to the crest of a hill. But when they charged the village at dawn, their blood-curdling war-whoops did no more than frighten a few wolves out of a rubbish heap, for the village lay deserted.[11]

With the men losing heart, voicing their discouragement, the chiefs held a council. In spite of the fear, fatigue, and dashed hopes that had marked the expedition, they wanted to proceed; the rule of vengeance required it. To restore morale, they formed the men in a circle and held an equipment swap. Taking turns, each man made one pass around the circle, displaying whatever item he needed—powder, balls, medicines—until someone offered to give up a portion of his own supply. If no one offered, a chief repeated the entreaty on the warrior's behalf. If still no one offered, then as a last resort the chief requisitioned the item from whomever in the circle he chose. In this way, everyone's critical needs were satisfied. Tanner stood in need of moccasins, for he had brought only seven pairs on the assumption that he would be riding horseback. Since the Assiniboine had stolen his horses, he had quickly run through his small supply. Although he was grateful to receive a new pair, his feet were already in bad shape.[12]

Continuing on the trail of the Sioux, the war party gradually pieced together where the enemy had gone. The Sioux had gathered everyone from the village; then, doubling back by another route so as to evade their pursuers, they had fled to the trader's fort on Lake Traverse. This independent trader was one Robert Dickson, a red-headed Scot who had lived among the Sioux for more than a decade and a half. Married to the sister of a prominent chief of the Yanktonai Sioux, he held considerable sway over his wife's people. The fort was Dickson's main residence. When the Ojibwas and their allies realized that they would have to attack their enemy in this stronghold, they lost heart. The war party finally disbanded. Together with Pe-shau-ba and ten remaining Ottawa warriors, Tanner returned to Pembina, having been absent from his family through the entire fall.[13]

As a military endeavor the war had been utterly fruitless: the war party had killed not one Sioux. But as a cultural endeavor the war succeeded, for it taught young men like Tanner the warrior ethic. It was one of the most important socializing experiences of his life. Emulating the veterans, he learned how to be brave, daring, tough, cunning, and resolute. The warrior's resolute defense of principle inspired Tanner above all else. Henceforth, when standing on principle, he often struck a warrior's pose.

His first opportunity to act in the warrior mold came the following spring, when he learned that the Assiniboines were boasting of having stolen his horses. Taking his brother with him, he embarked on a long and dangerous quest to recover his favorite black horse. In the course of this adventure he defied death threats, fought hand to hand with his antagonists, stole three different horses, and made three separate hair-breadth escapes. Wa-me-gon-a-biew, fearing for his own life after one of these close scrapes, finally deserted him. For this, Tanner branded his brother a coward. When it was all over with, Tanner arrived back home without a single horse. The first one that he stole he returned to its rightful owner. The second he rode so hard it burst a blood vessel and died. And the third—his favorite, the black—he gave to a passing friend in need. In the end, his warrior's quest was not so much about recovering his horse as it was about defending his honor.[14]

❈{IV}❈ McLOUGHLIN

Fort William

{ 13 } At the age of eighteen, Dr. John McLoughlin set out for his new post. His destination was the North West Company's new headquarters near the mouth of the Kaministiquia River on the north shore of Lake Superior. When McLoughlin arrived there in the summer of 1803, the impressive complex was in its third year of construction. Exploring his new home in the wilderness, he found a considerable area cleared of trees and enclosed within a large stockade. Several brick kilns were rapidly turning out bricks, and new buildings were going up in every area of the fort. Glass windows, cast iron stoves, and other furnishings of all kinds were being unloaded from the North West Company's new sailing ship, the *Invincible*. A handful of nearly completed buildings stood in a cluster around a central square: fur stores, dry goods and outfitting shops, a meeting hall for the partners, and a temporary kitchen. As no living quarters had yet been constructed, the partners and clerks were living in tents. The engagés had a separate encampment outside the stockade.[1]

Known simply as the New Fort or Kaministiquia in 1803, this grand post was eventually renamed Fort William in honor of William McGillivray, the head of the North West Company. In time it would grow to encompass about three dozen buildings including livestock barns, canoe sheds, a granary, and a powder magazine. The main council house was called the Great Hall. An imposing structure, it included living quarters for the partners on one side, quarters for clerks and apprentice clerks on the other, and a grand meeting room in the center.

McLoughlin soon went to work in the hospital. At times he worked under the watchful eye of the North West Company's only other physician, Dr. Munro. At other times he treated patients all on his own when Dr. Munro was away on other business. No letters written by McLoughlin during his first summer in the Northwest have survived, but an account book from the post contains numerous references to him dispensing "sundries" there.[2]

For the young apprentice, the rhythm of life at Fort William was highly seasonal. For most of the year, much of this forward base in the North West Company's far-flung operations stood empty and boarded up as the wintering population dwindled to about thirty-five employees—few more than the number who resided at a dozen other trading posts in the Northwest. But during the summer rendezvous the fort thronged with as many as a thousand employees. Then the Great Hall bustled with activity as the partners conducted business. In their leisure hours the partners dined on fresh game, corn, peas, potatoes, and white bread; drank copiously; played cards and gambled; and held an occasional dance. The employees did not lack for pleasures, either. Each new arriving brigade was met by a great regalement on the riverbank. Between times they played games and had friendly brawls. A good-natured rivalry existed between the year-round employees, or "winterers," and the seasonal hires who came up from Montreal. The former group condescendingly called the latter group "pork-eaters," and fights sometimes broke out in the commons between their two camps.[3]

McLoughlin was a little detached from this boisterous social milieu. Between his doctoring, his bookishness, and his habitual scowl, people often took him to be older than his actual age. Certainly he was unusual in appearance. Standing six feet, four inches tall, he was almost a foot taller than most of the other men, broad shouldered, and lanky. His tall, thin frame contrasted with the stocky, bow-legged build of the typical voyageur. One way in which he adapted to frontier life was to waste little effort on his grooming. He patched his clothes in a haphazard manner with whatever color of cloth came to hand. He let his hair grow long. In the few portraits that were made of him in later life, his hair came down to his shoulders or even down his back, framing his head like a lion's mane. His wild hair, along with his fierce stare, gave him a slightly mad appearance by middle age, and he may well have begun to acquire that intimidating look even as a young man.[4]

During the rendezvous McLoughlin kept up a busy medical practice. He was always on the lookout for cases to test his knowledge and skills. One such case involved a patient with scrofula. The ailment was also known as the king's evil, or what might be described today as tuberculosis of the neck or an infection of the lymph nodes. After curing this man using the juice of the sorrel plant, he proudly described his method in a letter to his uncle Simon.

> Pound [the sorrel] in a mortar till it is reduced to a kind of pulp, then put it into an unglas'd earthen pot and allow it to macerate in its own juice over a gentle fire until it becomes of a proper consistency. [Apply it in a poultice] as warm as the patient can endure to the naked sore. The patient I had complain'd it hurt him much and on the very first application the sore assumed a red colour. I have

adopted Dr. Darwin's theory i.e. that ulcers of this nature are from deficiency of irritability, and I imagine that there is an assumption of oxigene [*sic*] from the sorrel that gives the sore the red colour and irritates the part to a discharge of matter, in short, gives it the irritability it want'd before.

McLoughlin added that scrofula was common among the Indians and that he hoped to try his treatment on some of them as well.[5] Here was a glimmer of the humanitarian concern for Indians for which he would one day be remembered.

After the rendezvous, McLoughlin wintered at one of the smaller posts in the area as an apprentice clerk. This post may have been a mere cabin on a lake somewhere—a remote satellite to a larger post administered by a clerk or partner. Wherever he spent his first winter, he returned to Fort William the next summer for another season of doctoring the sick and injured. But again in the winter of 1804–5 the company sent him to a remote location. The rotation from doctor to apprentice clerk, from summer rendezvous to winter outpost, became the seasonal rhythm by which he marked his apprentice years. His winter posts cannot be identified with certainty, but probably all of them were in the region between Lake Superior and Rainy Lake. Certainly he acquired a familiarity with the country and a knowledge of the local tribes, for he later wrote a report titled "Description of the Indians from Fort William to Lake of the Woods."[6]

In his role as apprentice clerk, McLoughlin probably had charge of two or three engagés, whom he sent out each day to hunt, fish, chop wood, and drum up business with Indians, while he minded the store. His own tasks were to conduct trade, maintain accounts of goods going out and furs coming in, and report to whomever he was working under. He and his men may have been several days' march on snowshoes from the parent trading house.[7]

During the winter of 1807–8 McLoughlin was assigned to the outfit of fur trader Daniel Harmon—the same individual who encountered John Tanner at Fort Alexandria in 1801. McLoughlin and Harmon built their winter station on the shore of Sturgeon Lake, about 150 straight-line miles northwest of Fort William. The two clerks had one small cabin and the engagés another. Harmon was suffering from a stubborn ailment of some kind, an unspecified complaint, and it was hoped that McLoughlin could restore him to good health over the winter. Harmon was just a few years older than McLoughlin and in his seventh year in the Northwest. He proved to be a good companion through the wintry days and long, northern nights. The son of a Vermont innkeeper, he was better educated than most junior officers in the North West Company, and McLoughlin found his conversation pleasant. McLoughlin tried various medicines on him but could not find a cure. Yet Harmon bore himself well, accepting the inconclusive results with equanimity.[8]

McLoughlin shared the small living quarters with the Vermonter and his mixed-blood wife. It was not unusual for unmarried men and families to share the same quarters, especially at small outposts where cabins had been erected just in time for winter. In early December Harmon's wife gave birth to the couple's first child, a boy, and McLoughlin very likely helped deliver the baby. Such a compact living arrangement may have given McLoughlin his first close-up look at marriage between a white man and a mixed-blood woman. Harmon and his wife had been married for two years. As Harmon related, she had been offered to him one day at South Branch Fort on the Saskatchewan River, and after "mature consideration" he had decided to accept her. She was then fourteen, the daughter of a French Canadian, and far from her mother's people, who lived in the Rocky Mountains. Traders who intended to remain in the country for any length of time often took "a daughter of the country" as a wife. Indeed, the North West Company encouraged these marriages, since many mixed-blood women and girls were abandoned at the forts by their husbands and fathers, and without another trader or engagé to provide for them, they had to be maintained at company expense. If he and his young wife made each other happy, Harmon piously explained, then it was his intention to keep her as long as he remained in Indian country. When the time came for him to return to New England, he would then make every effort to find her another caring husband in the fur trade. For he firmly believed she would not be content living in civilized society.[9]

It was probably the following year that McLoughlin entered a similar marital arrangement of his own. Little is known about this union other than that it was short-lived and produced just one child, a boy, whom the couple named Joseph. Some sources on McLoughlin say that the woman was a full-blood Ojibwa, but that is unlikely. Although fur traders often sought full-blood Indian women as marriage partners in the eighteenth century, there was a decided shift in preference toward mixed-blood women as their numbers increased around the forts in the next century.[10] In 1806, the North West Company decreed that henceforth no employee could marry a full-blood Indian, the object being to encourage marriages with mixed-blood women, who would otherwise be a drag on company resources. The penalty for disobeying this decree was £100—as much as McLoughlin would earn in his entire apprenticeship—and surviving records indicate that the policy was enforced.[11] So it is more likely that McLoughlin married a mixed-blood woman from around Fort William. It would only be natural if, on returning from Sturgeon Lake, he decided to seek the kind of companionship that Harmon and his young wife had modeled for him that winter. Being unavoidably aware of sexual activities within the small space of the cabin provided a strong impetus for a young man to find a bed partner of his own.[12]

The marriage apparently lasted just a year or two at most. Perhaps the woman died in childbirth. Or perhaps McLoughlin, in his eagerness, married someone whom he soon found incompatible. Judging by his correspondence with his uncle, his emotions were in a tumult that summer of 1808. Although his letters focused on his terms of employment and said nothing about a marriage, the silence means little, because fur traders seldom acknowledged their country wives to relatives back home. What is known for sure is that McLoughlin took responsibility for the child and raised him.[13]

Fortunately, he had much better luck in choosing a second marriage partner two or three years later. She was the daughter of one fur trader and the widow of another. Her name was Marguerite Wadin McKay.

Marriage *à la façon du pays*

{ 14 } Marguerite Wadin McKay was the daughter of a Swiss Protestant man by the name of Jean Etienne Wadin and an Ojibwa or Cree woman whose name has been lost to history. Wadin probably came to North America with the British army during the French and Indian War. By 1772, he was trading with Indians west of Grand Portage, and seven years later he was among some two dozen traders who joined together to form the nucleus of the North West Company. He had a French Canadian wife and children back in Saint Laurent near Montreal. About 1775, his native wife gave birth to a baby girl, Marguerite. Some five years later, Wadin was shot to death at a remote trading post in the depths of winter, allegedly by another Nor' Wester. His demise left Marguerite fatherless at a young age, and she seems to have been reared by her Indian people in the vicinity of North West Company forts.[1]

At about age nineteen or twenty Marguerite married her first husband, a North West Company trader named Alexander McKay. In Canadian fur-trade society, marriages between fur trader and Indian were described as *à la façon du pays,* or "after the custom of the country." Marriage rites were a blend of Indian and European forms. When a trader wanted to marry an Indian woman, he was expected to approach her parents for permission. The parents then decided on a bride price for their daughter, such as a horse or a stock of blankets and kettles or other items of comparable value. After the required items were presented, a simple marriage ritual might conclude with the smoking of the calumet by the trader and the bride's family together with other members of her clan. This sealed the alliance between the trader and his wife's people. When the trader brought his new bride into the fort, his first act was to deliver her into the hands of the native women there, who put her through a cleansing ritual, taking away her Indian clothes and scrubbing off her face paint to signify that she now lived among white men. Reattired in European fashion, she was then escorted by her husband to his quarters and henceforth they were considered man and wife.[2]

If marriage *à la façon du pays* lacked the Christian ideal of lifetime commitment, it still involved a high level of commitment by both partners. Fur traders generally shunned polygamy and assumed that sexual fidelity was part of the marriage contract. As with husbands in Christian marriages, they accepted the role of sole provider within the monogamous relationship. Indian women, for their part, took their husbands' surnames and strove to adopt their husbands' culture and raise their children according to the norms of fur-trade society. The fur companies treated these unions as bona fide marriages and accorded the wives certain privileges as well as duties. The women made their homes with their husbands inside the trading post, and sometimes (more often in the case of officers' wives) they were allowed to travel with their husbands from post to post in the company's canoes. The women contributed to the general provisioning of the forts by gathering berries, catching small game, making moccasins and snowshoes, and performing numerous other tasks.[3]

Marguerite gave birth to Thomas, her first child by McKay, reputedly in 1796 at Sault Ste. Marie. Three daughters followed in succession over the next ten years as her first husband rose from clerk to partner, assuming overall direction of the English River Department. In 1805, after they had been together for ten years, Alexander McKay received his first "rotation," or twelve-month furlough, and went off to Montreal. For Marguerite, this was an anxious time, for among North West families the husband's furlough often led to the wife's abandonment. Although McKay returned to Fort William in 1806 for the rendezvous, he soon chose to retire from the business, tendering his shares in the company for £1,000. At that time he did abandon Marguerite and their three daughters in Indian country for good, taking twelve-year-old Thomas with him.[4]

Marguerite McKay and John McLoughlin formed their alliance in 1811. Their courtship probably occurred when he was on medical duty that summer at Fort William. No details of the courtship were ever recorded, but they may be imagined in the context of the summer rendezvous. The great annual gathering at Fort William was not only a time for renewing old friendships but also an opportunity to meet new people. White men and native women seldom were so free to mingle as they were during the rendezvous. They flirted with one another in idle moments during the work day, came together for the men's football games in the long summer evenings, and joined in dancing—a very popular pastime among both sexes. The fur traders' dances were truly a blend of cultures, the men high-stepping to the fiddle's fast tempo, the native women shuffle-stepping to their own internal rhythm.

Marguerite and John each entered the marriage somewhat seasoned in the ways of love, loss, and parenting. When they took each other as common-law husband and wife, she was about thirty-six years of age and he was twenty-six. He became a father to her three young girls and she became a mother to his boy, who was barely more than an infant. She had long dark hair, strongly Indian features, and a petite figure, which must have appeared even more so when she stood with her towering new mate.[5]

By coincidence, the year that they married was also the year that Marguerite's first husband, Alexander McKay, died in one of the deadliest acts of violence associated with the fur trade. Two years after retiring from the North West Company, McKay joined the Pacific Fur Company of John Jacob Astor and, with his son Thomas, boarded the *Tonquin* for a voyage around Cape Horn to the company's faraway outpost of Astoria at the mouth of the Columbia River. Fortunately, he left the boy at Astoria before reboarding the *Tonquin* for its ill-fated first run up the Pacific Coast. A few weeks later, this three-masted, ten-gun trading vessel was anchored in Clayoquot Sound, on the outer coast of Vancouver Island, when Indians, intent on avenging an insult made to their chief the previous day, talked their way aboard ship under the guise of wanting to trade but then attacked the ship's crew. After a bloody struggle, a wounded crew member, finding all his mates either slain or gone overboard, retreated to the powder magazine and blew up the ship. News of this incident could not have reached Marguerite until several months after she and John McLoughlin married, but whatever grief she felt at the death of her former husband must have been mixed with relief over the fact that her son was not among the victims. Young Thomas remained in Astoria until 1813, when the failing Pacific Fur Company sold out to the North West Company. Thomas then joined the Nor' Westers and returned to the Canadian prairie. And so John McLoughlin acquired a stepson.[6]

McLoughlin was not yet thirty years old and already he was responsible for five children. His situation was not uncommon. By the time McLoughlin entered the fur trade, children were as numerous as adults at many North West Company forts. Fort Vermilion on the Saskatchewan River in 1809, for example, had a resident population of thirty-six men, twenty-nine women, and sixty-seven children. Unlike the Hudson's Bay Company, the North West Company showed no interest in providing schools or teachers for this growing population of mixed-blood children. The company assumed that any traders who wanted to give their country-born offspring a formal education could send them down to Montreal. Few did, in part because of the great expense but also out of concern that they would not flourish in civilized society. In the absence of schools, parents were solely responsible for educating their children. Consequently, the influence of the mother's native culture featured strongly in the children's upbringing. Fathers generally hoped for their daughters to marry traders and for their sons to find employment as guides, interpreters, or clerks in the fur trade. John McLoughlin was no different, for at this point in his life he could not even think of financing a formal education for his children. He had no other choice than to contemplate their growing to maturity on the frontier.[7]

Based on the few surviving observations left by family, friends, and associates, it seems that McLoughlin and Marguerite were loving and tender companions. Both partners were noted for their moral rectitude, each adhering to the tenets of their own cultural traditions. People praised Marguerite for her generous spirit and sweet, mild temper. One man who was close to the McLoughlins later in life lauded Marguerite for "her numerous charities and many excellent qualities of heart." Her children would later remember the remarkable calming effect she had on her husband's stormy moods.[8]

McLoughlin, for his part, took a growing pride in providing Marguerite with what was, for a fur trader's family, an exceptionally stable domestic arrangement. Each fall, after the rendezvous, the McLoughlins packed their things and shipped out on the North West Company's main-trunk canoe route, crossing over the Height of Land (the divide between the Lake Superior and Hudson Bay watersheds) to McLoughlin's winter post at Rainy Lake. There they made their home either at the main trading house on the Rainy River just below the outlet of Rainy Lake or at a small, auxiliary outpost located at Vermilion Lake.[9] Each June or July, the family packed their things again and returned to Fort William, where McLoughlin saw to the health of hundreds of voyageurs and the few dozen partners attending that year's rendezvous. Eventually the McLoughlins were given their own private residence at Fort William, so valued were his medical services. Located just inside the large fort's main gate, it doubled as the apothecary.[10]

Twice in his seventeen years with the North West Company, McLoughlin maneuvered his way out of assignments that would have ended this happy arrangement and taken the family much farther afield. The first time, in 1811, he declined an offer to go to the Columbia River in Oregon. Then, in 1815, he refused a request by the partners to take over administration of the company's most valuable asset, the Athabaska Department. If McLoughlin gave his reasons for refusing the appointments, they are not known, as the minutes of council for those years have not survived. It seems clear, however, that his primary motivation was to maintain a stable home for his large family.[11]

McLoughlin's marriage *à la façon du pays* brought him the additional advantage of more direct links to native people. With his wife's help, he became fairly proficient in the Ojibwa language, and as the years passed he became an increasingly sensitive observer of Ojibwa culture, too. This was, of course, one of the main reasons the fur companies supported cross-cultural marriage, because these alliances were generally beneficial for the business. Marguerite had no kinship ties to the local Indian bands; by some accounts her own kin lived farther east around Sault Ste. Marie. Still, in the interactions between white and Indian that so permeated the fur trade, Marguerite's native background must have aided her husband in countless small ways. When Indians came to their winter post to barter, McLoughlin made it his business to learn a little about each one. By the time the McLoughlins left for the Columbia in 1824, he was acquainted with hundreds of Indians throughout the region stretching from Fort William to Lake of the Woods.

Bad Birds

❊ 15 ❊ Once, when McLoughlin was at his post on Vermilion Lake near Rainy Lake, an old Ojibwa chief and two young men came to see him with nothing to trade, bearing only a message. It was early April; the winter's snow lay in patches on the forest floor, and the ice had just begun to melt around the edges of the lake. The three visitors shared a pipe of tobacco with the young McLoughlin as they went through the customary ritual of exchanging compliments. At length, the old chief made a speech. He began by saying that his people were long acquainted with the white men, that he himself had been very young when they first came to winter on their lands, and that long before he was born his ancestors had encountered other white men in the East. In all this time the white men never caused his people any harm. But times had changed, and now his people were poor. And they had seen bad birds fly. McLoughlin interjected, what did he mean by "bad birds"? The Indian paused in his speech, sat on the ground and hung his head between his knees, apparently absorbed in thought. Finally, he lifted his head and said beseechingly, "Don't poison the waters of the lake!" McLoughlin was astonished that the Indian thought he would do such a thing, much less that he had the power, considering the enormous extent of the lake. As he tried to understand, he concluded that the Indians believed he was capable of sorcery and that their bizarre request had come in response to a stern warning he had given to a younger man of the Vermilion Lake band several months earlier. After this fellow had threatened the life of a trader, McLoughlin told him that if he repeated the offense he would be punished for it. But the Indian, it seemed, had misinterpreted his words, alerting the other members of his band that McLoughlin intended to punish the whole band. And so the chief had come to him, begging forgiveness.[1]

This kind of misunderstanding was becoming more common all the time, McLoughlin observed. The Indians were sunk in superstition, he wrote. If an Indian was unsuccessful in the hunt, or somehow injured himself, or if his child fell sick, he would attribute his misfortune to sorcery. And if his sick child should die, the Indian felt justified in seeking revenge on whomever might have cast the evil spell. Recently a prophet had come among the Ojibwa claiming that he was in direct communication with the Supreme Being. Such was the Indians' state of mind that they traveled in large numbers over long distances to see this prophet, to hear his stories, and to be forewarned of their collective fate.[2]

If McLoughlin disparaged the Indians for believing in sorcery and perceiving a spirit world in which bad birds flew, he shared the Indians' growing sense of unease over how their world was changing. All kinds of animals were becoming scarce, and most marked was the decline of beaver. Beaver, of course, was the "soft gold" that had lured him to this wild corner of the globe in the first place. It was the object of all his endeavors, his means to a better life, and they were hunting it to oblivion. Other furbearers—marten, mink, muskrat, otter—were becoming scarce as well. Year by year more traders and hunters came in pursuit of a diminishing supply of furs, and year by year the company's profits shrank.[3] While the promise of being promoted to partner in the North West Company was still McLoughlin's guiding star, he saw his prospects for becoming wealthy in the fur trade fading.

McLoughlin's newfound contentment in his domestic affairs was not enough to dispel his forebodings about this place he called Siberia. Outside the small circle of his new mixed-blood family, he saw his world in decline. The Indians were hungry and dispirited, the traders tired and cynical. When news reached Fort William in the summer of 1812 that Britain and the United States were at war, McLoughlin wrote dejectedly to his uncle Simon, "I have a promise of becoming a partner of the N W Co on the Outfit of the Year 1814—but I am Greatly afraid this war will injure this country if not ruin it entirely."[4] In fact, when the offer of partner was finally put to him two years later, he had to think hard on it, as the company's fortunes were sinking fast.

McLoughlin, in common with other traders, traced the decline to one source: rising competition among the fur traders themselves. To the fur traders' way of thinking, monopoly control of an area was an essential condition for a thriving trade. Competition, on the other hand, was an aberration and an evil. In the language of the fur trade, competition was called "opposition," and a rival trader was an "opponent." As the fur traders saw it, when Europeans first entered the wilderness they dealt with Indians in the absence of rivals, which gave them a free hand to develop favorable terms of exchange with their Indian trading partners. They needed that advantage in order to operate successfully so far from home. When a competitor came into the area and established a rival concern, evil consequences followed. First and foremost, Indians quickly took advantage of the situation by bargaining up the price of beaver. As traders found it necessary to give more yards of cloth, more iron pots, trinkets, and gifts of rum and tobacco for the same quantity of peltries, their profits diminished while their already high shipping costs rose. And as each separate trading post struggled for adequate returns relative to costs, overhunting of fur animals in the more marginal districts was the inevitable result.[5] Overhunting of beaver was made worse by the introduction of steel traps and the practice of baiting traps with castoreum (a substance made from the beaver's perineal glands). By 1800 fur traders began to recognize that beaver populations in the Northwest were in decline, and by 1812 the downward trend was conspicuous.[6]

Sadly, competition ultimately cost the Indians more than it did the traders. If Indians got any short-term benefit from the higher fur prices, it was soon cancelled out by the competition's ill effects. The worst of these was an increase in liquor trafficking. McLoughlin hated giving liquor to the Indians when he knew perfectly well what powerful and demoralizing effects it had on them. "While under its deleterious Effects the father and Son the Mother and daughter will fight together and Brothers Murder Each other," he wrote. "It is in my Opinion the Ruin of the trade." But he resigned himself to it anyway. In that respect he was no different from most traders. The use of liquor was firmly embedded in the system of exchange, and it was beyond the power of a single individual to do anything about it. "The Custom of giving presents of Liquor to the Indians was introduced by our predecessors in trade and every Opposition courted popularity by giving a Greater quantity of liquor to the Indians," he wrote dejectedly. "But now the country is poor. . . . If you take the Indians furs for liquor he will be destitute of the means of hunting and he and his family being naked will Starve—and make their way to the Fort. We cannot allow them [to] die of hunger alongside of the house and thus must support him."[7]

As the North West and Hudson's Bay companies squared off during the final years of their struggle for mastery of the fur trade, the volume of liquor shipped into Indian country threatened to reach all-time highs. In 1808, the North West Company shipped 9,000 gallons of rum and spirits. Most of this was "high wine," a highly concentrated form of spirits that was subsequently diluted with about six parts water, so the actual number of gallons plied to Indians was considerably greater.[8] The torrent of firewater was noted far beyond fur-trade society. That year, Britain's Parliament considered a bill to end all trafficking of liquor to Indians in British America. The North West Company's agents in London successfully petitioned against the bill, baldly stating that if the company were forced to submit to such a ban it would lose three-quarters of its trade on the upper Missouri to American traders.[9]

There was tension within the North West Company itself on this issue. The wintering partners, seeing with their own eyes how liquor destroyed Indian lives, felt the moral burden of it. The Montreal agents, on the other hand, saw with crystal clarity how the liquor affected the company's competitive position and profits and therefore tended to overlook the human cost. In 1810, the partners took up the difficult issue at their annual meeting at Fort William. McLoughlin, still a clerk at that time, was not allowed to take part in the discussion. The Montreal agents carried the debate. They decided that the quantity of liquor might be safely reduced from its then level of 10,000 gallons per year to half that much "should the *Saints in Parliament,* in their mistaken notions of Philanthropy, persist in the Intention of abolishing the use of that article."[10]

From the traders' standpoint, another evil of competition was the proliferation of Indian chiefs, or "trading captains" as they were sometimes called. The custom was to honor an exceptional hunter by giving him extra presents of liquor and tobacco and dressing him in a red coat and trousers with linen shirt, and perhaps a hat adorned with an ostrich feather. The idea was to increase these individuals' prestige among their people, so that the next time they came to the trading house they would be accompanied by more hunters with more furs. As rival traders competed with one another to cultivate these relationships, they were less and less discriminating about whom they made captains. Traders, bemoaning the rising cost of "clothing the Indians," muttered cynically among themselves that red-coated Indians in the forest became as thick as fleas on a dog.[11] Some worried about the social consequences of this practice as well, for it seemed to subvert the Indians' tribal organization, undermining the authority of bona fide chiefs. "It is much to be lamented that the natives in general in this Country have lost that respect and obedience which they formerly had for their principal Chiefs," wrote one Nor' Wester. "The consequences are of a serious nature to us at present, as every vice has got among them."[12] McLoughlin wrote in a similar vein in his report on the Indians inhabiting the area from Fort William to Lake of the Woods. "Most of their vices have greatly Increas'd of late Years from the escalation of traders." McLoughlin's answer to the problem was not just to reinstate monopoly control over the trade but to institute a kind of paternalism over the Indians alongside it. If the Indians had just one trader to deal with instead of many, he reasoned, then each trader would have it in his power and interest "to correct the bad morals of the natives" in his purview.[13]

Indians and traders were engaged in what the traders defined as a system of credit. Each fall, the traders advanced individual Indians a quantity of supplies with the understanding that the Indians would pay off their debt in furs over the course of the winter. The traders recorded the name of each Indian hunter together with the items and their assigned value in the post's ledger book. The supplies included powder and ball as well as cloth, ironware, trinkets, and other goods. All European goods together with all types of animal furs were valued according to a standard measure of "made beaver," this being the equivalent of a single prime beaver pelt. The amount of credit that the trader was willing to advance each Indian varied according to how much stock he put in that individual's hunting ability and trustworthiness. The markup on European goods was very high, and many debts did not get repaid in full, yet the credit system served to regulate a major portion of the trade. But this system, too, required monopoly control to function well. With multiple trading houses available to him, an Indian might take debt from one trader in the fall and then barter his entire winter's hunt to a rival trader in the spring. Traders for their part did not feel at all averse to bartering furs from an Indian whom they knew had been supplied through the winter by a rival trader. In the face of such cutthroat practices, traders anxiously appraised each Indian hunter on the basis of whether he would be "loyal" in hunting exclusively for him or a "cheat" by taking his furs somewhere else.[14]

For all of these reasons, McLoughlin blamed competition between traders for the sorry state of his world. Eventually, after the merger of the two companies in 1821, he would get to see monopoly restored more or less as he wanted. And, in his role as chief factor in the new concern, he would, to a degree, implement a kind of paternalism over the Indians in his department. In the decade beginning in 1810, however, the struggle for monopoly entered its most destructive phase ever. Ironically, McLoughlin would finally achieve his goal of becoming a partner in the very year when the North West Company's fortunes began to plummet.

The Restive Partnership

{ 16 } To appreciate the remarkable rise and fall of the North West Company, it is helpful to consider a few things about the geography of Canada. North and west of the St. Lawrence River valley, bent like a horseshoe around the enormous Hudson Bay, lies a vast plateau known as the Canadian Shield. Geologically, the region is the oldest part of the North American continent and constitutes the largest mass of exposed Precambrian rock found anywhere on Earth. Most of the shield is made up of hard crystalline bedrock of ancient volcanic origin. During the ice ages, continental glaciers covered the land, scouring the surface down to the bedrock and carving out depressions that became lakes as the ice sheets melted back. Today the western rim of the U-shaped shield features a chain of massive lakes of ice-age origin, stretching from the Great Lakes in the south to Great Slave Lake and Great Bear Lake in the Far North. Other big lakes in this far-flung chain include Rainy Lake, Lake of the Woods, Lake Winnipeg, and Lake Athabaska. Throughout this region soils are thin, outcroppings of bedrock are numerous, and drainage systems are geologically young and not well defined. The land is laced with an intricate maze of large and small lakes, rivers and streams, and sprawling marshlands.

In its competition with the Hudson's Bay Company, the North West Company was severely disadvantaged by geography. A royal charter of 1670 gave the Hudson's Bay Company an exclusive right to trade with North American Indians by way of Hudson Bay. Despite its high latitude, the bay afforded a relatively easy approach to the very heart of the continent. The Hudson's Bay Company's supply ships sailed from England across the North Atlantic up the Labrador Coast and through Hudson Strait into Hudson Bay, where they offloaded men and trade goods on the beach and picked up furs for the return voyage. For the first century of its existence, that was all the transporting that the Hudson's Bay Company needed to do, for it relied on Indian middlemen to bring peltries overland to its several forts situated on the bay. Two of these bayside forts did the bulk of the company's business. York Factory, on the mouth of the Nelson River, lay only 300 straight-line miles from Lake Winnipeg. Albany Factory, by the Albany River on the shore of James Bay (a Lake Michigan–size extension of Hudson Bay) lay a similar distance from Lake Superior. When the Hudson's Bay Company did begin moving its operations inland toward the end of the eighteenth century, it did not have far to go.[1]

By contrast, the North West Company, working out of Montreal, had no easy access to the heart of the continent. Instead of carrying furs, European goods, and men by ship, it had to exploit the Canadian Shield's remarkable network of inland rivers and lakes, devising an elaborate transportation system based almost entirely on the birchbark canoe. By the time McLoughlin entered upon his five-year apprenticeship, the North West Company had established a network of water routes that stretched over 3,000 miles from Montreal to Fort Chipewyan on the shores of remote Lake Athabaska, employed around 1,000 voyageurs, and involved hundreds of canoes. Flotillas of canoes were called "brigades," and their cargoes were identified as "inbound" or "outbound." The system not only transported European goods in one direction and furs in the other, it also provided passenger service and communications between posts.[2]

The central feature of this transportation network was a relay system in which the voyageurs passed the baton—exchanged inbound and outbound cargoes—at Fort William during the summer rendezvous. From the many posts in the interior the men set out in the spring in their *canots du nord,* each one laden with bales of furs collected over the winter. Coming down the Saskatchewan, the Assiniboine, the Red, and other rivers that eventually feed into Hudson Bay, the North West Company's canoes entered Lake Winnipeg. But rather than following the outlet of that lake to Hudson Bay as the Hudson's Bay traders were privileged to do, the Nor'Westers paddled to the southeast corner of the lake and continued their journey upstream, ascending the Winnipeg and Rainy rivers to Rainy Lake. From there, they traversed the chain of smaller rivers and lakes that stairstep over the Height of Land between the Hudson Bay and Great Lakes watersheds (the region known today as the Boundary Waters), which brought them finally to Fort William. Meanwhile, from Montreal came the *canots du maître,* the master canoes, which were nearly twice as long as the *canots du nord* and carried double the cargo. Packed with trade goods and other supplies, they came up the St. Lawrence River to Lake Ontario, then via rivers and lakes to Lake Huron, then up the St. Mary River and around the rapids at Sault Ste. Marie to Lake Superior. Hugging the north shore of Lake Superior in case of storms, they continued around to Fort William. At the rendezvous, cargoes were exchanged for the return trips. Among the northbound brigades, those with the longest journeys set out first. Brigades departed at two-day intervals in order to avoid backups at the many portages.[3]

So great was the distance from Montreal to the fur-rich Athabaska territory that the relay point for that supply line had to be pushed farther westward to the company's Rainy Lake post. At Fort Chipewyan on Lake Athabaska the voyageurs set out as soon as the ice melted from the rivers and lakes, sometimes as late as May, and they raced to get to Rainy Lake and back again before the waterways in the Far North froze up again in the fall. At Fort William, meanwhile, a contingent of voyageurs from Montreal transferred their cargoes to the smaller canoes and proceeded onward to meet the Athabaska men at Rainy Lake.[4] Thus, soon after the great rendezvous at Fort William, another rendezvous took place at the North West Company's trading house at Rainy Lake. Fort William was the company's great entrepôt in the wilderness, and Rainy Lake was its forward base.[5]

It might seem a riddle why the North West Company penetrated so far across the continent when its northern competitor possessed such an enormous geographic advantage in its position on the bay. The answer is that at the start of the nineteenth century the two companies each owed their relative breadth of operations to the previous 150 years of fur-trade history. Both grew organically out of the century-long contest between Britain and France in America that ended with France's ejection from the continent in 1763. The Hudson's Bay Company's passive position on the bay suited its shareholders well when France had dominion over the St. Lawrence River valley, the Great Lakes region, and the Mississippi valley. The company's London-based leadership was slow to shake off that conservative outlook in the latter part of the eighteenth century. The North West Company, meanwhile, organized itself to fill the vacuum left by the French. It was fundamentally expansionist. Structurally it was hardly a company at all but rather "a restive partnership of aggressive colonial merchants."[6] Each year a handful of the few dozen partners retired, while the most ambitious and energetic junior officers rose to take their place. The semiannual covenants by which these men bound their fortunes together were aimed at rapid growth of the business and speedy financial reward for the partners.

With few exceptions, the North West partners came from the English-speaking population of Canada. Most were of Scottish extraction. Many of the founding members maintained strong family ties in Scotland or England. They exploited those ties to leverage financial support from across the Atlantic and edge out their French Canadian competitors. Even after the North West Company was well established, those ties to the mother country mattered as much as a person's energy and ability in determining which clerks became partners.

That was especially true for the Montreal agents. From its start in the 1780s, the North West Company was a partnership between shipping agents in Montreal and traders in the interior, the wintering partners. While the Montreal agents' primary responsibility was to hire voyageurs and handle logistics, assembling ironware, guns, clothing, blankets, tobacco, liquor, and sundry items of trade and supply, their other function was to seek out fur buyers and investors in Britain and Europe. Control of the company was delicately balanced between Montreal agents and wintering partners. The Montreal agents held the largest individual shares, but the wintering partners collectively held the greater number of shares—the more so as the years passed.[7]

Besides its aggressive, entrepreneurial spirit, the Montreal-based company possessed another advantage over its London-based rival: it had access to an experienced labor pool. The company found no shortage of fit and experienced men in Lower Canada willing to indenture themselves for months or even years at a time. Most of these engagés were French Canadians. The oldest among them had begun their careers in the years of French control, and as time went on the company found plenty of new recruits among the French Canadian population who were eager to carry on the proud tradition of the voyageur.[8]

For a few short decades the North West Company enjoyed spectacular success. The historian Harold Innis, in his classic and meticulously researched work *The Fur Trade in Canada*, calculated that the company, at the height of its fortune, controlled something like 80 percent of the trade compared to 7 percent by its northern rival and 13 percent by independent traders.[9]

McLoughlin, for all of his gloom about the future of the enterprise, took pride in knowing that he was involved in one of the great business ventures of his time. Even as he complained about his desolate circumstances and inadequate pay, he yearned to become a partner. He still held out hope that a partner's share would someday yield him a sizeable nest egg—provided that the wealth of furs was not exhausted first. What he recognized only dimly if at all, however, was that the North West Company's domination of the fur trade would not last. With the Hudson's Bay Company now insurgent, the North West Company had become a teetering giant straddling an indefensible swath of the North American continent.

The Pemmican War

❋{ 17 }❋ The contest between the two big fur companies started in the 1790s and gradually deepened during McLoughlin's apprentice years from 1803 to 1808. The contest began when Hudson's Bay traders deployed west and south of Hudson Bay: west into the Saskatchewan and Athabaska districts, and south into the Red River and Rainy Lake districts. While the Hudson's Bay Company's advance into the fur-rich Saskatchewan and Athabaska made Nor'Westers uneasy, it was their rivals' southward push that really touched a nerve with them. New posts on the Rainy River and at the junction of the Red and Assiniboine rivers confronted the Nor' Westers precisely where their many branching canoe routes came together to form their main-trunk line from Lake Winnipeg to Fort William. As a transportation hub, the area was vital to the Nor' Westers' ability to keep their many posts in communication and supply. Not only that, the region from Lake Winnipeg to Rainy Lake yielded two resources that were essential to the North West Company's far-flung operations. One was birchbark for the construction and repair of canoes. The company's forward base of Rainy Lake, site of the rendezvous for the Athabaska brigades, doubled as a canoe-making center. The other essential resource was bison. The animal was hunted primarily for its meat, which was made into pemmican. Pemmican was a portable, high-energy food that was used to provision the voyageurs' canoes as well as to supplement the heavy diet of fish at the northernmost trading posts.[1]

Birchbark and pemmican were key products of what the fur traders called the "provisioning trade," a vigorous industry that supported the more conspicuous commerce in furs. Pemmican was the mainstay of the provisioning trade. It was produced by cutting the meat of buffalo and other large game into thin strips, drying the strips over a fire until they were hard and brittle, then pounding them into tiny flakes, and rendering the flakes with melted fat. Finally, the substance was wrapped in dried parchment-skin bags of ninety-pound weight (to match the standard ninety-pound packs of made beaver) and loaded in canoes like coal in a coal tender. Rich in calories, nonperishable, and portable, pemmican was the perfect high-energy food for fueling canoemen. A two-pound ration was sufficient to power a voyageur with his paddle all day long, while half that quantity could sustain an inactive passenger.[2] Pemmican formed a part of subsistence economies all over North America, but its factory production for the provisioning trade was unique to the parkland and prairie west of the Red River. There, a growing population of Métis offspring of the fur traders made bison hunting and pemmican the center of their economy.[3]

Since the Nor' Westers regarded the Red River country as an essential resource area and strategic hub for their vast operations, they were deeply concerned when the Hudson's Bay Company began to meddle in the area in a startling new way commencing around 1811. The source of their angst was the Scottish nobleman Thomas Douglas, Fifth Earl of Selkirk, who dreamed of founding an agricultural colony in the Red River valley for the resettlement of poor, dispossessed Scottish highlanders. Lord Selkirk, as he was commonly known, claimed to have a humanitarian interest in helping thousands of highland crofters who had been driven off their farms by Britain's agricultural revolution. His first attempts at colonization centered in eastern Canada. Then, in 1809, he came into possession of considerable shares of stock in the Hudson's Bay Company, and he began to consider the Red River country for another colonization scheme that would double as a place for Hudson's Bay employees and their families to live in retirement. Over the next two years he acquired a controlling interest in the fur company and persuaded the board of directors to grant him rights to a huge tract of land as a step toward implementing his plan. The grant in fee simple, executed in 1811, covered a staggering 116,000 square miles and took in swaths of the present states of Minnesota and North Dakota as well as portions of present-day Manitoba and Saskatchewan.

As all of this land fell within the Hudson Bay watershed, it was part of Rupert's Land under the Hudson's Bay Company's 1670 royal charter and was legally the company's land to give away. Nevertheless, the Nor' Westers were outraged when they learned of Lord Selkirk's scheme and the so-called Selkirk Grant. They considered the territory theirs by right of discovery (that is, it was theirs by way of the French, who were its first European discoverers). Equally important, a significant number of Métis considered the area to be the homeland of their rising nation. To both the Nor' Westers and Métis, it mattered not a whit that Selkirk claimed to be acting in a humanitarian interest. From their perspective, Selkirk's vision of turning the Red River valley into settled farmland clashed with their own interests in keeping the area wild for continued beaver and pemmican production.[4]

The North West Company tried to stop Selkirk's colonization scheme at its source, in the Scottish port towns where Selkirk expected to find his colonists. Simon McGillivray, the younger brother of William McGillivray, published a series of notices in the Scottish press aimed at frightening away prospective emigrants. Writing under the alias "Highlander," McGillivray portrayed the long journey as extremely perilous and the Red River country as a horrible place to scratch farms out of the wilderness. He warned that the Hudson's Bay Company would not be prepared to take care of the colonists when they arrived. They would likely lose their scalps to the warlike Indians if they did not die of starvation or drown in one of the ice-cold rivers first.[5] The North West Company's propaganda effort may have depressed the number of emigrants willing to risk all and face such perils, but it could not stop the emigration altogether.

The first party of Red River colonists sailed from Stornoway, Scotland, in the late summer of 1811. Numbering a few dozen men, women, and children, it landed on the shore of Hudson Bay, wintered over at the edge of the tundra, and in the spring made its way in clumsy bateaux up the Hayes River and Lake Winnipeg to the Red River, arriving there at the end of the summer of 1812 with scarcely enough time to prepare for the onset of the next winter. Although the settlers were woefully ill prepared for their new environment, they survived the harsh prairie winter on buffalo meat and merciful gifts of food from Indians, Métis, and even the North West traders. Other parties followed, and by the end of 1813 the colony stood at about one hundred strong. The settlement was located near the confluence of the Red and Assiniboine rivers, a place the fur traders called the Forks (the site of downtown Winnipeg today). It consisted of about twenty-five long lots, a cluster of settler homes, livestock corrals, and a log storehouse.[6]

Before the settlers arrived, the North West Company moved preemptively to occupy the Forks. The Nor'Westers built a trading house and large stockade at the very junction of the Red and Assiniboine rivers in 1810. Shortly after the first settlers arrived, the Hudson's Bay Company began construction of its own post two miles below the North West post. When the rival companies each developed a stronghold at the Forks, they showed their mutual intention to dig in there for a hard fight, winner take all. Their intentions were on display not only in the robustness of the forts, but in the names they picked for them. The Hudson's Bay Company named its post Fort Douglas after Thomas Douglas, the Earl of Selkirk, signaling that the company stood foursquare behind Selkirk's Red River colony. The North West Company named its post Fort Gibraltar, after Britain's island fortress at the entrance to the Mediterranean Sea, signaling that it valued the place no less than the British navy valued its strategic base on the isle of Gibraltar.

Selkirk's pick for governor of the Red River colony was Miles Macdonell, a native of Inverness, Scotland, and former captain in the Royal Canadian volunteers. He was a man of great courage but no diplomatic skill whatsoever. Everything he did seemed calculated to antagonize the Nor' Westers rather than conciliate them. His first official act was to invite the resident Indians, Métis, and Nor' Westers to a "seizin' of the land" ceremony. Standing on the empty, windswept prairie under a flapping banner, he shouted that the land would be known henceforth as "Assiniboia." He was their governor, and the Nor'Westers were there by his sufferance. On January 8, 1814, he issued his notorious "Pemmican Proclamation." As it was by then the dead of winter, he did not attempt to assemble the people again, but he had copies of his proclamation nailed to the gates of the North West Company posts in the area.[7]

In two long paragraphs the document described the territorial boundaries of Assiniboia and restricted exports of pemmican from the domain for the next year. The ostensible purpose of the control of exports was to provide food security for the growing population of settlers until they could establish farms and raise their own food. The Nor' Westers saw a more hostile intent. Calling it an embargo, they saw an effort to interdict the great quantities of pemmican the North West Company needed to fuel its voyageur-canoe-based transportation system. The Nor'Westers believed the Red River colony was simply a front for Selkirk's larger scheme, which was to put a stranglehold on the North West Company and take over its vast hinterland for the Hudson's Bay Company. The resident Métis, for their part, saw the Pemmican Proclamation as an attack on them. They considered the Red River valley to be their homeland and the provisioning trade with the North West Company to be the basis of their economy. A disruption of their pemmican exports would soon lead to their expulsion from the area.[8]

McLoughlin followed these developments from afar, being informed by Nor' Westers who passed through the Rainy Lake district in the early months of 1814. The Nor' Westers mostly resolved to ignore the order even as evidence mounted that Macdonell was arming and training the colonists to seize supplies of pemmican as necessary to protect the colony. Tensions in the Red River valley rose as spring came and the season for producing and distributing pemmican neared. With spring breakup, the Métis began rafting loads of buffalo meat down the Assiniboine River. In May, Captain Macdonell sent a force of fifty men with two field pieces to blockade the river. The Métis circumvented the blockade by transferring their cargoes onto carts and taking a road instead. A few days later, Macdonell dispatched his sheriff, John Spencer, with a warrant to seize pemmican stores held in North West Company posts before they could be shipped north. Spencer and his men broke into the trading post on the Souris River opposite the Hudson's Bay Company's Brandon House, where they confiscated 500 bags of pemmican, 96 kegs of grease, and 9 bales of dried meat. It was the opening action in what came to be known as the Pemmican War.[9]

In June 1814, five North West partners in or near the Red River valley met with Captain Macdonell and made a truce. The parties agreed to a temporary division of the Red River country's pemmican production: Macdonell would allow a certain quantity to be shipped out to feed the North West Company's northern posts, and the North West Company would guarantee that another quantity remained in the valley to feed the colony. Meanwhile, the two sides would await a decision by the colonial government for Upper Canada as to the legitimacy of Macdonell's governing authority.[10]

When the North West Company held its rendezvous at Fort William later that summer, William McGillivray blasted the agreement and denounced the five men as cowards for conceding anything to Macdonell after the violent actions he had taken against them. He called on the rest of the partners to censure the five. He insisted that the winterers must buck up and defend the company's rights and property at all costs. McLoughlin was not directly involved in either the truce or the recriminations that followed, but he was now close enough to the wintering partners to observe that they all "had their Belly full."[11]

The partners suspended their debate over how to retaliate against the Hudson's Bay Company to resolve another urgent item of business: bringing in new partners. Five clerks, including McLoughlin, were due a promotion. McLoughlin had long anticipated the day he would be promoted to partner. In becoming a partner, he would give up his annual salary of £200 in exchange for one share of profits plus living expenses. In former times that would have been a big raise in pay, but now the company's future was so uncertain it was a rather dubious proposition. The company was girding for war with its major rival. The partners were divided, with McGillivray calling for a fight to the finish and many of the winterers advocating restraint. But McGillivray and the other Montreal agents held a controlling number of shares. The two dozen wintering partners held just one or two shares apiece, amounting to about one-third of the total. Even if the winterers could all speak as one, they still held only a minority position in the company. McLoughlin well knew that McGillivray was marshalling the wintering partners to take up arms against the Hudson's Bay men if their struggle should come to that. It made him sick, yet he had so long set his sights on a company share he could not turn it down now. He took the offer of a single share, and afterwards transferred his entire account on the North West Company's books to a new account with McTavish, McGillivrays and Company. His accumulated savings from his clerk's salary came to 7,318 livres and 12 sous, or just over £600.[12]

As soon as McLoughlin and the other four clerks had committed to taking shares, the partners returned to the subject of the Red River colony. The Montreal agents insisted that Selkirk's colony must be crushed. William McGillivray's brother Simon, representing the firm of McTavish, McGillivrays and Company in London, had been urging them to oppose Selkirk's scheme for over two years now. "It will require some time, and I fear cause much expense to us," he had warned in 1812, "*yet he must be driven to abandon it,* for his success would strike at the very existence of our Trade."[13] The pemmican embargo gave proof of this. The Montreal agents insisted that if Selkirk were allowed to succeed in his real object of depriving them of provisions, "it would result in the total stoppage of the North West Company trade."[14]

There were two parts to the North West Company's plan for a counter-offensive. The first part would entail the removal of Miles Macdonell, leader of the Red River colony. The idea was to capture him, put him in chains, and haul him down to Lower Canada to stand trial on charges of illegal seizure of property. Toward that end, McGillivray presented a couple of the men with commissions for justice of the peace under the Canada Jurisdiction Act, which empowered them to make arrests in the Indian Territories and bring criminals to court in Upper or Lower Canada. One of them, Archibald McLeod, made out a warrant for the governor's arrest and gave it to another partner, Alexander Macdonell, who was tasked with bringing him in. By a strange twist, Alexander Macdonell was a cousin of the governor, Miles Macdonell. Though he and his cousin had already clashed several times and had no fondness for each other, the fact that he was given the task of arresting his own kinsman appears to have been a calculated move designed to test his loyalty to the North West. Like McLoughlin, he had just been promoted to partner. Like his blood relative the governor, Alexander Macdonell was endowed with more courage than cunning. As he was departing the rendezvous, he blustered to another partner: "One thing certain, that we will do our best to defend what we consider our rights in the interior. Something serious will undoubtedly take place. Nothing but the complete downfall of the colony will satisfy some by fair or foul means."[15]

Alexander Macdonell's "foul means" alluded to the second part of the North West Company's counteroffensive. One way or another, the Red

River colonists must be persuaded to leave. Alexander Macdonell would use his influence with the Métis to incite violence against the colony. Once the settlers were sufficiently terror stricken, the Nor' Westers would offer them protection from the Métis within Fort Gibraltar's palisaded walls. Then, when the settlers were utterly demoralized, they would offer them free passage in the North West Company's canoes down to Lower Canada. In this way the Nor' Westers hoped to effect the complete abandonment of the colony while giving the outside world the impression that they had rescued the colonists from a hostile native uprising.

But the chicanery did not end there. Another wintering partner, Duncan Cameron, was assigned to the Red River as well. While Alexander Macdonell incited the Métis against the colonists, Cameron would present the colonists an opportunity to join a militia. With the War of 1812 still on, William McGillivray came to the 1814 rendezvous supplied with a handful of officer's commissions for raising a frontier militia, a unit known as the Corps of Canadian Voyageurs. He assigned one of these commissions to Cameron, giving him the title "Captain, Voyageurs Corps, Commanding Officer, Red River." Dressed up in his red officer's coat with epaulettes, he was to pose as a recruiting officer for the militia. It was a bit of flimflam aimed at undermining the settlers' allegiance to the governor.[16] All in all the North West Company's plan for destroying the Red River colony was a tawdry mix of legal procedure, propaganda, terror, and subterfuge.

All the bombast and plotting at the North West Company's summer rendezvous in 1814 filled McLoughlin with dread. In a letter to his family in Quebec, he wrote that he felt "loansome, and quite low spirited." Now more than ever he regretted having ever gotten himself into the business. He had finally realized his ambition of making partner just when the company was in crisis, and it no doubt gave him a bad case of buyer's remorse over investing so much in a company share. But there was more. He felt moral indignation, and he wished he could be disassociated from the whole enterprise. "I Still call Canada my home and reckon myself only as a Bird of Passage in this," he wrote to his relatives back home.[17]

The following winter, as agents Alexander Macdonell and Duncan Cameron went to work harassing and haranguing the Red River colonists, many of them were frightened into deserting the colony and joining either the North West Company or the Métis. With the arrival of spring, the threats of violence intensified. Those colonists who were still loyal to the Hudson's Bay Company sought refuge inside Fort Douglas. When Captain Miles Macdonell returned to Red River from a trip to Hudson's Bay in June, he found the huts and fields abandoned and the few remaining settlers huddled within the stockade. Now the ground was prepared for the North West Company's main counteroffensive, taking the fort and capturing the governor.

Later that month, Duncan Cameron led a combined force of Nor'Westers and Métis to Fort Douglas and showed the baymen his arrest warrant. When Miles Macdonell refused to open the gates, Cameron laid siege to the fort. After a ten-day standoff, the governor surrendered. The Nor'Westers made him a prisoner together with his sheriff, John Spencer. With the governor in his custody, Cameron then offered the few remaining settlers a free passage down to Montreal. Some of them accepted and went with the two prisoners to Fort William. Others fled in the Hudson's Bay Company's york boats, descending the Red River to Lake Winnipeg, where they took refuge at another of the Hudson's Bay Company forts.

As soon as they were gone, the Métis pillaged the deserted settlement, tore down fences, trampled crops, and set fire to buildings. So ended the opening rounds of the Pemmican War. They were a prelude to greater violence ahead.[18]

❄

McLoughlin passed the winter of 1814–15 at Rainy Lake, somewhat removed from events on the Red River. Thankfully, he had other preoccupations. That year, Marguerite gave birth to Eliza, their second child together. Then, over the winter, he took on an unusual medical patient: a white man who had grown up among the Ojibwas and who called himself Shaw-shaw-wa ne-ba-se, the man he would soon come to know as "the American," or John Tanner.

McLoughlin's relationship with Tanner began after some Indians from Lake of the Woods informed him that one of their people had broken several ribs in a fall from a tree. McLoughlin directed his clerk, John Warren Dease, to go to the Indians' village and examine the man's injuries. His instructions to Dease were that if he found the injured man able to walk then he was to take him to the nearby outpost at White Fish Lake to convalesce. Dease did as he was told, and McLoughlin corresponded with him through the winter about the patient's up and down condition. When Dease appeared in the spring with his winter returns, he reported that the man's ribs had healed.

But a few days later Tanner showed up at McLoughlin's door. With him were two little girls, barely big enough to walk. In an instant, the doctor could see that Tanner was a very sick man, and he made him come inside. He soon learned that rather than returning to his people, the patient had attempted to follow Dease to the North West Company's house at Rainy Lake. His canoe had sunk while ascending a set of rapids in the Rainy River. He was lucky to get his two little daughters safely to shore, but then he had had to walk for two days with the girls on his back to reach the house. The exhausting ordeal had made him sick. Clearly his ribs were mended, but his strength was not yet restored. McLoughlin insisted that Tanner stay with him for as long as necessary to regain his health.[19]

McLoughlin gave Tanner and his two daughters a room in the house. The wee girls, who barely came up to the doctor's knees, mostly stayed by their father's side while he lay on the sickbed. As the condition of his patient improved and he and Tanner talked a little, McLoughlin asked him how he had come to live with the Indians. It was then that he learned how close Tanner had become with his Ottawa mother. When McLoughlin broached the subject of whether Tanner might someday return to his white folk, Tanner replied that he would not consider it as long as the old woman lived. When he asked Tanner about his wife, Tanner did not offer much. Only that the children still had a mother and that she lived with the Lake of the Woods Indians.[20]

The two men did not become friends, exactly, but they acquired a certain degree of familiarity and mutual respect.

Then one day, Tanner abruptly left with his children. *Lonely and dissatisfied*, was all he said. *Going back to Lake of the Woods to be with my wife*.[21]

The Battle of Seven Oaks

❈ 18 ❈ Despite the Nor' Westers' success in dispersing the Red River colony in June of 1815, they were hardly in a mood to celebrate victory when they gathered at Fort William in July. Largely because of the fighting, the Nor' Westers costs were up and their profits down. Relations between the wintering partners and the Montreal agents had never been so frayed. William McGillivray, sensing trouble, urged his younger brother Simon to come all the way from London to attend that year's rendezvous. Simon's job would be to engage with the wintering partners a few at a time and help his older brother collar the men one by one. In private dialogue with each wintering partner, William hoped to win back their allegiance.

Simon went at his brother's bidding and recorded his impressions in a private diary. "A good deal of conversation ensued about the gloomy times," he wrote one night. The partners talked of "the opposition, the consequences of dissention among ourselves, the information said to have been given to Lord Selkirk by proprietors, the presumption that some of them entertain a hostile feeling towards the Concern, which however all disavowed." He suspected, as did his brother, that there might be traitors among the wintering partners—men who secretly believed they would be better off if the Hudson's Bay Company prevailed in this struggle. Others were simply demoralized. "There seems a general wish to retire from the Country, some from getting old & tired of it, others from a dread of opposition."[1]

That month the Nor' Westers had two prisoners at Fort William: the deposed governor Miles Macdonell and his erstwhile sheriff, John Spencer. When Simon McGillivray went to interrogate the latter prisoner in his room on the morning of July 16, he asked McLoughlin to accompany him. As the interrogation concluded, McGillivray informed Spencer that it was the Nor' Westers' intention to prosecute either him or the ex-governor to show the Hudson's Bay Company that it could not seize the North West's property and get away with it. Spencer declared himself ready to cooperate with the prosecution to obtain his own freedom. He revealed to them a warrant and written orders, signed by Miles Macdonell on June 7, 1814. McGillivray took the two documents from him for evidence in court.[2] McLoughlin did not record his thoughts on this meeting, so his role in Spencer's "conversion" can only be conjectured. Perhaps Simon McGillivray expected that McLoughlin's giant physique would intimidate the prisoner. Or perhaps the younger McGillivray brother, in his careful surveillance of all the wintering partners, detected a note of dissension in McLoughlin, and deliberately involved him in the unsavory business of interrogating a prisoner to test his loyalty and resolve. If so, it was not the last time McLoughlin found himself under the McGillivrays' suspicion.

McLoughlin had resented William McGillivray since the days he was an apprentice clerk, but he was hardly alone in his resentment. Many wintering partners were weary of their leader's chidings, his misplaced sense of entitlement in gambling with their fortunes, his imperiousness. The McGillivray brothers were not insensitive to this. A few days into the rendezvous, Simon realized that much of the wintering partners' restiveness sprang from the recent poor returns from the Athabaska Department, where another member of the McGillivray family, John, was the partner in charge. Although John McGillivray was only a cousin to the brothers William and Simon, the wintering partners all knew that he owed his position to family connections. The McGillivray brothers concluded that the best way to placate the wintering partners was to remove their kinsman from his post.

When the partners met in private council to assign posts for the coming year, William McGillivray nominated McLoughlin to take over the valuable Athabaska. To the consternation of all, McLoughlin refused. Although his attachment to Rainy Lake and Fort William was well known, partners never refused assignments. McGillivray carried a unanimous vote by the other partners to compel his acceptance. Still McLoughlin objected. When McGillivray remonstrated that such behavior by a young partner was "presumptuous" and "extraordinary," McLoughlin replied that he would throw in his share and go to Montreal rather than be coerced. Archibald McLeod then reminded him that it was the partners' right under their agreement to expect his cooperation, and if he persisted in his rebellious conduct they could sue him for damages. McLoughlin remained obstinate. In an attempt to resolve the situation by compromise, the partners rescinded their earlier vote and reassigned him to a different northern post. On that sour note the session ended. But McLoughlin would not give in. In protest, he ceased seeing patients at the hospital. As much as McLoughlin's rebelliousness offended some partners, it tended to inspire others. The "doctor," as he was affectionately known, had a lot of salt. Over the next few days, McLoughlin's friends rallied behind him and blamed the McGillivrays for the impasse. Finally, he was quietly reassigned to Fort William for the winter of 1815–16.[3]

To brighten the mood of the rendezvous, the company put on a gala ball in the Great Hall. Besides the partners, those attending the dance included "all the Ladies of the Fort" (the Nor'Westers' mixed-blood wives and teenage daughters) plus a few dozen men and women colonists who were "guests" of the North West Company awaiting their free passage to Lower Canada. All those holding officer's commissions in the Voyageurs Corps dressed smartly in their red uniforms, and the "fun & good humour" continued until dawn. Unbeknownst to the colonists, their former governor Miles Macdonell endured this long night of merriment as a prisoner confined in one of the corner rooms adjoining the Great Hall.[4]

As soon as the rendezvous ended, the Nor' Westers faced new threats from the Hudson's Bay Company. Colin Robertson, a former North West Company clerk who had defected to the Hudson's Bay Company some years earlier, hired 100 voyageurs in Montreal and led a brigade up the Ottawa River, through the Great Lakes, and right under the noses of the Nor'Westers at Fort William and Rainy Lake en route to the Athabaska. Never before had the Hudson's Bay Company tapped the North West Company's labor pool in Montreal, and never before had it made such brazen use of its rival's transportation corridor. But this was not all. News arrived at Fort William at the end of July that the Red River colony was being resurrected. When Colin Robertson reached Lake Winnipeg on his way to Athabaska, he rallied the displaced colonists who were there and led them back to the Forks, where they rebuilt Fort Douglas and harvested what little remained of the crops. In October 1815, they were joined by more emigrants from Scotland—the fifth such party—together with a new governor, Robert Semple.

When spring arrived, the Hudson's Bay men took the offensive again. Robertson led fourteen men to Fort Gibraltar, where they burst in upon the fort's unsuspecting proprietor, Duncan Cameron. Rifling through Cameron's correspondence, Robertson found evidence that the Nor'Westers were once more attempting to organize an Indian and Métis assault on the colony. He placed Cameron under arrest and took him to nearby Fort Douglas as his prisoner. A few days later Robertson apprehended a North West light canoe carrying dispatches to the interior and ransacked that material for more evidence of a conspiracy. A letter from Alexander Macdonell to Cameron revealed with chilling brevity what Robertson already suspected: "a storm is gathering to the Northward ready to burst on the rascals who deserve it." In an obvious reference to the Métis the letter continued, "The new nation under their leaders are coming forward to clear their native soil of intruders and assassins."[5] Robertson apprised Governor Semple of the threat to the colony. As soon as the northern rivers were free of ice, Robertson left with his hundred voyageurs for Athabaska, taking his prisoner to York Factory on the way. On the day of Robertson's departure, Semple took thirty men to Fort Gibraltar and dismantled it piece by piece, rafting all the pickets down to Fort Douglas.[6]

With the two fur companies now seizing one another's forts and arresting one another's principals, this was turning into an ugly, messy affair. One side or the other, probably both, must be acting outside of the law, and the leaders began to think hard about how their stories would play in court. The Nor' Westers anticipated bringing their case before a judge and jury in Canada, while the Hudson's Bay men expected to find legal redress back in Britain. Up to this point in the conflict McLoughlin had had little direct involvement; if anything, he had let it be known that he had a distaste for such skullduggery. But now, as events moved toward a tragic resolution, he decided to act—another instance of his often abysmal timing.

In early June 1816 two partners, Archibald McLeod and Robert Henry, joined McLoughlin at Fort William. The information reaching them from Red River was sketchy, but they knew that Fort Gibraltar had fallen. The three men settled on an aggressive plan: with a force of voyageurs they would go to Red River, picking up some of their Indian allies at Rainy Lake on the way. Exactly what they expected to do when they got to Red River was a question that would later be examined in court. On the eve of their departure, the three partners explained their intentions in a letter to another partner. Like so much of the North West Company's correspondence, their letter would subsequently fall into the hands of Hudson's Bay men and be turned against them in court. Although the prosecution would cite the letter as evidence that McLoughlin and his partners planned an attack on the colony, its careful wording obscured their purpose: "We shall, and will, be guarded and prudent; we shall commit no extravagances, but we must not suffer ourselves to be imposed upon; nor can we submit quietly to the wrongs heaped upon us by a lawless, unauthorised, and inveterate opponent in trade."[7] A defense witness in the eventual trial, a voyageur who was on the expedition, would testify that the Nor' Westers' purpose was merely to safeguard the supply of pemmican at Red River. They were to "go fetch those provisions [and] if not molested, pass the Settlement singing, and return in the same way; but, if attacked, they were determined to defend themselves."[8] But this sounds like a whitewash after the fact. Robert Henry's statement in a letter to his uncle in Montreal probably came closer to the truth: "It was our intention to storm the fort. Our party consisted of 100 men, 70 fire arms and two field pieces."[9]

At Rainy Lake en route to Red River, McLoughlin tried to persuade some of the Indians to join the expedition, and a handful did join. The expedition picked up another partner with all of his men from the post on Rainy River, and yet another partner with more engagés when it came to Lake Winnipeg.

As the expedition started up the Red River toward the Forks, it caught sight of eight boatloads of colonists coming downstream. On first impression, it looked like the colony had been routed again and the whole population was evacuating. The Nor' Westers gave a victory yell and started thumping the sides of their canoes. But when they drew up alongside the lead boat and asked where the governor was, the colonists gave them the shocking news that Robert Semple and twenty-one of their number had been killed in an attack by some sixty or seventy mounted Métis. Only one Métis had fallen in the lopsided fight. The partners were horrified, knowing that they themselves were implicated in the slaughter. McLeod, who was in command, detained the colonists for questioning. He seized the late governor's trunk, broke the lock with an axe, and rifled its contents looking for any captured North West letters of an incriminating nature. In addition, he took four colonists into custody who admitted to having witnessed the battle. Finally, McLeod allowed the rest of the colonists to go on their way while the Nor' Westers hurried on to the Forks.[10]

At the Forks they found the Métis occupying Fort Douglas. McLeod immediately took charge, assembled everyone in the mess house, and congratulated the Métis on their victory. Sickened by the heavy loss of life though they were, the Nor' Westers assured the Métis that the North West Company stood with them in their defense of their homeland against the English. The mixed-blood Métis were, after all, mostly the Nor' Westers' own progeny. The partners had promised gifts of clothing to all those who would join in driving out the colonists, and now McLeod had those presents distributed. He also opened a keg of liquor so that everyone could drink to their shared success.[11]

Later that day, a party of Métis and Nor' Westers rode down to the battlefield to review what had happened. The fight had occurred about two miles north of Fort Douglas, among the settlers' long lots. A nearby copse would give the incident its name in history, the Battle of Seven Oaks. McLoughlin and his companions found that the dead had been stripped of their clothes and left on the ground to be scavenged by wolves. As nearly a week had passed since the event, there was not much left of the corpses but skeletons. In the presence of those human remains, the Nor' Westers queried the Métis about what had taken place. While each Métis recounted his part in the battle, the Nor' Westers nodded their approval and voiced admiration for their brave deeds. Then, satisfied that the bloodletting had all been in self-defense, everyone returned to Fort Douglas, where another four kegs were opened for a final victory celebration.[12]

The Surrender of Fort William

❊{ 19 }❊ Returning from Red River, the Nor' Westers arrived at Fort William to find the rendezvous already in full swing. With news of the Battle of Seven Oaks preceding them, they found the other partners all atwitter at Robert Semple's folly in provoking the Métis to attack. Everyone agreed that the poor fellow had brought about his own death and the destruction of the colony through his rash and overbearing actions; none dared to suggest that they themselves were the least bit culpable.

William McGillivray, meanwhile, fulminated against the opposition. He declared that the war with the Hudson's Bay Company must now be pushed to the hilt. He wanted McLeod to go to Athabaska and face off against the turncoat Colin Robertson. Meanwhile, he would return to Montreal and keep an eye on their biggest enemy, Lord Selkirk.[1]

Selkirk had crossed the Atlantic the previous fall and had passed the winter in Montreal. That spring, he was reported to be hiring a combined force of voyageurs and Swiss mercenaries—the latter recently discharged from the British army—for an expedition to Red River. Now, as July turned to August at Fort William, the Nor' Westers speculated about what their adversary might do next. Had Selkirk's expedition set out? Had Selkirk yet learned of the Battle of Seven Oaks and the destruction of the colony? What would he do when he got to Fort William? The partners had all heard Selkirk's name cursed and reviled for so many years that it was now hard to imagine confronting the devilish British lord in the flesh. McLoughlin shared in the general feeling of suspense. Unlike the other partners, however, he had more at stake than his financial fortune. As the proprietor of Fort William, his own post and family's home lay smack in Selkirk's path.

The anticipation grew when Selkirk's scouts were observed in birchbark canoes paddling up the Kaministiquia River. Brazenly, these men passed in front of the fort, landed about a half mile above the gate on the other side of the river, and right there, in plain view of the Nor' Westers' rendezvous, began to clear ground for Selkirk's military-style encampment.

On August 12, a cry from the watchtower signaled that the rest of Selkirk's expedition was arriving. First appeared Selkirk in a Montreal canoe with a bodyguard of seven soldiers and a crew of sixteen Iroquois canoe-men. Following him were a dozen canoes strung out in a line, carrying 100 soldiers with muskets and bayonets, four light six-pounder guns and two nine-pounders, more than a ton of gunpowder, over 100 barrels of salted pork and lard, 500 gallons of high wine, and numerous packs of flour and other supplies. Most of the soldiers were Swiss mercenaries of the De Meuron Regiment—veterans of the Napoleonic Wars who had fought in Wellington's army in Spain before being redeployed to North America in 1813. Another contingent included men of the Glengarry Fencibles and De Watteville Regiment, who had joined the expedition at Kingston. All these soldiers, mustered out of service in the spring, had responded to Selkirk's offer of soldier's pay and a tract of land when the expedition reached the Red River valley. Among Selkirk's recruits were four officers, with Captain P. d'Orsonnens in overall command. Also with the expedition was Miles Mac-donell, now free on bail for a few months pending a trial before the King's Bench in Montreal. Selkirk also tried to enlist two justices of the peace to provide his expedition with legal counsel and the important weapon of arrest warrants, but when both men backed out he assumed those powers himself.[2]

The Nor'Westers watched the long line of canoes glide past the fort and nose up to the beach one by one upstream on the opposite bank, where the expedition's scouts had already cleared ground for a sizeable encampment. As soon as the cargoes were unloaded and the tents erected, Selkirk sent a canoe across the river with a message for William McGillivray: release all of the colonists and employees of the Hudson's Bay Company whom you are holding prisoner. McGillivray replied with a note that there were just four men of that description and they were not prisoners, but he would send them over forthwith. Despite McGillivray's claim that they were not being held prisoner, however, two of the men reported to Selkirk that they had been kept in close confinement and another claimed that he had been kept in irons. And all were eyewitnesses to the destruction of the Red River colony.[3]

The next morning an officer of the Glengarry Fencibles by the name of John McNabb appeared at the gate with a guard of nine soldiers, claiming to have a message for McGillivray. McLoughlin, as the fort's proprietor, allowed the man to enter. In company with his friend Kenneth McKenzie, he escorted McNabb to their chief's private quarters, which occupied a cor-ner room in the Great Hall. The instant they entered the room, McNabb pulled an arrest warrant from his jacket and thrust it toward McGillivray. McGillivray, who was sitting at his desk writing a letter, remained calm;

he had expected as much. He assured McNabb that he would cooperate as a gentleman. Turning to McLoughlin and McKenzie, he requested that they accompany him to the enemy camp. If necessary, he explained, the two partners would offer themselves as "bail" (hostages) so that he could return to Fort William. McLoughlin must have bristled at this conceit—the idea that he should make himself Lord Selkirk's prisoner in place of the precious McGillivray! Nonetheless, he consented to the plan. McGillivray, imperious to the last, then insisted that McNabb stand by while he finished writing his letter.[4]

As soon as the three Nor' Westers landed on the opposite bank of the river, McNabb coolly placed them all under guard and reported to Selkirk alone. Shortly, he returned from Selkirk's tent with warrants for McLoughlin and the other partner as well. Whatever qualms McLoughlin had about giving up his own freedom to secure his leader's release, now he saw with perfect clarity what a foolish idea it was. McGillivray's ploy had simply gotten all three of them put in chains.

Selkirk then sent a force of fifty men in two big canoes back across the river to Fort William. From where McLoughlin sat in chains in the enemy camp, he could only wait and wonder. By and by he heard a bugle call, then nothing—just the thrum of crickets and the murmur of the river flowing past—until finally, late in the day, back came Selkirk's men with the remaining North West partners all under arrest. To the partners' shame and amazement, they had allowed Selkirk to take Fort William without giving him any resistance. Captain d'Orsonnens, with a squad of soldiers, went through the company offices placing seals on all desks and crates containing documents. The two hundred or so voyageurs were made to retire outside the stockade, and a handful of De Meurons were left behind to stand guard over the cannons, powder magazine, and armory.[5]

And after all that, McLoughlin and the other partners had not yet laid eyes on Selkirk himself. All they had seen was his slanting signature scratched across each of their arrest warrants and his officers' soldierly bows as they went in and out of his Lordship's tent. Finally, late in the day, Selkirk sent for them. When McLoughlin stooped inside the tent and faced him, he saw a man who was visibly unwell, with a sallow complexion and sunken eyes. When he spoke, he paused between sentences to cough into a handkerchief.[6]

The partners' collective interview with Selkirk must have struck them as a farce, for here was their archenemy posing as an impartial magistrate. The British lord addressed each of them in turn, asking if the accused understood the charges laid against him. The most serious charge was accessory to murder, on the grounds that the Nor' Westers had aided and abetted the

Métis in the "massacre" at Seven Oaks. As captives of their enemy, the partners had little choice but to say they understood the charge. With Selkirk fussing over his absurd attempt at due process, each partner in turn agreed to his terms of parole. Each gave his word of honor not to resist the soldiers occupying the fort nor disturb anything that had been sealed for evidence. Then all the partners were allowed to return to their sleeping quarters in Fort William.[7]

That night, the partners made a last-ditch attempt to control the damage. Scurrying about in the dark so as not to alert the De Meurons, and quietly breaking seals (as well as their oaths) they carried armloads of letterpress books and other documents to the kitchen basement, where the potentially incriminating material was fed into the ovens as fast as it would burn. When Selkirk arrived in the morning, all that remained of a large part of the North West Company's records were so many piles of warm ashes.[8]

Selkirk immediately ordered a search of the premises. His men found that the partners had also busied themselves stashing arms and ammunition. Forty fowling pieces, all loaded and primed, were uncovered in a hayloft, and eight barrels of gunpowder were discovered in a nearby stand of willows. In addition, a few dozen packs of furs marked with the Hudson's Bay Company stamp were discovered in the fur store. Although each pack also bore the North West Company insignia, the original stamp identified them as the very same packs that had been seized from Hudson's Bay men by a Métis captain on the Qu'Appelle River in May. Most damning of all, in Selkirk's eyes, were thirteen bales of clothing found in the equipment office that were tagged for Red River. With them was an account book that had escaped incineration. Inscribed therein was a list of Métis who had received gifts of clothing from Archibald McLeod following the Battle of Seven Oaks. Beside each name was a check mark. At the bottom of the list were the names of thirteen Métis who had not yet received their reward. The numbers lined up: thirteen names and thirteen undelivered bales of clothes. That clinched it. The Nor'Westers were a pack of "robbers and murderers," Selkirk wrote to the governor general of the Canadas a few days later.[9]

The De Meurons were called in, and the partners were once more placed under guard. Little by little, Selkirk revealed his intentions. The partners would be taken down to Lower Canada to stand trial for conspiracy in the destruction of the Red River colony. Selkirk and his mercenaries would occupy Fort William through the coming winter. In the spring Selkirk's expedition would continue on to Red River, where Selkirk would further investigate the North West Company's crimes and personally oversee the restoration of the colony.

But the partners sensed that Selkirk's designs did not end there; with Fort William in his hands and a mercenary army at his back, their archenemy had it in his power to take every North West Company post from Fort William to Red River and completely sever their supply line. Fortunately for the Nor' Westers, most of the inbound brigades had set off in the days just preceding Selkirk's arrival, so the interior posts would not lack for supplies through the coming winter. The outbound traffic was another matter. The fur stores at Fort William held £100,000 worth of peltries awaiting shipment to Montreal. Without those shipments, and the sales in England that would follow, the North West Company would face a critical shortage of capital in the coming year.[10]

On August 18, 1816, McLoughlin bid farewell to his wife and children. No account of their parting exists, but it can be imagined how distressing it must have been for the trader and his wife and probably their children as well. Not only was McLoughlin being taken away with criminal charges laid against him, but it was also likely that Marguerite and the children would be turned out of their home now that Fort William was to serve as winter quarters for Selkirk and his men. The young family would be hard-pressed to survive. There were now six children: Marguerite's three daughters and McLoughlin's one son by previous marriages plus a four-year-old son and two-year-old daughter. And another child was growing in Marguerite's womb. Great must have been McLoughlin's anguish as he and the other partners were marched out of Fort William under guard and forced to take seats in three of the company's own Montreal canoes. In each canoe, two pairs of Selkirk's soldiers sat fore and aft with muskets at the ready, while a dozen voyageurs sat port and starboard, their paddles raised over the gunwales, awaiting the signal from their new masters to set off down the Kaministiquia River.[11]

Lord Selkirk's Prisoner

{ 20 } On the eighth day of the voyage from Fort William, as the canoes carrying McLoughlin and his fellow prisoners wended their way along the north shore of Lake Superior, disaster struck.

Around noon the party stopped to eat. During the meal the wind picked up, but since the men were on the leeward side of an island they did not realize how strong it really was. The commanding officer, Lieutenant G. A. Fauche, asked William McGillivray if he thought it was safe to proceed. McGillivray replied that it would be safe as long as the soldiers allowed the guides to do their duty. With that goading remark from his lead prisoner, Fauche decided to chance it. But as soon as the canoes pushed off from the shelter of the island and were out on open water, the men realized their mistake. The fierce westerly made it impossible to turn back, so they steered for the nearest mainland. But the heavy chop was too much; the big canoes began to take on water. Changing course again, they paddled for a small island lying to the north.

It was McLoughlin's bad luck to be in the smallest canoe, which was so low in the water by the time it approached the island that it could not be maneuvered through the shoals. With icy water swirling about the men's ankles and breakers crashing on all sides, the canoe turned broadside to the surf and foundered. Plunged into the frigid water and tossed amongst ninety-pound packs and flailing men, McLoughlin went under. By the time some other crew members hauled him out of the lake he was half-drowned and unconscious. He lay as if lifeless on the shore for many long minutes before the men managed to resuscitate him. The other two canoes came to the rescue, but by the time they arrived the overturned canoe was smashed to pieces in the surf and only twelve of the twenty-one men on board could be accounted for. A wider and wider search was made for the missing men and finally, sometime later, the bodies of the other nine were found washed up on a nearby beach. The dead included one partner, two soldiers, and six Iroquois canoemen.[1]

Amidst the heavy loss of life, the survivors could at least rejoice over the fact that their friend still lived. They stripped off the doctor's wet clothing and warmed him by a fire and were thrilled when his first teeth-chattering utterances offered proof that he was coming around to his old cantankerous self again. Although drowning and near-drowning accidents were not uncommon in the fur traders' experience, it still seemed almost miraculous to them that McLoughlin had revived after lying motionless without so much as drawing a breath for so many minutes on end.

Medical science now tells us that when drowning victims are submerged in cold water they may undergo what is called the "mammalian diving reflex," a set of bodily reactions found in various mammals and especially in sea mammals. These include a slowing of the heart rate by as much as 50 percent in humans; a restriction of the blood flow to extremities so as to increase the blood and oxygen supply to the vital organs, especially the brain; and a blood shift to the chest to avoid collapse of the lungs. Near-drowning victims may go without breathing for many minutes—in rare cases even as long as an hour—without sustaining brain damage. Even so, the more usual result is hypoxemia, or shortage of oxygen in the blood, causing damage to the brain or lungs.

Medicine in McLoughlin's day had just begun to address the treatment of near-drowning victims. In earlier times, medical practice limited itself to the treatment of the sick, and there was no tradition of emergency medical response, or first aid, for accident victims. By the end of the eighteenth century, first aid was becoming a regular part of a physician's education, and most doctors knew a little about first aid to near-drowning victims because drowning was a relatively common accident. Various methods were used to resuscitate a person, though the modern treatment of cardiopulmonary resuscitation, or CPR, was not developed till later. McLoughlin saw plenty of drowning or near-drowning accidents in his medical practice, and he surely would have known that he was a lucky man to have survived and escaped brain damage.[2]

He seems to have been less fortunate with his lungs, however. In the months and years following the accident, he suffered repeated bouts of serious, sometimes protracted, illness. Once, several weeks after the accident, while still detained in Lower Canada, he was laid up for a month in the care of a tavern keeper. The illness may have been a case of bacterial infection and pneumonia brought on by his having had water in his lungs. Or perhaps it was a different complication from the near-drowning: he may have damaged some lung tissue, bringing on a case of what doctors would now call acute respiratory distress syndrome, a chronic shortness of breath, which also leads to pneumonia. Whatever the ailment was, it struck again and again until McLoughlin came to believe that he was never completely recovered from it. Some five years after the accident, he finally committed himself to a long convalescence of about six months to try to shake it for good, and the treatment worked. In all likelihood his lungs were indeed impaired as a result of the accident.[3]

The Nor' Westers held Lord Selkirk responsible for the disastrous loss of life, since they were his prisoners when the accident occurred. It rankled them deeply that Selkirk had placed his mercenaries, the De Meuron Regiment, in control of their lives, and that the commander of the prisoner escort, Fauche, had acted with such callous disregard for their safety. The Nor' Westers lamented that the soldiers of the De Meuron Regiment were nothing but a bunch of "worthless plunderers and deserters from Buonaparte's armies in Spain." The disaster would never have happened were it not for the De Meurons' mishandling of the canoes.[4]

Following the disaster, Fauche and the surviving prisoners still had many miles to travel together. On September 3, they arrived in York, the capital of Upper Canada, where Fauche expected to turn over his charges to the attorney general. But the attorney general was out circuit riding, so their journey continued, to one town and then another, in a vain effort to catch up with this official. "At Kingston we were informed that the Attorney-General was at Brockville," Fauche later stated by affidavit. "We soon arrived at that place, where I hoped to be unburdened from so disagreeable a charge; but the prisoners having applied for a Writ of Habeus Corpus, I was charged to convey them to Montreal, where we arrived on the 10th of September, and where the prisoners were all admitted to bail."[5]

In Montreal, McLoughlin had to go through four grueling days of questioning, mainly concerning his role in the deaths at Seven Oaks in June. After he and the others were arraigned, they were released on bail to await trial. Because the trial was not scheduled until 1818, McLoughlin returned to Fort William in the spring of 1817—that is, after his month-long illness when he had to hole up in a tavern.[6]

In the meantime, the strife between the two rival companies continued. As charges and countercharges flew, the number of cases pending before the colonial courts multiplied. The Nor' Westers managed to obtain a warrant for the arrest of Selkirk himself on charges of abusing his legal authority and unlawfully seizing the company's property at Fort William. When Selkirk refused to submit to arrest, his own legal troubles mounted. By the time McLoughlin returned to Fort William in the spring of 1817, Selkirk and the De Meurons had already vacated the premises and were at Red River. Selkirk spent that summer taking depositions and making further efforts to restore the colony. In the fall, he journeyed back east through the United States. His route was by minor waterways and the Mississippi River to

St. Louis, then up the Ohio and across the Alleghenies to Washington. Although Selkirk had legitimate business with the American government (he met with Secretary of State John Quincy Adams in hopes of getting compensated for the portion of his land grant that lay south of the forty-ninth parallel), his decision to return east through the United States exposed him to the charge that he was avoiding arrest in Canada. Writing to his attorney that he was offended by those allegations, he returned to Montreal in January 1818 to face his accusers.[7]

McLoughlin and the other Nor' Westers who were called to stand trial began to assemble in Montreal later that year. The many trials became a sensation. With prosecuting and defense counsel lined up on both sides of the conflict, Selkirk's personal attorney remarked, "All becomes a perfect chaos." A comprehensive list of over a hundred separate cases printed in the *Montreal Courant* showed the Nor' Westers facing charges of murder, arson, robbery, grand larceny, and malicious shooting, while Selkirk and the Hudson's Bay Company stood accused of riot and larceny, false imprisonment, and assault.[8]

Although public opinion in Lower Canada favored the North West Company—the Montreal-based fur company was, after all, the home team in this contest—McLoughlin felt none too sanguine about his own pending day in court. The clash at Seven Oaks and the shocking death of the governor and colonists continued to lie at the center of the government's interest in the whole matter, and the charge of murder hung on McLoughlin menacingly like a steel trap. But as the months passed and no new indictments were issued against the Métis who had fought on that fateful day, he took it as a sign that Canadian officialdom was becoming skeptical of Selkirk's characterization of the incident as a massacre of noncombatants.[9] There was more good news when attorneys for the North West Company succeeded in moving most of the trials to York, where, it was hoped, more witnesses from the Northwest could be brought to testify.

The trials of the Nor' Westers finally took place over the last two weeks of October. McLoughlin had to sit through several days of proceedings before his own case came up. First on the docket was the case of two Métis, Paul Brown and François Boucher, who had participated in the Battle of Seven Oaks. Witness testimony covered a wide gamut of alleged misdeeds by both fur companies but focused most heavily on the Seven Oaks affair. The attorneys for the Crown attempted to show that the North West Company and the Métis had conspired to destroy the colony and that this conspiracy had culminated in a murderous attack on Governor Semple and innocent colonists. The attorneys for the North West Company, two brothers by the names of Samuel and Livius Sherwood, presented a different story. Skillfully playing to the sympathies of the jury, they constructed a narrative in which the Red River colony was nothing but a hunting camp peopled by Hudson's Bay Company partisans. In their version, the battle was a spontaneous combustion, or "great riot," that occurred following a string of provocations and aggressions by the Hudson's Bay Company going all the way back to the founding of the Red River colony and the so-called Pemmican War. In closing arguments, Samuel Sherwood declared that the killings at Seven Oaks amounted to acts of self-defense, not unprovoked manslaughter.[10]

The direction of the court's verdicts began to emerge when both men were acquitted of the charge of murder. Their two-day trial was followed by others involving incidents of alleged theft and arson in 1815, which ended in acquittals as well. Finally, McLoughlin's case opened on October 30. At bar with him were four other partners and one clerk, John Siveright, who had been at Fort Gibraltar during the summer of 1816. The partners were charged with being accessories to murder after the fact, while Siveright was charged with being an accessory to murder both before and after the fact. The prosecution called several witnesses who had already testified in the trial of Brown and Boucher; in the partners' trial their testimony was directed toward establishing each of the defendants' presence or absence at various points along the now-familiar timeline. Several witnesses identified McLoughlin as having been among the Nor'Westers who had traveled to Rainy Lake in June 1816 to recruit Indians for an assault on the Red River colony. Two witnesses testified that the doctor had taken part in detaining the colonists as they fled down the Red River after the Battle of Seven Oaks. One witness stated that McLoughlin had joined in the council at Fort Douglas in which the Nor'Westers congratulated the Métis on their victory. If this was a conspiracy, then there could be little doubt that McLoughlin had taken part in it. But as the jury had already acquitted Brown and Boucher of murder, it seemed unlikely that the charge of accessory to murder brought against McLoughlin and his five co-defendants would be any more convincing to this court. Closing arguments were heard late on the second day of the trial, then the jury retired. After only three-quarters of an hour, they returned. When all had taken their seats and the courtroom was once again quiet, hushed with anticipation, the foreman delivered a verdict. *Not guilty.*[11]

For the first time in over two years, McLoughlin was a completely free man. But he was in no mood to rejoice. Even though he had been more and more confident of the outcome of the trial toward the end, the strain of living under an indictment for murder had soured what little enthusiasm for the fur trade he had remaining.

Time of Reckoning

{ 21 } A time came in the life of most fur traders when they had to make a choice about where they intended to retire. After a person had spent so much of his life in the wilderness, wintering year after year in the cold heart of the continent, he had to wonder if it would be his lot to remain. Would he live out the rest of his years in the raw society that was emerging on the frontier, or would he cash in his earnings in the fur trade and go back to a more genteel life? It was a stark choice. If he had an Indian family, the choice could be a shattering one. More often than not, fur traders decided to return to white society and leave their family behind.

The abandonment of family was seldom total and unmitigated. Depending on the circumstances, the trader might determine that his wife and children would go back to her native people. Alternatively, he might assume that his family would remain at the fort and come under the guardianship of another trader. Sometimes a marriage to another trader was arranged before the husband left. A few traders chose to take their families with them back to white society, bracing against the culture shock and racial prejudice that would inevitably beset them. Starting around the time that McLoughlin entered the fur trade, a growing number of traders avoided all of these unhappy choices by choosing to retire with their families in Indian country. Known as "freemen" because they were no longer attached to the company, they eked out a living as subsistence farmers and hunters.[1]

McLoughlin was completely torn about his options. To his business associates, he displayed a somewhat outsized devotion to his mixed-blood family. He fought stubbornly to give his family a stable home at Fort William, and he declared his intentions to give his sons a formal education. Woe be to anyone who brought any insult or injury to Marguerite or the children. Stern, righteous, and hot-tempered, the doctor did not shy from using his towering frame and brute strength to browbeat or inflict corporal punishment on any "damned rascal" who deserved it.[2] Many years later, in Oregon, he would give a clergyman a severe caning for making racial slurs against his wife.

But in letters home, McLoughlin gave full play to his desire to return to civilization. The Northwest was a dreary wasteland, he insisted, and the fur trade was a rough and dirty business from which he would retire at the earliest possible moment. He never wrote a word about his wife and children to his family in Quebec. Just days before his trial in York began, McLoughlin wrote to his uncle Simon in Terrebonne: "Between you and me I have an offer to enter into Business in the civilized world. If I do not accept the proposal it will be from want of capital. This is between us—no one else must know it."[3] Was McLoughlin privately contemplating a break with his mixed-blood family? His insistence on secrecy may have been purely to protect his position in the North West Company. One wonders, though, if it related in some way to his domestic affairs.

Nothing further came of the business offer McLoughlin confided to his uncle. Possibly a "want of capital" was, as he claimed, the primary reason it never materialized. After a decade and a half in the fur trade, he still did not possess the nest egg he had long sought. If he had made partner a few years earlier, he might have expected an annual income of around £400, plus another £1,000 or more upon retirement when he tendered his share to the other partners. But as the Nor' Westers entered into economic warfare with the Hudson's Bay Company at the very time that McLoughlin acquired his single share, profits disappeared and McLoughlin received not a penny in annual dividends from 1815 onwards. A surviving ledger book of the North West Company, in which McLoughlin's account takes up a single page, seems to indicate that he received nothing more by way of compensation than to be reimbursed year after year for living expenses. These expenses were paid to his account by McTavish, McGillivrays and Company. One historian, in examining this account, concluded that McLoughlin "would probably have been better off financially if he had remained on a salary with the North West Company, and refused to become a wintering partner."[4] No doubt the doctor himself was tormented by that prospect.

Yet there was more to McLoughlin's decision to stick with the fur trade than mere impecuniousness. It would seem he had come to that fork in the road that many fur traders found so agonizing. His actions over the next two years suggest that his mind was in just such a dark place and that he was appealing to his better angels to keep his commitment to Marguerite and accept a lifelong career and retirement on the frontier.

Moreover, loyalty to Marguerite was not the only issue weighing on him. Maybe it was no coincidence that McLoughlin leaned into his marriage at the same time that he prepared to break with the arrogant William McGillivray and his ham-fisted leadership of the North West Company. To McLoughlin and a growing number of wintering partners, McGillivray appeared more and more reckless and vain in his desire to vanquish the Hudson's Bay Company. Increasingly, the others looked to the doctor as the one man in their group with the courage to stand up to McGillivray. In February 1819, a close observer of the situation wrote that there was none among the wintering partners "possessing firmness of character" except McLoughlin and perhaps one or two others. "A good dinner, a few fair promises would waltz the remainder about, to any tune the McGillivrays chose to strike up."[5] Sometime during that year, McLoughlin began to conceive a plan for how to accomplish a radical break with McGillivray and the Montreal agents.

In the spring of 1819, the doctor returned to Fort William, rejoining his family after another long absence. Marguerite had somehow managed to care for the children through the period of Selkirk's occupation of the fort. Their youngest child, Eloisa, was now two years old. Marguerite's three daughters by her first husband were in various stages of becoming independent. One of these daughters, Nancy McKay, had married the captain of the North West Company's schooner that ferried goods and men up and down Lake Superior. Another daughter, whose name has been lost, had probably married by this time as well. By one account, she married a lieutenant in the British army and went to India.[6]

Though the partners' trials were now over, the war between the two great fur companies went on. The main theater of conflict moved from the Red River valley to the rich Athabaska district, the ultimate prize of the Canadian fur trade. Reports from that remote country told of more false arrests, more illegal imprisonments, more forts seized. Meanwhile, the rivals continued to do battle in the courts and in the public sphere, hammering one another with pamphlets and book-length tirades. The costly and embarrassing litigation bled both companies of their financial reserves and led politicians and governing officials in Canada and Britain to consider the need for a union of the two antagonists to end the strife.[7]

When all the North West partners convened at Fort William in the summer of 1819, the company's acute financial problems were laid bare. The wintering partners found the Montreal agents hard-pressed to keep them in supply for the coming year. For once, McGillivray was not so cocky. He could sense the old partnership coming apart. Most of the partners were signatories to a twenty-year agreement that was set to expire in three more years. Day after day McGillivray tried to talk the partners into renewing their commitments, but many of them balked. McLoughlin encouraged dissension. Speaking to the partners privately, he intimated that they might do better, when the time came, to negotiate with the Hudson's Bay Company instead. According to intelligence passed between agents of the Hudson's

Bay Company, McGillivray went home from Fort William that summer in
a terrible funk, convinced that if he could not get the agreement with the
wintering partners renewed by the following year, then "the whole North
West Company concern would be annihilated."[8]

After the rendezvous McLoughlin made his opening move toward
leading a revolt among the wintering partners. He wrote confidentially to
George Moffatt, a prominent Montreal merchant and partner in a supply
house with ties to the Hudson's Bay Company. He asked Moffatt to inquire discreetly whether the wintering partners, if they stood together in
refusing to renew their agreement with McTavish, McGillivrays and Company, would then be able to forge an alternative arrangement with the Hudson's Bay Company. Moffatt communicated this question to Samuel Gale,
a Montreal attorney, who conveyed its substance in a letter to Lady Jean
Selkirk, the wife of the earl. Lady Selkirk forwarded Gale's letter to Andrew
Colvile, attorney for the Hudson's Bay Company and a leading member of
its governing London Committee. Gale's letter kept McLoughlin's identity a secret, describing him only as "a wintering partner now in the Indian
Country." Gale stated that this anonymous individual possessed "influence
to withdraw almost every useful member of the North West Association"
who was fearful of being cheated or abandoned by his Montreal suppliers.[9]
In other words, he thought McLoughlin could lead a revolt against Mc-
Gillivray and end the conflict if only the Hudson's Bay Company responded
with the right overtures.

Gale's letter was explosive, for it arrived in London at the very time when
William McGillivray and his brother Simon were pursuing back-channel
negotiations with the Hudson's Bay Company to resolve the conflict in their
own way. With the help of their London contacts, the McGillivrays offered to buy Selkirk's controlling interest in the Hudson's Bay Company.
They reasoned that if Selkirk were removed from the equation, the Nor'
Westers would be rid of their enemy while the London-based company
would be unburdened of the distraction of Selkirk's colonization scheme.
More important, the Nor' Westers would at last gain access to the Hudson Bay supply route, and the competitors could join as one. Unbeknownst
to McLoughlin and the other wintering partners, several members of the
Hudson's Bay Company's governing committee had mutinous designs of
their own as they looked for a way to throw over Lord Selkirk and accomplish a union of the two companies. But when they received Gale's letter,
they suddenly dropped all talk of conveying Selkirk's controlling interest
to the Nor' Westers. Why negotiate with the enemy when the enemy was
itself on the verge of surrender? The Hudson's Bay Company rejected its

rival's offer, adopting the policy that by standing firm for another year or two it could bring the North West Company to its knees. Selkirk died a few months later, in April 1820, but it made no difference for the negotiations; the governing committee retained its resolve.[10]

McGillivray suspected McLoughlin of betrayal, for it was clear from the way the Hudson's Bay Company officers had suddenly broken off negotiations that they had learned of the dissension among the wintering partners. Who else might have given them their intelligence but the nettlesome doctor? His suspicions grew when McLoughlin hosted George Simpson, a rising officer in the Hudson's Bay Company, at Fort William the following spring. What really rankled McGillivray about this meeting was that the British government had tasked Simpson to deliver a communiqué to the North West Company and Simpson had handed the communiqué to McLoughlin as the company's representative officer in the interior instead of bringing it to McGillivray as head of the company. Clearly, Simpson's action was intended to build up McLoughlin and undermine McGillivray, and McLoughlin had played along with it. The junior partner and the powerful Montreal merchant had always been wary of each other; at last their antipathy was out in the open.[11]

At the rendezvous that summer of 1820, McGillivray's waning influence over the wintering partners was evident. He could only prevail upon a handful of them to renew their contracts with McTavish, McGillivrays and Company. Vindictively, and as a test of his remaining power, he called for a vote to remove McLoughlin from his longtime post as proprietor of Fort William. He knew how attached the doctor was to that place for the sake of his family. With his tight hold on the Montreal merchants' shares in the company, McGillivray could just muster the votes to punish his rival. The vote was taken, and McLoughlin was removed from his post. But in taking that action, McGillivray pitted the doctor against him. And the rendezvous was not yet over.

Now stripped of his post, McLoughlin called the wintering partners together in a separate meeting to discuss his idea that they collectively join the Hudson's Bay Company. It was a mutiny against the Montreal merchants that he now incited. Although the Montreal house of McTavish, McGillivrays and Company owned a majority share in all of the company's far-flung assets, everyone knew that the company's real strength lay in the energy and experience of the men who dwelt in the interior. The wintering partners were ready. They elected McLoughlin and one other of their number, Angus Bethune, to go on a secret mission to London and represent them at the Hudson's Bay House. Eighteen men assigned powers of attorney to those two, and handed the documents over to the doctor.[12]

As the rendezvous broke up, McLoughlin made arrangements for his family. For the time being, Marguerite would remain at Fort William with their youngest, little Eloisa, while he would take the older two, John Jr. and Elizabeth, ages eight and six, to Montreal to begin their formal education. Each of the older children would be assigned to a separate guardian, and he would establish an account with his uncle Simon to cover their expenses. He and Marguerite prepared for their third long separation in four years.[13]

Arriving in Montreal in September, McLoughlin and Bethune went to the trading house of George Moffatt. A former clerk in the North West Company, Moffatt now held a controlling interest in the firm of Gerrard, Gillespie, Moffatt, and Company. Eager to support the two North West partners' scheme, he provided them with a generous expense account for their mission to London. He then introduced them to Samuel Gale, the Selkirks' former attorney in Montreal, who gave them the necessary contacts in London. McLoughlin still insisted on the secrecy of their mission, but it was ever more apparent that he and Bethune were being treated as envoys to negotiate terms with the opposition. After their meeting, Gale wrote a letter to Andrew Colvile, the attorney on the Hudson's Bay Company's London Committee, to inform him about the nature of McLoughlin's and Bethune's forthcoming visit.[14]

London

{ 22 } In November 1820, McLoughlin and Bethune set sail from New York aboard the American packet *Albion,* bound for Liverpool. As McLoughlin began roaming the deck to acquire his sea legs for the five-week voyage across the Atlantic, he discovered that among the ship's other passengers, ironically, was their old rival, Colin Robertson. The tall, proud, bewhiskered Hudson's Bay man stood out in a crowd quite as much as the lanky, white-haired doctor did, and in spite of their past enmity and present need for discretion, the two became good friends aboard ship. As the days and weeks went by, McLoughlin found himself calling more and more regularly at Robertson's state room for convivial conversation.

Like McLoughlin, Robertson was frustrated that he had not risen faster and higher in his company's hierarchy. A onetime clerk in the North West Company, he had crossed to the opposition around 1810, just as Lord Selkirk began to increase his interest in the Hudson's Bay Company. Together with Selkirk and Andrew Colvile, Robertson helped pull the company out of its century-old lethargy and seek primacy. Robertson was more bellicose than either Selkirk or Colvile. His strategy for defeating the North West Company was simple: hit the Nor' Westers where it hurt them most—in the fur-rich Athabaska—and make them bleed. He once summed up his line of attack by quoting a Russian proverb, *If you live among wolves you have to howl like a wolf.* He had acquired a deserved reputation among the Nor' Westers as a fighter, a schemer, and an amazing escape artist. In the past three years, the Nor' Westers had taken him prisoner twice, and each time he had managed to make a bold getaway.

During an altercation outside Fort Chipewyan in the summer of 1818, Robertson had discharged his pistol—by accident, he claimed—prompting the Nor' Westers to arrest him and lock him inside a small shack next to the fort's privy. In that confined space they had held him prisoner for eight months, awaiting such time as they could transport him to Lower Canada under guard. In an amusing story he undoubtedly shared with McLoughlin during their Atlantic crossing, Robertson told how he made the most of his long imprisonment by sending secret intelligence that he gleaned about the

Nor' Westers to his own people at nearby Fort Wedderburn. He sent his intelligence in coded messages, which he managed to stash in a rum keg that went back and forth semiregularly between the two forts. He was very proud of the clever hiding place he devised to hold his ciphers.[1]

Robertson's adventures continued when his captors attempted to transport him to Lower Canada in the spring. His canoe suspiciously capsized in rapids near Île-á-la-Crosse. Though two guards who were both capable swimmers drowned, Robertson in manacles somehow survived. Once ashore, he found refuge in the Hudson's Bay Company's nearby Cumberland House. In the following year, the Nor' Westers ambushed him at the Grand Rapids on the lower Saskatchewan River and once again clapped him in irons for the long passage by canoe to Lower Canada. As their journey lengthened, Robertson studied his chances. During a meal break, he flung a dish of biscuits into his captors' faces, grabbed a gun, and made his second escape from the Nor' Westers. As there were warrants out for his arrest this time, he fled over the border into the United States. And that was how he came to be aboard the *Albion,* he explained to McLoughlin, for now he was on his way to London to make a report.[2]

But that was not the whole truth. While in New York, Robertson had received the intelligence that the Nor' Westers were looking for a way to make peace and merge the two companies. He had come aboard the *Albion* anxious to take part in the upcoming negotiations in London. He had a good idea why McLoughlin and Bethune were aboard ship, in spite of their secrecy about it, though he was too sly to challenge them directly.

McLoughlin, for his part, would not reveal his purpose in going to England. Once, at the risk of revealing his secret mission, he tried to steer their conversation to the character of the men on the London Committee, the very men with whom he would soon be sitting down to negotiate terms. What were they like? Were they affable and easy in their manners? Robertson saw right through the questions and could not resist taunting his new friend, who was still, after all, his rival. "You will see them Doctor, by and bye, and you will tell us all about it yourself," Robertson said. "*Me—me?*" McLoughlin stammered back, his face flushing. "*How, how* am I going to see them?"[3]

By the end of their sea voyage, all attempts at secrecy had become a mere pretense. On the last day aboard ship, McLoughlin, Robertson, and Bethune dined with John Caldwell, a public official in the government of Lower Canada and close friend of William McGillivray. Robertson baldly challenged Caldwell to name the purpose of the two Nor' Westers business in London. "Come, come," Caldwell replied, "you know very well, as you are going to introduce them to the Hudsons Bay Co." Robertson denied it, but

Caldwell would not be taken for a fool. "Oh, I believe so," he insisted, "and William McGillivray himself sets no value upon them." He paused, waiting for McLoughlin and Bethune to absorb this insulting remark. When they did not rise to it, he added, "Oh yes, I know they are radicals."[4]

The verbal sparring only made McLoughlin angry, but it was the sort of thing Robertson greatly enjoyed. As land came in sight, the ship's stewards brought everyone a glass of wine followed by a subscription (collection) for the stewards and other servants. McLoughlin signed the subscription and passed the pen to Robertson. Robertson started to sign and then stopped, noting the fact that Bethune was next in line. He turned to a clergyman, one Monsieur Carriera, and quipped: "Come Abby put down your name. I don't like to sign between two North Westers." "Never mind," the abby replied, without missing a beat, "remember our Saviour was crucified between two thieves." McLoughlin reddened but held his temper.[5]

In London, McLoughlin and Bethune soon located the Hudson's Bay House at Numbers 3 and 4 Fenchurch Street in the heart of the East Side's mercantile district. The company headquarters occupied both levels of a two-story stone building. On the ground level, a high central archway led to cavernous fur stores; on the level above, offices and filing rooms were ranged down a narrow, musty hallway. The fur stores were stuffed to the rafters with rack upon rack of beaver, marten, fisher, otter, mink, wolverine, bear, lynx, wolf, fox, and muskrat skins. All were arranged in such a way as to facilitate an occasional "sale by the candle," or public auction. At these events, buyers would pack the floor, and bidding for each lot of furs would go on for as long as it took a one-inch candle to burn down. Whoever got in the last bid before the candle flame guttered out secured the lot for sale.[6]

Through its royal charter, the company owned rights to dock its ships at Deptford, one of the oldest shipyards in the Port of London. Furs were landed dockside and were trundled from there down narrow lanes to Fenchurch Street, a thoroughfare thrumming with traffic and trade. Together with Cheapside, Cornhill, and Gracechurch streets, Fenchurch Street formed one of the radiating spokes within the ragged perimeter of the ancient, walled section of the city. From those four main trunk roads branched the many little crooked alleyways and cobbled mews that comprised the better part of the old city's bewildering maze of streets. The mercantile district was the commercial heart of London, jammed with dockyards, warehouses, produce markets, and livery stables. Above the jumble of roofs and chimney pots and columns of smoke loomed the massive dome of St. Paul's Cathedral.[7]

The shipyards stretched for miles eastward along the Thames, a good many of them built since the start of the Napoleonic Wars. Besides the old shipyards at Deptford and Millwall, there were the East India Docks at Blackwall, the New West India Docks of the West India Dock Company, and the recently completed Commercial Docks at Surrey. Barks and brigs and sloops of all sizes were packed like sardines in their berths, while the many vessels slowly coming and going on the river made a veritable forest of masts and sails.[8]

In the eyes of the two Nor' Westers the London streets were a chaos of noise and confusion. Horse-drawn wagons, handcarts, hackney coaches, two-wheeled hansoms, and sedan chairs vied for openings in the slow-moving traffic, their drivers shouting and cursing at one another. Pedestrians thronged the sides of the street, jostling past the innumerable street vendors, who had in their stalls or their baskets every imaginable item from articles of furniture to roast potatoes and gingerbread. Bobbing along in this endless, roiling stream of humanity were the numerous messenger boys and pickpockets. And the throng went on day after day in all kinds of weather. When the cold, damp fog rolled off the Thames, the people just bent into it. When it rained, all the pedestrians jockeyed to take the wall to avoid the curtains of water pouring off the shingle roofs.

McLoughlin could not help but notice all the dandies around him. London was the center of fashion in 1820, and both he and Bethune had little idea of what was new in Englishmen's dress before they took their sudden plunge into London society. Most English gentlemen now wore trousers instead of breeches—not the loose-fitting pants worn by peasants and working men, but skin-tight trousers designed to show off a man's legs. The model new look was to dress in a smart, black waistcoat fitted snugly over a white linen starcher, skin-tight trousers, Wellington boots, and, of course, a beaver felt top hat. Society men accessorized: in place of the old sword scabbard hanging from a waist belt, they now carried a fancy umbrella.[9]

Unfortunately, no official record of McLoughlin's and Bethune's negotiations with the London Committee is known to exist, and we are left to imagine what kind of impression the two rough-hewn Canadians in their rustic finery made on their London hosts. It is likely that after their initial contact the meeting place moved from the Hudson's Bay House to one of the nearby coffee houses, since that was where merchants and businessmen conducted most of their business affairs. A favorite meeting place among the Hudson's Bay men was Garraway's Coffee House on Broad Street. Also popular were the numerous coffee shops tucked into every nook and alleyway around the Royal Exchange, at the center of the mercantile district. These establishments catered to the middle-class merchants, bankers, and lawyers of London's East Side, providing coffee and a place to sit, smoke, read the newspapers, and discuss business for just a penny a cup. It is likely that McLoughlin and Bethune found themselves frequenting one of these establishments sometime during the month of December, trudging back to their private lodgings for each long winter night.

They must have soon realized, however, that the London Committee was holding them at arm's length. Almost on the day the two men arrived in England, William and Simon McGillivray intensified their own efforts to forge an amalgamation of the North West and Hudson's Bay companies. John Caldwell, the colonial government official whom McLoughlin and Bethune had met aboard the *Albion*, brought the McGillivrays the news that the two Canadians had arrived from New York to strike a deal on behalf of the wintering partners, whereupon the McGillivrays determined to preempt them. The men of the London Committee perceived their advantage. With two teams of negotiators from the fractured North West partnership in London at the same time, they saw that they were in a very strong bargaining position. If either the McGillivrays or the wintering partners demanded too much, the Hudson's Bay Company men only had to turn to the other party. Andrew Colvile of the London Committee decided that the McGillivrays held the balance of power in the rival company, and so he would deal mainly with them. His main interest in parleying with McLoughlin and Bethune, therefore, was to hold them in the wings until his negotiation with the McGillivrays was concluded.[10]

The key negotiator on behalf of McTavish, McGillivrays and Company was Edward Ellice, a wealthy Londoner, investor, merchant, and member of Parliament. Ellice had dabbled in the fur trade as early as 1803, when a short escapade to North America earned him the nickname "Bear." By 1819, he had become a major shareholder in the North West Company and its principal London agent. Near the end of that year, Ellice had put together an offer to buy all the Hudson's Bay Company shares held by the dying Lord Selkirk as a way to position the two companies so they could broker a merger. Andrew Colvile had spurned that offer, but Ellice had patiently stayed in the game. Now, one year later, the McGillivrays looked to him to negotiate a deal.[11]

In early January, "Bear" Ellice and John Caldwell visited Colin Robertson at his East Side lodgings to discuss the prospective merger. Ellice said he greatly resented McLoughlin and Bethune coming to London with powers of attorney to negotiate on behalf of the other wintering partners; it was very damaging and it put him in a bind. Neither he nor Robertson knew whether the doctor was parleying with the Hudson's Bay men right then or not. Evidently Ellice went to Robertson in the hope of finding out. When Robertson claimed not to know, Ellice turned their conversation to another topic. The next day Robertson went to Andrew Colvile, reported the fact that Ellice was curious whether McLoughlin was currently negotiating with the London Committee, and asked Colvile point blank whether he was talking to McLoughlin. Colvile would neither confirm nor deny it.[12]

A few days later, Simon McGillivray joined Robertson for breakfast. Like Ellice, he soon inquired as to what McLoughlin and Bethune were up to—were they in touch with the London Committee? Robertson said he could not enlighten him on that. Simon McGillivray then got spitting mad, referring to the matter of the eighteen powers of attorney that the doctor held in his pocket. As Robertson wrote afterwards, he railed against the doctor "with the utmost contempt."[13]

On February 6, Andrew Colvile informed Robertson by letter that the London Committee was very close to a deal with "the N.W. Co."—by which he meant the McGillivrays and Ellice. Perhaps McLoughlin received the news as well, for around that same time he left London and sailed across the English Channel to visit his brother David, who was also a doctor and had a successful medical practice in Boulogne, France. He sojourned with his brother for about one month, returning to London in March. If he had any expectation of participating in the final stage of negotiations in the latter part of March, he was disappointed. The gentlemen of the London Committee and the McGillivrays and Ellice signed the instrument forming a union of the two companies on March 26, 1821. McLoughlin and Bethune were not invited.[14]

Simon McGillivray would later insist that without the untimely defection of McLoughlin, Bethune, and the eighteen winterers, and their meddling in the negotiations, the North West Company would have succeeded in buying control of the Hudson's Bay Company in 1821. That may have been so, but in the judgment of history the actual outcome was probably better for everyone than an outright victory by one side or the other would have been. "The union of the North West and Hudson's Bay companies created an enterprise of power unequalled in the history of the fur trade," the historian John S. Galbraith has written. "The resources, experience and business acumen of the Hudson's Bay Company blended with the energy of the Nor' Westers to give unusual vitality to the monopoly that came into being in 1821."[15] If McLoughlin's role was that of a spoiler, he nonetheless came out on the right side of history. His concern that the McGillivrays acted too much in their own self-interest was not misplaced.

Despite the fact that McLoughlin's actions gave the Hudson's Bay Company the upper hand in the negotiations, Andrew Colvile steered the parties toward an equitable settlement. In the final accord, annual profits were to be divided into 100 shares with 20 distributed to the Hudson's Bay directors, 20 to the Montreal partners, 40 to the wintering people, 5 to the heirs of Lord Selkirk, and 5 to Simon McGillivray and Edward Ellice. The remaining 10 shares were to be kept in reserve. Colvile recognized that it was not in his company's long-term interests to be vindictive. Historians E. E. Rich and R. Harvey Fleming praised Colvile's "good sense" in refraining from using the winterers' revolt to destroy McTavish, McGillivrays and Company. To cut the Montreal merchants out of the fur trade would not have served the company's interests in the long run.[16]

The union's most important result was that it reconstituted a monopoly over the fur trade in British North America. Reorganizing the trade as a monopoly was necessary in order to restore its profitability, provide security for investors, and fend off American traders. In particular, the rise of John Jacob Astor's American Fur Company posed an increasing threat to British and Canadian interests. Fur-trade historian Harold Innis went so far as to assert, "American trade after 1815, in a sense, squeezed the two large Canadian companies into one unit."[17]

Another important effect of the amalgamation was to create a more rational and efficient system of supply and transportation based on Hudson Bay. Gaining access to Hudson Bay was, next to ending the strife, the North West Company's greatest incentive for forming a union with its rival. The 3,000-mile relay system for transporting goods and furs between Montreal and the Athabaska may have been the pride of the North West Company, but it was wildly impractical. Costly both in time and money, it was a poor substitute for the Hudson's Bay Company's privileged position on the bay. When the two companies combined, the Hudson's Bay Company's most significant contribution to the new enterprise was its royal charter of 1670, granting exclusive rights to trade with Indians in the vast Hudson Bay watershed. It was chiefly to protect the royal charter that the Hudson's Bay name was retained for the reorganized company.

McLoughlin surely understood that as soon as the system of transport and supply was revamped, Fort William would become a minor post. The four-week canoe run between Montreal and Lake Superior would become a mere tangent to the main flow of goods to and from Hudson Bay. He knew not where his next posting would be, but he did know that managing a hospital for the thousand-odd canoemen who gathered for the rendezvous each summer at Fort William was now a thing of the past.

The part of the agreement of most consequence for McLoughlin personally, as it was for all traders in the two companies, was a document known as the Deed Poll. The Deed Poll spelled out which men from each company were to be retained as officers in the reorganized company. Since one object of the union was to eliminate redundancies, all traders were anxious to know who would be included in this select group of officers, to be known henceforth as "chief factors" (district administrators) and "chief traders" (their deputies). Those not selected faced either demotion to the rank of clerk or a forced retirement. Altogether the Deed Poll named thirty-two Nor'Westers and twenty-one Hudson's Bay men to these coveted positions. To many Nor' Westers, the selection seemed skewed in favor of the Hudson's Bay men, who were far fewer in number and on the whole considerably less experienced than the Nor'Westers. Still, the Deed Poll was balanced enough. By combining the senior personnel of both companies, it turned many former adversaries into new associates.[18]

The Deed Poll identified a total of twenty-five chief factors and twenty-eight chief traders. The roster of chief factors included McLoughlin as well as Angus Bethune and Colin Robertson. Among the twenty-eight men selected as chief traders, the name of Simon McGillivray jumped out. This was not Simon McGillivray of McTavish, McGillivrays and Company, but rather his nephew. Born in 1790 to William McGillivray and his Cree wife, Susan, the younger Simon McGillivray joined the North West Company in 1813 and was a wintering partner in 1821. His selection as a chief trader in the reorganized company is notable, not only as a final act of nepotism by the McGillivray clan, but also because his subsequent career with the Hudson's Bay Company would intertwine closely with McLoughlin's.[19]

The Deed Poll provided for a new system of administration. Virtually all of British North America was divided into four departments, with a governor appointed for each one. Each department's governor and chief factors were to meet in council on an annual basis. The meeting in council was analogous to the North West Company's annual meetings at Fort William. It established regulations, planned the next year's operations, and dealt with personnel matters. The difference was that each governor and council would report to the board in London, where ultimate authority for all company actions resided.[20]

Following the amalgamation, the British Parliament gave its approval and support to the new Hudson's Bay Company in a statute passed later that year. Enlarging upon the royal charter of 1670, it extended the company's monopoly over the Indian trade to all of British America east of the Rocky Mountains as well as the Oregon country west of the Rocky Mountains insofar as British subjects were concerned. In addition, the act empowered the company to administer all criminal and civil law cases in British America outside of Upper and Lower Canada and the Maritime colonies. The judicial powers were granted with the proviso that the company act to regulate and restrict the trade of liquor to the Indians.[21]

As soon as the agreement was signed, McLoughlin and Bethune left London and took a coach to Liverpool. On March 31, they boarded the American packet *Amity* and sailed for New York. During the voyage, McLoughlin suffered another bout of the recurring malady that had afflicted him ever since his near-drowning in Lake Superior. He did not lay over in New York to rest and recover but immediately took passage on a schooner up the Hudson River, thinking he must get home to his Marguerite. But as his condition worsened, thoughts of what still lay ahead of him—days and weeks bent into a canoe, nights on the ground, cold spray in the face from the dark storm-tossed waters of Lake Superior—he changed his mind. In his present state the arduous journey from Montreal to Fort William would probably kill him. Instead, he transferred to another schooner headed back down the Hudson, had a brief stay in New York, and then boarded another sailing ship for Boulogne, France. His purpose in taking this extraordinary step was to put himself in the care of his brother David. He reached his brother's place in June. As he had anticipated, his brother insisted that he convalesce there for as long as needed to restore his health.[22]

Although McLoughlin had barely seen his younger brother since they were young, the two had faithfully corresponded through the years. David had received his medical education at Edinburgh while McLoughlin was still serving his four-year apprenticeship with the North West Company. Twice during his apprenticeship, McLoughlin tried to send his younger brother £100 when David was in danger of falling into debt. (He sent instructions to his uncle Simon to draw on his account and send the money to Edinburgh, but it seems his request was never acted upon.) During the years 1808 and 1809, McLoughlin feared that his brother's financial difficulties might prevent him from completing his medical degree, or worse, land him in debtors' prison. Whatever or whoever saw David through his difficulties, he received his degree of medicine in 1810, got an army commission in 1811, and served as a surgeon in Wellington's army in Portugal and Spain for the next three years. In 1814 he was stationed in Boulogne, and upon completing his military service four years later he returned to that city to establish his own medical practice.[23]

When McLoughlin was crossing the Atlantic the first time, he invited his new friend Colin Robertson to call on his brother in Boulogne. Robertson, curious about McLoughlin and his kin, acted on this suggestion and had dinner with David McLoughlin at his home in Boulogne some months later. In a letter to their mutual friend George Moffatt, Robertson remarked that the younger brother "bears a strong resemblance to our friend but it is a polished likeness. What an astonishing difference a little intercourse with the world makes in a man's manners! Dr. McL. is an elegant, gentlemanly young man, stands high at this place, and seems to be a great favorite with the good folks of Boulogne."[24] Judging by Robertson's description, David gave an idea of the sort of person John might have become had he not gone into the fur trade.

McLoughlin never expressed anything but admiration for his younger brother's superior medical education and burgeoning success as a private physician. Despite the fact that they were both doctors, their circumstances in 1821 could not have been more different. Chance had placed the two of them on divergent paths, and although they remained emotionally close they would be worlds apart, both geographically and socially, until the end of their lives. Whereas John McLoughlin would end his days in Oregon as an undervalued administrator, his younger brother would later move to Paris and write a number of distinguished medical treatises before eventually retiring in London. David McLoughlin never returned to Canada.[25]

Early in 1822, while John McLoughlin was still in his brother's care in Boulogne, a letter arrived for him from George Simpson, the new leader of the reorganized Hudson's Bay Company. "I shall be glad to learn that you are long ere now recovered from your severe illness," Simpson began hopefully. He went on to explain that he wanted to appoint him chief factor of the Hudson's Bay Company's Rainy Lake district. He wanted him back in time to join the outbound movement of men and supplies at the end of summer.

It must have been very good news to McLoughlin. The Rainy Lake district was his old turf, almost as well known to him as Fort William. He had occupied the North West Company's Rainy Lake post for a number of years until 1816. The Hudson's Bay Company had built its Rainy Lake House in 1817. From what he was told, the Hudson's Bay post was located about a mile below his old place. It stood on a prominence beside the Rainy River, where it overlooked the portage around Koochiching Falls. Simpson's letter was the closest thing to a summons home that he could have expected.[26]

Simpson also indicated in his letter that the Rainy Lake district was a critical one for the company, worthy of McLoughlin's talents. Although the district was no longer on the Athabaska supply route, nor rich in furs, it now acquired strategic importance of another sort. The American traders had just begun to push into the region from the south. Simpson wanted to cut them off. If necessary, he would place a chief trader in the area as well, giving McLoughlin a second in command and ensuring that the Americans would make no inroads with the Indians there. He identified Rainy Lake House as "our principal Frontier establishment"—using "frontier" in the Old World sense of that word as a border between nations. Nowhere else in North America was Britain's position in the fur trade more exposed to the restless ambitions of its neighbor to the south.[27]

❈{V}❈ LONG

The Wonder of the Steamboat

{ 23 } Stephen Long dreamed of exploring the western rivers in a steamboat. Not a big, wide "river queen" of the sort that would later be associated with Mark Twain, but a much smaller craft. Yet, a vessel eminently more capacious and powerful than the keelboats used by Lewis and Clark. What a triumph it would be to take a steamboat on unchartered waters through the western prairies.

A sometime inventor, Long admired the steamboat as one of the great, influential inventions of his day. It was an engineering marvel. How clever to harness the steam engine to the waterwheel! With the new power of steam, the familiar action of the waterwheel was thrown into reverse, buckets were turned inside out and made into paddles, and the paddlewheel, churning against the current, drove the boat upstream. Clearly, the newly invented vessel would soon play a big role in inland navigation. There was no better way for the army to open the West, in Long's view, than to send an exploring expedition on a steamboat to demonstrate how the new boats could ply the western rivers.

The steamboat posed certain possibilities for exploring the West in a big new way. Foremost was its power to ascend rivers. It was well known what a tedious, hazardous, and costly undertaking it was to ascend the Missouri River in keelboats propelled only by oar and sail. To harness the power of steam on that mighty river would be a great stroke. It would collapse distance—put the city of St. Louis nearly at the threshold of the Rocky Mountains. Traveling by steamboat, an exploring expedition would travel faster, cover more miles, make more discoveries, and reduce costs for the government.

Exploration by steamboat suggested exciting new prospects for scientific investigation, too, Long thought. A riverborne steamboat expedition would be able to carry more scientific instruments and collect a far greater quantity of specimens than one that traveled by keelboat or horse. More important, he would take on board a few gentlemen of science. Lewis and Clark, his illustrious predecessors in western exploration, had had to perform their scientific inquiries by themselves. They had had to collect specimens and take field notes alongside their other responsibilities, and with scant training as naturalists at that. Long conceived of scientific exploration more grandly. He wanted to take bona fide men of science with him and have them do the collecting. He would be their guide, introducing them to the West like a teacher introducing inquisitive young minds to new fields of knowledge. He was still a New England schoolmaster at heart. His six years of teaching at the West Point, Germantown, and Salisbury academies did not lie too far behind him.

He found the idea of a steamboat expedition on the western rivers compelling for yet another reason: it would be a glorious endeavor. The steamboat had already begun to catch the nation's imagination as a potent symbol of economic progress. Belching smoke and hammering its way forward against the current, it exuded strength and power. If Long could get command of a steamboat expedition to explore the Missouri and its major tributaries, it would bring prestige to the army and glory to the nation.

Long first proposed his idea in a letter to James Monroe soon after Monroe became president in the spring of 1817. "I would build a small steamboat about 40 feet in length and 7 feet beam, drawing no more than 14 inches of water," he wrote to the president. "With this I would navigate all the rivers of consequence . . . meander their courses, and take the latitude and longitude of their mouths and heads of navigation."[1] Long did not receive a reply. He then put forward his plan to his commanding officer, General Smith, and to his mentor, the chief of engineers, General Swift. The problem, Long realized, was that neither of those officers would be able to advance his proposal past their superior, Major General Andrew Jackson, commander of the army's southern division.

Around the time that Long wrote to President Monroe, he found himself in the middle of a controversy between General Jackson and Acting Secretary of War George Graham. Jackson protested the order that Secretary of War Crawford had given to Long to explore the Illinois country. Jackson argued that the purpose of the Topographical Engineers was merely to produce maps for the army, not to explore the West. More importantly, Jackson objected to Crawford's having given Long an order without informing him of it, that is, without running it through the military chain of command. Graham retorted that the secretary of war had that prerogative; to suggest otherwise was to question the constitutional principal of civilian control over the military. The argument continued for months until Monroe finally weighed in on the side of the secretary of war and requested Jackson to cease and desist. On his next trip to St. Louis, Long was ordered to detour through Tennessee and visit General Jackson at his headquarters so they could patch things up between them. Jackson received Long graciously, for the general's quarrel had been with the secretary, not the major. Still, the controversy had given Jackson an axe to grind that made it harder for Long to realize his vision of army exploration of the West.[2]

In January 1818, while Long was stationed at Fort Belle Fontaine in Missouri, he learned that Congressman John C. Calhoun of South Carolina had become secretary of war. A former War Hawk (he had advocated going to war with Britain in 1812), he was strongly identified at that time with the nationalist program of westward expansion, internal improvements, and protective tariffs. To Long, Calhoun's move from representative in the US House to secretary of war in Monroe's cabinet was excellent news. The prospects brightened for getting his plan of exploration past General Jackson. For the second time, Long outlined his plan to General Smith, who forwarded the communication to Calhoun with an endorsement. General Smith told Calhoun that Long was "the most skillful, industrious and enterprising officer" in the Corps of Engineers whom he knew.[3]

Calhoun not only liked the idea of a scientific expedition, he expanded on it. The army would also send a military expedition far up the Missouri River to establish a fort at the mouth of the Yellowstone. Its purpose would be to awe the Indians, wrest control of the upper Missouri fur trade from the British, and secure the nation's hold on that territory. The military force would include 200 new recruits from Pennsylvania and Ohio plus whatever contingent of riflemen General Smith wanted to assign from his own command at Fort Belle Fontaine, and it would carry four light howitzers. In addition, the expedition would requisition up to $3,000 worth of goods in St. Louis for making presents to the Indians.[4]

Calhoun called Long back to Washington in the spring, and their plans for coordinated military and scientific expeditions began to take shape. Calhoun thought, too, perhaps the military force would use steamboats for its advance up the Missouri River, and Long encouraged his thinking on that score. Rather than marching troops hundreds of miles on foot and hauling supplies up the river by keelboat, the army would contract for services by one or two steamboat operators. Although western steamboats had barely ventured up the Missouri by that point in time, they were proving their mettle on the Mississippi and Ohio rivers. Long was reasonably confident that the transport by steamboat could be done. But make no mistake, he advised Calhoun, the Missouri was a uniquely challenging river. With its surging waters and logjams and sandbars bristling with downed trees, it was a horrific stream to navigate. The army's occupation of the upper Missouri would involve, he expected, "one of the most arduous undertakings that ever was encountered in the military operations of the Country." It would require "a proportionate expense of treasure and labor" and, considering the fighting spirit of the Plains Indian tribes, "possibly of blood."[5]

Meanwhile, Long prevailed on Calhoun to give him command of a topographical and scientific expedition that would ascend the Missouri at the same time as the military expedition. Long's expedition would be borne on a steamboat of the major's own design. He already had in mind the boat's dimensions, its approximate cost, and the various scientific instruments it would carry. He would take a small group of scientists with him, and besides making a survey of the Missouri and ascertaining its geographical position relative to the boundary with British America, his expedition would gather information about the geology, botany, zoology, and Indian tribes of the area. With the aid of the steamboat, they would explore the Missouri, the Yellowstone, the Platte, and possibly other western rivers. He envisioned a lengthy exploration of as much as four years. This plan was similar to the one he had put to President Monroe a year and a half earlier, but now it centered on the upper Missouri instead of the upper Mississippi.[6]

After discussing his ideas with Calhoun over the summer, Long put them into a formal proposal which he submitted to the secretary on August 31. He only had to wait two days for a reply. Calhoun not only approved the idea of coordinated military and scientific expeditions, he authorized Long to draw upon the services of the Quartermaster's Department in Pittsburgh to build his steamboat. Long's new orders were to report to the army's Allegheny Arsenal located two miles up the river from Pittsburgh, where he would assemble a team of shipwrights and mechanical engineers to help him build it.[7]

Long, now in the prime of life, at last had command of the expedition he had been dreaming of since his first trip to the West in 1816. But there was one more thing he wanted to do that winter of 1818–19 before embarking on what would surely be the grand adventure of his military career. He wanted to marry a young Philadelphia woman named Martha Hodgkis.

A Christian Marriage

{ 24 } Stephen Long was thirty-four and Martha Hodgkis was not quite nineteen years old when they were married on March 3, 1819. They no doubt made an attractive couple. Long was tall and rail-thin. His rounded chin and full lips had a refined quality befitting his bookishness, and the soft expression in his eyes was more like a schoolmaster's than a soldier's. Yet he groomed himself like an officer, trimming his dark side-whiskers into mutton chops, and cutting his hair short and combing it forward in the Napoleonic style. There is no known portrait of Martha, but her sister was painted as a young woman by Thomas Sully. If the sisters looked alike, then Martha would have been thin and fine-featured with porcelain skin and dark, curly hair.

Martha was born in 1800 in Philadelphia to Michael and Sarah Dewees Hodgkis. Her father and two older siblings died in a yellow fever epidemic when she was five, leaving her fatherless and an only child. A baby sister, born later that year, had to be given up for adoption. The adoption was, in modern terms, an "open" one, with the adoptive family residing only a few blocks away, so Martha formed a close relationship with her younger sister despite the fact that the two girls were raised in separate households. Her widowed mother, meanwhile, went to work as a dressmaker and managed to keep them afloat financially. In 1812, her mother married a steel manufacturer, and year by year, Martha's family returned to relative prosperity. By 1818, her stepfather worked as an agent for the Schuylkill Glass-Works and they lived in a house at 401 High Street, four blocks from City Hall. Martha resided at that address when Stephen Long courted her.[1]

One imagines Long, the suitor, wooing Martha with his characteristic suaveness, deliberation, and efficiency. He had had several years to prepare for it, and he may have been conscious of his relative maturity as a bachelor officer. Better than four-fifths of army officers were already married at his age. Like them, Long had to overcome certain obstacles to marriage that were unique to military life. For one, it was difficult to pursue a lengthy courtship when new orders could precipitate a transfer at any time. A young lady of the middle class regarded courting as no trifling thing; indeed, the choice of a marriage partner was usually the most important decision she would make in her adult life. Many army officers balked at courting under those weighty conditions and chose to put off marriage or avoid it altogether. Still, most of them did aspire to having a middle-class wife and family, and Long was no different.[2]

Another challenge to marriage for army officers was the relatively low pay they received. At the rank of major, Long was paid a salary of $60 per month plus four rations per day. A single ration was worth twenty cents, bringing his total pay to about $84 per month, or $1,008 per year (equivalent to about $20,000 today). That was virtually the same salary he had earned while teaching at the Germantown Academy, which paid him $1,000 per year. In both instances, it was assumed by his employers that he might supplement his meager income through additional work.[3] While employed by the Germantown Academy, Long held odd jobs as a surveyor and raised small crops of vegetables for the market. As an army explorer, he had fewer opportunities to obtain extra income. When he courted Martha Hodgkis he had no real property to his name. All he could promise her was a secure income. The one advantage an army wife had over most middle-class women was her husband's relative job security. One historian has described the army of the early Republic as "the first major public sector employer on a national scale in the United States" and suggested that many officers went into the army to insulate themselves from the anxiety and stress of the emerging market revolution.[4] Perhaps Martha found the financial security and stability in marrying an army officer attractive, since she had passed several years of her childhood in a fatherless household, frequently changing residences.

The biggest challenge for most army marriages arose from the long periods of separation involved. Many army officers who were stationed on the western frontier either found marriage partners in the West or expected their wives to accompany them there.[5] But even if an officer's wife lived with him in officers' quarters, the couple still had to endure frequent partings and long separations when duty called the husband away. And life in an army garrison could be isolating. Officers' families usually formed a small social circle while shunning intimate contact with the families of the rank and file.[6] In Long's case, the couple decided to make their home in Philadelphia, not the West. There, Martha enjoyed the ongoing support of her extended family, the Deweeses of Germantown and Philadelphia, while Long had opportunities to broaden his contacts with the eastern elite.

Long brought to the marriage a gregarious and positive nature, qualities that probably helped to bridge his and Martha's fifteen-year age difference. He was quick to make friends. His fellow officers were very fond of him.

Testimonials to his "suavity of manner" and "amiableness of disposition" and remarks about his sunny optimism followed him wherever he went.[7] It is easy to imagine how the affable major in the Topographical Engineers might have impressed the middle-class young woman.

Stephen and Martha were married on a Wednesday evening in Philadelphia's old Christ Church. Although the wedding was no more than a small ceremony, it was a big step in Long's quest to become a part of Philadelphia society. The elderly Reverend William White, who performed the service, had been rector of the church for more than forty years, having served as chaplain of the Continental Congress from 1777 to 1789 and chaplain of the US Senate from 1790 to 1800. He was a member of the American Philosophical Society and a revered humanitarian, and over the years his congregation had included such luminaries as George Washington and Benjamin Franklin. The grand church, with its towering white steeple, was said to be the tallest building in America. Martha's mother, Sarah Dewees, had been baptized in this church, and her father and two siblings had been laid to rest in the church burial ground.[8]

While Long's marriage into the successful Dewees family of Germantown and Philadelphia carried a certain cachet with well-to-do citizens of the city, that was not his avowed reason for marrying Martha Hodgkis. Marriages in the United States in the early nineteenth century were founded on romantic love. When Stephen and Martha made their wedding vows, they did so with the understanding that they had each come to that moment through their own volition. The marriage compact was their own, not something arranged between their respective families. They were probably a little self-conscious knowing that it had not always been so—that in early colonial times marriages were typically based on considerations of property or inheritance. By 1819, arranged marriages were virtually nonexistent and romantic courtship had become the norm. While each partner's economic assets and prospects surely counted for something in a couple's decision to marry, most husbands and wives justified their commitment to one another on the basis of love or affection.[9]

The change in marriage pattern had manifested during the ferment of the American Revolution. The generation of Americans who reached adulthood in the Revolutionary era—Long's parents' generation—regarded traditional arranged marriages as authoritarian, the more so because property ownership vested in the husband. Finding such a heavy imbalance of power between husband and wife to be repugnant, couples sought to redefine marriage as a partnership between equals. Indeed, they aimed to free themselves from the patriarchal relationship in the same way that the colonies freed themselves from the authoritarian rule of the king. They developed a new ideal for marriage that historians have called "companionate marriage." Although men and women were not equals under the law, companionate marriage aimed to resolve that tension by allotting the husband and wife separate spheres of influence. Husbands held sway in all matters outside the home (work, politics, civic affairs), and wives exercised their superior judgment in matters relating to the household and family. The trend toward companionate marriage reached full force in the early national period, when Stephen and Martha married, and they became exemplars of the companionate marriage couple, for instance, studiously taking turns in choosing names for their children.[10]

How did Stephen Long's sentiments on marriage affect his response to the domestic affairs of the white Indian, John Tanner, when the two met at Rainy Lake House? According to the account Tanner gave of his life, Long initially took him "for one of those worthless white men who remain in the Indian country from indolence, and for the sake of marrying squaws."[11] Whether or not this harsh statement is accepted at face value, there are a few hints in Long's own writings that would indicate he took a disparaging view toward interracial marriages between white traders and Indian women. If that was his prejudice, he was hardly unusual among white Americans of his day.

Whites were struck by the fact that Indian marriage forms differed markedly from the companionate ideal, or "Christian marriage," as it was then known. Among Indian peoples the nuclear family of husband, wife, and children was usually subsumed in the larger social unit of the extended family or clan. Children in such families might address all of their birth-mother's sisters as "mother" or all of their birth-father's brothers as "father." Furthermore, Indian children made no distinction between siblings and cousins—all were considered "brothers" and "sisters." Some Indian cultures were patrilineal and some were matrilineal, meaning that clan and lineage might be reckoned through the male or female line. Marriage partners had to come from outside of the clan. By the time of Long's western explorations, ethnographers had only begun to decipher the many complex systems of kinship found among Indian tribes, so a large part of what they observed was unintelligible to them. The cultural norms that Long and his contemporaries tended to focus on were the relations between Indian husband and wife. Yet even that bond could appear quite foreign. While monogamous marriages were the prevailing form in many tribes, polygamous marriages were not uncommon, and in no tribe did one form exist to the exclusion of the other. Moreover, all Indian tribes showed a liberality toward divorce and remarriage that white observers found exotic. All of these differences contributed to white Americans' perceptions that Indian peoples were a "savage" race.[12]

Even more troubling for whites was how Indian cultures exhibited an entirely different division of labor between the sexes. In an Indian marriage, the husband was the hunter and the wife was the agriculturalist. Indian men saw agriculture as women's work, so they had little interest in emulating white men who worked on their farms all day. Moreover, in many Indian cultures the women owned all of the material wealth including fields, gardens, dwellings, and even the village itself, making Indian men all the more averse to becoming freehold farmers like white men. Government officials and missionaries took note of these profound cultural differences. Intent on assimilating Indians into American society through a process of individual land allotment, they found that Indians must first be taught the virtues of monogamous Christian marriage. Only then, they thought, would Indians accept the American model of the single-family farm as a social and economic unit.[13]

To these observers' dismay, white traders who lived among the Indians were seldom themselves exemplars of monogamous Christian marriage. On the contrary, traders were apt to adopt Indian marriage customs. Often they took Indian wives to improve their standing with the local tribe. Then, furthering their own economic self-interest, they might take additional wives in other tribes as often as they changed locations. Modern research has shown that a significant number of marriages between Indian women and white men in the fur trade were both monogamous and enduring, but the government officials' and missionaries' view of these marriages was quite the opposite.[14] White men who took Indian wives were called "squaw men," with the term "squaw" usually being a pejorative that meant whore or concubine. One missionary wrote disparagingly of white men on the frontier who lived with half a dozen Indian wives. Secretary of War Calhoun was troubled by his perception that Indians learned practically everything they knew about whites' morals from traders. "From this source," he sniffed, "they have learned nothing but the most libidinous and abandoned licentiousness."[15]

Calhoun commissioned a Protestant missionary, the Reverend Jedediah Morse, to investigate the "moral condition" of Indians living near the white settlements and advise how to reform the Indian trade. Morse's idea was to establish a "mission family" or "education family" adjacent to every licensed trading house. These education families would consist of husband, wife, and children, and they would model a Christian marriage for their Indian neighbors. Morse thought the good example set by the education families would especially impress Indian women, whom he saw as universally in a "degraded state." Under the influence of the education families, Indians would soon give up polygamy, which was not only an affront to God but an obstacle to Indian advancement. "Let in the light on the Indians and the abolition of the practice will follow," he predicted.[16]

Long would use that same metaphorical language of light and dark, good and evil, and civilization and savagery to describe the Indian tribes he encountered on his expedition to the Rocky Mountains in 1820. The "shade of barbarism" found among those tribes tended to "exclude the light of civilization," he would observe in his official report, adding that the Indians' ways were not "equally dark and malignant in all cases."[17] This dismal view of Indians reflected the common attitudes of Long's white contemporaries and doubtless stemmed in part from his own rootedness in a conventional, white, middle-class marriage.

Up the Missouri

❊ 25 ❊ In the weeks leading up to and immediately following his wedding day, Long was furiously busy with preparations for the expedition. Besides working on the design of his steamboat and overseeing its construction, he was assembling supplies, forming his boat crew and military escort, recruiting the scientific members of the party, and corresponding with Calhoun and various officers in charge of the military arm of the combined expedition. The Yellowstone expedition, as it was now called by the nation's press, was the most ambitious operation the army had ever undertaken in peacetime. It had the triple aim of establishing army posts on the upper Missouri, experimenting with steamboat technology, and expanding scientific knowledge about the West. Long's arm of the expedition was to be the first army exploration in the Trans-Mississippi West with trained scientists on board.[1]

Long saw the expedition up the Missouri as a springboard to a comprehensive scientific survey of the region that would stretch over a number of years and would entail multiple trips. The steamboat would carry the party up and down the main stem of the Missouri and its major tributaries, returning to St. Louis for more supplies between trips. He himself would return to Washington and Philadelphia from time to time. With this grand view in mind, he aimed to recruit scientists who would commit to the project for three to five years. Initially he thought they might serve without regular salary, volunteering their time in exchange for the privilege of having all their travel expenses paid by the government. Only after the first of the year did he receive authorization to nominate civilian scientists for a handful of paid commissions. In the meantime, he turned to the American Philosophical Society for advice on likely candidates. One of his early picks, a New York physician and amateur geologist by the name of John Torrey, backed out because of uncertainty over the terms of compensation. Finally, in February and March, the issue of pay was cleared up and the roster of scientists began to take shape.[2]

A total of five civilians were commissioned. Dr. William Baldwin was to serve as botanist as well as physician and surgeon for the expedition. One of the most eminent American scientists of the day, he had been schooled in medicine at the University of Pennsylvania, practiced medicine for some years in Wilmington, Delaware, and then moved to Savannah, Georgia, where he sought a warm climate to improve his health. Despite his health problems, he thought he could survive the rigors of the expedition.

Thomas Say was the expedition's zoologist. The owner of a Philadelphia apothecary, possessing little formal education, Say had distinguished himself as the founder of the Philadelphia Academy of Natural Sciences. He had recently published the first volume of his three-part tome, *American Entomology.*

The position of geologist vacated by Torrey was assigned to Augustus E. Jessup. An amateur scientist like Torrey, he was a wealthy Philadelphia merchant who had made his name in the scientific community through his membership in the Philadelphia Academy of Natural Sciences.

Titian Ramsay Peale was to serve as assistant naturalist to the first three men, collecting, preparing, drawing, and maintaining specimens. He was the youngest son of Charles Willson Peale, the Philadelphia portrait painter and museum curator.

Finally, there was Samuel Seymour, a Philadelphia painter and engraver, whose task was to provide the expedition with sketches of the more dramatic landscapes through which it passed and to make portraits of Indian chiefs and scenes of Indian life.[3]

Besides the five civilians, the expedition included Lieutenant James Duncan Graham and Cadet William Henry Swift, topographical engineers who were to assist Long in taking astronomical readings and making surveys, and Major Thomas Biddle, Jr., who was assigned to keep the official journal of the expedition. Benjamin O'Fallon, US Indian agent, was to join them in Missouri. Filling out the expedition was a military escort of eight privates and one sergeant, and a six-man crew for the steamboat.[4]

Calhoun wrote to the American Philosophical Society for advice on the scientists' instructions. The Society responded by appointing a committee to develop a list of topics for inquiry. Long's new in-law, Dr. William P. Dewees, was on the committee. The committee's "Suggestions for Inquiries by the Scientific Members of the expedition to the Yellowstone river" ranged across many topics relating to Indian life—including such specific questions as whether Indians practiced circumcision and what were the customs attending menstruation, pregnancy, and childbirth. It recommended two essential texts that the expedition members should pack along: Jonathan Carver's *Travels through the Interior Parts of North America* and Benjamin S. Barton's *New Views of the Origins of the Tribes and Nations of America.* It also presented Long with a copy of the first volume of the Society's

Transactions and an unpublished dictionary of the Osage language. To these items, Calhoun added former president Jefferson's instructions to the Lewis and Clark expedition.[5]

The army did its part to draw public attention to the endeavor. It had special uniforms designed for the expedition members, and it commissioned artist Charles Willson Peale to paint individual portraits of the commander and the five civilians seated in their smart new uniforms. Long was first to sit for Peale, and when the artist had finished with him Baldwin went next. Baldwin was surprised how much time was devoted to this exercise when there was so much else to be done; he had to sit for the artist for nearly twelve hours. While Baldwin sat, Peale confided to him that Long had not been an easy subject—always fidgeting and impatient. On Long's last session with the artist, shortly after his wedding day, he was drowsy from lack of sleep and explained that his wife had been ill. Baldwin thought the drowsiness showed in Long's portrait, which he described to a friend as "defective—particularly about the eyes."[6]

Toward the end of March, the members of the expedition began to gather in Pittsburgh, where Long's steamboat, the *Western Engineer,* was undergoing trial runs and final adjustments. Measuring seventy-five feet long and thirteen feet across the beam (almost twice the size originally envisioned), the craft drew thirty inches of water fully loaded, much more than hoped. Its paddlewheel was placed in the stern to give the paddles maximum protection from damage by snags and floating debris. Its engine featured a cam cutoff, a device of Long's own invention, which increased the amount of steam compression by cutting off the steam's flow into the cylinder before each stroke was completed. This innovation was soon adopted in other steamboat designs.[7]

The boat's superstructure had another unusual feature. The bow was in the form of a serpent's head, its long neck jutting forward menacingly. It looked like the bow of a Viking ship but with an added touch of the new industrial age: with the aid of an exhaust pipe below deck the serpent's head could be made to belch black engine smoke from its mouth. One newspaper correspondent, observing a demonstration of the steamboat in action, tried to imagine for his readers how the noise and exhaust would awe the Indians. "Neither wind or human hands are seen to help her; and, to the eye of ignorance, the illusion is complete, that a monster of the deep carries her on his back, smoking with fatigue, and lashing the waves with violent exertion."[8] Just in case the serpent's head failed to intimidate the Indians, the *Western Engineer* carried five small cannon on deck, three mounted on wheeled carriages and two on swivels.[9]

The expedition members left Pittsburgh on May 5, 1819, following a month's delay as various bugs were worked out of the *Western Engineer*. Problems with the steamboat were to dog them all the way. Descending the Ohio River, they had to make frequent stops for engine repairs, and on one stormy night a severe gust of wind toppled the mast. Below deck, the quarters proved to be leaky and damp. The men could not keep their clothes dry, and Baldwin's fragile health began to fail. In Cincinnati, they halted for six days for repairs and then another three days for Baldwin to get well enough to continue downstream. Twice the boat took the wrong river channel and ran aground on sandbars. When they reached the Mississippi and turned upstream, the steamboat made slower progress than expected even against the rather languid current. It was June 9 when the expedition at last reached St. Louis, and the *Western Engineer* had not yet been tested against the much stronger current of the Missouri.[10]

If these problems and delays were not disappointing enough, Long now learned that the military arm of the expedition was experiencing even greater transportation difficulties. The previous December the army had contracted with James Johnson of Kentucky to furnish at least three and perhaps as many as five steamboats in the spring for transporting men and supplies from Pittsburgh to the Missouri. Like the *Western Engineer*, Johnson's steamboats suffered numerous delays in getting from Pittsburgh to St. Louis. Worse yet, there were just two operable steamboats. A third boat had been impounded and the fourth and fifth never got out of the shipyard. Johnson's problems were not so much technological as financial. He was caught in the sharp economic downturn known to history as the Panic of 1819. As the national economy faltered and credit became scarce, Johnson came up short of funds. By June he was heatedly demanding advances on his government contract on one hand while fighting off bank creditors on the other. When the first of Johnson's steamboats arrived at Fort Belle Fontaine laden with supplies, he would not allow its cargo to be offloaded for inspection by the Quartermaster's Department, as he feared that the Bank of Missouri would try to seize the goods and hold them against his debt. This standoff was still unresolved when Long arrived in St. Louis on the *Western Engineer*. Given the mounting difficulties over the use of steamboats, Colonel Henry Atkinson, the expedition commander, informed Long that he would resort to keelboats and proceed with the troops only as far as Council Bluffs that year—far short of the Yellowstone. Long had no choice but to adjust his plans accordingly, since the two separate arms of the expedition were supposed to be coordinated.[11]

The *Western Engineer* left St. Louis on June 21 and began its tortuous ascent of the Missouri. The effect of the current was even greater than Long had anticipated. In places the strong current brought the chugging steamboat almost to a standstill. Every bend in the river was an obstacle: the outside current was apt to be too strong, while on the inside the boat might run aground on shoals and snags concealed beneath the surface of the roiling, muddy waters. The great volumes of mud carried by the stream clogged the boilers and played havoc with the joints and cylinders of the engine. It was necessary to stop about every fifteen hours to cleanse the boilers and readjust the engine valves. At each stop the soldiers went ashore to replenish the supply of wood fuel. Felling trees, chopping them into cords, and loading the cords in the steamboat took much time and, as the wood was unseasoned, it did not burn efficiently. Still, despite these adversities, Long believed the steamboat offered distinct advantages over the alternative. Steamboats were considerably safer than keelboats, which were exposed to the hazardous tangles of driftwood floating down the river, and as pilots gained experience with the river there would be many fewer delays caused by running aground.[12]

The expedition's progress was so slow that Long assigned half of the men to a shore party—both to lighten the load and to give the scientists more opportunity to observe the country. Under the leadership of Major Biddle, Long's second in command, the shore party traveled up the Kansas River, where it was welcomed by the Kansa Indians at their main village. However, a few days after leaving the Kansa village the shore party was robbed by a group of about 140 Pawnee warriors. Although the men got through this incident unscathed, it caused them to abandon their plan of continuing overland to the mouth of the Platte River. Instead, they beat a retreat back to the Missouri to catch the lumbering *Western Engineer*. Finding that the steamboat had already passed upstream, Biddle divided the shore party in two, sending the stronger members ahead to overtake the steamboat while the slower group followed behind. When the faster group at last caught up with the *Western Engineer*, Long called a halt to await the remainder of the ill-fated shore party.[13]

Before the expedition reached Council Bluffs, Long had to contend as well with the loss of one scientist and the insubordination of his second in command. Baldwin became so ill he had to remain behind in the frontier settlement of Franklin, Missouri. This left the expedition without a surgeon and botanist. Baldwin hoped to work on reports while he convalesced and then rejoin the expedition later, but his condition only worsened and he died two months later.[14]

Major Biddle, meanwhile, had decided that Long's idea to navigate the

Missouri by steamboat was ill conceived. He believed Long was so stubbornly wedded to the idea that he was unfit for command. Moreover, Biddle blamed Long for the shore party's humiliating "defeat" by the Pawnee,
which he believed might prejudice his own chances for promotion in the
officer corps. At one point Biddle even challenged Long to a duel. (He was
deadly serious; the hot-headed army major met his end a decade later in
a duel with another man.) Long avoided a duel, but his relationship with
Biddle was irreparably damaged. Faced with such an unending string of
setbacks and frustrations, Long felt profoundly discouraged as the summer
drew to an end, so much so that other members of the expedition noted it
and observed that his seemingly indomitable spirit of optimism had finally
deserted him.[15]

Reaching Council Bluffs in September, Long and his men made winter
quarters at a point on the river about five miles below where Colonel Atkinson established his own winter quarters. With the men's quarters built
and the *Western Engineer* safely tucked away in a cove for the winter, Long
prepared to float back down the Missouri in a canoe with one soldier and
Jessup (who decided he had had enough). He gave instructions to the remaining scientists to pursue their studies in the surrounding area through
the winter; meanwhile, he would travel back to the nation's capital to report
on the expedition's travails and set new objectives for the coming year. He
left the engineers' cantonment in the middle of October, visited his family
in Philadelphia at Christmas, and was back in Washington around the first
of the year.[16]

By the time Long reported to the War Department, he had recovered
his characteristic enthusiasm. On January 3, 1820, he gave Calhoun an account of the expedition's numerous setbacks during the past summer: the
steamboat's many defects at the outset of the journey, the surprising force
of the Missouri River ("far greater than the most exaggerated accounts had
authorized us to expect"), the plundering of the shore party by the Pawnee,
the illness and eventual death of Dr. Baldwin, the insubordination of Major
Biddle. Yet in spite of all those mishaps, he proposed an ambitious plan for
the coming year. First, he wanted to return to his men by way of a more
northerly route. He would set off at the head of Lake Superior, travel overland to the mouth of the St. Peter's River, proceed up that river and overland
again to the Great Bend of the Missouri, and float down the Missouri to
Council Bluffs. Once reunited and supplied with horses and provisions, the
expedition would then follow the Platte River to its source in the Rocky
Mountains, head south to the source of the Red River of the South, and
down that river to the Mississippi, and finally homeward by way of New

Orleans. As for the *Western Engineer*, he no longer thought it the preferred "mode of service" for exploring the West.[17]

Long soon learned that his plan was far too expansive. With the nation's economy still in a sharp downturn, Congress aimed again at slashing the War Department budget. On December 21, 1819—just two weeks before Long submitted his report—the House committee on military affairs began an investigation of the Yellowstone expedition and its costs, starting with the botched contract with Johnson for steamboat transportation. Calhoun duly assembled this information during the month of January and submitted it to the House committee on February 3, 1820. Calhoun did not begrudge Long for the army's problems with steamboats the previous summer; indeed, the secretary of war still wanted Colonel Atkinson to use steamboats on the upper Missouri in the coming year, for he believed that they would add color to the expedition and impress both the British and the Indians with the power of the United States. But in the following weeks, as Congress moved to slash the expedition's funding, Calhoun became convinced that the whole military operation must be recast. The original objective of establishing a fort at the mouth of the Yellowstone was too ambitious. He apprised Long that the scientific expedition would have to be scaled down as well.[18]

Long worked with the secretary of war to develop a plan that would keep the scientific expedition going and still meet with Congress's approval. In the meantime, he forged ahead with preparations. First, he had to attend to the unpleasant duty of delivering Baldwin's personal letters and other effects to Baldwin's widow. Then he turned to finding a junior officer to replace the insubordinate Biddle, who had been quietly transferred to Colonel Atkinson's command. The man he chose was Captain John R. Bell, an instructor of tactics at West Point Military Academy. Long also required a single individual to replace the two scientists no longer with the expedition. He made an excellent choice in his selection of Dr. Edwin James of Vermont. Although just twenty-two years of age, James had studied medicine and had published papers in both geology and botany. He not only filled the roles of surgeon, geologist, and botanist, he would eventually assume the role of lead author and editor of the official account of the expedition.[19]

At last, in early March, Long received his new orders from Calhoun. He was to return to Council Bluffs by way of St. Louis and the Missouri River. After sending the *Western Engineer* back down the Missouri for repairs and purchasing horses for the expedition's further travels, he was to proceed up the Platte River to its source in the Rocky Mountains, then explore southward to the Arkansas River. From that point the expedition would split up, with one party continuing southward to the Red River. The two separate parties would then head eastward across the southern plains, descending the Arkansas and Red rivers respectively, rejoining on the Mississippi.[20] Calhoun did not need to remind Long of the geographical significance of the Arkansas and Red rivers. Each formed a section of the transcontinental boundary between the United States and New Spain under the terms of the Adams-Onís Treaty signed in February 1819. Besides compiling topographical and scientific data about the West, the expedition would be surveying the new territorial limits of the United States.[21]

To the Rocky Mountains

❋ 26 ❋ Long's expedition of 1820 shared important features with the Lewis and Clark expedition of 1804–6. Fundamentally, both expeditions were aimed at strengthening the young Republic's claim to territory in the Far West. In each case, the explorers were expected to make important geographical discoveries. For Lewis and Clark, the principal objective was to find a useable water route across the continent to the Pacific Ocean. For Long, the main objectives were to trace the course of the Platte, Arkansas, and Red rivers across the central plains and, if possible, to find the source of each river. Lewis and Clark focused on the Missouri and Columbia rivers, the greatest rivers on either side of the Rocky Mountains, while Long's explorations focused on the next three largest rivers draining the eastern slope of the Rocky Mountains. Since rivers formed the principal corridors of travel and commerce across continents in the early nineteenth century, they were vital to sovereign claims of territory under the doctrine of discovery.

This doctrine, recognized by European states for hundreds of years and embraced by the United States as well, held that the discovery of territory by one Christian state before any other state had knowledge of it gave that state a sovereign claim to the territory. Included in this claim were all the indigenous, non-Christian, non-European peoples who inhabited the area. The doctrine was another aspect of that Eurocentric worldview that divided all of humanity into civilized and savage peoples, and it posited that indigenous peoples, being in a "savage state," had no comparable sovereign interests of their own.[1] It provided a rationale for European colonization of the rest of the world and a system for managing imperial rivalries. While the Lewis and Clark expedition was aimed at preempting a potential British claim to the Pacific Northwest, Long's expedition of 1820 aimed to challenge the Spanish claim to the Southwest. Long himself would urge that the United States lay claim to as much of the Rocky Mountains as possible.[2]

Another strong parallel between the two expeditions was their commitment to scientific as well as geographical discovery. President Jefferson's instructions to Lewis were famously expansive, requesting that the expedition collect information on soils, minerals, climate, plants, animals, and much more.[3] "Taken altogether," historian Stephen E. Ambrose has written, "the instructions represented a culmination and a triumph of the American Enlightenment." Although Lewis was not a scientist, Jefferson found him a good observer of natural phenomena, and the president saw to it that he received considerable scientific preparation, mostly under his own tutelage, before setting out.[4] Clark, the expedition's second in command, had less formal education than Lewis, but he too was a keen scientific observer. As the more skilled cartographer of the two, Clark made many significant contributions to the expedition's study of Indian tribes and its recording of new animal species, among other things.[5]

Long's expedition and the Lewis and Clark expedition also took similar account of the fur trade and Indians. Jefferson, like Calhoun, perceived a long-term threat to US interests if Britain achieved control of the fur trade and thereby secured a dominant influence over the western Indian tribes. Early in the planning of the Lewis and Clark expedition, Jefferson wrote to Lewis: "The commerce which may be carried on with the people inhabiting the line you will pursue, renders a knolege [sic] of these people important." And in his final instructions: "You will readily conceive the importance of an early and friendly intimate acquaintance with the tribes that inhabit the country." As diplomats, Lewis and Clark were to convey to the Indians that the United States was a rising power and a worthy supplier of trade articles for them.[6] With a view to giving American citizens a stronger entry into the fur trade, Lewis and Clark were instructed to learn the names of the various tribes and their numbers, the extent of their possessions, their relations with other tribes, their languages and customs, their means of subsistence and material conditions, and most pointedly, "articles of commerce they may need or furnish, & to what extent."[7]

The avid pursuit of both scientific knowledge and cross-cultural understanding that Jefferson envisioned for the Lewis and Clark expedition set a standard for subsequent army exploration of the West for decades to come. Long's primary contribution as an army explorer was his almost single-handed effort to renew the government's commitment to scientific exploration in the era following the War of 1812. In the words of his biographers, Nichols and Halley, "Long hoped to rekindle the spark of curiosity" embodied in Jefferson's instructions to Lewis and Clark.[8]

Long's feelings of kinship with the Lewis and Clark expedition were not just intellectual but personal. Although Long never met Lewis, he considered Clark to be a mentor. When Long reached St. Louis on his way to Council Bluffs in the late spring of 1820, he took Dr. James and Captain

Bell to meet the venerable explorer. Clark, then in his last year as governor of the Missouri Territory, was fifty years old. The young and impressionable Captain Bell described their meeting, and in his eager recitation there is a glimmer of the emotional bond between Long and Clark: "The Govr who is very sociable and pleasing in his manners, shew us the rifle, powder horn, bullet pouch, hunter knife etc—which he carried on his tour with Capt. Lewis from this place to the Pacific ocean. . . . I looked upon them with more veneration, than any other of his curiosities—because I was about commencing such a journey. . . . He conversed freely with the Major of the incidents of his tour, and particularly described the manner of constructing and managing a skin canoe of buffalo hide."[9]

Long's expedition to the Rockies never acquired the fame of the Lewis and Clark expedition. It lacked the epic sweep of Lewis and Clark's journey across the continent and back. More importantly, the members of the 1820 expedition came back with an overall negative assessment of the country they explored, announcing that the plains were parched, barren, and impossible to farm. Long is most often remembered in history as the explorer who described the western plains as the "Great American Desert." He inscribed this unfortunate misnomer boldly across the map of the western territories he produced in 1822, and it has stuck to his reputation like tar. The truth of the matter is more complex. Long based that negative characterization of the region on his assessment that its arid climate and dearth of timber would be an obstacle to the westward advance of agricultural settlement. "I do not hesitate in giving the opinion," Long wrote after the expedition, "that it is almost wholly unfit for cultivation, and of course uninhabitable by a people depending upon agriculture for their subsistence." Since American farmers would not experiment with irrigated or dry farming methods until several decades later, it was not an unreasonable assessment at the time. So, criticism of Long for describing the southern Great Plains as a "Great American Desert" did not emerge until many years after his lifetime.[10]

Historians have rightly pointed out the 1820 expedition's many other shortcomings. In the first place, Long did not find the source of the Arkansas River. This was a significant omission, since the Adams-Onís Treaty defined the border between US and Spanish territory as running along the south bank of the Arkansas to its source. To trace the river all the way to its source would have required the expedition to penetrate the Rocky Mountains more than a hundred miles, and Long decided there was not enough time for that. (Calhoun's instructions allowed him that discretion, calling for him to find the source or explore to the West as far as he could "with safety.") The expedition's second major shortcoming occurred on the homeward journey. After dividing the expedition into two parties and putting Bell in charge of the party that was to follow the Arkansas down to Fort Smith, Long headed on to find the source of the Red River of the South. What he thought was the Red turned out to be the Canadian, a fork of the Arkansas. The Red River lay farther to the south. By the time he realized his mistake, they were low on provisions and there was no time to look for the elusive stream. Long pushed the expedition along at a furious pace even as his men grew weak from hunger.

In some respects, the expedition fell short in its scientific objectives. To hold down expenses, Calhoun gave Long just four months to explore the central plains. This prevented the scientists from making more than cursory observations over much of the territory they covered. Adding insult to injury, the scientists in Bell's detachment lost their journals and scientific notes when three soldiers in the escort deserted and mistakenly made off with the scientists' packhorses instead of other packhorses that might have been more useful to them. Long offered a reward for the lost journals, but they were never recovered.[11]

Historians have pointed out in Long's defense that he completed the expedition under very trying circumstances. Funds that were promised him by the War Department failed to reach him in time, which forced the expedition to take off from Council Bluffs late in the season and short of provisions. Some members of the Otoe tribe who were present at the departure remarked that the party was too small (the soldier escort was a fraction of what Long requested) and grimly predicted that the major and his men would be wiped out by hostile Indians before they reached the mountains.[12]

Long responded to these challenges with courage and ingenuity. To defend against night attack, he had the men regularly pitch the expedition's three tents in a line, all facing the same direction, with the baggage placed in heaps to the left and right of each of the tent entrances to serve as breastworks. Occasionally, "to test the coolness and self-possession of the party," he ordered the sentinel to sound the alarm in the night, waking the men from a dead sleep, whereupon they scrambled to take up their weapons and positions. And to thwart predawn attacks, he had everyone rise long before sunrise each day so they were on the march by five o'clock in the morning.[13]

As for provisions, the men started out with a light supply of sea biscuit and parched maize, which they expected to supplement with game. Long paid close attention to rationing, having learned from his experience on the upper Mississippi. First the sea biscuit was distributed, starting with three shares per day to each man, then two, then one; then one for two days; and at last one for three days, until the stock was exhausted. Then they resorted to the parched maize, beginning with one pint per day for four men and slowly cutting back according to a similar formula. The officers and scientists always received the same quantities as the soldiers and interpreters. Meat was never as plentiful as had been anticipated, and on their return trip they endured terrible hunger.[14]

They suffered most from heat and thirst. Due to their belated start in late spring, they had to traverse the southern plains on their homeward march in August. By that month, the Arkansas River flowed below ground and all that was left in the riverbed was an occasional stagnant, fetid waterhole. Marching mostly down the dry bed of the river, they saw no running water except for a trickle here and there following a thunderstorm. As daytime temperatures soared to 100 degrees Fahrenheit, they halted each midday, desperately seeking out even the smallest shade tree for relief from the scorching sun. When none was to be found, they pitched their one remaining tent. Because the tent did not afford everyone complete shade, they resorted to lying in a circle with their heads together and their legs protruding out in every direction into the hot sunshine.[15]

In spite of these trying conditions, the scientific members of the 1820 expedition compiled some of the fullest descriptions of Indian tribes produced in the early decades of the nineteenth century. Thomas Say, Titian Peale, and Samuel Seymour visited with the Otoes, Missouris, Ioways, Kansas, Pawnees, and Omahas near Council Bluffs during the winter of 1819–20 and made the first significant studies of those tribes. Although the scientists had much less time for ethnographic investigations as they made their way to the Rocky Mountains and back, Long did allow visits of a day or two at some Indian encampments en route, and on more than one occasion the expedition traveled with or alongside hunting parties, giving the scientists an opportunity to observe the tribesmen on the move. As these observations were subsequently published and widely disseminated, the ethnographic studies should be reckoned as one of the expedition's most valuable contributions.[16]

Long set down his own observations on Indians in a handwritten report of 109 pages entitled "Report of the Western River Expedition." Directed to the War Department and the army, the section of the report entitled "Indians" was an unvarnished, hard-headed, mostly negative appraisal. It was not ethnographic description so much as a distillation of his overall impressions. In this piece, there was a strain of contempt toward Indians that was not present in his earlier writings. It betokened a change of attitude, a rising racial prejudice. Where the racial prejudice came from cannot be known. It may have arisen as a result of his actual experiences with Indians, and the uncomfortableness of encountering strange cultures; or, from time spent in the western territory, with its surfeit of Indian haters whose attitudes rubbed off on others; or, from longer-held values connected to his religious up-bringing, now brought into sharper relief by his Christian marriage. Perhaps it was some of each. What is clear is that he was not alone in experiencing a change of attitude. Sadly, in the coming decade a wide swath of the American people would join him in turning to a more racist and pessimistic view of the western tribes and their likely future.

Long began his remarks in his 1820 report by noting how hard it was to obtain accurate knowledge of Indian cultures without actually living among the Indians. Based on his own experience in talking with Indians, he was skeptical about the "delicate trains of thought and reflections" sometimes attributed to them by other writers. Indians, he said, generally spoke only of immediate concerns, whereas "in regard to matters of an abstract or meta-physical nature their ideas appear to be very limited." Most Indians believed in a Supreme Being whom they referred to as the "Master of Life" or "Great Spirit." But when asked to describe the Creator's attributes, they could only express "vague and confused" ideas. They had some general notion of the immortality of the soul, but they had no conception of Heaven or Hell. Indeed, they were much more concerned with supernatural powers in the here and now. They were highly superstitious and believed in magic. He discussed the role of the "crier," a holy man who would go through the vil-lage exhorting his followers. The holy man's claim to "medicine" amounted to nothing more than magic tricks, yet it formed the whole foundation of his influence.[17]

The Indians were almost universally "addicted to habits of extreme indo-lence," Long continued. Little besides hunting, war, and recreation stirred them to action. The white man's way of life, with its emphasis on work, a private home, and accumulation of personal property, held almost no appeal for them. Yet they were hardly free from want, either, for living by the hunt they could never be sure of their food supply. Not only was their subsistence "precarious," they lived in constant dread of attack from enemy tribes. These elemental concerns produced in their minds a highly developed sense of intrigue, cunning, and artifice, and a conviction that ends always justify the means. They used their stratagems, Long wrote, "not just in warfare but in the management of domestic concerns." As a result, the life of the tribe was fraught with rivalries, factions, and the rise of pretenders.[18]

Long's remarks on the Indians' character paralleled those of many of his fellow officers. Although army officers tended to attribute to the Indians such unflattering qualities as indolence, superstition, treachery, and brutality, they were not racist in the sense of believing in immutable, racial differences between Indian and white man. Rather, they tended to assume that the Indians' "savage" nature stemmed from environmental factors. Indian cultures were what they were because Indian peoples had lived so long in primitive isolation under harsh conditions. These historical circumstances placed them far down the scale among the world's civilized and savage peoples.[19]

One of the most common observations that military men made about Indians was that they were vengeful. Long agreed with that assessment. "Their reluctance to forgive an injury is proverbial," he wrote. "Injuries are revenged by the injured, and blood for blood is always demanded if the deceased had friends who dare to retaliate upon the destroyer." Long heard of instances where the revenge had become hereditary and quarrels were finally settled after the original parties to the quarrel were long dead.[20]

He closed his remarks by saying that the great variety of western tribes should not distract from their essential sameness. There were certain traits and characteristics common to all. The western Indians were a "race of barbarians."[21]

Long's commentary added to the army's internal discourse about Indians, but it did not reach beyond that to the general public. What it reveals is that Long's personal attitudes toward Indians had turned quite negative, even by the standards of his peers, and probably grew more so the longer he served in the West.[22]

Mapmaker

❊ 27 ❊ When Long returned to Washington in November 1820, he still thought of his expedition to the Rocky Mountains as only the first in a series of explorations that would come to embrace the entire region. On reporting to Calhoun, he immediately offered suggestions as to what they might undertake in the coming year.[1] But his great reconnaissance of the West was not to be. Nearly two and a half years would elapse before Long set out on his next and last expedition in May 1823. This was the journey that would take him to Rainy Lake House and his encounter with John Tanner.

There were two reasons why his ambitious plan of exploration never unfolded as he envisioned. The first was political. Long's explorations piggybacked on the expansionist impulse that drove US diplomatic and military policy following the War of 1812. About the same time that Calhoun announced plans for the army to build fortifications on the upper Missouri, the United States and Britain resolved a number of issues left hanging after the Treaty of Ghent, the foremost of which was the boundary between US and British territory from the Great Lakes to the Continental Divide. In an instrument known as the Convention of 1818, this boundary was demarcated by the forty-ninth parallel. Adjusting the frontier to conform to this latitude, Britain ceded to the United States the southernmost reach of the Hudson Bay watershed, that being the upper Red River valley in what is now Minnesota and North Dakota, while the United States ceded to Britain the northern tip of the Louisiana Purchase, it being the northern edge of the Milk River valley in present-day Alberta and Saskatchewan. One year later, the Adams-Onís Treaty settled the boundary between the United States and Spanish territory in the Southwest. After the two treaties were concluded, the United States had less need to buttress its territorial claims by right of discovery. It also had less need for extensive military fortifications to protect its western frontier. When the nation's economy slumped in 1819 and Congress looked for ways to reduce government expenditures, the War Department presented an obvious target. All through 1820 and 1821, Calhoun tussled with Congress over how to reduce the size of the army. Thus, Long's ambitious plan for army exploration of the West fizzled.[2]

The second reason is to be found in Long's personal life. On his return to Philadelphia at the end of 1820, he found that he was now a father as well as a husband. Martha gave birth to their first child on October 11 while he was at Cape Girardeau on the Mississippi River. By the following summer, she was pregnant with their second child, who was born in February 1822. Family life was rewarding for Long, but it also brought him no small amount of anxiety, as Martha and the children were often sick. Martha was sometimes confined to her bed for weeks. Her health was always precarious, never more so than in late summer and early fall when yellow fever stalked the city.[3]

Long suffered a protracted illness himself that put him out of commission through much of the first year after his expedition to the Rocky Mountains. He had no doubt that he had contracted the illness in the West. The onset of the illness occurred as the expedition was preparing to disband at Cape Girardeau. While the rest of the party waited there, lacking funds to complete the journey home, Long rode a horse to St. Genevieve, half the distance from Cape Girardeau to St. Louis, in order to visit the Bank of Missouri and negotiate the US Treasury note that was supposed to have reached him at St. Louis the previous May. At St. Genevieve he fell violently ill. Although he soon recovered enough strength to travel, he had recurring bouts of fever and vomiting over the next twelve months. His physician in Philadelphia eventually diagnosed the illness as an infection of the liver.[4]

Through 1821, he struggled between the demands of his work and the need to tend to his health. Convalescing at home, he thought he was sufficiently recovered in the spring to make a brief visit to Washington. But as soon as he was back home he relapsed. His physician prescribed bed rest, and when that failed to cure him, a course of mercury. The latter treatment was a strong purgative aimed at flushing excess bile out of his body. The chemical acted on him so powerfully that he was soon limited to a diet of skim milk and tea. After three weeks of this drastic regimen, he became emaciated, his normally spare frame "reduced to a skeleton." He was so weak and dehydrated that he could barely talk above a whisper. The doctor assured him, however, that the purgative had removed the cause of his disorder and he would now begin to recover. By October he was shuffling about on his feet but still thin and weak. A persistent pain in his right side prevented him from riding horseback. At the end of the year he described his health as "tolerably good though not perfectly re-established."[5]

Throughout his prolonged illness Long's arrangement with the War Department amounted to a mix of light duty and paid sick leave—a de facto healthcare benefit when no such thing existed officially. If ever there was a time when Long was thankful for the relative job security he had found with the army, this was it. Upon returning to Washington in November 1820, he received orders from Calhoun to go to Philadelphia and prepare his report of the expedition; thus, he continued to work under special orders from the secretary of war, answering to no army officer other than his friend Isaac Roberdeau, who was now chief of the Topographical Engineers. For the next year, he worked mostly at home. Although he finished the report in February, the map project dragged on. At least twice he apprised Calhoun that due to illness he was behind in his work. But he never requested any relief from his duties and continued to draw his officer's pay throughout the period of his convalescence. This was in contrast to the two junior officers assigned to the expedition, Lieutenants William H. Swift and James Duncan Graham, both of whom became ill also and requested sick leave. In June 1821, Swift asked for a three-month furlough for the sake of his health, which had been "considerably impaired in consequence of his exposure in an unhealthy country," and the following month Graham requested sick leave through the end of the year, likewise on account of illness incurred as a result of the expedition.[6] When Long gave an account of his life many years later to a biographer, he frankly admitted that his illness "rendered him unfit for service for nearly an entire year."[7] But at the time of the illness he made no such admission.

In the summer of 1821, Long considered applying for an assistant professorship at the military academy at West Point, a move he would not have countenanced had he been firmly committed to completing his reconnaissance of the West.[8] In an unguarded moment, he confided to Roberdeau that he had begun to fear that four years of exploring the West had permanently broken his health.[9]

So, understandably, Long put concerns for his family's financial security and his own health ahead of his ambition to continue the great work he had begun. The choice was not only a personal disappointment but awkward for him as well, since it was only by virtue of his special orders from Calhoun that he was able to get by with such light duty on an officer's pay for so many months following the expedition.

Not that his work life was free of pressures. Soon after he was home in Philadelphia, a letter from the War Department brought the request that he provide a recapitulation of the several orders he had received over the past year, a source of his authorization for employing scientists on the expedition, and a detailed accounting for expenses. Long duly provided an accounting down to the last half-penny. Total costs incurred through January 1, 1821, amounted to $19,778.67½. He collected affidavits from military personnel to address the question of per diem expenditures. As for his authorization to employ scientists, he informed the War Department that the authority had never been put in writing but had come from none other than the secretary of war. If this verbal authorization had come from anyone else, he stated, he would feel "alarmed" that the War Department was now requiring him to identify the source.[10] Long's statements did not satisfy the clerks at the War Department, who kept after him with more niggling questions all through the year.

As Long's health improved in the fall of 1821, he focused his energies on bringing out a popular account of the expedition. Preparation of the manuscript was to be a collaborative effort by the leading civilian members of the expedition, Thomas Say, Samuel Seymour, and Edwin James, while publication of the book was to be placed in the hands of Philadelphia's leading publisher, Henry Carey. Calhoun committed the War Department to this project to the extent of paying per diem wages for the three gentlemen's efforts, providing them office space, and subscribing to a dozen copies of the book. In November 1821, Calhoun instructed Long to have the quartermaster in Philadelphia supply him with a room and heating fuel for the coming winter so the men would have a place to meet and work. In due time, Long appeared in the Philadelphia city directory as "Stephen H. Long, U.S. Major Artillery" (this was in error, as he was with the Engineers) with an office at 240 Filbert Street.[11]

By the beginning of 1822, he had reassembled the three civilian members of the expedition. James took the lead in writing the narrative while Say worked up his notes on natural history and ethnography and Seymour developed illustrations from his many sketches. Long's role was mainly administrative, as he saw the project through a series of difficulties with the publisher. When *Account of an Expedition from Pittsburgh to the Rocky Mountains* finally appeared in 1823, James was credited as the compiler while Long's name was included as commander of the expedition.[12]

In addition to overseeing this publication, Long launched into his own cartographic project. He wanted to make the most accurate map of the United States to date based on latitudes and longitudes established by astronomical survey. Using a scale of ten miles to one inch, it would measure fifteen feet by thirteen feet. He envisioned it mounting on the wall of the secretary of war's office or Roberdeau's office when completed.[13] To get started, he built a fifteen-foot-square drawing table, together with a giant "beam compass" with a thirty-three-foot adjustable arm. Sweeping this beam across the full length of the room and over his tabletop, he etched a series of concentric curving lines on his blank canvas to mark the twenty-five degrees of latitude from Maine to Florida. Then, with notebooks, measurements, and drawing utensils, he set to work mapping the nation's coasts, rivers, and cities. Crawling back and forth over the giant tabletop, working on hands and knees, he labored hour after hour, sometimes day after day. He worked on "the big map" intermittently through the winter and spring of 1822. He was still working on it one year later when he left Philadelphia on his last expedition.[14]

Long produced a smaller map of the western territories during this time as well. In preparing this map the matter of the western boundary with Spanish territory soon arose. Having failed to locate the source of the Arkansas River on his expedition, Long was uncertain where to mark the western boundary line through the Rocky Mountains. He finally resolved the issue by taking the map only as far westward as the Front Range of the Rocky Mountains. He depicted the Spanish boundary as running along the Red and Arkansas rivers and exiting the western edge of the map short of the river's source. This was the map on which Long wrote the words "Great Desert." The Philadelphia publishing house of Carey and Lea made an engraving of it and printed the map in its American atlas of 1822.[15]

During his correspondence with Roberdeau over the Spanish boundary question, Long emphasized that he was only offering a technical opinion as to where the boundary might lie. As a matter of policy he thought the United States should aim to have as much of the Rocky Mountains as possible. The mountainous terrain was valuable "on account of the fur it is calculated to yield," he wrote. The fur trappers who operated out of St. Louis normally passed over the arid plains and went straight to the mountain streams, where they found beaver aplenty. The Great Plains had marginal value; the Rocky Mountains were the grand prize. As in earlier pronouncements, Long expressed strongly nationalist and expansionist views.[16]

Even as the Long family struggled through illnesses in 1821 and 1822, it prospered financially. As a brevet major, Long's annual income climbed to $1,625. And being stationed in Philadelphia, he was able to develop other sources of income to augment his officer's pay, not an uncommon practice in that era. He and Martha moved into a country residence on the outskirts of Philadelphia, where he was able to enjoy the role of gentleman farmer, growing small crops of buckwheat and potatoes for market, riding to and from town on his wagon, and doing commerce with a sea captain who regularly docked his schooner on the Delaware River a few blocks from Long's office on Filbert Street. Long proudly showed off his miniature country estate to one of the two top generals in the army as the general came through Philadelphia in September 1822.[17]

Long's household at that time included not just the major and his wife and their toddler and infant sons but also an unnamed cook and another servant whom Long referred to as "the black boy." While nothing is known about the cook, the servant was soon to accompany the explorer on his last expedition, so he must have been a grown boy or young man when he joined the Long household in 1821 or 1822. This person was an indentured servant, not a slave, though the distinction was a fine one under Pennsylvania law.[18]

In March 1823, Long was asked by General Alexander Macomb, chief of engineers, if he was "agreeable" to leading another exploring expedition, one that would focus on the territory lying to the west of Lake Superior. Long accepted the assignment, but this time he felt no elation. Instead, he admitted to feelings of ambivalence, informing General Macomb that he was "extremely anxious" to provide for the "reasonable provision and protection" of his rising family. Nonetheless, he would answer the call of duty.[19]

Long made swift and even somewhat improvised preparations. On this expedition there would be no steamboat; the party would travel mostly by horseback or canoe and would procure supplies at the western forts as it proceeded. Long's minimal technical equipment consisted of a patent lever watch, a surveyor compass, a plotting instrument, and a small box sextant. As in his previous exploration, he planned to find scientists and a painter to accompany the expedition, but this time he would have just one assistant officer. Long would hire guides and interpreters along the way, and the small party would pick up a soldier escort at Fort Crawford. He estimated the costs for this expedition at $2,000, one-tenth the cost of his previous expedition. He based this figure on the expectation that the journey would be completed in just eight months. By necessity, they would be traveling light.[20]

Long invited three members of the 1820 expedition, Thomas Say, Samuel Seymour, and Edwin James, to join him again. All three enthusiastically agreed. However, since James was in Albany, New York, that spring, he and Long had to make arrangements by long-distance correspondence and time ran out before they were able to fix on a point where James would join the expedition en route. Recognizing that James's participation was problematic, Long recruited another scientist, William H. Keating, to serve as James's backup. When the half-formed plan for James to join the party did indeed fail, Keating became the expedition's literary journalist in his place. Keating was just twenty-three years old in the spring of 1823 but he possessed an exceptional education, having studied geology and mining in France, Savoy, Germany, Switzerland, Holland, Scotland, and England. Since returning to the United States in 1820, he had written a book on American mines and mining and had joined the science faculty at the University of Pennsylvania.[21]

Long named Lieutenant Andrew Talcott, a veteran traveler on the upper

Mississippi, to be his second in command. But at the last minute the War Department gave Talcott different orders and substituted James Colhoun, a midshipman in the navy and cousin of the secretary of war. Colhoun (he spelled his name with an "o") would capably serve as astronomer and assistant topographer.[22]

Long's final instructions from the secretary of war were to journey to the Red River of the North; make a general topographical description of the route; ascertain latitudes and longitudes of all major points of interest; compile a scientific record of the animals, plants, soils, and minerals; and inquire into the customs of the Indian tribes inhabiting the country. Starting in Pennsylvania, the route to the northwest would largely be overland through northern Ohio, Indiana, and Illinois, then up the Mississippi and St. Peters (Minnesota) rivers to the Height of Land at the head of the northward flowing Red River. It would then follow the Red River (the modern state line between Minnesota and North Dakota) to the point where it struck the forty-ninth parallel. From there, the expedition would turn eastward, follow the international boundary to Lake Superior, and return by way of the Great Lakes to Pennsylvania.[23]

Secretary Calhoun's instructions to Long reflected a keen desire on the part of nationalists to advance US interests in the fur trade in the northern borderlands. Two important developments in 1821 and 1822, one in British America and the other in the United States, altered the terms of the Anglo-American rivalry in the fur trade. Ultimately, the developments on either side of the international boundary strengthened the hand of each government in dealing with Indian tribes. They marked a turning point in white-Indian relations that would come to affect Long's political outlook and reshape the lives of both John McLoughlin and John Tanner.

American nationalists like Calhoun and Long followed events north of the border with interest. When the Hudson's Bay Company and the North West Company merged into one, the reorganized Hudson's Bay Company emerged as one of the greatest companies in North America. It had a board of directors sitting in London and far-flung field operations extending from the Great Lakes to the Pacific Ocean and from the American borderlands to the Arctic. The merger ended a destructive competition and placed British interests in the North American fur trade on a much stronger footing. The British government had, in fact, insisted on the merger as a defense against US expansionism.[24]

Meanwhile, in the United States, Congress finally abolished the government-run trading houses, or factory system, by an act of May 6, 1822. Though the factory system had always struggled, it had been at the heart of US Indian policy since the mid-1790s. The end of the unpopular system paved the way for John Jacob Astor's American Fur Company to expand operations throughout the Old Northwest, including today's Wisconsin and Minnesota, a region where the two large British fur companies, US factories, and small American trading outfits formerly competed. With a controlled monopoly established in Canada and a competitive marketplace unfettered in the United States, the fur trade in each country entered a new phase. Both the United States and Britain put their internal affairs in order so that they could face off against each other along the forty-ninth parallel in the midcontinent and in the Far West.

Calhoun and other US officials were especially interested to know where the forty-ninth parallel lay in relation to the British settlements in the Red River valley. They wanted a better understanding of the potential for agriculture there, since the Hudson's Bay Company and the North West Company, in their fierce competition over the area, had produced conflicting reports on the matter.[25]

Along with his instructions from Calhoun, Long carried a letter signed by Britain's envoy to the United States addressed to officers of the Hudson's Bay Company. In the event that Long entered British territory and visited any Hudson's Bay Company post, the letter gave assurances that the British government looked with favor on the expedition, and it called on the company's officers to render whatever assistance Long might request.[26]

On April 30, 1823, Long set out on his last scientific exploration, accompanied by Say, Seymour, and Keating, and his black servant. The men rode out of the city of Philadelphia in two light carriages, aiming to go as far as Wheeling, Virginia, at the western terminus of the National Road, before continuing the journey on horseback.[27]

The Northern Expedition

✳ 28 ✳ Stephen Long's observations of the fur trade in 1823 began at Fort Wayne, Indiana. There, the party halted for three days to inquire into the manners and customs of the local Indian tribes. A village had grown up in the shelter of the square palisade fort, which had long since ceased to hold any troops but now served as the residence of a US Indian agent. The village population consisted mostly of Indians and French Canadians engaged in the fur trade. The explorers were surprised to pass so suddenly from the American settlements in Ohio to this predominantly French-speaking community in neighboring Indiana. Most of the French Canadians appeared to be part Indian, and what with the numerous Indian languages they spoke, the place was a veritable Babel. It was as if the explorers had entered a foreign country even though they were still within the United States.

The Fort Wayne community impressed them much the way Prairie du Chien had affected Long six years earlier. Just as Long had found the mixed-race people of Prairie du Chien in a state of "degeneracy," Keating, the expedition's journalist, described the inhabitants of Fort Wayne as being in a "degraded condition."

Keating noted with particular disgust the sight of a French Canadian dressed in breechcloth and blanket stooping to weigh the hides that he and his Indian partner had brought to the trader. The French Canadian was an engagé, an employee of the fur-trade outfit, whose role was to accompany Indians on their summer hunts and provide them with equipment, while making sure they did not betray the outfitter by taking their peltries to another trading house somewhere else. What Keating found offensive about this scene was that the "little Canadian" kept making vain attempts to adjust his breechcloth so that it would properly cover his private anatomy as he maneuvered his bundle of hides onto the trading-house scales. The Indian hunter who accompanied this man stood "in an erect and commanding posture" off to one side, while a number of Indian women and children who were looking on snickered over the French Canadian's difficulty with his native garb. For Keating, Long, Say, and Seymour, the sight of numerous

French Canadians walking around Fort Wayne, Indiana, in Indian dress just seemed wrong. There was no place for that kind of cultural crossover in American society, not even on the frontier. It was, Keating wrote, as ridiculous and disgusting as "the Indian who assumes the tight body coat of the white men."[1]

The explorers' response to seeing white men in breechcloths reflected a hardening of American attitudes toward Indian culture that began in the 1820s. Essentially the explorers were troubled because they saw the white men's use of Indian clothing as a sign of cultural degeneracy. They were unable to perceive this example of cultural exchange in neutral terms but judged it by the moral standards of savagery and civilization. Since "civilized" ways were superior to "savage" ways, they condemned what they saw. Logically, the mirror image of the Indian in ill-fitting white man's clothes that Keating conjured up by way of comparison should have been a positive rather than a negative image; the fact that he found both images "ridiculous" and "disgusting" was telling. He felt shame for the white man in a breechcloth and mistrust toward the Indian in a waistcoat. Writ large, this was the emotional foundation for a policy of apartheid. As more Americans came to believe that the two races should be kept apart, it led in a few short years to broad public support for "Indian removal," or government-directed expulsion of all Indian peoples from areas settled by whites to an "Indian territory" lying west of the Mississippi River.

Not that Long or the other explorers were themselves advocates of Indian removal at this time. Long still supported the program of Indian assimilation. Like many of his countrymen, however, he put less and less stock in the traders and believed that Christian missionaries must take the lead in civilizing the Indian. A few days after leaving Fort Wayne, the expedition visited a mission recently founded by the Baptist Missionary Society. The establishment consisted of a residence for the mission family, a one-room school house, and a blacksmith shop. The log buildings were set in about fifty acres of cleared land, with forty acres or so being fenced and planted with corn. The mission school served some forty to sixty Indian children, of whom fifteen were females. The plan of the mission was to instruct the children in the arts of civilization rather than attempt to bring Christianity to the Indian families at the outset. The explorers thought this was a sensible plan. To attempt to Christianize the Indians before they had been civilized would be to expect "a maturity of reasoning" far beyond what they presently had. "In his present state of wildness and ignorance," Keating wrote, "it is impossible for the Indian to appreciate the vast difference which exists between his heathen superstitions and the pure morality of the gospel." In due time, after the Indian acquired a taste for civilized life, he would recognize the superiority of the Christian faith to his own religion.[2]

Long and his companions saw the trader as an obstacle to the Indian acquiring civilized values. In contrast to the missionary's mostly charitable nature, the trader was typically avaricious. The trader only reinforced the Indians' tendencies toward cunning and artifice. The trading house itself was "one of the worst schools for morals," a sink of iniquity where the Indians got drunk and were swindled, abused, and injured. During the three days that the expedition spent at Fort Wayne, two Indians received grave tomahawk wounds to the head. The first assault was by a French Canadian engagé during a so-called drunken frolic on the night of the expedition's arrival; the second incident occurred the next morning, when an intoxicated Indian man struck his wife. In the view of the explorers, these Indians were victims of the trader who sold them liquor.

Traders were the main suppliers of liquor, but US Indian agents imported quantities as well, using it to obtain the Indians' friendship or to placate them when they begged for it. Long and his companions felt the US government could do much more to suppress the trafficking of liquor to Indians. "All Indians concur in considering intoxication as improper, and as the source of every evil," Keating wrote. On this expedition, Long refused to provide Indians with any liquor whatsoever, even if it was customary to offer small quantities as a gift. The expedition carried a supply of tobacco for that purpose instead.[3]

If Long held a jaundiced view of the trader as a corrupting influence on the Indians, he was still keen to learn how the American traders as a group were faring economically. He found the fur trade in decline from Fort Wayne to Prairie du Chien. Deer skins now made up the bulk of the product, as the valuable beaver was largely depleted. More important, the Indian populations were ravaged. Wherever the number of Indians fell, the traders faced a shortage of labor, for they relied almost entirely on Indian hunters to bring in the animal pelts. When Long reached the prairie lands in what is now western Minnesota, he encountered a different situation. There, beaver was still abundant and the supply of big game was greatly enhanced by the presence of buffalo. The region belonged to the Sioux nation, a powerful and numerous people who were still peaceably disposed to the Americans. Following the rapid withdrawal of the North West Company from the area two years earlier, an American outfit called the Columbia Fur Company had formed to take its place.[4]

Entering this new country, Long's expedition was accompanied by a military escort of one officer and a dozen enlisted men, together with two interpreters, one who spoke Sioux and the other Ojibwa. The party was also joined by an enigmatic Italian adventurer, Giacomo Beltrami, who was on a personal quest to find the source of the Mississippi River. All of these men joined the expedition at Fort Snelling, the last military installation on the upper Mississippi River, set on the high bluff overlooking the junction of the Mississippi and St. Peter's rivers. The fort occupied a site Long had surveyed in 1817. In the middle of July, the expedition started up the St. Peter's River. They traveled up this river valley in two detachments, one in canoes and the other on horseback and foot, the better to observe the surrounding country as well as scout for Indians. But they saw no Indians; the Sisseton Sioux, considered potentially troublesome and with whom Long hoped to parley, were absent from their village on a buffalo hunt. Two weeks after leaving Fort Snelling the expedition arrived at Lake Traverse, situated just north of the low continental divide between the Gulf of Mexico and Hudson Bay watersheds. It was here the Columbia Fur Company had its principal establishment.[5]

One of Long's two interpreters, Joseph Renville, was a mixed-blood Sioux, a former Nor' Wester, and a partner in the newly formed Columbia Fur Company. Renville invited Long and his companions to inspect the retired North West Company post returns. Examining the large bound ledgers of the former company, Long could see that the region lying south of the forty-ninth parallel had been highly productive in recent years. The returns included some 4,000 buffalo hides, which accounted for a fourth of the total dollar value of all furs and hides shipped out of the area. In addition, the meat of the buffalo could be made into pemmican and sold to the Hudson's Bay Company to supply that company's operations in the Far Northwest. In coming years, Renville explained, the new company hoped to expand its operations east to the headwaters of the Mississippi and west to the Mandan villages despite its rather small capital stock. Long thought the Columbia Fur Company showed good prospects for success, providing it could stay on amicable terms with the much larger American Fur Company.[6]

After meeting with the Columbia Fur Company, Long and his men visited a band of Yanktonai Sioux who were encamped nearby. The chief, Wanatan, invited them to partake in a dog feast. Long's men observed how their host treated the cooked dog carcasses with reverence, each bone being meticulously cleaned in preparation for burial. The Sioux buried the bones to show respect for the species and to encourage more dogs to come into the world. After eating copious amounts of the greasy dog stew, Long and his men watched a dance.[7]

During the dance, the expedition's artist, Samuel Seymour, took out his drawing materials and made a sketch of Wanatan. Keating later wrote of him: "We have never seen a nobler face, or a more impressive character, than that of the Dacota chief, as he stood that afternoon, in this manly and characteristic dress, contemplating a dance performed by the men of his own nation." Thankful for Wanatan's friendship, Long invited him and his people to accompany the party for the next two days as it marched from Lake Traverse to the Bois des Sioux River, the northern edge of the Sioux's hunting territory.[8]

On the morning of its departure from Lake Traverse, the party made its first buffalo sighting. A ripple of excitement passed through the whole command as Long dispatched three mounted soldiers to give chase and secure fresh meat for everyone. On the following day excitement rose again as the buffalo herd reappeared on the prairie hills all around them. This time, Wanatan offered to take some of the soldiers with him and demonstrate the use of his bow and arrow. After the hunt and another night camped with Wanatan and his band, Long and his men were once more on their own, marching north. Early the next morning they crossed the Bois des Sioux. As Wanatan had said before they separated, the Sioux never went north of this river without being prepared for war with their enemies, the Ojibwa.[9]

Entering the southern reaches of the Red River valley, the expedition encountered more and more "tree islands," or patches of forest intermingled with open prairie. Soon they sighted their first herd of elk, numbering sixty to eighty head. Long sent Colhoun and two soldiers to kill and butcher one elk from the herd while the rest of the party continued on.

Late in the afternoon, and before the party was reunited, Long and his men were riding quietly across the prairie with their eyes on some distant buffaloes when their attention was suddenly diverted by the crack of a gun and the sight of two Indian braves running their way. Soon others appeared, about a dozen tribesmen dressed for war, wearing nothing but breechcloths, each armed with bow and arrows or a gun or both. Despite what Wanatan had said, these were Sioux.

Their initial greeting was friendly, but the braves soon adopted a more belligerent tone as more men came running up. By this time, the Sioux outnumbered the Americans. They wanted Long and his men to detour and spend the night at their encampment. As an inducement, they offered that the men could sleep with their women. The offer convinced the explorers that this was a degenerate band of Sioux, for they understood from Wanatan and other informants that in general the Sioux Nation scorned the practice of sharing its women with strangers. When Long declined the offer, their leader pointed to the setting sun and then to a cottonwood grove and insisted that he and his men make camp in the nearby wood. While this conversation was taking place, other Indians were overheard talking about the expedition's horses, admiring the bigger ones, and inquiring as to which might be the best to ride. Say observed that as they did so they slyly positioned themselves so that at least two of their number surrounded each member of the party. Long presented them some tobacco, but at the earliest possible moment he mounted his horse and gave the command to march. As the expedition moved out the Indians did not oppose but followed behind on foot.[10]

A short distance farther on, about forty mounted Sioux warriors came over the horizon up ahead. The group on foot signaled them that these were white men, whereupon those on horseback approached. Long halted his men to exchange greetings with these additional warriors. But upon learning that their chief was not present, he once more set his expedition in motion. This time several of the Indians who had been following the Americans on foot ran to the front of the column and fired warning shots in the air. The Indians on horseback formed a crescent in front of the Americans' path. Outnumbered as well as surrounded, Long had no choice but to reopen the parley about where his party would camp that night. He pointed to a large wood in the distance, and after some taut back and forth he agreed that the Americans would camp there while the Indians would camp at their present location. Then, in the morning, the Americans would accompany them to their main encampment and meet their chief.

But as the men began to march they were confronted again. One of the warriors stepped in front of the lead soldier in the column and cocked his gun. This soldier immediately responded by cocking his own gun. Long spurred his horse to the head of the column and brushed past the belligerent warrior to lead his men forward himself. The Indians, observing his courage and recognizing that his men would not surrender their horses without a fight, chose to let them go.[11]

Long and his men reached the wood after dark. Placing sentinels around the camp, he had all arms examined and loaded in case of attack, and the horses staked with short ropes. Still worried about Colhoun and the two soldiers, who had gone elk hunting prior to their encounter with the warriors, he had a beacon fire built to draw them to their camp. He was greatly relieved when they arrived shortly afterwards without having stumbled into the Indian camp first. As soon as the men had cooked and eaten the fresh elk meat, they extinguished the fire. They were aware that a number of Indians had followed them to their camp and were concealed nearby. Long reckoned that if the Indians wanted to steal their horses they would attempt to do so just before dawn. Therefore, they rested the horses until midnight and then stealthily loaded up for an early departure. One Indian who had gone to sleep in their camp awoke as they were packing, saw what was happening, and trotted off, apparently with the purpose of arousing his compatriots. The men watched anxiously as this solitary figure receded across the prairie and was swallowed up in the darkness. Then all was quiet; the lone man was the last they saw of the Sioux war party.[12]

Following this encounter Long took the precaution of posting sentinels each night as they continued in a northerly direction down the Red River valley. These were bright, moonlit nights that all of the men experienced with heightened senses, straining eyes and ears to catch anything strange or threatening coming across the prairie. One night they seemed to hear voices amidst the lowing of the buffalo, another time they mistook a wolf for a man in animal hides on hands and knees. But each night passed uneventfully, and after eleven days' travel they arrived at the settlement of Pembina on the international border. On this leg of the journey, a solid march, they managed to cover an average of twenty-three miles per day, sometimes setting off so early that they walked by the light of the moon.[13]

When they arrived at Pembina they found the place nearly deserted, all but a few of the inhabitants being away on a buffalo hunt. Whole families —men, women, and children, together with horses and dogs—had been out on the prairie for forty-five days. An old man, a Mr. Nolen, ferried the expedition across the Red River and invited Long and his men to make use of his home. Nolen lived in a log cabin like most other residents of Pembina. Altogether the settlement had about sixty log cabins together with a number of tepees. Long, together with his two officers, the scientists, and Mr. Beltrami, made use of one tepee, while the enlisted men pitched their tents around it. Confident that this camp was located just south of the forty-ninth parallel, Long planted a flagstaff, hoisted the colors, and named the place Camp Monroe in honor of the president.[14]

Since a primary object of the expedition was to ascertain the location of this settlement relative to the forty-ninth parallel, Long and Colhoun lost no time in taking astronomical readings. They took two measurements, one at Mr. Nolen's house and the other at Camp Monroe, and determined that the community lay within a whisker of the international line on US territory. They marked the line with two oak posts, each bearing the initials "U.S." on one side and "G.B." on the other. Long read a proclamation, and the soldiers discharged their weapons in a national salute.[15]

Earlier that year the Hudson's Bay Company had determined the same thing using its own astronomers. Resigned that the Americans would soon take control of the area, it had closed its Pembina trading post and taken everything transportable downriver to Fort Douglas (the site of modern Winnipeg). At the same time it had persuaded the Catholic priest in Pembina to remove his mission downriver as well. Ostensibly the company acted to save its property, but its larger motivation was to encourage the population of Pembina to relocate north of the border, as it feared that these settlers, once under US jurisdiction, would all go over to the American fur-trading outfits. Some of the residents had duly followed the priest to the Red River settlements around Fort Douglas, but most of the population still remained at Pembina in the summer of 1823.[16]

On their second day in the village, Long and his men were treated to the spectacle of almost the entire population returning home en masse, joyous at the conclusion of their successful hunt. To behold such a large number of settlers in that distant and empty prairie-land came as a surprise to the explorers. They counted 115 carts loaded with dried buffalo meat, and they estimated the number of horses at 200. Twenty mounted hunters rode abreast leading the procession. The Pembina settlers, having heard in advance of the visit by the American expedition, proudly fired a salute as they passed the Americans' camp.[17]

Most of the settlers were of mixed race, descended from European fathers and Indian mothers. Later known as *Métis,* they were identified to Long as *Bois brulé* (Burnt Wood), so named for their dark complexions. Although Long and his companions were not well informed on the Métis, they recognized that they were a unique people, combining different elements from their paternal and maternal lines. Keating noted, for example, that their dress was "singular, but not deficient in beauty . . . a mixture of the European and Indian habits." Every man wore a long, blue cloak secured around the waist by a military sash, a shirt of calico or painted muslin, and leather moccasins and leggings fastened around the leg by garters that were ornamented with beads. The men were also distinct in physical appearance: their eyes were "small, black, and piercing; their hair generally long, not infrequently curled, and of the deepest black; their nose short and turned up; their mouth wide; their teeth good; their complexion of a deep olive." Even as Keating recognized the Métis as a distinct people, he could not resist commenting on what he perceived to be the ill effects of racial mixing. "The great mixture of nations, which consist of English, Scotch, French, Italians, Germans, Swiss, united with Indians of different tribes, viz. Chippewas, Crees, Dacotas, &c. has been unfavorable to the state of their morals; for, as is generally the case, they have been more prone to imitate the vices than the virtues of each stock; we can therefore ascribe to this combination of heterogeneous ingredients, but a very low rank in the scale of civilization. They are but little superior to the Indians themselves." As evidence of the Métis' cultural deficiency, the explorers noted the state of agriculture in Pembina: several households had small garden plots, but the residents did all of their gardening by hand. Not a single oxen or plow was observed. For the farm-oriented Americans, that was enough to stamp the Métis as an inferior people.[18]

From Pembina, Long expected to march due east on the forty-ninth parallel to Lake Superior. His local informants quickly talked him out of that plan. The country to the east was an impenetrable maze of lakes, rivers, and swamps. The only practical way to travel through this region was to follow its waterways. Long needed to trade the expedition's horses for canoes and make a short but necessary excursion through British territory. They would descend the Red River to Lake Winnipeg and then ascend the Winnipeg River to Lake of the Woods. At that point the route of the expedition would intercept the international line, which left the forty-ninth parallel to follow the main water route used in the fur trade up the Rainy River to Rainy Lake and beyond.[19]

Now there was a change in the composition of the expedition. The Italian, Beltrami, bought two of the expedition's horses and, with a guide, set out to find the source of the Mississippi. The officer of the escort who had joined the expedition at Fort Snelling turned back with three of the enlisted men. Long sold the remaining horses for an excellent price, purchased three canoes, and hired the services of a river pilot, nine voyageurs, and a new interpreter—one Charles Brousse. Altogether the party now numbered twenty-nine men.[20]

The canoes were of the variety known as *canot du nord* (northern canoe), a vessel thirty feet long and four feet wide at the beam. After his experiences with steamboat navigation, Long took particular interest in the northern canoe. Perfectly adapted for the needs of the fur trade for transporting people and goods on the vast interior network of rivers and lakes, it was made of large pieces of birchbark spread over a skeleton of cedar ribbing, the sections of bark sewn together with long fibrous threads derived from the root of the spruce tree, and the seams caulked with pitch to make them watertight. Each one could carry up to 3,000 pounds yet was light enough to be lifted and carried over the head by two men. This was important because the canoe had to be hauled out of the water at frequent intervals during travel, both for portaging around obstacles and for drying out the birchbark periodically. Piloting the canoe took great skill, for the bark was easily torn or punctured if it struck logs or rocks.[21]

On August 8, they set out down the Red River, entering the territory of the Hudson's Bay Company. A week later they were at the former Fort Douglas, renamed Fort Garry, where the expedition paused to resupply. Long purchased from the Hudson's Bay Company 1,000 pounds of pemmican and four bushels of wheat flour, along with vegetables, buffalo fat, and other victuals. Continuing down the Red, they entered Lake Winnipeg and followed its southern shore around to Fort Alexander, where they delayed for a day to repair the canoes. On August 20, the party started up the Winnipeg River.

As they penetrated the geologic province known as the Canadian Shield, Long was impressed by the amount of exposed bedrock and the number of falls and rapids. Both the Winnipeg River and Lake of the Woods, which they traversed on August 27 and 28, were "among the most singular and curious of Natures works in the formation of rivers and Lakes," he wrote in his journal. Everywhere, they saw shorelines of gently tilting bare rock, clear streams cascading over polished slabs, and conifer trees growing on boulders. "The country, both main and islands, is so cased and covered with rocks that no part of it appears susceptible of cultivation," Long marveled. It was hard to imagine how men could ever plow and fence such a land. He predicted that the rockbound wilderness would yield slowly, if at all, to white settlement, remaining of little use other than for sustaining the fur trade.[22]

It was on their way down the Red and up the Winnipeg rivers that Long and his men began to pick up curious pieces of information and gossip about "the American," a onetime captive of the Indians and citizen of the United States who had recently returned to the area to reclaim his two half-Indian daughters. They were told the fellow had been ambushed and gravely wounded by a young Indian man while he paddled his canoe up a rapid. When the assault happened, he was making his retreat from Indian country with his daughters and their mother. It seemed the man who attacked him was somehow in league with the girls' mother. Now the American convalesced at Rainy Lake House—a few days ahead on their journey.

❊{VI}❊ TANNER

The Coming of the Prophet

{ 29 } If there was a time in Tanner's life when he reached an apex of being Indian—when he found maximal acceptance among his adopted kin and all but gave up thoughts of returning to the white man's world—it came around the time of the Lewis and Clark expedition. In the year 1804, when Lewis and Clark set out up the Missouri River, Tanner was in his twenty-third year, hunting across the northern prairie in what is now Manitoba. Ensconced in an Indian way of life, he had set aside his ambition to return to the United States, take up the white man's ways, and leave his Indian wife and mother behind.

There came a test of his resolve in the fall of that year. On a visit to the Hudson's Bay Company's Brandon House, the British traders informed Tanner about Lewis and Clark, saying that they were encamped near the Mandan villages less than 200 miles to the south. Evidently the traders supposed that he would be tempted to go south and join his erstwhile countrymen. The information stirred a feeling of some kind in Tanner's breast, because it unsettled him for a spell. Yet he allowed the opportunity to pass.[1]

Though he was a little curious to visit the American expedition, Tanner put off going to Fort Mandan in part because he mistakenly assumed they were establishing a permanent trading post among the Mandan rather than simply wintering there. He had no conception of the expedition's purpose. His ignorance is not surprising when one considers that he lived among Indians in British territory and received his information through Hudson's Bay Company interpreters. He had little more sense of what Lewis and Clark had accomplished when the explorers passed back down the Missouri a year and a half later. Yet the Lewis and Clark expedition marked the start of a new phase of American expansionism that would change the shape of the fur trade and shake Tanner's world. No sooner had Lewis and Clark completed their expedition than American traders began advancing into the borderlands, challenging the British wherever they operated inside US territory, brewing a storm that would finally break in the War of 1812.

Meanwhile, distant thunder sounded from another source. The year that Lewis and Clark completed their journey was also the year that Indians all over the Old Northwest learned of the Shawnee Prophet, an Indian messiah who performed miracles and preached a message of native revival. The holy man called himself Tenskwatawa, the Open Door, a name that underscored a message of divine revelation. Indians, he declared, should renounce white culture and return to the old ways. If Indian peoples embraced this new religion, the Great Spirit would overturn the land and cover up the white people, restoring the Indians' world.[2]

The apocalyptic message resonated with Indians of various tribes, who felt downtrodden by white culture and threatened by land-hungry Americans in particular. While the new, pan-Indian religion was critical of virtually all European influence, the Shawnee Prophet reserved his harshest invective for the Americans. Tenskwatawa said that the British, French, and Spanish had been brought into the world by the Master of Life and were the Indians' friends, whereas the Americans were the spawn of the Great Serpent and a scourge on the land. The Master of Life had revealed to him that the Americans "grew from the scum of the great Water when it was troubled by the Evil Spirit. And the froth was driven into the Woods by a strong east wind." He preached that "they are numerous, but I hate them. They are unjust. They have taken away your lands, which were not made for them."[3]

The heavy strain of anti-Americanism in the Shawnee Prophet's pronouncements did not go unnoticed by American and British officials. As the religious movement gained in strength, the British invited Tenskwatawa to Canada. They hoped to make him a tool of their Indian diplomacy, which aimed to block US expansionism. Tenskwatawa declined the invitation, but his older brother, Tecumseh, went instead. A rising Shawnee chief, Tecumseh dreamed of establishing a sovereign Indian nation within the Great Lakes region, possibly under British protection. But Tecumseh's immediate goal was the same as Britain's: to maintain peace with the Americans.[4]

The Shawnee Prophet began to attract believers from various tribes in the winter of 1805–6. In the spring his disciples fanned out across the country to spread his message. It was probably in the summer or fall of 1806 that one of these disciples, an Ojibwa, hailed Tanner as he was out hunting on the Canadian prairie. Subsequently this disciple spent time in Tanner's village, initiating the people into the ceremony of "shaking hands with The Prophet," winning many converts to the new religion. The account Tanner gave of this episode stands as one of the most valuable historical sources on the Prophet's commandments, the secret handshake ritual, and the early spread of his religious movement.[5]

When Tanner related the episode years later, he began by saying that he first mistook the Prophet's disciple as an enemy Sioux when he approached across the prairie. Tanner's apprehension slowly turned to curiosity as the man came up and showed himself to be "strange and peculiar" in manner, avoiding his eyes while telling him by sign language to return at once to his lodge. Tanner's way of storytelling, which employed techniques he had learned from the Ottawas and Ojibwas, made frequent use of premonitions, dreams, and omens to foreshadow later developments. In this instance, his premonition that the man was a foe served to foreshadow the grave problems he would have with other holy men starting a few years later. Even at this point in his life, religion seems to have become a matter of friction for him. There are hints in Tanner's *Narrative* that religious differences with Red Sky of the Morning were an undermining factor in their marriage. What is clearer is that Tanner's growing religious skepticism eventually undermined his second marriage and finally drove him out of the tribe. Although he could not possibly have foreseen it at this juncture—when the Shawnee Prophet's peculiar messenger arrived in their midst—in hindsight Tanner must have viewed the coming of the Prophet as a major turning point in his life, one that would eventually strip him of his Indian identity.

The Prophet's disciple accompanied Tanner to his lodge and joined him in a smoke. Then, after a long silence, he began to expound on the Prophet's teachings. Indians should give up the white man's firewater. Men should never strike their wives or children. They should not steal or lie or make war on their traditional enemies. Ojibwas who practiced the new religion would be able to hunt in the Sioux lands without fear, for they would be invisible to the enemy. As a proof of their fidelity to the new religion, practitioners must kill their dogs, throw away their medicine bags, and make fire the old way by rubbing two sticks together instead of with the white man's flint and steel. When they felt ready to follow this path they should light a new fire in their lodge, which they must henceforth keep burning at all times. "You must remember that the life in your body, and the fire in your lodge, are the same, and of the same date," the messenger intoned. "If you suffer your fire to be extinguished, at that moment your life will be at its end." Although Tanner thought the man crazy, he respectfully listened to his pronouncements long into the evening. However, the next morning he could not contain himself. Rousting his guest, he pointed out that the fire had gone out while everyone slept. Get up, he told the man, and observe for yourself how many of us are alive and how many are dead! The messenger responded to his jest without emotion, saying only that Tanner would feel differently once he had had the opportunity to shake hands with the Prophet.[6]

The messenger stayed with Tanner only one night. But, proselytizing from lodge to lodge, he remained with the tribe for some time. As the weeks

went by Tanner saw the population of dogs in the village plummet. Many
Indians were killing their dogs in obedience to the new strictures. It was
the clearest sign he had that the Prophet's religion was taking hold. Apparently he did not feel comfortable discussing these matters with other members of the tribe, or they with him. Unnerved by what was happening and
feeling increasingly isolated, he went to the trading house to consult with
the whites. Did they think it possible the Creator might be revealing new
truths to this Shawnee holy man? The traders insisted that such a notion
was blasphemous and ridiculous. To think God would choose a poor Shawnee medicine man to be His prophet! Tanner was relieved when the traders
confirmed his doubts, yet the meeting left him feeling even more alienated
and alone than before. He refused to kill his own dogs, but he did not openly
challenge the new doctrine. And he did follow along to the extent of laying
aside his flint and steel and medicine bag.[7]

In time, the chiefs announced that their guest would be given an opportunity to present the Prophet's message to the whole village. A ceremonial
lodge was built for the purpose and everyone was invited to come. Upon
entering the lodge on the appointed day, Tanner saw an effigy covered by a
blanket. Two men sat guard by it, and though the object presented a curious
sight, lying in plain view in the center of the floor, no one was permitted to
approach it or turn back the blanket. The messenger then rose and made a
long speech describing the Prophet's revelations. At the conclusion of his
speech, he drew four strings of beans from under the blanket, saying that
these were made of the flesh of the Prophet. Then, selecting certain men in
the assembly, he invited each one in turn to hold the four strings of beans
at one end and gently draw them through his hand. He called this action
shaking hands with the Prophet. Only those men who had already killed
their dogs were allowed to partake in the ritual. In doing so, they pledged to
obey the Prophet's injunctions and accept his teachings as divine revelation.
Tanner was unimpressed, noting that the beans were moldy.[8]

By the time the Prophet's messenger moved on, the new religion had
acquired a considerable following. Many of the male practitioners stopped
drinking, gave up talk of war, and began treating their wives and children
with extra kindness. But when winter came and everyone felt the pinch of
hunger, Tanner reckoned those same practitioners must now have regrets
about killing their dogs. After his own dogs helped him find and kill a bear
one day, he tried to get his fellows to admit their folly. But his words met
with cold silence.[9]

The wedge created by the religious excitement must have been doubly
frustrating for Tanner, as it coincided with his coming fully into manhood.

It probably denied him a certain status he might otherwise have attained in the tribe. Now in his midtwenties, he had twice gone to war against the Sioux. He had taken an Ojibwa wife, who had by this time given him a son. He had become a skilled hunter, as evidenced by the remarkable growth of his lodge. His lodge now contained not only Red Sky of the Morning, their firstborn child, and old Net-no-kwa but also a half dozen orphan children. The adoptions were probably made on Net-no-kwa's initiative; nevertheless, they were proof that Tanner had come into his own as a principal hunter. Yet he did not get the respect that taking on so many dependents should have afforded him.[10]

About this time, the Ottawas and Ojibwas began to hunt beaver in the upper reaches of the Red River. Hunting that far south carried greater risk of attack by the Sioux, but it brought greater reward, too. Pe-shau-ba, the old Ottawa chief who had once been like a father to Tanner, was the first to attempt it. With a companion, he hunted at Otter Tail Lake and along the Pelican River in the spring of 1806, returning to Pembina with 300 beaver and 40 otter. Though the pair saw some Sioux at a distance, they managed to avoid them. The following year, Tanner went with a large party to the same area, then ventured with his family still deeper into the disputed territory. Sure enough, the beavers were plentiful, and he managed to take 100 in a single month. But Tanner's wife, mother, and adopted children lived in constant fear of attack. One night they heard rustling outside their lodge. Imagining Sioux sneaking up, they lay terror-stricken in their beds. Tanner quietly got his gun. In a low voice, he urged his family to be brave, saying their time had come and they would all die together. Then, squatting at the door of his lodge and pointing the muzzle of his gun in the direction of the foe, he slowly raised the flap. The unseen foe turned out to be nothing but a porcupine.[11]

Tanner and his family were lucky. Numerous Ojibwa and Sioux hunting parties clashed that year, and both sides suffered fatalities. Tanner supposed that one reason so many Ottawas and Ojibwas accepted the risk of hunting in that country was that they were persuaded by the Prophet to believe they were invisible to their enemies.[12]

Another reason for their southward advance was that they had depleted safer hunting grounds farther north. With more Ottawas and Ojibwas migrating west each year, competition between traders in the Red River country was peaking in the early 1800s. Beaver populations in the lower part of the watershed were decimated. Moreover, an extraordinarily wet spring and summer in 1806 caused the buffalo to move southward. That year, the fur trader Alexander Henry wrote in his journal, "I hear of nothing but famine throughout the Country."[13]

The largely Ojibwa advance on the Sioux frontier may have signaled something even more portentous than a quest for bountiful hunts. Often those areas that tribes fought over contained more abundant game precisely because they were less hunted-out than the tribe's home territory. Some Indian scholars go so far as to suggest that tribal warfare had evolved as a function of human ecology. War zones unintentionally served as game refuges. Hunted species found relative sanctuary in these areas and propagated, and the excess population of these species moved out and replenished the tribes' hunting grounds.[14] The incessant warfare between Ojibwas and Sioux was, according to these scholars' interpretation, a cultural evolution that tended to reduce overhunting and famine. If so, then the Ojibwa advance into this area is an example of how the fur trade disordered Indian peoples' relationship to their environment.[15]

Environmental stresses contributed to the overall climate of foreboding that allowed the Shawnee Prophet's teachings to make such rapid inroads among the western Ottawas and Ojibwas. Tanner saw the Indians' fear and gloom and recognized that in some way it made him vulnerable. The combined effects of famine and religious fervor caused the Indians to be more suspicious of outsiders. In spite of his many years living with them, he was still an outsider. And he had scoffed at the Prophet's teachings.

Returning to the upper Red River with another large party of Ojibwas in the spring of 1808, Tanner was not altogether surprised when one of his own party challenged his right to hunt in the area. The leader of the expedition was a chief named Ais-ainse, the Little Clam. One night the Little Clam's brother, Wa-ge-tone, entered Tanner's lodge and woke him from a sound sleep. Half-drunk and brandishing a knife, he threatened to kill Tanner if he did not give up his plan to hunt with them. "You are a stranger," he declared. "You are driven out from your own country, and you come among us because you are too feeble and worthless to have a home or a country of your own." Tanner rose from his bed and answered that his right to hunt in that place was as good as any man's. As Wa-ge-tone continued to bluster, someone else seized him from behind and muscled him outside. Afterwards, the Little Clam told Tanner to pay no attention to his brother's words. But the incident still rankled. Only once before had anyone challenged Tanner's right to hunt in a given territory. That challenge had come from an Iroquois hunter attached to the North West Company, so Tanner had disregarded it. This was different since it came from an Ojibwa—a member of his wife's tribe and an individual he could almost call a kinsman.[16]

Seldom before had anyone rejected Tanner for being a non-Indian. Following the excitement over the Shawnee Prophet, however, he began to experience it more often. Not long afterwards an Ottawa man by the name of Wah-ka-zhe counseled Tanner to go back to the whites. Wah-ka-zhe spoke from experience, for he had spent ten years in the Rocky Mountains and other places far from his own people, mostly in association with white traders and missionaries, but had finally returned to his homeland. A sympathetic old man, he advised Tanner that if he went back to the whites he could not become a trader, since he did not know how to read and write. He could not become a farmer, since he would detest the endless toil involved. However, he could likely find a good situation as an interpreter. Wah-ka-zhe did not mean anything unfriendly by his counsel, but his words surely gave Tanner food for thought.[17]

Indeed, Tanner was already pondering such a move. On one of his journeys to the new hunting grounds, he met an American trader who urged that he return with him to the States. The man informed him that one of Tanner's relations had been to Fort Mackinac in search of him. How the fellow knew this is unclear; apparently the story of Tanner's capture had spread by word of mouth and was still widely known more than a decade and a half after his disappearance. Upon reflection Tanner declined the trader's offer; but he did take the opportunity to dictate a letter to his American family, even though he thought it likely they had been wiped out long ago by his original captors. The trader, whom he trusted, told him he would do his best to get the letter delivered.[18]

After mulling over the trader's offer for about six months, Tanner finally decided to act on it. Presumably his purpose was to look for his white family as well as to test the appeal of the white man's way of life. How he felt about leaving his Indian wife and children Tanner never divulged. As it happened, he did not complete the trip. On his way to find the American trader, British traders told him the United States was at war with Great Britain. The Americans were making attacks all along the frontier, they said, and he would have difficulty getting through. One year later, Tanner tried to make the journey again, this time by way of the Great Lakes, but was turned back by similar reports received at the trading house on Lake Winnipeg. Both times the intelligence was not true; there was no war. But on each occasion Tanner aborted his trip, accepting the British traders' advice at face value.[19]

The British traders had their reasons for deceiving him. In June 1807, a British warship attacked a US frigate off Chesapeake Bay and seized four of her crew for deserting from the British navy, sparking an international incident that soon brought the two nations to the brink of war. Since British officials anticipated an American invasion of Canada in the event of war, they signaled the Indian Department to do whatever it could to shore up alliances with tribes throughout the Old Northwest. The Indian Department duly dispatched a communiqué to the traders: make sure the Indians are loyal and prepared to fight in case of attack. The traders took these instructions as carte blanche to manipulate the Indians through a campaign of misinformation. Rumors of war flew.[20]

Amidst these war scares, the excitement over the Shawnee Prophet spread like a prairie fire. In the summer of 1807, an eastern Ottawa convert and skilled orator named Le Maigouis went on a mission to the western Ottawas and Ojibwas. Threatened with arrest by the American commander at Fort Mackinac, he defiantly held his first assembly on Mackinac Island beneath the walls of the fort. From there he crossed over to Sault Ste. Marie, carrying the Prophet's message from village to village around the southern shore of Lake Superior. That year, US agents reported hundreds of western Ottawa and Ojibwa pilgrims trekking eastward to witness the Prophet's miracles. In one notable instance, the Indians carried a dead child in hopes that it could be restored to life. In the summer of 1808, a vast throng of believers gathered at Chequamegon Bay, Wisconsin, where they ceremoniously pitched their medicine bags into the lake before setting out in 150 canoes. However, when they were halfway around the lakeshore they met with disturbing news: many eastern Ottawa and Ojibwa pilgrims were returning to their villages disillusioned. This large party then turned back. In the winter of 1808–9, those Ottawas and Ojibwas who had proceeded all the way to Prophetstown in Indiana suffered an even crueler disillusionment. A coughing sickness entered the settlement and killed 160 of their number. Strangely, the outbreak took the lives of only five Shawnees. Fearing black magic, the surviving Ottawas and Ojibwas fled. When news of this disaster reached the Red River valley, the Prophet's influence ebbed.[21]

Three or four years after the "Shawano excitement" began, the Prophet's ideas were so discredited that many of Tanner's kinsmen hung their heads in shame or lied about their past involvement whenever the subject came up. However, the western Ottawas and Ojibwas remained anxious and susceptible to the idea of a coming apocalypse. In the aftermath, at least three, and quite possibly more, holy men arose from among their own people, each claiming to be a messenger of the Great Spirit. Tanner regarded them as charlatans and resisted their influence. His opposition stemmed in part from religious conviction, in part from self-preservation. Their vision of a coming apocalypse and the restoration of a world without white people could only bring him trouble.[22]

Around this time, Tanner fell out with his wife, Red Sky of the Morning. Although he avoided the subject when he gave an account of his life many

years later, there is a suggestion in the *Narrative* that the rupture had something to do with the new prophets, that their revolutionary teachings drove
a wedge into his marriage. At this point in his life, Tanner had come to embrace his tribe's traditional religion, with its focus on prayer and medicines
for invoking the Great Spirit's blessings. He addressed his prayers primarily
to Nanabozho, whom the Great Spirit long ago sent to Earth to create fur
animals, edible plants, and healing herbs for the benefit of humankind. Or
he prayed to the Earth itself, the great grandmother Nokomis, whom the
Great Spirit bid stay home in her lodge forever. In the traditional view, these
two were the primary intercessors between human beings and the Great
Spirit. Tanner felt indignation toward those who now claimed to be in direct communication with the Supreme Being. As time passed he ridiculed
the new prophets more openly, even when his contempt offended some of
the more credulous Indians around him. Once, when Tanner was bursting
with sarcasm about these pretenders, Red Sky of the Morning coldly shut
him down in front of their relatives. After that, she no longer confided her
own spiritual leanings to her husband but instead joined the conspiracy of
silence slowly forming around him.[23]

A Loathsome Man

✦ 30 ✦ In the spring of 1808, the Nor'West trader Alexander Henry left Pembina after an eight-year residence. Another Nor' Wester, Daniel McKenzie, occupied the post through the winter of 1808–9. Then, in the summer of 1809, the North West Company leadership decided to abandon the place and establish a new post at the Forks. The Nor'Wester assigned to the task was John Wills. He arrived in the year 1810 with a force of twenty men and proceeded to build a large fort where the Assiniboine River flows into the Red, the site of today's Winnipeg. This impressive installation, named Fort Gibraltar, consisted of a square palisade about fifteen feet high made from oak logs split in two, with a pair of bastions at opposite corners, and eight buildings arranged within the fort's walls. The interior buildings included a residence for the trader, two houses for the engagés, a blacksmith shop, a stable, a kitchen, and an ice house. A watchtower rose from the roof of the ice house. The Red River Indians watched with interest as Wills superintended construction and the new fort took shape. As Wills was a very large man, the Indians nicknamed him "The Sail" for his wide beam.[1]

The North West Company had two purposes in view in establishing Fort Gibraltar at the Forks. One purpose was to support the movement of Métis into the area and thereby secure the company's important provisioning trade in pemmican. Its second purpose was to prevent the Hudson's Bay Company from making a southward advance up the Red River valley. Wills aimed to oppose the trader Hugh Heney, who was lately in charge of the Hudson's Bay Company's Brandon House.

Wills returned from the Nor' Westers' rendezvous at Fort William in the fall of 1810 to find his anticipated rival absent. He assumed that the construction of Fort Gibraltar over the preceding months had convinced Heney and the Hudson's Bay Company to abandon the area. Rashly, Wills took the opportunity to drive a hard bargain with his Indian trading partners and call in some of the Indians' debt. While giving the Indians their customary "fall drink" when they gathered at his trading house before the winter, he used the occasion to announce a new limitation on credit: no material items would be provided to them until they brought in skins during the coming winter.[2]

Tanner avoided the Indians' drinking bout according to his pattern, so he missed Wills's announcement. At the onset of winter, he went to the newly occupied fort for his first encounter with the new trader. Ushered into the trader's house, he asked for woolens to clothe his family. He was taken aback when the trader refused. Tanner pleaded on behalf of his children, saying that they were hungry and ill clothed and might die without the trader's assistance. Wills rudely cut him off and told him to leave the house. Tanner then placed eight silver ornaments on the table. Having purchased these items a year before at twice the standard price of a *capote* (a hooded coat), he proposed to pawn them for a single capote. Wills could hold the ornaments as collateral until such time as he could return with the necessary skins to pay for the capote and get them back. Wills found Tanner's offer to be as impudent as it was irregular. With a sweep of his arm, he scattered the ornaments on the floor.[3]

Tanner took great offense at this treatment. When Wills's competitor, Heney, showed up in the valley after all, several weeks later than usual, Tanner decided to get back at Wills. He would broadcast to the Indians his intent to trade his skins with Heney, not Wills, at the end of the winter season. In the language of the traders, he would be going over to the opposition—breaking trust—even though he currently owed no debt to the North West Company. With that in mind, Tanner wintered on the Rat River, a tributary on the lower Red, where he took large numbers of beaver, otter, marten, and muskrat. Early in the spring, he went to the Forks and ostentatiously set up camp on the east bank of the river directly opposite Fort Gibraltar, expecting to intercept Heney as the Hudson's Bay trader made his way back northward from Pembina.[4]

Wills soon learned of Tanner's presence across the river and sent him repeated invitations to come over and trade. Twice Tanner refused, but on the third invitation a kinsman persuaded him to go. Leaving his furs behind, he took only a little tobacco as a peace offering. Wills greeted him respectfully and offered him brandy and whatever provisions he might need. Tanner had not been visiting long when some of Wills's engagés came through the door toting his packs of furs—the very same that he had intentionally left in his lodge. Not stopping or saying a word as they passed by him, they placed the packs in a back room. Tanner knew this trick. The traders at Grand Portage had attempted to take possession of Net-no-kwa's packs in just that way many years before. But he said nothing, pretending to be oblivious both to the seizure of his peltries and the surliness that suddenly came over his host as soon as they were stowed away. Calmly he waited until the engagés were out of the house. Then, when Wills stooped to get something out of a trunk,

Tanner slipped past him into the back room. The fat, old trader was too slow to stop him. Tanner gathered his packs in his arms and, staggering under the immense load, made for the front door. Wills interposed himself. In their short struggle, one of the bundles fell from Tanner's grasp, breaking apart when it hit the floor. As Tanner went to gather up the skins, Wills fetched his pistol, cocked it, and pointed it at Tanner's breast. Tanner momentarily froze, thinking he was about to be shot and killed, since the trader was so obviously frightened. But Wills only stood there, shaking. Tanner grabbed his wrist and turned the pistol aside with one hand while drawing his knife with the other. In an instant he was holding the trader at knifepoint.[5]

Wills called out to his wife and interpreter. Very soon they entered the room, together with his French Canadian engagés. Tanner held the trader hostage in the middle of the floor while Wills's allies stood back against the wall. With their numbers, the French Canadians could have overpowered him. Yet when Wills growled at the men to disarm Tanner and get him out of the house, no one made a move. At length, Wills started bargaining. He offered Tanner an even split: half the skins for the Hudson's Bay trader, half to the North West. Released from knifepoint, he began separating them into two piles.

Never in his life did Tanner find a trader more loathsome than this man. Answering him through the interpreter, Tanner reminded Wills of his refusal to provision his family at the start of winter. He informed him that he had obtained all of his ammunition on credit from Heney; therefore, all the skins would go to him. Then he excoriated Wills for being such a coward.

> You have not so much courage as a child. If you had had the heart of a squaw, you would not have pointed your pistol at my breast, and have failed to shoot me. My life was in your power, and there was nothing to prevent your taking it, not even the fear of my friends, for you know that I am a stranger here, and not one among the Indians would raise his hand to avenge my death. You might have thrown my body into the river, as you would a dog, and no one would have asked you what you had done, but you wanted the spirit to do even this.[6]

As the interpreter finished translating, Wills retreated to the company of his wife and took a seat. He looked so pale and shaken, Tanner thought he might collapse. When the fat, old man at last regained his composure, he went outside. Tanner retied his skins, loaded them on his back and took them to his canoe, saying no more to Wills as they passed in the yard.

The next day, Wills sent his interpreter over to Tanner with a peace offering: he would give him his horse if the unfortunate matter could then be forgotten. Tanner refused. Tell the man he is a child, Tanner responded, since he expects to quarrel with me one day and pretend that it never happened the next. Tell him I will keep my skins, and I will not forget how he pointed his pistol at my heart and lacked the courage to shoot me.

Wills persisted. A few days later he sent four armed men to claim Tanner's skins. The clerk in charge of this gang stated that the skins rightfully belonged to the North West Company because ten years ago Tanner's brother, Wa-me-gon-a-biew, had failed to repay a debt, and that this old debt still attached to Tanner as his close kin. To this, Tanner replied that he would pay his brother's debt if in turn the North West Company would pay him for the four packs of beaver his family had shipped to Mackinac around the same time. He referred to the promissory note that had burned up in their wigwam. The clerk ignored this and moved to take the skins by force, but as Tanner remained sitting on them he changed his mind and led the men back to the fort.

When more days went by with no sign of Heney, Tanner packed up and went down to the mouth of the Red River to do some more trapping. When Heney finally did come down the river a few days later, passing by Fort Gibraltar, Wills went after him with a canoe of armed men. Heney saw he was being pursued and landed his canoe. Telling his men to stay with the canoe and its cargo, he walked alone to a spot above the river where he could confront Wills face to face. Seeing him there, Wills landed his canoe and approached with an escort. Heney made him stop at a distance of ten paces, and the two men argued over their respective rights to the territory. Finally, Wills agreed to let Heney continue on unmolested. Farther downriver, Heney found Tanner and related to him what had happened. Tanner traded him all of his skins as he had intended. Heney gave him a gun as a token of their new alliance.

Up until that time, Tanner had traded almost exclusively with the North West Company. There were one or two exceptions. He traded at the Hudson's Bay Company's Brandon House until its former proprietor, John McKay, promised to sell him a horse and sold it to a Nor' Wester instead. Miffed, Tanner ceased going to Brandon House. He probably traded at Swan River House, another Hudson's Bay Company post, as well. All of his trading at Grand Portage, Rainy Lake, Pembina, Prairie Portage, Lake Winnipeg, Lake Manitoba, and Red Deer River was with the North West. He accepted the traders' notion of company loyalty to a certain extent, but he based his own loyalty on personal relationships with individual traders. When Wills betrayed his trust, Tanner punished him for it by "crossing over" to the opposition. He then allied with Heney and the Hudson's Bay Company for as long as the thieving North West trader still lived.[7]

Sorcery and Sickness

{ 31 } Around the time of his break with the North West Company, Tanner also broke up with his first wife. As he and Red Sky of the Morning grew apart, Tanner acquired a rival. His wife's suitor was one Gi-ah-ge-wa-go-mo of the Red Lake band of Ojibwas. It seems that when Tanner and Red Sky of the Morning chose to part ways, she went and joined Gi-ah-ge-wa-go-mo in his lodge near Red Lake about one day's journey from the Red River band's wintering place, which was near the mouth of the Red River on the south shore of Lake Winnipeg.

All might have gone smoothly with the divorce but for the former couple's disagreement over who should take the children. Evidently Red Sky of the Morning took the two girls, who were then toddler age, while Tanner kept the boy, their firstborn, who was then around six years old. But Red Sky of the Morning was not satisfied with the arrangement.

Gi-ah-ge-wa-go-mo made two attempts in four months to steal Tanner's son. In both occurrences, Tanner returned from a day's hunt to learn that Gi-ah-ge-wa-go-mo had come into his lodge and absconded with the child. Both times, Tanner leapt onto his horse, chased his rival down, and recovered the boy unharmed. When he caught up with his son's captor the second time, he dismounted from his horse, handed the reins to his son, and advanced on Gi-ah-ge-wa-go-mo on foot with his knife drawn. Rather than attack him, however, he stabbed Gi-ah-ge-wa-go-mo's horse in the neck twice until it fell. Then he challenged Gi-ah-ge-wa-go-mo to shoot his own horse if he dared. His rival did not make a move, nor did he ever again attempt to steal the boy.[1]

Tanner's confrontation with Gi-ah-ge-wa-go-mo stands out oddly in Tanner's *Narrative*. Tanner presented the episode out of sequence with the rest of his story. It was the only point in his long narration of his life where he felt compelled to go back in time to an event he had omitted to mention earlier. It would seem that his description of this episode was as much as he could bring himself to say about the breakup of his first Indian family. In the end Tanner did not keep his son. How he later lost the boy to his mother he declined to say. What Tanner's *Narrative* does make clear was that in hindsight, at least, Tanner regarded the clash with Gi-ah-ge-wa-go-mo as an important harbinger of his mounting difficulties with the Indians.

Just as Tanner found it expedient to form a new trade relationship with Heney and the Hudson's Bay Company when things soured between him and the North West trader, so too did he feel the need to form new alliances among the Indians after his breakup with Red Sky of the Morning. In 1809, his old friend Pe-shau-ba, the Ottawa chief, died of an illness. Pe-shau-ba was the closest person to a father he ever had among the Indians. Tanner stayed with Pe-shau-ba's band for about a year and then joined another band led by the Ottawa chief Sha-gwaw-koo-sink. Sometime after that, Tanner moved with Sha-gwaw-koo-sink's band to Lake of the Woods.[2]

At the urging of his companions, Tanner took a new wife. It seems to have been largely a marriage of convenience. He needed a young woman in his lodge to help care for his aging mother and the many small orphans she kept adopting. This young woman had no children of her own when they married. In telling his life story some years later, Tanner never stated her name even though they remained married for a decade and a half and had six children together. Toward the end of their marriage, after she converted to Catholicism on Mackinac Island, she took the name Therezia.[3]

Not long after Tanner married Therezia, a new prophet arose in their midst. This man, Ais-kaw-ba-wis, had no prior experience as a medicine man. Before his sudden emergence as a spiritual leader, Tanner knew him only as a poor hunter who had allowed his wife to starve to death. Indeed, the circumstances surrounding his wife's death, two winters past, were suspicious. Tanner, for one, believed he had eaten her to save his own life. Had Ais-kaw-ba-wis admitted to such a thing, the other Ojibwas would have put him to death. Ever since that time, he had been withdrawn and listless. Then one day this marginal member of the band announced that he had received a message from the Great Spirit. Calling the principal hunters together, he produced from under his garment a perfectly round cobblestone about five inches in diameter, painted red, which he claimed the Great Spirit had given him with the injunction that he must show the way in making the whole Earth clean and new like the red ball—or like the Earth was when Nanabozho created it.[4]

Tanner wasted no time telling his fellow tribesmen that Ais-kaw-ba-wis was a faker. How ridiculous, he said, to think the Great Spirit would choose one so lazy and spiritless as this man to serve as divine messenger! Meanwhile, Ais-kaw-ba-wis retired to his lodge, where he began loudly singing, crying, praying, and beating his drum. The incantations went on for days and weeks. Occasionally he stopped to make a round of the village, sharing with each family his latest word from the Great Spirit. Twice he predicted that one of the hunters would kill a moose that day. The first time he was mistaken; the second time he guessed right. His error in the first instance seems to have cost him little, while his lucky guess the second time got much attention. Building on that success, he made a ceremony of collecting and cleaning the bones of the moose and hanging them in a tree out of reach of wolves and dogs. Tanner disparaged Ais-kaw-ba-wis and his pretensions of holiness at every turn, yet his criticisms had little effect. Much to his dismay, the prophet acquired a strong following among the band.[5]

As soon as Ais-kaw-ba-wis thought he had sufficient influence, he made a bid to drive Tanner out of the band. In the middle of winter, he sent messengers to all the hunters to return to the village for an important announcement regarding the Swallow. Tanner duly complied with the prophet's request, reckoning that he must face his adversary directly. Ais-kaw-ba-wis had planned an elaborate ceremony. All the wigwams were reconfigured into one large lodge. At Ais-kaw-ba-wis's signal the whole village filed into the lodge. Forming a circle inside, the people danced four times around while Ais-kaw-ba-wis sat in the center with his eyes closed, singing and beating his drum. At the culmination of this ceremony, Ais-kaw-ba-wis somberly announced that the Swallow would soon die. The Great Spirit had told him so in a vision. Drawing in the dirt with a stick, he made a long straight line to represent the life of a good Indian, and beside it he drew a short, crooked line falling away: this was Tanner.[6]

Tanner put no credence in the medicine man's prophecy of his own imminent death. But the representation of his life as a crooked path was much more troublesome. It cast a pall over his relations with other members of the band. Even his wife's mother and father began to treat him with suspicion. In all likelihood this was not a sign of disrespect so much as apprehension. They may have suspected that Tanner would resort to sorcery in his conflict with Ais-kaw-ba-wis. The Ottawas and Ojibwas believed that in personal feuds of this kind, supernatural powers might be put in play. According to their worldview, any person was capable of putting a curse on another. And since they believed the Great Spirit had made all of Creation, and that every plant, animal, rock, and water body had a spiritual dimension, it followed that any object under the sun could be summoned by the sorcerer to harm his enemy. A thing as small and insignificant as an insect could be summoned from many miles away to injure or kill the intended victim.

In Ottawa and Ojibwa culture, resorting to bad medicine might at times be justifiable. It could be used, for example, to punish a wrongdoer who could not otherwise be held to account. In that way, the fear of sorcery was a powerful incentive to treat others well; it operated as a deterrent against unethical conduct much like the revenge principle did. But the power of bad medicine was not to be invoked lightly. Most people refrained from its use altogether. Indeed, the very subject caused such anxiety that they avoided even talking about it. In general, bad medicine was thought to be the province of bad people. Tanner, for his part, never considered using it. He prayed for divine assistance many times in his life, but never, it would seem, for the purpose of smiting an enemy. Still, it would have done him no good to forswear the use of sorcery, for just to raise the subject aloud was to engender fear of it.[7]

Tanner hoped that Ais-kaw-ba-wis would soon discredit himself. Once in the early spring, when Tanner and some other hunters were returning from a trip to the trading house, they espied Ais-kaw-ba-wis chasing a woman through the willows a little distance from camp. When they questioned the woman about it, she confided that he had made several attempts to catch her alone in the woods, that she had always eluded him, yet she feared what he might do to her if she voiced a complaint. The principal hunter then requested Ais-kaw-ba-wis to account for himself. But the prophet refused, saying if he was to be questioned it must be in his own lodge. So the hunters sent him a gift of rum—a portion of what they had just obtained at the trading house—to see if he would then condescend to come and speak with them. Ais-kaw-ba-wis still refused, but he accepted the gift and got so thoroughly intoxicated he was observed later that night stumbling around the village stark naked. Tanner got a good laugh over Ais-kaw-ba-wis's foolishness. Yet he was disappointed to observe that the incident did nothing to diminish the man's influence.[8]

That year the several bands of western Ojibwas and Ottawas abandoned their summer village site at Netley Creek in favor of an island in Lake of the Woods. Tired of seeing their crops pilfered each year by the North West Company, they decided the island location would afford them greater protection. At the new site, Tanner set to work clearing land for cultivation. He hoped that amidst the sizeable community of Indians gathered on the island his breach with the ridiculous medicine man would not be taken so seriously. However, Ais-kaw-ba-wis continued to undermine him. Tanner sensed it most clearly in the cold treatment he got from his wife's family. When his feelings of alienation finally became unbearable, he left the new village with his aged mother, her adopted children, and his young wife, and went to hunt on the upper Red River.[9]

※

Near the summer's end, Tanner witnessed the arrival of the first Scottish colonists in the Red River valley. They came in York boats from Hudson

Bay. Numbering about 100 people, they included half a dozen families and four or five young, single women—the first white women he had seen since he was a boy. The colonists camped briefly at the Forks, where their leader, Governor Miles Macdonell, performed a flag-raising ceremony and "seizin'" of the land; they then moved upriver to Pembina and immediately set to work constructing cabins, a storehouse, and a stockade, to be known as Fort Daer. Tanner observed their activities with mounting skepticism, for the colonists were clearly ill prepared for winter. They had only a few horses and dogs and knew nothing about how to hunt buffalo. Their situation would have been extremely perilous had they not been under the semiprotection of the Hudson's Bay Company. Tanner was not surprised, then, when the trader Hugh Heney approached him with an offer to hunt for the Hudson's Bay Company through the coming season. Largely out of sympathy for the colonists, he accepted the offer.[10]

The first problem facing the colony was that the bison happened to be herding in the Pembina Hills that winter, 100 miles west of Pembina. Tanner made his hunting camp at an abandoned trading post near the head of the Pembina River, approximately ten days' journey from the settlement. There, he lived with four Hudson's Bay men, including one interpreter, for the next four months. The men assisted Tanner in killing and butchering bison, while about twenty colonists worked in teams, transporting the meat back to Pembina in carts. Due to the size of the operation and distance that had to be covered, less than half the meat ever reached Pembina. By January, the shortage of food at Pembina was so severe that families without small children and most of the single men who were not already employed in the relay system were sent forward to the hunting camp. As these people settled in with them, Tanner was appalled by their wretched condition and bestial manners. Even when there was plenty of food, they ate like ravenous dogs and fought over their rations. The baymen had to beat them to maintain discipline.[11]

It was the first time Tanner actually lived with traders, and in his view it was they, not the Indians, who behaved savagely. These men, having no women or children to care for, acted almost entirely in their own self-interest. His experience had taught him to put the welfare of the family group before all else. He had taken care of his aging mother for the better part of ten years. He had provided food and shelter for numerous orphan children through many winters. His wife Therezia had recently borne their first child, a daughter whom they named Martha, which Tanner dimly recalled as being the name of his long-deceased white mother. None of that brought him any esteem among the traders. They showed him little respect and treated his wife insufferably. Indeed, one of the Hudson's Bay men, a clerk named McDonald, behaved so badly toward Therezia that he finally had to be sent away. For two months in the middle of winter this troublemaker was posted to another hunting camp, where his sole occupation was guarding a mound of frozen buffalo carcasses against scavengers—a fitting punishment for his abusiveness, Tanner had to admit. For Tanner, sharing quarters with these men through the long winter season was indeed a trial, though it did give him the opportunity to relearn some English. It would be years before he could speak it fluently, but at least he had made a start. When spring came, Heney offered to hire him as an interpreter for the Hudson's Bay Company. Heney said he would have his own cabin in Pembina. Tanner declined, and at Therezia's urging, they prepared to return to Lake of the Woods. Old Nct-no-kwa, choosing to remain at Red River, went to live with her other son, Wa-me-gon-a-biew.[12]

On the eve of their departure, Tanner bought a shirt from one of the colonists that was probably contaminated, most likely with smallpox virus. After they had paddled about twelve days down the Pembina and Red rivers— roughly the incubation period for smallpox—he fell violently ill. His skin broke out in large sores, and in no time he was prostrate. Soon Therezia became ill as well, though she was not quite so severely afflicted. Therezia set up their lodge on the riverbank, and the family subsisted mostly on fish as they struggled through the illness. Tanner lay in the canoe day after day, with pukkwi mats laid across the gunwales to protect him from the weather, and a fishing line coiled around his hands. Whenever he hooked a fish, he called out weakly to his wife to bring it in. Meanwhile, she tried various herbal medicines on him, but nothing seemed to work. Tanner found some relief by mixing gunpowder with water to make a salve that he smeared over his sores. Finally, after about a month, the illness passed. As they were still weak from hunger, they moved on up a tributary of the Red River to a small lake where Tanner knew he would find good hunting. Once they had eaten plenty of fresh meat and recovered their strength, they headed on across the remaining expanse of muskeg to Lake of the Woods.[13]

At the island village, bad news awaited them. The smallpox, or whatever it was that Tanner had caught from the colonist, had been passed to the general Indian population as well. Spreading among the western Ottawas and Ojibwas that spring of 1813, the disease had taken many lives. Therezia's three younger siblings had all succumbed. Therezia's parents were devastated by their loss, and they held Tanner responsible for it. Therezia's father accused him of having caused the deaths by sorcery. The evil prospect frightened Therezia and probably confused her, too, after the ordeal she and her husband had just been through together. Fearful and grief-stricken, she took the baby and returned to her parents' lodge.

As Tanner suspected, the accusation of his evil-doing ultimately came from Ais-kaw-ba-wis. About a month earlier, when Therezia's young siblings had fallen sick, the parents had gone to the medicine man for help. Ais-kaw-ba-wis had confirmed in their minds that their son-in-law was probably behind it. As Tanner was far away from the village still, the medicine man had determined to channel his spirit and interrogate his spirit as to what evil he had done to make the children sick. The Ojibwas had a ritual for such occasions. It involved the use of a temporary, booth-like structure they called a *jiisakiiwigaan*. The structure was built like a wigwam but was smaller and more conical in shape. Normally the conjurer would get inside it, and when the spirit of the dead or distant person was summoned, the structure would lift off the ground and sway from side to side. The English term for the jiisakiiwigaan was "shaking tent." When Ais-kaw-ba-wis performed the ritual and emerged from the structure, he told the distraught parents that Tanner's spirit had confessed to having "shot bad medicine" into the children. Their wayward son-in-law, he indicated, was exercising the power of life and death over their helpless little offspring. When all three children subsequently died, the parents were convinced that their son-in-law was responsible.[14]

As Tanner saw it, at least in hindsight, the epidemic spread not only death but fear, which worked to strengthen the medicine man's influence against him. At the time, he seemed to be unsure whether to confront this new challenge or try to distance himself from it. While not everyone in the village believed the evil things Ais-kaw-ba-wis said, a considerable number did, including Therezia. After just four days back in the village, Tanner found an excuse to go away again, joining a war party against the Sioux. Clinging to the familial connections, though, he announced that his reason for going was to protect his "little brother"—that is, Therezia's brother, his brother-in-law—who was taking the warpath for the first time. As this young man was in mourning over the deaths of his small siblings, he was apt to be reckless with his own life and would need a protector. The young man accepted Tanner as his guardian, notwithstanding the fact that he lay under a cloud of suspicion with the rest of the family.[15]

As often happened, the war party wandered about for several months without ever coming across the enemy. The Assiniboines and Crees contributed great numbers of warriors to the enterprise, and as the intertribal force spawned its own set of internal conflicts, acts of bravery were demonstrated against other members of the expedition instead of the enemy. In one brawl, three Ojibwas died; in another, two horses belonging to the Assiniboines were killed. As this particular war party numbered several hundred men, the casualty rate was not high.

The war party threw Tanner and his brother Wa-me-gon-a-biew together after a separation of some years. Their old sibling rivalry had grown even more bitter in their adulthood. In Tanner's view, Wa-me-gon-a-biew was shamefully deficient in the cardinal Indian virtues of bravery and generosity. His face was disfigured—some six years earlier a man had bitten off the end of his nose in a drunken brawl—and he did not bear this indignity well. Quarrelsome by nature, he picked fights with weaker men. Near the outset of the expedition, he threatened to kill Tanner's young brother-in-law, alleging that he was a remote kin of the man who had mortally wounded their father with a thrown rock so many years earlier. When Tanner warned that he was determined to defend the young man even if it meant fighting his own brother, Wa-me-gon-a-biew settled for breaking Tanner's gun instead.[16]

The war party returned to Pembina in the fall, where a big bout of drinking preceded the general dispersal. Although Tanner usually disparaged such occasions, this time he joined in the spree. On his last night with his brother, they were sitting with a group around a fire, quite intoxicated, when one of those present recalled how Wa-me-gon-a-biew had insulted Tanner by breaking his gun. Finding the man's remark an affront to his honor, Tanner grabbed a wooden skewer from beside the fire, ran over to his brother's horse, and stabbed it in the neck. The horse folded to the ground, bleeding to death. Wa-me-gon-a-biew did not react, yet the expectation of further violence loomed. The five men with whom Tanner had expected to journey back to Lake of the Woods the next day did not want to be drawn into a fight between brothers, so they set out later that night rather than waiting till sunup. Tanner delayed his own departure until his brother was up the next day so as not to be called a coward later. That morning, he loitered near his brother's lodge until the two had exchanged several meaningful glances, then, feeling satisfied that the matter of his gun had been put to rest—one outrage suitably answered by another—he took off after his companions.[17]

The country between Pembina and Lake of the Woods was at that time one vast muskeg. The word "muskeg" comes from Ojibwa and refers to a type of peat bog, flecked with tussock mounds, which covers extensive areas in the boreal regions. It is generally too lumpy and spongy to walk across, yet too clogged with decaying matter and vegetation to float a canoe. When the fur traders traveled between Pembina and Lake of the Woods, they avoided the muskeg altogether and followed the Red, Winnipeg, and Rainy rivers, their route making a wide detour around the area. Tanner and his compatriots preferred a more direct route across the muskeg, as they possessed an intimate knowledge of the area's connecting lakes and streams. But this time they had no sooner got out into the middle of it than the temperature plummeted and a thin ice formed over everything. The ice was not solid enough to hold their weight, but it was too thick for their canoes to get through. They seemed to be hopelessly stranded there.

By chance, Tanner's wife, together with three other women, started across the muskeg from the other direction almost on the same day as their men did, thinking that they would either find them at Pembina or encounter them along the way. The men were sitting on their haunches on a bit of high ground, pondering what to do, when they sighted the four women dragging a pair of light canoes toward them through knee-deep muck and snow. The women, who had brought a generous supply of food and did not feel any alarm at the weather, enjoyed a hearty laugh when they came up and found their returning warriors looking so crestfallen. Taking counsel, they all decided that they would go to Red River for the winter.[18]

In this way Tanner was reunited with his wife. But the resumption of their marriage was more along the lines of a truce than a reconciliation. When they returned to Lake of the Woods in the spring, he found the medicine man, Ais-kaw-ba-wis, still poisoning the people's minds against him and his wife's parents still under his spell. Through the following year, Therezia vacillated between counting her husband her enemy or her intimate. Though she and Tanner mostly lived apart, they did produce two more children in close succession. It was around this time that Tanner broke some ribs in a fall from a tree and found himself under the care of Dr. John McLoughlin, the North West trader at Rainy Lake. Over the winter, when Tanner convalesced at a small trader's house on White Fish Lake, Therezia refused to live with him. But she did visit him there on occasion. Toward the end, she placed their two toddler-age girls in his charge while she cared for their nursling.

In the spring, as he was going up the Rainy River to see the doctor, his canoe struck a rock and sank. He managed to keep a grasp of his children as they went into the rushing water, and as he found his footing in the waist-deep channel he was able to carry them to safety. But the dousing in the cold river made him sick again. McLoughlin took them into the trading house and invited him to stay until he was well. He lingered only long enough to recuperate, for he was anxious to get home to his wife. Then, back in the village at last, he was disappointed to find that Therezia still kept her distance from him.[19]

Once, some months later, when another sickness ran through the village,

Tanner's mother-in-law attacked him with a hoe while he slept. Fortunately, he was able to ward off the blows and avoid serious injury. Though the attack took him by surprise, the fact that his mother-in-law would actually assault him came as no surprise at all. He had even anticipated it. Indeed, to a certain degree he sympathized with her. Later he was told how she had been standing in the cornfield when she suddenly began to wail over the loss of her little children. The sickness in the village reminded her afresh of the earlier sickness that had taken their lives. She still suspected that Tanner had had something to do with their deaths. So she acted on impulse from grief, charging into his lodge with her hoe raised to strike. Tanner held her less accountable for the attack than he did the medicine man.[20]

When the village dispersed for the winter, Tanner set out with his three children in one canoe, Therezia with her parents in another. Whether by accident or design, Tanner went ahead with some other canoes, and he and his wife failed to join up again. Left to his own resources with three tiny children—the oldest, Martha, was only three—Tanner was in a tenuous situation. He might have joined another subsistence group, but shame and pride prevented it.

One of the chiefs, having observed Tanner's dysfunctional marriage from afar for some months, urged him at this point to take another woman to wife rather than risk going to the winter hunting ground with only his small children and no helpmate. Tanner refused to take the chief's advice. Instead, he went to a trader for provisions, and with a pair of sled dogs he managed in two trips to set up camp in his prearranged hunting territory. There, he performed the work of two people all through the winter: tending the fire, preparing food, bathing and clothing the children, dressing moose skins, making moccasins, chopping wood, and bringing home game. Each time he went out on his trap line, he hastened back to the lodge as quickly as possible lest a wolf discover his unattended children, or the low fire he left burning in the lodge should happen to die. Escaping those perils, the children luckily survived. Among the Ottawas and Ojibwas it was customary to divide into small groups for the winter, but never a group this small. This was aberrant. Alone with two toddlers and an infant, Tanner had virtually cut himself off from the tribe.[21]

Taking Fort Douglas

❊{ 32 }❊ By 1816, the Ottawas and Ojibwas grew so much corn and other produce on their island in Lake of the Woods that the traders called the place "Plantation Island." Tanner had his own crop of corn in a field that he cleared for himself. Like other families in the village, he cultivated his own piece of ground and treated his individual crop as a commercial product, taking it to the trading house as he would skins. In doing so, he practiced a form of agricultural production that the Ottawa had pursued for many years around the shores of Lake Huron and Lake Michigan. However, in the Ottawa culture, women normally performed virtually all of the labor of cultivation, tilling the soil, planting seed, harvesting the crop, and disposing of the product at the trading house. Perhaps it was Tanner's early memory of his father and brother working in the cornfield on their Kentucky farm that prompted him to take on tasks most Ottawa men disdained as women's work. Apparently he had no qualms about it. And yet, it was another choice he made that marked him as different. It may have contributed to his growing sense of alienation from the tribe.[1]

Ottawa and Ojibwa agricultural production on Plantation Island was not large, but it had already become an important source of food for the fur traders. A Hudson's Bay Company trader who was a contemporary of Tanner described the crops as being laid out in a "regular manner" and tended in a way that "would have done credit to many farmers." Some years later, another white visitor reported that the island was about half cleared of forest with agricultural fields covering the whole eastern half and that "an air of great neatness prevailed over the whole of the cultivated portion of the Island." Growing corn at that northern latitude was no small achievement. Historian D. W. Moodie has remarked that it heralded "the final stage in the northward diffusion of Indian domesticated plants (or cultigens) in North America, a process that had begun several millennia before the arrival of Europeans." Without the presence of the fur traders the Ottawas would not have introduced agriculture in that place, and without Indian agriculture the fur trade would not have penetrated northward and westward as it did. Indian agriculture provided the essential foundation for more extensive crop production by white settlers in the Red River colony in the coming years, which in turn helped sustain the fur trade in the Far North. Some historians go so far as to say that the spread of agriculture was vital to the success of the fur trade everywhere in Canada with the one exception of the plains area, where hunting buffalo and making pemmican sustained the fur trade at the outset.[2]

Since the Ottawas and Ojibwas bartered most of their agricultural produce to the fur traders, they more or less welcomed the Hudson's Bay Company's move into the Red River region because it gave them more opportunity in the provisioning trade as well as the fur trade. Along with their agricultural enterprise on Plantation Island, the Ottawas and Ojibwas began hunting buffalo every winter to supply meat and pemmican both to the traders and the colonists coming to the Red River valley. The resident Métis wanted a corner on the latter activity, but the Ottawas and Ojibwas challenged them for it. The Ottawas and Ojibwas did not share the concern of the Métis that the Red River colony posed a threat to their commercial interests or their new homeland. As a result, they wanted no part in the conflict between the North West and the Hudson's Bay companies. When the Nor' Westers tried talking them into making war on the Red River settlement and driving the settlers out of the country, most of them refused to get involved. Even when the Rainy Lake trader, Dr. McLoughlin, exhorted them to join the Nor' Westers in going against the colony, only five of their number went.

Tanner heard the Nor' Westers' harangues and shared the Lake of the Woods Indians' prevailing view about it. He did not want to get mixed up in what seemed like an unnatural quarrel between relatives. His young brother-in-law, however, was one of the handful of Ojibwas who did agree to fight. By the time this group reached Red River, the Métis, acting as the North West's proxies, had already clashed with the Hudson's Bay people near the Forks, killing many settlers as well as the governor. After this bloody affair—the Battle of Seven Oaks of June 19, 1816—the Indians were sent to stand guard at the mouth of the Red River in case the Hudson's Bay people tried to counterattack. The Indians soon tired of that duty and went home. When Tanner learned of these events from his brother-in-law, he felt he had made the right decision to stay out of the traders' war.[3]

That summer, as the conflict between the two fur companies continued to escalate, Tanner tried to settle back into his life with the Indians. He hunted in the area around Lake of the Woods, caught fish, gathered wild rice, and worked in his cornfield. Still persecuted by his old antagonist, Ais-kaw-ba-wis, he now tried a new tack with him, pretending to be oblivious to the medicine man's constant efforts to undermine him. Therezia moved back into his lodge, acting as though the two had never been estranged.[4]

Hudson's Bay men began visiting the Lake of the Woods Indians, preaching war as the Nor' Westers had done earlier. One of the Hudson's Bay agents, a Canadian-Ojibwa interpreter named Charles Brousse, spoke to Tanner on a number of occasions during the summer and fall. He told Tanner about the British chieftain, Lord Selkirk, entering the Northwest at the head of a small army. Selkirk had seized Fort William, taking many prisoners and sending them to Upper Canada to stand trial. Brousse convinced Tanner that the Hudson's Bay Company was in the right, or at least it had the might of the British government behind it. He also educated Tanner on the state of US-British relations, revealing that the War of 1812 was long over and that there was nothing to prevent him from returning to the United States.[5]

Tanner was so impressed by the worldly Brousse that he entrusted him with transporting twenty sacks of corn to Rainy Lake. Tanner intended to follow in a light canoe several days later. His plan was to winter with his family near the North West trading house and then push on alone to Mackinac in the spring. From there he aimed to go down into the Ohio country to search for his white relations.[6]

When Tanner arrived at Rainy Lake, he found that the North West trader, John Warren Dease, had just surrendered the fort to one Captain d'Orsonnens and a party of Selkirk's soldiers. Most of Selkirk's men remained with the British chieftain at Fort William. Tanner soon understood Selkirk's purpose for taking the fort at Rainy Lake: he had sent his men to seize its food stocks, which he needed for feeding the many soldiers who were set to pass the winter at Fort William. D'Orsonnens informed Tanner that Dease had dispersed most of the fort's food stocks to the Indians to avoid letting them fall into enemy hands. So Tanner's twenty sacks of corn, which he had sent ahead with Brousse weeks earlier, were now gone.[7]

Behind d'Orsonnens came Miles Macdonell in charge of a second contingent of soldiers from Fort William. All these men took up quarters in the small North West fort. D'Orsonnens calculated that he could not sustain such numbers at Rainy Lake through the winter, so they must press on to Red River to hunt buffalo. He asked Tanner to guide his men through the maze of frozen waterways in between, promising him a generous reward and the Hudson's Bay Company's future goodwill for his service. This time, d'Orsonnens explained, the North West traders must not know they were coming. In particular, he wished to catch the Nor' Wester who was holding Fort Douglas and take him prisoner. In order to gain the element of surprise, he wanted Tanner to lead them by way of the muskeg, taking the route known only to the Indians. Tanner agreed to do it, boasting that he could make a road from where they now stood right to the door of the Nor' Wester's bedroom.[8]

As snow began to fall, Tanner set out with an advance party of twenty men on horses. They halted at Lake of the Woods, where they engaged a number of Indian hunters, sent back the horses, and made snowshoes for everyone. Soon d'Orsonnens and Macdonell arrived with the rest of the soldiers and two small fieldpieces on sleds. Now they had to wait until the ground was well frozen to proceed across the muskeg. By the time they finally set out, the snow lay deep, the days were very short, and the nights freezing cold. Partway across the muskeg, they ran out of meat. When no game could be found, the soldiers grumbled about being made to march on rations of wild rice, and there was even talk of mutiny. Yet the expedition made good time, striking the Red River a short distance above Pembina on December 31, 1816. The Hudson's Bay Company's Fort Daer, which had been abandoned to the Nor' Westers following the Battle of Seven Oaks, was retaken without a fight. Its only occupants were a few old French Canadians and their wives and children. The soldiers plunged ravenously into the fort's food stores.[9]

While the expedition rested for a few days, Tanner made arrangements for his family to stay with the Red River Indians. In relating his life story many years later, Tanner was vague about who accompanied him at this point, saying only that he left his *children* at Pembina, and that he returned there to his *family*. Often in recounting events Tanner used the first-person singular without saying precisely who was with him, so this minor inconsistency is not surprising. It seems probable that Therezia and their three children, who were then between the ages of two and four, were with him on the expedition from Rainy Lake to Pembina, even though the difficulties of traveling under such harsh conditions with very young children can well be imagined.[10]

More perplexing is what became of Tanner's mother. Net-no-kwa simply faded from his account. In autobiography, what gets left out often deserves scrutiny. In spite of Tanner's devotion to his Indian mother, she seems to have ended her days with her biological son, Wa-me-gon-a-biew. Why this was so can only be guessed, but Tanner's silence on the matter suggests he was not at peace with it. The last time he alludes to her she is living with the Red River band of Ojibwas in 1813 and 1814. Ironically, the only record of Net-no-kwa's death comes not from Tanner but from John McLoughlin. McLoughlin later wrote in the Rainy Lake House post journal that the reason Tanner would not take the advice of various traders and return to the United States earlier was that he had such a strong attachment to the old woman who had adopted him. McLoughlin continued: "At last in 1817 she died and he went in search of his friends." If McLoughlin was right about the year, then it is likely Tanner saw Net-no-kwa for the last time in January 1817, when the expedition passed through Pembina.[11]

It was four days' march from Pembina to the Forks. With the temperature plummeting again, the men faced into a cutting north wind. Near the Forks, before they got within sight of Fort Douglas, they were joined by Be-gwais, chief of the Red River band of Ojibwas. This much-respected leader had been a friend of the colonists since their first winter, when he led them on Indian ponies from the Forks to Pembina. After the Battle of Seven Oaks, he openly supported the Hudson's Bay against the North West. Be-gwais advised d'Orsonnens to march onward without delay and array his men and two fieldpieces in plain view of the fort before nightfall, as he was confident the Nor' Westers would surrender when they saw the size of the force prepared to attack them. But d'Orsonnens wanted to reconnoiter the situation and ordered his men to make camp for the night.[12]

Tanner felt slighted when d'Orsonnens left him out of the council with Be-gwais. He had promised to lead d'Orsonnens right to the enemy's bedroom door, and he felt certain that they could take the fort with a surprise attack at night. As the soldiers bedded down, he confided to the interpreter his impatience with their commander. This fellow agreed that the fort lay practically in their grasp, and the two began to whisper it about among the soldiers. Soon they had a small party of volunteers ready to go. At Tanner's urging, they set out without informing d'Orsonnens.[13]

Approaching to within view of the fort, the men chopped down a small tree and cut its branches to four-inch nubbins to make a single-pole ladder. Then, hoisting it onto their shoulders, they waded across an open expanse of moonlit snow toward the fort, trusting that the night was so extremely cold no one would be manning the watchtower. Reaching the outside of the stockade and hearing no one stirring inside, they leaned their scaling ladder against the wall and climbed up and over, one at a time, dropping onto the snow-covered roof of the blacksmith's shop and then to the ground. Once they were all inside the fort everyone was assigned a position, two or three men standing guard at each door so that the occupants, once alerted in their various quarters, would be unable to combine against them. Tanner was anxious to find the Nor' Wester who was in charge of the fort and make his capture, but he could not tell which door was his. So the men waited for daylight.[14]

The man they hoped to take prisoner was Archibald McLellan, a partner in the North West Company. He finally burst through his door in a rage, armed with a pistol and primed to fight. The soldiers standing on either side of the doorway jumped him and wrestled the pistol from his hands. When the other occupants of the fort heard their leader shouting and saw that he had been captured and disarmed, they gave up without firing a shot. D'Orsonnens and Macdonell entered through the gate with the rest of their troops and accepted the fort's surrender. The crimson flag of the Hudson's Bay Company was run up the staff. McLellan continued to yell, hurling insults at the two Hudson's Bay officers and anyone else he happened to recognize. This included Tanner, whom he berated for turning against the North West. D'Orsonnens and Macdonell finally had enough of his ranting and ordered him tossed into the snow outside the fort with his hands bound behind his back. After a time, they let him back in and allowed him to warm up by a fire. As soon as his teeth stopped chattering he resumed his cursing. Finally, he was placed in confinement along with two other men, while the rest of the fort's occupants were released at large.[15]

It soon became known among the Métis that Tanner had taken the Hudson's Bay's side against the North West. As the Métis remained staunch allies of the North West, several of their leaders stated that Tanner should be killed for his treachery. When Tanner heard their threats, he taunted them that they would have to catch him sleeping, just as he had caught the Nor' Westers sleeping, or else they would never have the courage to try it. After collecting his family in Pembina, he went with the Red River Indians to hunt buffalo along the Assiniboine. Then, finding himself in the heart of the Métis homeland, he worried that all his brave talk had been too provoking. Each night his family remained in that country, he had to be vigilant against attack. He thought he saw a few Métis spying on their camp from time to time, but none came near.[16]

Lord Selkirk arrived in the spring and spent the next six months at Fort Douglas, where he personally took charge of efforts to restore the colony. In frail health and unequal to the hard physical labor of putting the colony back together, he spent most of his time taking depositions from numerous individuals who had witnessed one phase or another of the colony's struggles with the North West and Métis. His aim was to build an overwhelming legal case that would finally vanquish the opposition by way of the British courts. He was assisted in this work by a supposedly neutral commissioner sent from Montreal, William B. Coltman.

Over the course of the summer, Lord Selkirk developed a keen interest in Tanner. Coltman informed the Scottish nobleman of Tanner's role in guiding d'Orsonnens through the muskeg and his personal initiative in re-taking Fort Douglas. At Coltman's urging, Selkirk presented Tanner with a cash reward plus the promise of a small lifetime annuity from the Hudson's Bay Company. Apparently, the company duly paid him his annuity for the next five years, but the payments ceased after he entered a contract with the American Fur Company in 1822.[17]

Selkirk was intrigued not only by Tanner's recent exploits for the company but his unusual story as well. He persuaded Tanner to talk about himself, even though Tanner's command of English was still so limited he had to use his native tongue and speak to the Scottish lord through an interpreter. In spite of their difficulty communicating, they must have spoken for several hours, for Selkirk learned details of Tanner's early life and of his capture that were found nowhere in print at that time. From what he subsequently wrote about him, it seems Selkirk responded to Tanner in two ways: both as a white captive deserving of rescue and as a noble savage worthy of publicity. At one point, he broached the idea of taking him to England—an offer Tanner had heard before. Tanner, for his part, was impressed by Selkirk's evident wealth and power. He indulged the British chieftain's curiosity in the hope that it might help him in some way.[18]

By the end of summer Selkirk was anxious to return to Montreal, but he was in a quandary about how to get there. He feared that if he attempted the usual route through the Great Lakes, the Nor' Westers would try to arrest or assassinate him. But if he took the alternative route through the United States, the Nor' Westers would paint him as a fugitive from British justice, winning points in the court of public opinion in Canada. There was no good choice, so he opted for the latter course. He would arrange some official business in Washington to give him an excuse for going through the United States.

Selkirk invited Tanner to accompany him, as he would be traveling by way of St. Louis and the Ohio River, where they would stand a fair chance of tracking down some of Tanner's white relations. Tanner weighed the offer and finally rejected it. His ambivalence was akin to that experienced by many fur traders preparing to retire from the fur trade. His closest attachments, like theirs, were among the Indians, and his true home was in Indian country. Even if he promised to return, he could not leave his family so late in the fall with winter coming on.[19]

Frustrated, he went to Selkirk and dictated a letter instead. Or, perhaps he just gave his blessing as Selkirk composed it. The letter has not survived. Later Tanner would recall that it included some identifying particulars of his early life, and it may have been these same details that Selkirk inserted in correspondence and newspaper notices in his efforts to locate Tanner's family. The letter Selkirk wrote for him seems to have been only the second one Tanner ever sent from British America to the United States. The first he had sent off with an American trader ten years earlier, giving it little chance of success. But this second letter had the weight of the British chieftain behind it. And this time it found its mark.[20]

The combination of Lord Selkirk's fame, humanitarianism, and tenacity made him an effective messenger. Soon after Selkirk arrived in St. Louis, he placed a notice about Tanner in several newspapers in the western states. In this notice he got one crucial fact wrong: Tanner had misremembered his white family's name as Taylor. This, it turned out, was the name of some close family friends. One Mrs. Taylor of Lexington, Kentucky, read the notice and thought she recognized some details reminiscent of the capture of a boy whom she had once known as John Tanner. She contacted Selkirk, who traveled out of his way to meet her and confirm that the man whom he had befriended was indeed named Tanner, not Taylor. Selkirk wrote another notice with the name corrected, and this time it came to the attention of Tanner's relatives.[21]

Thus Tanner's family learned at last that the boy who had been taken by Indians some twenty-seven years earlier was still alive, living among the Ottawas and Ojibwas on the northern prairie. The news confirmed what John Tanner, Sr., had been told when he went searching for his son long ago: he had been traded from tribe to tribe and taken west. Although Tanner's father had since died, his brother Edward and sisters Agatha and Lucy still lived. Edward, in fact, had never given up hope of finding their brother. During the War of 1812, he had served as a captain in the frontier militia. On his travels from one frontier post to another on the upper Mississippi, he had often spoken of his brother's captivity. Since then he had attended Indian treaty councils in the hope of ferreting out some bit of information that would lead to his brother's discovery. At last, in March 1818, Edward received a letter from one Mr. Castleman, enclosing a note from Selkirk, which left no doubt in his mind that the white Indian in question was John. Being reliably informed that he lived among the Red River Indians, often hunting for Selkirk's colony or the Hudson's Bay Company, Edward resolved to set out the following summer to find him.[22]

Rough Justice

{ 33 } John Tanner passed the winter of 1817–18 hunting bison along the Assiniboine. He now planned to go in search of his white relatives in the coming year, and since it would entail a long separation from his wife and children, he wanted to leave them well provisioned in his absence. So he killed a great number of bison, drying the meat and pounding it into pemmican, and preserving the tongues and other choice parts in tallow in ten-gallon kegs. By the end of winter, he had made twenty large sacks of pemmican and filled ten kegs with tallow and meats.[1]

Late in the season, he and Therezia received an urgent message from Therezia's mother: they must both come at once to see her. Their band was then somewhat scattered over the prairie, and the old woman had recently encamped a few miles away from Tanner and Therezia with another small band of three lodges. Therezia wanted to leave the very next day, and Tanner consented. But that night he had a dream in which a young man came down through the smoke hole in his lodge and warned him not to go to his mother-in-law's camp. He knew this person, this *pawaganak*, or dream visitor. He was the same figure who appeared to him in dreams whenever he made preparations for a medicine hunt. "You must not go to the place you propose to visit tomorrow," the man intoned. "Look there," he said, pointing, and Tanner saw some of his friends running toward him. Then the man pointed skyward. Looking up, Tanner saw a hawk with a banded tail circling above. Tanner awoke from the dream feeling apprehensive. He told Therezia she must go to her mother by herself.

Therezia insisted that he come, and he finally agreed, thinking he must not add to his mother-in-law's suspicions. He and Therezia had barely started down the trail, however, when he saw the same hawk, flying close by. This stopped him dead in his tracks, for he saw at that moment with perfect clarity that the bird was his guardian spirit sent to warn him of evil. He told his wife a second time that she must go without him. Therezia would not agree to it. She belittled him for being afraid of her mother. Finally, he relented, saying nothing of his dream, and they continued on. The warrior ethic rose in him, and he resolved to face whatever challenge lay ahead.[2]

Just as he feared, his mother-in-law had laid a trap. When he got to her lodge he left his gun at her door, went in, and sat down beside Therezia's two older sisters. He was wearing a capote with a large hood made of moose hide, and as he did not immediately remove the hood from his head he did not see his mother-in-law's accomplice step from the shadows and raise his tomahawk. This man went by the name Waw-be-be-nais-sa, or White Bird (no relation to the lazy hunter of the same name who he had known many years before). Lately, Waw-be-be-nais-sa had become his antagonist, telling everyone that Tanner was a stranger in their village and that he bragged too much of being a great hunter. The two had come to blows twice, and when Tanner got the better of him in those scuffles Waw-be-be-nais-sa had tried to even the score by stabbing one of Tanner's dogs.[3]

Now this man's tomahawk came crashing down on the crown of Tanner's head, and the blade would have surely split his skull in two had it not been for the thick hood. The blow knocked Tanner out. When he came to, he found himself surrounded by several women. He recognized the frightened faces of his two sisters-in-law but not his wife's. Neither his mother-in-law nor the man with the tomahawk were anywhere to be seen. Oddly, he felt no pain, just the warm and sticky blood oozing from his scalp. The women were holding his arms, trying to pin him to the floor. As soon as he could raise himself up, he pulled away from them and stumbled out of the lodge, thinking that he must find his assailant. But he was no longer in possession of his gun. When he realized—still in a daze—that no one was coming forward to help him, he bolted from his mother-in-law's camp and made for his own.[4]

The sight of Tanner staggering into camp without his wife brought the principal hunter, Sha-gwaw-koo-sink, running. The moment Tanner reached out and took him by the hand, his scalp wound opened and blood streamed down his face. Three of Sha-gwaw-koo-sink's young men quickly gathered around, and one of them, Oto-pun-ne-be, with whom Tanner had often hunted, vowed to take revenge on the man who had tomahawked him. Safe among his friends, Tanner crawled into his lodge to rest.[5]

The next day, Therezia appeared at the door of their lodge with her mother. Tanner's heart sank when he saw them standing there together, for he knew that his mother-in-law wanted him dead and he had to conclude that his wife must now be in league with her. His mother-in-law announced that the Ojibwas were making haste to leave, as it was thought that a Sioux war party was coming. Tanner said he was too weak to travel, that they should take the children and go without him. This they did. Many other families fled that same day, abandoning their lodges, their belongings, and their sunjegwuns hung with buffalo meat. Soon the entire encampment was deserted except for Tanner, his friend Oto-pun-ne-be, and a fourteen-year-old boy who was Oto-pun-ne-be's cousin. Tanner lay prone for ten days while his friends took turns attending him or watching for signs of the enemy.

As soon as Tanner could travel, the three set out for Lake of the Woods. Their sole purpose now was to find Tanner's assailant, Waw-be-be-nais-sa, and punish him. In two small canoes they threaded their way through the muskeg to the shore of the lake. There, they made camp and held a council. Oto-pun-ne-be and his cousin would canoe across to Plantation Island, where they felt confident of finding the guilty party in the Ottawa-Ojibwa village. Tanner, meanwhile, would pay a visit to the local trader. It was deemed easier for Oto-pun-ne-be to accomplish his mission if Tanner did not accompany him. On an agreed upon day, the three would meet back at their present camp and then return to Red River.[6]

Oto-pun-ne-be was a big, strong man with a generally peaceable disposition. People knew him as one who rarely fought unless it was in another man's behalf. As soon as he entered the village, the Indians recognized the purpose of his visit. He went to the lodge of one of the principal chiefs, sat down, and waited for the man he was looking for to come meet him there. After a while, Waw-be-be-nais-sa appeared and sat down across from him. While the chief listened, Tanner's assailant stated that he understood Oto-pun-ne-be's purpose. He did not deny his part in the affair, nor did he offer an explanation, excuse, or apology for it. Rather, he gave his challenger a warning and an opportunity to reconsider. He pointed out that Oto-pun-ne-be had no brothers, for they had all been killed by the Long Knives (the Americans). He said it was foolish for him to count the Swallow as his brother, for the Swallow was himself a Long Knife, who masqueraded as an Indian. In answer, Oto-pun-ne-be said it was not true that the Long Knives had killed any brothers of his. But it was true he called the Swallow his brother, and regardless of his opponent's view of the matter, he would avenge him as he would an Indian brother.[7]

With that, Oto-pun-ne-be stood up and pulled his opponent outside the chief's lodge for a fight. Waw-be-be-nais-sa had some friends standing by, and as he and Oto-pun-ne-be began to circle one another these other men moved in closer. Seeing he was outnumbered, Oto-pun-ne-be drew a knife. The chief was right behind him and with a quick movement he caught his arm and made him drop the weapon. But with another vigorous gesture by the chief Waw-be-be-nais-sa's seconds stepped back from the two combatants. Big Oto-pun-ne-be was allowed to charge his opponent and pummel him to the ground. Soon the men jumped in and overpowered him but not before he landed a few powerful blows and cracked some ribs. Thus, with the help of the chief and Waw-be-be-nais-sa's seconds, the punishment was kept within bounds commensurate with the injury done to Tanner. After the combat was over, Oto-pun-ne-be and his young cousin were permitted to leave the village unmolested.[8]

While Oto-pun-ne-be was avenging his friend, Tanner's condition improved enough that he was able to hunt and bring down a large animal. When the three men met up at their previous camp as planned, he gave them a feast. Tanner felt satisfied that two cracked ribs squared with a cut head, so the matter was settled. He was pleased to count Oto-pun-ne-be as his friend. And yet, the cause of the fracas was not lost on him: many in the tribe had come to regard him as a Long Knife, an alien, and even looked upon his friends with a jaundiced eye. With so much prejudice against him, he doubted that those like Oto-pun-ne-be would rally to his side forever.

Tanner and his two companions got back to their original encampment shortly before all the other Ojibwas returned. During their absence, no Sioux had ransacked their camp; the lodges remained just as they had left them. Tanner joined with everyone else in loading the canoes with their dried meat and possessions for the slow trip back to the village. In a few weeks, the move was complete. Now his family was well stocked with provisions to last a year or more. At last he was ready to go in search of his white relatives.[9]

In Search of Kin

❴ 34 ❵ In the summer of 1818, Tanner left Plantation Island in a small birchbark canoe bound for the States. He did not go directly south, for that would have taken him through Sioux country, which he considered too dangerous. Instead, he headed east toward Lake Superior, intending to backtrack over the route he and Net-no-kwa had taken more than twenty years earlier, when they first came west from Lake Huron.

The Hudson's Bay people told him to expect rough treatment from the Nor' Westers as he passed by their forts, as they were "much enraged" over his involvement in retaking Fort Douglas. But when Tanner met them in person they were more forgiving. At Rainy Lake, the trader John Warren Dease hailed him from the riverbank and invited him to come inside. Once they were in the house, Dease gave him a chiding, saying by rights he should have barred the door against him. "Why do you not go to your own people of the Hudson's Bay Company?" he asked reproachfully. Tanner replied that he was now on his way to the States; he had decided the time had come to go search for his American relatives. Dease cogitated on that for a while, and gruffly responded, "It would have been well had you gone long ago." However, letting bygones be bygones, he offered him a seat in his canoe and took him to Fort William.

At Fort William, Tanner was reunited with Dr. McLoughlin for the first time since lying in a sickbed in his care some four years earlier. When Tanner informed him of his intentions to go to the States, the good doctor was obviously affected. Looking him up and down, as if studying Tanner's light complexion, long reddish hair, and buckskins for the first time, he said he had something to give him for his journey. He went to the apothecary and came back with some tartar emetic to add to his medicine bag. It was in case he ate something poisonous along the way or contracted dysentery in the unfamiliar country, the doctor explained.

With McLoughlin's assistance, Tanner rode in a company boat from Fort William around the north shore of Lake Superior to Sault Ste. Marie, where he presented himself with a letter of introduction to the independent trader Charles Ermatinger. A former clerk in the North West Company, Ermatinger had become a successful farmer and middleman, selling grain and other supplies to his former employers. He provided Tanner with lodging in the big house that he occupied with his Ojibwa wife and eight children, and on his next trip to Mackinac he took Tanner along.

At Mackinac, Tanner met with yet more kindness. The US Indian agent, William Puthuff, gave him provisions and a letter addressed to the governor of Michigan Territory, then put him on a schooner bound for Detroit. The agent also furnished him with a canoe for the journey from Detroit to the Ohio. The canoe was lashed to the side of the schooner. After a five-day voyage down Lake Huron, Tanner was in Detroit.[1]

With just over a thousand residents in 1818, Detroit was the biggest white settlement he had ever seen. Coming down off the boat, he stood for a long time just gazing about him at horse-drawn wagons and carriages moving up and down the muddy streets and crowds of pedestrians clomping over the boardwalks. At length he began asking passersby for directions to the governor's house, but no one would respond to his labored attempts at speaking English. So he started walking and soon came to a mansion that looked like the place. It was fifty feet long, two stories high, and had a grand porch facing the street. A rotund man whom Tanner took to be the governor was sitting on the porch. Walking up to him, Tanner held up his letter from the Indian agent. Sure enough, this man was Governor Lewis Cass. After reading the letter, the governor held out his hand in welcome and immediately sent a man to get an interpreter.[2]

By a remarkable coincidence, the interpreter who was summoned turned out to be none other than Kish-kau-ko, the son of Manitoo-geezhik, Tanner's long ago captor. Tanner could barely recognize this interpreter as the young man whom he had once called his brother. Kish-kau-ko was naturally reticent about their past relationship. Indeed, he probably avoided communicating to the governor the fact of his own involvement in Tanner's capture, for Governor Cass remained ignorant of the two men's past connection; he made no mention of it in the description of Tanner that he gave to the newspapers. Tanner, for his part, had no way of knowing what got translated and had to assume that Kish-kau-ko corroborated his testimony when he told the governor about his capture and two-year stint with the Ottawa at Saginaw. Nonetheless, the governor learned enough to write a lengthy account of Tanner's background and capture in 1790. This went into the newspapers under the headline "A Captive Found." It was dated August 2, 1818, and was signed "Lewis Cass."[3]

Cass was one of two territorial governors who played important roles in Tanner's transition back into the white man's world. The other was Governor William Clark of Missouri. Both governors were deeply involved in Indian affairs, gathering information about tribes, negotiating land-cession treaties, and enforcing the Indian Trade and Intercourse laws. Both men had led troops in the War of 1812 and remained profoundly suspicious of British intentions after the Treaty of Ghent. Both advocated strong US involvement in the fur trade, partly to spur economic growth in their respective territories and partly to take the trade out of British hands and quash British influence over Indian tribes in US territory.

The governors differed in how they sought to reorganize the fur trade, however. Cass was a great friend of John Jacob Astor and the American Fur Company. After the company moved its field headquarters to Mackinac in 1816, the Michigan governor decided Astor's organization was the one best suited to compete with the British. He used his authority in issuing traders' licenses to further the American Fur Company's monopoly throughout the Michigan Territory. Governor Clark, meanwhile, wanted to Americanize the fur trade through the creation of a government-owned company based in St. Louis. Government ownership was important, he believed, to ensure that the enterprise was sufficiently capitalized to achieve a monopoly position. The St. Louis location seemed necessary to Clark if the Americans were to compete effectively with the British in the upper Missouri. In 1818, the Missouri Territory took in all of the Louisiana Purchase minus the state of Louisiana, while the Michigan Territory included the future states of Michigan, Wisconsin, and part of Minnesota. These were the two big western territories in the United States at that time. As a result, the governors' ideas carried enormous weight in federal Indian policy.[4]

Both governors saw the fur trade as an extension of statecraft. They hoped to shape it in ways that would help secure peaceful relations between white Americans, Indians, and the British. To that end, they were keenly interested in how the fur trade functioned. Yet, when they encountered John Tanner, the subject never came up. Where they might have recognized in him a white-Indian hunter who knew the business from an Indian perspective, instead they regarded him in more conventional terms. Here was the boy who had been stolen from his home by Indians many years before. The humane thing to do, then, was to restore him to his family.

Regarding Tanner through the nineteenth-century prism of civilization and savagery, the governors were unable to form a more nuanced view of the man. Governor Cass presented him with a set of American-style clothes and sent him on his way. A few years later Governor Clark did the same thing, entering the expenditure in his account book with the following notation: "four handkerchiefs, $2; four pair socks, $2; four yards cloth, $16, furnished

John Tanner and family, *returned from the Indians, with whom he was a pris-oner.*"[5] Tanner accepted their gifts with gratitude, but the sentiment behind them did not bode well for him. The governors thought they were helping him reclaim his white heritage, and they assumed the transformation would be quick. They had no conception of a person in his circumstances trying to bridge two cultures. Even as the fur trade formed a meeting ground for Indian and white America and encouraged a mingling of the two races, American society as a whole remained closed to the idea of either a bicultural, white-Indian identity or an interracial family. The governors of Michigan and Missouri territories were as well placed as any US leaders to understand this contradiction and do something about it. That they expected Tanner just to shed his Indianness like a set of clothes was significant.

Meanwhile, Tanner's white relatives made heroic efforts to help him. Edward Tanner left his home in New Madrid, Missouri, on August 31, 1818, to go look for his brother in the Red River valley—unaware that John had already arrived in Detroit at the beginning of that month. Edward went first to St. Louis, where he informed Governor Clark of his purpose and obtained papers and instructions for traveling due north through Sioux country to the Red River. When he got to Prairie du Chien, the trader told him that a man fitting his brother's description had reportedly reached Mackinac. So Edward, hoping to intercept him there, changed his route and proceeded via the Wisconsin and Fox rivers to Green Bay, where he hired an Ojibwa interpreter and boarded a schooner for the passage up Lake Michigan to Mackinac. Only when he reached Mackinac in November did he learn that his brother had met with Governor Cass in Detroit some four months earlier. Changing his route again, he made for Detroit.[6]

A few weeks after Edward set out, one of John Tanner's sisters read in a Kentucky newspaper the notice issued by Governor Cass, and she immediately sent her son to Detroit. By then John had left Detroit with a group of Indians but had fallen sick with a fever while descending the Big Miami River. His nephew found him in the care of a farmer, still quite ill. The nephew took him in a skiff down the Big Miami and Ohio rivers to a cluster of farms on the Kentucky side of the river, where John met numerous relatives, including the sister, another grown nephew, and a younger half-brother whom he had never known. He was still so weak that he had to be carried from the skiff to the house, and when he was finally situated in the home of his half-brother, he lay sick for another month.[7]

John could communicate with his relatives only a little, but when a letter from Edward arrived he understood from their conversation that his older brother had gone to look for him in the Red River country. The information in Edward's letter was out of date and did not disclose how he had changed course and gone to Mackinac. Though John was still unwell, he was walking around again and could ride a horse. Fearing for Edward's safety, he insisted that he must go north at once to find his brother—they had swapped places! His relatives reluctantly consented to his plan. With about a dozen neighbors, they took up a collection and gave him a purse of silver coins for the journey.[8]

Edward met with Governor Cass in December, more than four months after John did. Though his brother's trail had grown cold, he hoped that John might have found his way to their sister's place in Kentucky. But soon after Edward acquired a horse and started for home, he received some distressing information. At Fort Meigs, two days south of Detroit, he was told that John had passed by in the other direction just a few days earlier, heading back to the Red River. Turning about, Edward rode swiftly back to Detroit to catch John before he boarded a ship for Mackinac. John, meanwhile, on reaching Detroit, went again to the governor. Fortunately, Governor Cass insisted that he stay there and wait for Edward to return for him. Three days later Edward arrived as the governor had guessed he would. Finally, after months and indeed decades of searching, the two brothers were reunited. As John later recounted, "He held me a long time in his arms."[9]

After twenty-eight years of separation, the brothers were now well into middle age. John thought that Edward bore a strong resemblance to their father. Edward noted a scar on the left side of John's face and neck that he remembered from their childhood. A newspaperman remarked that the brothers looked very much alike, though John still had long hair past his shoulders like an Indian. Throughout his adult life, he had kept his hair parted in the middle and either braided or loosely tied on each side of his head with a string of broaches made of animal bone. However, before the two paid a final visit to the governor, he allowed his brother to cut off his long braids. Governor Cass approved of the haircut, commenting that he was pleased to see that John had laid his Indian costume aside and was now dressed like a white man.[10]

John lived with Edward at his home in New Madrid, Missouri, through the winter and spring. Edward was keen to rehabilitate John. As his brother's English improved, Edward developed big plans for the two of them. He applied to the American Baptist Board of Foreign Missions to serve as a missionary among the western Indians, with John to act as his interpreter. Edward already had some acquaintance with the western tribes by way of his military experience, and on his journey from Prairie du Chien to Green Bay he witnessed a few of the Indians' religious ceremonies. These he described in a long letter to the Reverend John M. Peck, who headed the Baptist mission in St. Louis. Peck published the letter in *The Latter Day Luminary* and sponsored Edward's application to the board. When the board met in Baltimore in April 1819, it resolved to give his application serious consideration. "This is encouraged by the peculiar circumstances of his brother, who is acquainted with several Indian languages, and whose aid, most probably, may be obtained," the minutes of the board recorded.[11]

John seems to have genuinely entertained the prospect of joining Edward on a mission, but in the meantime he had a more pressing object in mind. Since reuniting with Edward in Detroit, he had been telling his brother that he needed to find his Indian family and bring them to the States. He had in mind not just his young children by Therezia but also his first set of children by Red Sky of the Morning. As for his two wives, he now felt estranged from both of them.[12]

In the summer of 1819, the brothers met with Governor Clark to consider how John might reclaim his children from Indian country. Edward told the governor that he wished to accompany John to the Indian village at Lake of the Woods where the children would likely be found. As a former captain in the army, he requested the command of a company of soldiers so that they could seize the children from the Indians should force be necessary. Without acknowledging it, the brothers proposed to deal with the Indians much as the Ottawa-Shawnee war party had dealt with the Tanner family a generation before. Of course, there was one major difference: John Tanner was the biological father of these children. There was, in addition, a significant distinction in tactics: the Indians used stealth to take child captives, whereas Edward Tanner proposed to use intimidation and state power. Despite those differences, the outcome would be strikingly similar: children forcibly removed from their birth cultures, permanently separated from their mothers, and thrust into a new life.[13]

Governor Clark must have demurred from granting Edward Tanner's request for a military escort—if for no other reason than that these were British Indians who clearly resided outside his jurisdiction. Moreover, while US troops were often deployed to reclaim white captives, there was no such tradition of sending soldiers after mixed-blood children. Still, there was substantial precedent for white settlers snatching Indian children. Mostly it had been done under the pretext of converting the little innocents to Christianity.[14] So, if Edward's plan did not win approval from the governor, it almost surely met with some sympathy.

Whatever the governor's response, John would not agree to Edward's plan in any case. Following the meeting, he visited Clark again without his brother and informed him he wished to go alone. It was necessary, he said, because no white men, not his brother nor any soldiers, would be able to endure the hardships of the northern winter. He expected to live in an Indian lodge all through the winter and bring his children out after the spring breakup. Clark supported him, writing him a letter of endorsement to show to the traders whom he would meet in the course of his journey.

However, Clark still did not understand the Indian side of John Tanner's personality. Clark expected Tanner to travel due north through Sioux country, failing to see that those Indians were Tanner's mortal enemies. If the Sioux learned he was culturally Ojibwa or Ottawa, it could be his death warrant. In the end, Tanner found it expedient to accept Clark's offer of assistance, boarding a keelboat laden with provisions, guns, and army tents and manned by a large crew of sixty men. They were going north anyway and would take him as far as the upper Mississippi. Edward, who was by then reconciled to staying behind, wished his brother Godspeed. But as soon as the keelboat passed a little above the mouth of the Missouri, Tanner asked to be put ashore. With two men and a small canoe, he started up the Illinois River—making for Chicago, Lake Michigan, and thence the familiar route via Mackinac. That way, he would avoid the territory of the Sioux.[15]

Between Two Worlds

✳ 35 ✳ Tanner made two separate expeditions to claim his children from the Indians, the first in 1819–20, the second in 1822–23. On the first expedition, he succeeded in claiming the younger ones, his children by Therezia. On the second, he went back for the older three, the children of Red Sky of the Morning. In narrating these events a few years later for his book, he made it quite clear that his sole purpose for going back both times was to get the children. Yet in the first instance, with regard to his children with Therezia, he gave no details as to how he obtained custody of them. He made no mention of opposition by his mother-in-law, which must have been vociferous, or action of any kind by the village chiefs. We have only this terse comment on how it transpired: "My wife refusing to accompany me, I took the three children and started without her. At Rainy Lake she overtook me, and agreed to accompany me to Mackinac."[1] Probably what happened was that on his return to the village, Therezia fell back into a tumult over whether she loved him or hated him. Sometime near the end of 1819 she must have allowed him to make her pregnant, for by the time the two of them left for Kentucky together the following June or July, her pregnancy was quite far along. As her condition made it evident that their marriage was, if dysfunctional, still not completely over, the chiefs probably saw Tanner's claim to the children as a family matter.

So Therezia rejoined Tanner at Rainy Lake and consented to his plan of taking the family to the United States, at least as far as Mackinac. Therezia gave birth to a baby girl just a few days before they reached Mackinac. When they came to Mackinac Island, Tanner set up their wigwam on the beach in front of the small settlement. Soon an old woman came down from the nearest house to investigate. Tanner invited her into his lodge, showed her the newborn, and explained that they needed to rest there a while. When she asked where they were going, he told her they were on their way to Kentucky to join his brother. She went back to her house and returned with a set of white man's clothes for Tanner to put on.[2]

The woman was Thérèse Schindler, the daughter of a French fur trader and an Ottawa woman. She was married to George Schindler, an American trader. Around 1810, her husband had had a stroke, which left him partially paralyzed. Since then, she had taken over the business and expanded it. When the American Fur Company entered the upper Great Lakes fur trade in 1816, it enlisted her as a supplier. By 1820, she had become one of the wealthiest citizens on Mackinac Island.[3]

After a few days, Tanner called on the Schindlers and asked if they would be willing to care for the newborn. He proposed that they keep the girl for three years, at which time he would return for her. Reluctantly, the Schindlers agreed. He brought them the baby on a cradleboard and they drew up an indenture, which Tanner signed with a mark. A few days later the Schindlers baptized the newborn in the Roman Catholic faith. A record of the baptism, signed by the two godparents, was preserved by the Schindler family. It read: "On this 4th day of August, 1820, Lucy Tanner, aged sixteen days, has received lay baptism from George Schindler, Mackinac, Michigan."[4]

Tanner's actions in giving up the baby shocked Therezia. In her culture, children were treasured from the moment of birth. Placing an infant in the care of a relative was not unusual, but giving it to a stranger was a desperate act. She was in a torment over what to do next: whether to accompany her husband to Kentucky, or await his return at Mackinac, or abandon both him and the children and go back to her people at Lake of the Woods. Tanner finally convinced her to continue on, but she was now as depressed and unstable as ever.

In Tanner's *Narrative*, neither the infant daughter, Lucy, nor Thérèse Schindler receives any mention. Despite his candor about so much else, Tanner kept this episode to himself. In a letter Tanner sent to President Van Buren in 1837, however, he did allude to giving up his daughter that year: "I lost [her] on Mackinaw iland—she is [now] 16 years old and I dont know what is become of her." In the letter, he exonerated himself. "My family is Dear to me more than my own life."[5]

Apparently, Tanner thought the infant would likely not survive the remainder of their journey. Or, that if the rest of them were so encumbered, it would imperil the lives of his other three children, whose ages were approximately eight, seven, and six. It was not an unreasonable judgment. Having already made the journey to Kentucky once, he knew what a lot of sickness and hardship they were apt to experience. Perhaps, too, he had begun to sense the depth of the whites' racial prejudice and how it would make this journey even harder than his last. Twice while they were at Mackinac he tried to obtain passage for his family on schooners bound for Chicago. Both times the captain refused him—presumably on account of the family being Indian, for Tanner had the money to pay their fare. He now saw how much better the whites had treated him on his previous trip through the Michigan Territory, when he had come alone.

Giving up on the schooners, Tanner bought an old canoe from some Indians and set off with his family down the Lake Michigan shoreline. A little way south they came to an Ottawa village, where they fell in with a group of Ottawas going south to the Illinois country as well. A few days' short of Chicago, they learned from some Indians coming from the opposite direction that the swampy portage between the Chicago and Illinois rivers was very difficult on account of low water. It seems that these Indians may have alerted them to the presence of a bad sickness in the area as well, for the Ottawas decided then and there to turn back. Therezia wanted to turn back, too, but Tanner would not. Moreover, he insisted on taking his children with him. Therezia, still in despair, got into the northbound canoes without her children. Of this latest breakup of his family, Tanner would only say in his *Narrative* that his wife returned with the Ottawas.[6]

A few days later, as they arrived at the tiny settlement of Chicago, Tanner fell ill with a fever. Considering the season, the location, the fever's severity, and the fact that he did not pass it to his children, the ailment was most likely yellow fever. (Although yellow fever is highly infectious, it is not usually contagious between people, being transmitted by the bite of a mosquito.) The infection rendered him too weak to move, much less hunt, and soon he and the children had run out of provisions.

Feverish and anxious for the health of his hungry children, Tanner finally went to the US Indian agent at Chicago, a man named Alexander Wolcott, Jr. Tanner had met Wolcott briefly one year earlier, when he made his way north. He was certain Wolcott would remember him. However, Wolcott took one look at his sallow face and refused to let him into his house or offer him assistance of any kind.

The Indian agency stood on the north bank of the Chicago River just above Fort Dearborn. A little farther upriver there was a wild rice marsh where hundreds of redwing blackbirds were feeding on the rice grains, filling the air with their noisy chatter. With the last of his failing strength, Tanner towed their canoe to a piece of dry land in this place and erected a shelter in which to lie down out of the sun. For several days he lay in his sickbed, occasionally summoning the strength to raise himself to a sitting position and shoot a blackbird for the children to divide and eat.

When his fever at last subsided, Tanner made another attempt to get help from the Indian agent. Using two sticks for walking canes, he hobbled the short distance back to Wolcott's house and begged him for food for his starving children. Once more, Wolcott drove him away. This was the point at which Tanner nearly broke, crying like a woman—as he thought—because he could not contain his sorrow.[7]

They were discovered by a French trapper and his Ojibwa wife, who agreed, for a fee, to carry the four of them and their canoe over the portage in their horse-drawn cart. But after this couple had conveyed them several miles beyond the end of the Chicago River, the trapper was suddenly seized with fever and diarrhea. He insisted on offloading his passengers and turning his cart around right there. Now they were marooned with their canoe midway across the portage, which, in that low-water year, was reckoned to be a distance of sixty miles.

An old Potawatomi man came along on foot and offered to help. Tanner put his children and baggage back in the canoe, and the two men began towing it through the shallows, Tanner pulling at the bow and the older fellow pushing at the stern. This soon proved too slow and arduous to get them anywhere. When they rested, Tanner had to admit that they were well and truly stuck. But while they were sitting there, another Potawatomi man with two horses happened by. The older man, who was called the Smoker, spoke to the younger man in their Potawatomi tongue, bargaining on Tanner's behalf. The younger man finally offered to transport the children and baggage on his horses in exchange for a blanket and a pair of leggings. He would go one way while the Smoker and Tanner went another with the empty canoe and they would meet where the stream once again became navigable for the fully laden canoe. Tanner was suspicious of his proposal, especially since the rest of the baggage that he would entrust to the man had value. Yet what choice did he have? They were stranded in the middle of a vast swamp, sick, hungry, and exhausted. The Smoker promised him that this other Potawatomi was trustworthy. Tanner finally agreed to the arrangement, saying not another word as the younger Potawatomi put the three children on one horse and the baggage on the other. In three days, the man said, he would meet them at the mouth of a certain stream—the Smoker knew the one.

When Tanner and the Smoker came to the designated place, they found the man with his two horses waiting for them, the children all in good shape. At last they had reached water deep enough to float their canoe. Tanner paid the man, who went off with his horses, while he and his family, accompanied by the Smoker, threaded down the stream to the Illinois River. As they navigated this river across the prairie, Tanner was able to kill plenty of game. Finally eating well again, they recovered their strength and regained their health.[8]

It was mid-October when they reached St. Louis. They had been traveling nearly four months since departing Lake of the Woods, and they had covered more than a thousand miles, nearly all of it in small, birchbark canoes. Considering all the sickness, the children's young ages, and the necessity of hunting for food as they went, the journey was a remarkable feat. Tanner must have felt some pride in their accomplishment, even though the ordeal had nearly killed them all, and had driven away his wife. Docking their last canoe on the waterfront in St. Louis, Tanner led his children and the Smoker to the Indian agency to inform Governor Clark of his return.

The complex of buildings that made up the Indian agency covered over half a block along Main Street and included the governor's private residence, office building, factory house, blacksmith, gunsmith, and council house. The latter building, constructed according to Clark's personal specifications, featured a long meeting hall with a conference table down the center and display cases along the walls. The many glass cases exhibited more than 200 Indian artifacts collected from all over the West. Clark had designed the hall specifically for receiving Indian visitors and tribal delegations.[9]

Clark received them warmly. The governor doted on the children, presenting each one with a comb. Then he thanked the Smoker for his help in seeing the family safely to their destination, gave him a present, and offered assistance for his homeward journey. The old Potawatomi soon departed, while Tanner and the children remained in the city several days as the governor ordered a set of clothes made for each one of them. Clark also gave Tanner another letter, this time to the Indian agent at Cape Girardeau.[10]

When Tanner came to the Mississippi River town of Cape Girardeau, he happened to see the explorer, Stephen H. Long, then returning from his expedition to the Rocky Mountains. Tanner gave this incident only passing mention in his *Narrative,* so it would seem that he merely observed the members of the expedition from afar. That he had this encounter at Cape Girardeau three years before meeting Long for a second time at Rainy Lake House in 1823 was a coincidence and nothing more, though it speaks to what a small world the United States was in 1820, when the nation had fewer than ten million people.[11]

Tanner's white kin lived on both sides of the Mississippi River around Cape Girardeau, some in Missouri and others in Kentucky. They formed a large clan—perhaps a dozen brothers, sisters, and nephews, together with their spouses and many offspring. In the thirty years that John had been absent from the family, they had migrated from eastern Kentucky down the Ohio River valley to its junction with the Mississippi. They were part of a great migration of "southern plainfolk" who trekked across the Appalachians following the American Revolution and down into the Mississippi valley after the Louisiana Purchase. Southern plainfolk were yeoman farmers who typically cleared their own land, grew a patch of corn, raised a few dozen head of livestock, and subsisted their families by a combination of farming and herding. As their mode of living was well adapted to the sparsely populated frontier, they often pulled up stakes and moved farther west when other families settled nearby. A few, such as Tanner's father, owned slaves, but as they never owned more than a few at a time they were not part of the Southern slaveholding aristocracy. Although they often migrated in clans, like the Tanners did, generally each nuclear family worked its own land. As a people, they put a high value on self-reliance.[12]

Tanner did not thrive in this new environment. Despite the love and affection his relatives had shown him during his previous stay, he seems to have been ill at ease on his return. For whatever reason, he did not go back to his brother Edward's place. Edward's idea of their going on a mission together fell by the wayside. John lived with one sister on the Missouri side of the river for four months, then with another on the Kentucky side. He and his children were often sick. They suffered most in fall and winter, when the houses became stuffy and dank. They felt a terrible craving for fresh air. On Tanner's prior visit to the region, he had finally taken to sleeping outdoors, finding that it improved his health. But now his children were not permitted that option. His sisters, determined to raise them like white children, made them sleep in a bed indoors. That winter, all three children became ill with a fever that swept through the local population. The older two finally recovered; the youngest one died.[13]

After a year went by, John Tanner decided he could not stay there. He was simply not interested in farming, and as he remained quite odd to the Tanner clan in many ways, it is likely he wore out his welcome.

Perhaps most revealing of his inability to assimilate is this: his relatives finally quarreled over how they should collectively provide for him. At issue was the family's slave property. Several of John's relatives wanted to sell the slaves and put the proceeds into a trust fund, while another faction opposed that plan. The slaves had once belonged to John's father and now belonged to the father's estate; in other words, they were the property of the whole clan. Probably the several Tanner households took turns keeping these slaves and owning their labor; such an arrangement was not unheard of, and it would explain why no one had authority to sell them outright. The matter came to a head when John's stepmother took matters into her own hands and sent the slaves to the West Indies—apparently under lease, to keep them off the auction block in St. Louis. Those in the family who advocated setting up a trust fund for John took her to court, challenging her right to have done so without their consent. The matter had not yet been settled by the time John left.[14]

With his two daughters, Tanner made the long journey back to Mackinac. He knew that Therezia was living there, working as a domestic for Thérèse Schindler. In his *Narrative,* Tanner stated that a principal reason for going to Mackinac was to secure a job as interpreter for the US Indian agent, George Boyd. He had had repeated invitations from Boyd to come back and serve in that position once his English-speaking ability improved. After sixteen months with his white relatives, Tanner's proficiency with the language had indeed become much better. However, Tanner's own actions point to two other reasons for returning to Mackinac that he was disinclined to acknowledge. The first was to reconnect with Therezia. He was loath to admit it, but he missed her. In fact, the two resumed their tumultuous marriage as soon as he got there and she quickly became pregnant again. His second reason for settling in Mackinac would have been more difficult for him to explain in that era, but it was probably no less real for that. He wanted a community in which interracial, white-Indian families were not freakish, where he and his wife and children would suffer less prejudice.[15]

Mackinac would allow him to straddle two worlds. Existing at a crossroads between white and Indian peoples, the small settlement with its military fort, trading post, and boarding school was home for a few, a meeting place for many more, and a jumping-off point for still others. Both whites and Indians regarded Mackinac as a portal into the world of the other. The tragedy for Tanner was that he had known one world and then the other, yet he had become estranged from both. Paradoxically, his unusual experience bridging two worlds had come to limit his options rather than broaden them. The old Ottawa man, Wah-ka-zhe, who once told him he would have to make his way among the whites as an interpreter, had turned out to be right. It was almost the only occupation left to him. And going hand in hand with that, the little village of Mackinac, with its predominantly Métis population, must have seemed like one of the few communities still open to him. Alienated from both his Indian people and his white heritage, he may have hoped to find some sense of belonging there. At the very least, it would be a refuge.

In the summer of 1822, he and Therezia set about building a new life together. They found a dwelling on the island and bought a few modest furnishings for it. According to the Schindler granddaughter, whose memory may have been skewed on this point, Therezia then requested that her husband marry her in a Catholic service. Like so many white-Indian couples who married in Indian country and later came to live among the whites, the two came under pressure to sanctify their nuptials in the Christian faith. Whether or not Therezia accepted the Church's position that they were living in sin, she may have wanted a Christian ceremony simply to ease their way in their new community. Tanner refused. As the Schindler granddaughter recollected: "He said he had married her as they were all married in the Indian country, and she was his wife."[16]

Meanwhile, Tanner pursued a wage-earning job. It was not the first time he had worked for wages (the Hudson's Bay Company had paid him in cash when he hunted for the Red River colony, and he may have worked for wages in Kentucky as well). But now he considered taking wage work as a mainstay in place of his usual occupation of hunting. Boyd, the Indian agent, was as encouraging as ever about Tanner's long-range prospects for employment as an interpreter for the US Indian Office. Though he could not yet offer him a position, he proposed to put Tanner on as a striker in the blacksmith shop until he could find him one. Tanner was still weighing this offer when he went to see Robert Stuart, the American Fur Company agent at Mackinac.

The company offices were located in a brand new, three-story building on Market Street. Stuart was a second-generation fur trader whose father and uncle had both worked for the North West. He himself had sailed aboard the *Tonquin* around Cape Horn to serve two years at the Pacific Fur Company's outpost near the mouth of the Columbia River. At the end of that stint he had led an overland expedition from the Oregon country eastward. Since then, he had become prominent in John Jacob Astor's rising empire, overseeing the American Fur Company's expansion into the upper Great Lakes region. When Tanner inquired with Stuart about work, the trader could appreciate Tanner's unusual circumstances. In particular, he understood Tanner's desire to reclaim his children from Indian country.

Stuart drew up a labor contract tailored for Tanner's particular needs. He was to join William Morrison's Fond du Lac outfit. From Fond du Lac (modern day Duluth, Minnesota) he would go with the company of men to Rainy Lake, where he would hunt and trade with Indians through the winter. In late spring, when the others returned to Mackinac, he would be released to go to Red River to find the children of his first marriage and bring them out. In this last endeavor, he would be strictly on his own. For his services to the American Fur Company, he would be paid $225 per annum plus one set of clothes and a daily allowance of food.[17]

Tanner signed the contract with his mark, and walked out of the building with a renewed sense of purpose. This was to be his last journey to Red River.

❋{VII}❋ McLOUGHLIN

Chief Factor

❋ 36 ❋ John McLoughlin settled easily into his old post at Rainy Lake. In the eight years since he previously resided there he had proven himself to be a strong, intelligent manager, and he was comfortable in his new position of chief factor. In some ways, being chief factor of the Rainy Lake district was like being seigneur of his grandfather's Mount Murray Seigneury. There were elements of the job that must have reminded him of his late grandfather Fraser's preoccupations. He was running a farm as well as a trading post; he was overseeing a multiethnic community of men, women, and children; and he was directing a sizeable labor force. He was husband and father to a growing family and, as he saw it, patriarch to a considerable body of Rainy Lake Ojibwa, too.

McLoughlin's youngest daughter, Eloisa, was five years old, and his youngest son, David, was one-and-a-half when the family moved to Rainy Lake in 1822. In an interview more than a half century later, Eloisa recalled that her father "took charge of a little fort there" and the family "stayed two years." Her recollections are valuable because in McLoughlin's two years at this post he did not once mention his family in the official post journal or in his correspondence. Eloisa's statement confirms what would otherwise be left to supposition: his family was there with him. That the family is never mentioned in the company records is not surprising. McLoughlin always made it his practice to keep his wife and children separate and apart from his official duties. Whenever he entertained visitors, Marguerite did not dine with him and the children were kept in the family's private rooms. "The families lived separate and private entirely," Eloisa recalled with regard to their subsequent years at Fort Vancouver. "We never saw anybody."[1]

The Rainy Lake House that the McLoughlins occupied in 1822 was not the same trading post that they had lived in before. It was a newer set of buildings situated a few miles upriver from the old North West post, now abandoned. The Hudson's Bay post stood on a low promontory overlooking the Rainy River, the Koochiching Falls, and one end of a well-trodden portage that led around the falls. On the riverbank below the post there was a yard for making birchbark canoes, and a landing from which a path ran up the slope to the gate. The post itself consisted of a square stockade with two bastions situated at opposite corners and three buildings arranged around an interior courtyard: the officers' house, the servants' quarters, and a storehouse for skins and supplies. Above the palisaded stockade fluttered the crimson flag of the Hudson's Bay Company. And next to the flagpole stood a spindly watchtower from which a sentinel could observe Indians canoeing up the river from the west or portaging around the falls from the east. Behind the fort was a small clearing planted with corn, wheat, potatoes, peas, pumpkins, and melons, and beyond this patch of cultivation spread a field of stumps where trees were chopped down for firewood.

Rainy Lake House had a wintering population of around thirty male employees plus an unknown number of women and children. This small community cleaved into three distinct groups: an English-speaking officer class of four men, a French-speaking laboring class, and the mostly Ojibwa-speaking women and children. But the community was like three compact islands connected by a hundred bridges. Most of these people spoke at least two languages and some, like McLoughlin, spoke all three. A few of the men, and perhaps all of the women and children, were of mixed blood. Even in the matter of religion there was a crossing over of sometimes hard differences. McLoughlin himself had been baptized Catholic and then raised in the Protestant Church (at his grandfather Fraser's insistence). As practically the only literate person at Rainy Lake House, he took it upon himself to read aloud from the Bible on Sundays to his mostly Catholic employees.[2]

McLoughlin's three officers included one former Nor' Wester and two Hudson's Bay men. The former Nor' Wester was Simon McGillivray, the Métis son of William McGillivray. George Simpson described Simon in his notorious "Character Book." This notebook, which contains a series of personality sketches of Simpson's many associates, is well known by fur-trade historians for its raking personal remarks and cynicism. Concerning the younger McGillivray, Simpson wrote:

> Possesses a good deal of superficial cleverness and is very active but conceited, self-sufficient and ridiculously high-minded. Very Tyrannical among his people which he calls "discipline" and more feared than respected by men & Indians who are constantly in terror either from his Club or his Dirk. Would be a very dignified overbearing man if he was in power; fond of little convivial parties and would soon fall into intemperate habits if he had an opportunity of indulging in that way. Has a good deal of the Indian in disposition as well as in blood and appearance, and if promoted would be likely to ride on the top of his commission and assume more than it is either fit or proper he should have an

opportunity of doing; in short I think he would make a bad use of the influence
he would acquire by promotion and be a very troublesome man.[3]

One wonders what Simpson had in mind when he assigned McLoughlin
and McGillivray to work together. Not only were the two men both ill tempered, the doctor's feud with Simon McGillivray's father was well known.
Yet, despite their differences, the men's two-year partnership at Rainy Lake
succeeded.

Besides Simon McGillivray as chief trader, McLoughlin was assigned
two clerks, William Clouston and Charles Bouck. Both were Hudson's Bay
men who had been at Rainy Lake since the company moved into the area
in 1817. Clouston came from the Orkney Islands, the rain-swept archipel-
ago off the northern tip of Great Britain, where the Hudson's Bay Company recruited heavily in the early nineteenth century. Orkneymen were
found to make good employees, being for the most part loyal, temperate,
and hardworking. At the time of the merger in 1821 an estimated 40 percent
of Hudson's Bay employees came from the Orkney Islands. Bouck, on the
other hand, was Canadian. In the service of the Hudson's Bay Company
since 1815, he had taken a wife *à la façon du pays*—a marriage that stood him
in good stead with the Rainy Lake Ojibwa. McLoughlin wrote of Bouck,
"knows every Indian in this place—their character and disposition—is a
good trader and respected by the Indians but has no education." He wrote
of Clouston, "has no education—is a good trader—a very fit person for the
charge of small outposts."[4]

Among the two dozen laborers at Rainy Lake House were at least two
mixed bloods, Jean Baptiste Jourdain and Charles Roussin, and one full-
blood Indian by the name of Peninshin. Besides Peninshin and a man named
William Schelling, all the other men had French names, reflecting the fact
that the reorganized Hudson's Bay Company still drew heavily on French
Canadian voyageurs as well as Métis for its labor supply. The Rainy Lake
House annual account books and journals contain a wealth of information
about this population; for example, Jean Baptiste Auger was a guide and
canoe builder who served at Rainy Lake House beginning in 1820 and performed a wide variety of tasks around the fort; Jacques Beauvais and Pierre
Chalifoux, both at Rainy Lake starting in 1821, were two strong-backed men
who often worked together as woodcutters; Nicholas Chatelain, though new
to the place in 1823, must have been an energetic and trustworthy individual,
for McLoughlin sent him out frequently on fishing and trading expeditions.
McLoughlin regarded all of his laborers as unique individuals, recognizing
that their skills and physical strength differed widely.[5]

McLoughlin likewise treated the Rainy Lake Ojibwa as individuals. In his report on the Rainy Lake district for the fall, winter, and spring of 1822–23, he listed more than a hundred hunters by name. Next to each name he included a brief notation as to their hunting skills and character: "a tolerable Hunter but doubtful Character," "a good Hunter & honest," "a poor Hunter and Great Rascal," and so on. After each notation he jotted two numerals followed by an "N" or an "S." The numerals indicated how many women and children were with each hunter, and the letter indicated whether the person hunted north or south of the US border. Altogether he enumerated 118 hunters, 230 women, and 455 children. Not many traders made such an effort to know every Indian hunter within their districts.[6]

McLoughlin correctly observed that the extended family group formed the basic social and economic unit in Ojibwa culture. Family groups typically stayed together through the winter, hunting and taking care of domestic chores as a unit. Often the group consisted of one old man, his adult sons, and their spouses and children. McLoughlin's list of Indian hunters reflected this social structure; for example, the fifty-first name on his list was "Two Hearts Senior" and the next two names were "Two Hearts 1st Son" and "Two Hearts 2nd Son." The largest extended family group was that of Old Premier, a chief renowned for his excellent hunting skills and many brave deeds fighting the Sioux. In McLoughlin's 1822–23 census, Old Premier was the first person listed. He was followed by three brothers, two sons, and one stepson, with a total of ten women and twelve children attached to these seven men.[7]

McLoughlin recognized that the Ojibwas also had higher levels of social organization beyond the extended family group. The Ojibwas were grouped into clans, each clan being identified with a totem animal. Kinship was determined by patrilineal descent, and marriage partners had to come from outside the clan. Moreover, the Ojibwas came together in larger numbers during various seasonal food-gathering activities such as making sugar in the spring and fishing for sturgeon in the fall. They also gathered in large numbers each summer for the Midewiwin, a religious ceremony, and sometimes to form war parties against enemies such as the Sioux. McLoughlin and his contemporaries referred to the Ojibwas as Saulteaux (the name derived from the Ojibwa ancestral homeland around Sault Ste. Marie) and recognized them as a distinct Indian nation (a *nation* in the nineteenth-century sense of that word was a people united by culture). However, McLoughlin naturally focused on the smaller Ojibwa groupings because of their singular importance in trade. When he provided the Indians with ammunition and other supplies on credit, he did so in the expectation that they would return at the end of the hunting season in the same extended family groups.

At the start of October, Ojibwa family groups began arriving at Rainy Lake House, seeking to obtain goods on credit for the approaching winter. But now that they could trade their furs to the Americans on the other side of the river, McLoughlin could not be sure that the Indians would honor their debts at the end of the winter. He had no doubt that the Americans lacked the wherewithal to outfit the Indians as they were accustomed to being outfitted by the British. Yet these American interlopers (as he saw them) would do everything in their power to obtain the Indians' furs, irrespective of the fact that the Indians owed those furs to the British. McLoughlin's answer to the problem was to impress upon the Indians that they must henceforth respect the line between the British and American traders. If they took credit from the Hudson's Bay Company, then they must hunt on the British side and bring their furs to the British trading post. But if they went to the Americans for credit or trade, then he would not incur the expense of provisioning them because they were no longer the Hudson's Bay Company's Indians to trade with. For this strategy to succeed, all depended on establishing credit with the right Indians. "I will only endeavor to keep the Best hunters—The poor hunters and cheats I will allow [to] go to the Americans," he wrote in the post journal. "It will answer a double purpose— Clear us of a set of Indians who never pay us and if these Americans give them Debt it will clean them of a good lot of Goods and drain off their attention from others."[8]

McLoughlin first put his plan into action when Old Premier appeared with his band in early October. As was customary, on the evening of his arrival Old Premier sought out McLoughlin and they smoked the calumet. This ritual signified that the trade relationship was not just a matter of material exchange but carried social and political implications as well. Since Old Premier was a prominent chief, with a big following, he was used to generous treatment by the traders. McLoughlin did not disappoint him, filling his canoe the next morning with goods and a keg of rum—but only after he had used the occasion to announce the new regime: the Indians must repay their full debt to the British and have nothing to do with the Americans. When one of Old Premier's sons unwittingly disclosed that he had just obtained credit from the Americans, McLoughlin denounced Old Premier for his son's action and insisted on taking everything back, returning it to the store. Old Premier was astonished by this disrespectful treatment. As a token of his hurt, he took off his Hudson's Bay Company trade medal and hung it on a peg in McLoughlin's office. Then he went off and slept that night in his canoe.

The next day Old Premier returned, apologizing for his son's action and promising his loyalty to the British, at the same time reminding McLough-lin that he and the British traders had known each other a long time. McLoughlin granted this, admitting "it was true we had brought him and all his [family] up," but he stressed that the British traders did not want the Indians to be "slaves" to that relationship. Old Premier and his people were free to take credit from the Americans instead. In other words, McLough-lin sought to deflect Old Premier's characterization of their relationship as a social contract and make it more of a commercial relationship. Feeling that he had made his point, McLoughlin ordered his men to load the chief's canoe with goods all over again. "I think it was necessary to treat him in this unceremonious manner," McLoughlin wrote afterwards. "By acting in this manner with the principal man of the District, it will show the others that if they value our favour & approbation they must deserve it."[9]

Europeans and Indians knew that whenever they engaged in trade rit-uals the transaction involved more than a simple exchange of goods. Each exchange of furs for goods, or goods for credit, in addition to bringing ma-terial gain, entailed various shades of influence, interdependence, status, and obligation for both parties. However, if both parties saw clearly enough that their trade included all of these complex facets, they could never see eye to eye on what the ritual symbolism or terms of trade meant precisely. Their different cultures prevented it. Ojibwas viewed their trade relations with Europeans through the prism of their kinship relations, in which mutual gift giving had important social and even spiritual meanings aside from its economic benefits. European traders viewed the same transactions from the standpoint of commerce in a global economy. They operated within a com-pany structure that was primarily organized to respond to market forces and maximize profit. McLoughlin and Old Premier were able to communicate with one another only up to a point; then their opposing mindsets con-founded them.[10]

Part of why communications were so challenging was that the conditions of the fur trade were constantly changing. If a ritual such as smoking the calumet could embrace a world of meanings, it could not begin to regis-ter the profound impact of an ever more dominant European presence in North America, or the effect of European power and influence on Indian cultures.[11] McLoughlin and Old Premier each struggled for words to ex-plain how the fur trade was changing in their particular place and time. Old Premier used the analogy of a child growing under its parents' protection, while McLoughlin used more abstract terms such as "pity" and "charity" to explain the moral obligation that sometimes entered into the exchange.[12] If

McLoughlin's effort to reset trading practices between the Hudson's Bay Company and the Rainy Lake Ojibwas was in one sense naïve (since he had only a partial grasp of the Indian perspective), his effort was in another sense quite realistic: it took into account the new realities imposed by the 1821 coalition and the coming of the American Fur Company.

Providence

{ 37 } Everyday life at Rainy Lake House revolved around the changing seasons.[1] The annual cycle of activity began at the end of summer, when the chief factor arrived with his brigade of voyageurs and several tons of goods to be traded for furs in the coming year. As soon as the voyageurs had offloaded their cargo and carried it into the store, these same men became farm laborers, artisans, traders, hunters, and fishermen. The large north canoes were stowed out of the weather until the following spring, and local transportation needs were met by a combination of light canoe, foot, snowshoe, and sled as the seasons progressed.

Fall was spent stocking the fort with provisions for the long, cold winter ahead. In September most of the men and women went to work in the fields, cutting and drying hay and reaping and threshing wheat. Other men ran the mill, rolling the grain and loading flour into kegs. By October women were digging potatoes in the garden. Gradually, as the mornings turned frosty and days grew shorter, the food bins began to fill. By mid-November the barn would be crammed with bundles of hay and sheaves of wheat, and the corn bins would be packed with kegs of flour, potatoes, and garden produce.

The fall harvest included Indian crops as well as crops grown around the fort. The most important food obtained from the Indians was the seed of the water grass, *Zizania palustris,* commonly known as wild rice, which grows around the shores of shallow lakes from the Great Lakes region westward through southern Manitoba. The Ojibwas harvested this grain by going about the shallows in their canoes, bending the reeds over the gunwales of the canoe, and gently brushing the rice grains from the stalks. Rainy Lake House purchased a considerable store of this food through trade. Some of it the Indians brought to the fort, and some the traders purchased among the Indian camps. The Rainy Lake traders went to Plantation Island in Lake of the Woods to purchase corn, pumpkins, potatoes, and onions. They purchased corn from the Lake of the Woods Indians at the price of one three-point blanket for a bushel. In the fall of 1822, the clerks Clouston and Bouck each made separate trips to Plantation Island and returned with more than twenty kegs of corn apiece.[2]

Inside the fort, too, there were preparations for winter. The men replastered the walls and chimneys and repaired the roofs. The women made moccasins and snowshoes. Everyone worked on building up the enormous woodpiles.

As winter set in, the traders' attention focused on two imperatives: obtaining furs and ensuring that the food stores would last till spring.

Around the first snowfall, Indian hunters or their surrogates started coming in, animal peltries loaded on their backs or towed behind on sleds. Their loads (a mix of beaver, marten, mink, muskrat, bear, moose, lynx, otter, and fisher) sometimes amounted to just a few pieces, or, at other times, dozens or even hundreds. After the fur traders' careful planning and preparations through the preceding months, it all came down to this: passing a bitterly cold winter at the trading post and waiting anxiously for the Indian hunters to bring in furs. "On the 9th [January] the Little Deer's young Wife & daughter arrived," McLoughlin recorded. Much to McLoughlin's chagrin, the mother-daughter pair presented him with just one lynx skin and five marten skins—a very poor showing for their own and Little Deer's efforts thus far that winter and a paltry return on the family's credit of sixty skins. In one of his bleakest entries in the post journal of that winter, McLoughlin went on to relate that the mother and daughter told him the Little Deer remained behind in their winter camp "starving." McLoughlin gave the Little Deer's wife ten quarts of flour to take to her husband, who was waiting for her at the Manitou Rapids, plus two quarts "to feed her on the way."[3]

But even if the Ojibwas did virtually all of the hunting, the fur traders did not wait idly in the fort for the hunters to come in. Rather, they maintained contact with their Indian partners in every way possible. Rainy Lake House supplied two satellite outposts, one to the east and one to the west, each staffed by a handful of men, while those at the main fort took turns going out in parties of two or three to search for Indians and trade with them wherever they could be found. One of the most miserable duties was to man the guardhouse. This one-man shelter was maintained throughout the winter at the outlet of Rainy Lake, three miles from the fort. There a sentinel was expected to scan miles of lakeshore hour after hour watching for the least little flicker of human activity. As if the desolation of this post were not enough, the watcher often had to face into a cutting wind.

All winter long the fort's occupants obsessed about food. Their diet consisted mostly of porridge flavored with animal fat, augmented by an occasional helping of dried or freshly caught fish. Such a monotonous diet was vastly preferable to the alternative: hunger and dread of starvation. The traders lived on rations, and as the winter progressed and their Indian hunt-

ers more and more often came to the fort to beg for food, they found themselves in the uncomfortable position of drawing down their own food stores
to pay for those coveted furs.

If one reads the Hudson's Bay Company's records from this era too literally,
one easily gets the impression that fur traders and Indians alike were very
often desperately hungry. McLoughlin's post journals, like many others, are
filled with references to people starving. "Baballiards two sons with their
families and their followers arrived here starving," he wrote at one point.
"The Barque and another . . . are suffering the greatest degree of starvation
—which they give as the cause of their poor hunt," he wrote in another
entry.[4] All such references must be interpreted with care. Ethnographer
Mary Black-Rogers made a close study of the various meanings and contexts of the word "starving" in Hudson's Bay Company records and found
that these references fall into three broad usages. First, there was the *lit-
eral* usage, which described people who were actually dying of hunger or
suffering horribly because they had no food. Second, there was a *technical*
usage (unfamiliar to the modern reader because it belonged to a specialized
fur-trade glossary), which referred to a condition in which the quest for
food became so precarious as to allow no time or energy for other pursuits.
In this sense, starving Indians were those living too close to the edge to be
effective fur hunters. Viewed in this light, McLoughlin's statement, "They
are suffering the greatest degree of starvation—which they give as the cause
of their poor hunt" takes on a very different meaning. The third usage that
Black-Rogers identified was *manipulative* in intent. This involved declaring
oneself to be starving, whether it was literally true or not, in order to receive
food or some other compensation. Often the Ojibwas called out that they
were starving even as they approached a fort. As Black-Rogers pointed out,
European traders and Indian hunters had different cultural perceptions of
begging and supplicating. While Europeans tended to view an announcement of one's pitiful condition or helplessness as ignoble behavior, Indians
generally regarded it as merely disarming or nonaggressive. (Another ritual
greeting that both sides adopted was to fire guns in the air when approaching, the purpose being to show that all guns were unloaded as the parties
drew close.) Perhaps when McLoughlin wrote that the Baballiards "arrived
here starving" it was his shorthand for recording such ritualized behavior
when the Ojibwas approached the fort.[5]

Taking into account that not all references to "starving" were as dire as
the word suggests, it is still true that starvation loomed as a frightening
prospect for the fur traders. The Indians faced this threat each winter with
far greater equanimity, in part because actual death by starvation, which was

rare from the Europeans' standpoint, was fairly common in their experience. No one among the Ojibwas was immune to the danger. Old Premier, the prominent chief, starved to death with his entire extended family in the winter of 1825–26.[6] The Indians' seeming indifference to the prospect of starvation could be unnerving to the European fur trader. In contrast to the disciplined way in which the trading house laid in stores and measured out rations, the Indians displayed a feast-or-famine mode of living that struck the fur traders as recklessly improvident.[7]

The Rainy Lake region was a particularly hungry land in the early nineteenth century. The once abundant moose and caribou had largely been hunted out. Farther westward, on the prairie, fur traders and Indians still ate elk and buffalo during the winter months, but the Rainy Lake region afforded only meager amounts of animal protein from fishing, snaring rabbits, and occasionally killing a large mammal. "This is a miserable place for provisions," McLoughlin remarked in the post journal in 1822. In this instance, he recorded an objective fact.[8]

Spring was the most welcome season of the year at Rainy Lake House, but it came on at an agonizingly slow pace. As the days lengthened and the sun rose higher in the southern sky, weeks passed and the enormous mantle of snow and ice remained locked in place. The snow might not completely leave the ground until the latter part of April, and ice would remain on the lakes and swamps for some while after that. During the long thaw, travel became exceedingly difficult. McLoughlin observed that although the climate of the Rainy Lake region was similar to that of his native Quebec, the flatness of the terrain meant that there was no appreciable current in the rivers to dislodge the ice and carry it away. Instead of a sudden and noisy spring breakup, the lake ice slowly thinned and loosened into plates that lingered for weeks. These "flakes," as McLoughlin called them, drifted to and fro across the lake with the least breath of wind, so that a shore offering clear passage for a canoe one day might be jammed with ice the next.[9]

Notwithstanding the difficulty of travel during the long spring breakup, it was precisely at this time that the traders redoubled their efforts to go out and find Indians, who were then concluding their winter hunts. Those still at the fort kept busy filling the ice house, and cutting and hauling wood and birchbark for building and repairing canoes. The actual manufacture of canoes had to wait on warmer weather, as warm days were needed for stretching the birchbark. During the month of May, the men of the fort were variously employed making canoes and plowing and sowing the fields.[10]

With June came preparations for the outbound journey. First, the chief factor made final inventories of furs, goods, and provisions and settled the men's accounts. Then all of the furs in the fur store were sorted and bundled into ninety-pound packs under a wedge press, and these were carried on strong backs down to the canoe landing and placed in the big north canoes.

With the departure of the chief factor and his brigade, Rainy Lake House was left in the hands of the chief trader, two clerks, and a few laborers together with all of the wives and children. With its total population of men, women, and children reduced to about half what it was in winter, the trading house then passed through the normally quiet summer months.

Opposing the Americans

❊ 38 ❊ While the merger of the two great fur companies in 1821 secured a monopoly over the country from Hudson Bay to Lake Athabaska, the reorganized Hudson's Bay Company still faced competition along the international frontier with the United States. Nowhere was this threat greater than in the Rainy Lake region. The company's aggressive new leader, George Simpson, recognized two sources of competition there: the American Fur Company and the independent traders. Of the two, Simpson saw a more urgent need to oppose the latter, the "petty Traders of Lake Superior." Competition from such people could not be tolerated, for if they were permitted to chip away at the company's territory then others would follow.

The largest independent trader in the area was George Johnston. Based in Sault Ste. Marie, Johnston established two posts in the Rainy Lake region in 1821. One post was on Crane Lake in American territory and the other on Mille Lacs in British territory. Johnston put two brothers, Paul and Bazil Beaulieu, in charge of the first post and a former Nor'Wester, Joseph Cadotte, in charge of the second.[1]

By the time McLoughlin took over Rainy Lake House in September 1822, Cadotte had been driven out of British territory by an Indian attack that claimed the lives of two of his men. But the Beaulieu brothers still had their trading house at Crane Lake. McLoughlin's first impulse was to send his chief trader, Simon McGillivray, to Crane Lake with a force of men to undercut their trade. En route, however, McGillivray learned that a US customs agent was in the vicinity, so he left his men inside British territory and returned to Rainy Lake House to confer with McLoughlin. Since 1816, the US government had banned British traders in American territory, but as yet there had been no enforcement of the law west of the Great Lakes. Now both men agreed that they should not risk the arrest of their men or the hefty $1,000 fine for trading without a US license. Instead, McGillivray established an outpost at nearby Basswood Lake in British territory, still with the object of capturing most of the trade and driving off the American competition.[2]

With McGillivray and his Hudson's Bay men aggressively trading nearby, the Beaulieu brothers soon ran out of provisions at Crane Lake. All their hired men deserted them. Some of these deserters appeared at Rainy Lake House in December, "starving" and offering to work for food. McLoughlin refused to employ them, but on humanitarian grounds he gave them each two days' rations and sent them on their way. The Beaulieu brothers stayed at Crane Lake through the winter, though by spring they were reduced to eating animal skins to keep alive.[3]

The Hudson's Bay Company faced a far more formidable rival in the American Fur Company of New York financier John Jacob Astor. This company operated on a different business model than either the Hudson's Bay Company or the North West Company. Astor acted as import-export agent for the American Fur Company, which in turn served as liaison to the traders in the field. Each trader was assigned a department, or "outfit." The trader normally assumed all risk of profit or loss, although the company would sometimes share in profit or loss on a 50–50 basis. The American Fur Company tried to minimize competition between its own traders but was never completely successful.[4]

Although Astor liked to suggest that his fur company was a US equivalent to the Hudson's Bay Company—"the only respectable one of any capital now existing in the country," he once wrote to Senator Thomas Hart Benton of Missouri—in fact, the American Fur Company behaved more like the rapacious independent traders with whom it competed.[5] Its decentralized capital structure ensured that its traders would emphasize immediate profits over long-term interests. At a time when the reorganized Hudson's Bay Company began taking small steps toward conserving wildlife, reducing imports of liquor, and improving the welfare of its employees, the American Fur Company did nothing of the sort.[6] The only thing that distinguished it from George Johnston's outfit was its size. As the American Fur Company had far more capital behind it, McLoughlin could not expect to defeat this rival so much as hold it at bay.[7]

In the fall of 1822, the American Fur Company established new posts at Grand Portage, Rainy Lake, Vermilion Lake, and Lake of the Woods—a line of posts running more or less along the US border with British America. (The US-British Convention of 1818 defined the international border from Lake Superior to Lake of the Woods as not along the forty-ninth parallel but following the main voyageur route through the maze of lakes and streams now known as the Boundary Waters. This description of the boundary line was unambiguous to most traders and Indians in the region, although it would not be officially surveyed until 1823 and not finally settled until the Webster-Ashburton Treaty of 1842.) The whole area from the shore of Lake Superior across what is now the northern tier of Minnesota counties was included in the American Fur Company's Fond du Lac Department and placed in the capable hands of William Morrison, another former Nor'Wester. In George Simpson's judgment, Morrison was "one of the best and most experienced Salteaux traders in the country."[8]

Informed by Simpson of the American Fur Company's plans, McLoughlin waited for Morrison to come up the Rainy River in the early fall of 1822. Morrison sent a pair of clerks instead. One was Pierre Côté, a mixed blood from Fond du Lac, and the other was Joseph Cadotte, the former Nor'Wester who had worked for George Johnston at Mille Lacs the previous winter. When the outfit finally arrived without Morrison on October 5, McLoughlin counted fourteen men in seven small canoes, the lead canoe flying the American flag. As he soon learned, the fourteen included the white Indian, John Tanner, whom McLoughlin still knew by his Indian name, Shaw-shaw-wa ne-ba-se, the Swallow. They camped on the south side of the river almost exactly opposite Rainy Lake House. The next day the men set to work building a post, which rose within sight of the Hudson's Bay establishment. Morrison visited the new post only once during the winter, and although McLoughlin recorded his arrival and departure from across the river, he made no mention in the journal of any courtesy call between them.[9]

Côté and Cadotte proved to be wily foes for McLoughlin. The chief factor asked the Americans to refrain from trading with Indians on British soil, but the Americans refused. After enduring several months of the Americans' trespasses, he called Côté and Cadotte over to Rainy Lake House on a ruse and took them prisoner as soon as they set foot on the British side of the river. The tactic was reminiscent of the old struggle between the Hudson's Bay Company and the North West Company. McLoughlin wished not to venture too far down that road, so after keeping them confined for ten hours he extracted a promise from Côté in writing that he would not allow his people to trade with the British Indians any more, and then he let the two go. Writing at length in the post journal that evening, McLoughlin cogitated over the day's excitement and what it meant for the future. Had he done wrong in holding the men prisoner? "Taking them after asking them to come over," he wrote, "it may be said I broke my word—but it must be recollected that they first broke theirs by coming to our side." If he could not treat his unscrupulous American rivals as roughly as he might have liked, neither could he stand by passively when they trespassed. And yet, as he tried to force a change in the American company's practices, he still worried that it might provoke retaliation or expose him to legal action by higher authorities.[10]

But McLoughlin's tactic seemed to do the trick. The Americans ceased trespassing on British territory. And with the Hudson's Bay Company's greater capacity for supplying the Indians their wants, he soon had the lion's share of the trade. In his year-end report on the district, McLoughlin stated with obvious satisfaction that the Americans departed in June with twelve packs of furs (nine of them underweight) compared to the Hudson's Bay Company's twenty-nine. When McLoughlin reported in person to the governor and council of the Northern Department at York Factory that summer, he boldly predicted that the Americans would not be back the next season.[11]

❋{VIII}❋ COLLISION

Working for Wages

❋{ 39 }❋ Two years after leaving Indian country with Therezia, and four years after leaving it the first time, Tanner returned to Rainy Lake in the role of a fur trader. John McLoughlin observed the arrival of Tanner's group from the British side of the Rainy River and recorded the event in the post's journal. "About one PM Messrs Cote and Cadotte made their appearance in the Canoes with the American flag flying. They camped at the South side halfways between the two Forts. Several Saulteur Canoes brought up the rear, and seemed loaded with provisions." The date was October 5, 1822.[1]

Tanner may have been the only American citizen in this outfit. The other dozen or so men were probably all French Canadians. The American Fur Company, like the Hudson's Bay Company, found French Canadian voyageurs to be an indispensable source of labor in the Great Lakes region. The American Fur Company's Northern Department was staffed almost entirely by these people. Tanner was the odd man out. He did not speak French like the others, nor did he understand their manners. He was little more at home in the close quarters of the American trading post at Rainy Lake than he had been the year before among Kentucky farmers.[2]

The clerk in charge of the post, Pierre Côté, soon sent Tanner to Manitou Rapids, a place on the Rainy River where the Indians gathered and caught sturgeon during the fall migration. Traders normally took a quantity of liquor along to trade for part of the Indians' catch rather than seine for sturgeon themselves. In years past, Tanner's friends had entered into this exchange both at Manitou Rapids and at the rapids on the inlet into Rainy Lake, a place the traders knew as Kettle Falls. Tanner had seen the traders make off with so much of the Indians' dried sturgeon that their canoes could barely stay afloat, while the Indians got nothing for their work but a day of debauchery. He also remembered the time at Kettle Falls when he indulged in a drinking bout, passed out drunk, and awoke hours later to find all his possessions stolen. Contemplating these practices from his new vantage point, as a non-Indian engaged in stocking the fort with winter provisions, he felt as averse to the use of liquor as he had ever been. Refusing to take any whiskey in his outfit, he went to the rapids and caught 150 sturgeon by his own efforts.[3]

Soon after Tanner returned to the post, Côté assigned him and five other men to scour the country in search of Indians with peltries. They were to load up with trade goods and not return until they had exchanged every last item for furs. This aggressive mode of trade—taking the goods to the hunters rather than waiting for the hunters to bring their peltries to the post —was called "running *en dérouine.*" Traders increasingly employed the practice in order to maximize their returns and get an edge over their competitors. Tanner was to be the group's guide and interpreter. He proposed to wait until the first snow so that they might use dog sleds to carry their freight. Côté insisted that they leave without delay. Tanner prevailed on another point, however: their outfit, like the one he took to the fall fishery, contained no liquor.[4]

On their fourth day out they ran into a snowstorm. Tanner called a halt while everyone made snowshoes. When the weather finally cleared, the land lay deep in snow. Tanner wanted to go on, but several in the party thought this foolhardy. The group finally split in two. Four men insisted on returning to the post, while Tanner and one other chose to keep going. This fellow, who went by the name Veiage, impressed Tanner as an exceptionally hardy one of his kind. The two men loaded as much of the outfit as they could on their backs before parting company with the others.

Tanner and Veiage each carried a substantial quantity of wild rice. This was their sole sustenance unless they could augment it by hunting or, should they become desperate, by trading some of their goods for food instead of furs. After struggling on through the deep snow for several more days, Tanner and Veiage grew weak on their meatless diet. Tanner led them to an Ojibwa encampment. These Indians were nearly as destitute as they. Leaving Veiage in their care, he trekked on to the next encampment, which the Indians told him lay some distance ahead. When he arrived at the second encampment, he found those Indians to be just as hungry and poor as the first group; they could offer him nothing. Wearily he turned back, for the first group had been willing to give Veiage and him shelter at least. But stumbling into the camp late in the day, he found the lodges were gone and neither the Indians nor the French Canadian were anywhere to be seen. Their trail led off through the snow, but Tanner was too spent to follow it. As dusk came on, he could not summon the will to make a fire. Foreseeing that the night would be an extremely cold one and he would likely freeze to death, he composed himself to die.

Tanner was alone but not abandoned. Just before dark, an Indian hunter returned to the site to look for him. He roused Tanner from his torpor, helped him build a fire, and huddled with him under his blanket through the still, frigid night. In the morning the man left him tending the fire while he went to check his trap line, returning with one beaver. Then he led Tanner to their new camp, where the flesh of the single beaver was cooked and divided among the twenty people of the band plus their two guests. Marginally fortified, Tanner and Veiage set out once more.[5]

As the winter progressed, they slowly converted their loads of goods and trinkets into furs. When the snow on the ground consolidated, they acquired dogs and a dogsled. There were more desperate days: sometimes it seemed they threaded a line between purposeful work and a sheer fight for survival.

Once, as they followed the trail of a band of Indians, they were reduced to gnawing on animal bones and scraps of leather that the Indians had discarded a few days before. Though the Indians' tracks were now covered by snow, Tanner and Veiage began searching under the snow's surface as they walked, looking for worn-out moccasins or anything else that could provide the least bit of sustenance. By and by they found two dead dogs, each one lying under a telltale snowdrift. These they dug out and ate.

On another occasion their wanderings brought them to the lodge of Oto-pun-ne-be, Tanner's old friend who had avenged him on Plantation Island some four years earlier. Tanner was taken aback when Oto-pun-ne-be's wife cried out at his emaciated appearance.[6]

Back at the American Fur Company post on the Rainy River, Côté wondered what had become of Tanner and Veiage. He figured either they had perished or they had gone to hunt buffalo. At last he sent eight men to look for them. This relief party found Tanner and Veiage shortly after they had departed from Oto-pun-ne be's lodge. As they were many miles from the post and low on food, Tanner proposed that they go to the buffalo grounds. The others agreed to it. There, they killed several buffalo, ate copiously of the fresh meat, and regained their strength. Being at last well-provisioned, they were able to complete their mission of searching out Indians and trading goods for furs. Winter was more than half over when they returned to the post, Tanner's dogsled loaded high with peltries.[7]

Although the load weighed in at 600 pounds, Côté fumed over what a lousy return it was on the value of goods they had started with. For this, he blamed Tanner for refusing to include whiskey in the outfit. He also groused because the men had eaten one of the company's dogs to get through their ordeal. Even though they had decided as a group to consume the animal, Côté made a point of charging ten dollars to Tanner's personal account to cover it. And, finally, he ordered the men to make a second run *en dérouine*, insisting that they take a supply of whiskey this time to ensure a better return. Under Côté's bullying, Tanner acquiesced and accepted whiskey in the second outfit. As much as he resisted plying the Indians with liquor, he dared not give Côté any grounds for cheating him out of his year's pay. He even agreed to lead the party to Lake of the Woods to trade with the very Indians whom he had once counted as his friends. And, to everyone's chagrin, the whiskey did smooth their way with the Indians. In short order, they returned to the post with twice as many furs as they had obtained the first time out. Tanner felt ashamed by what he had done, and he told Côté he would never consent to the same thing again.[8]

The hand-wringing and hypocrisy that marked this outfit's trafficking of liquor to the Indians was no isolated affair. The issue played out across the whole northern frontier that season, causing consternation among governing officials in both Detroit and Washington. With the United States deploying customs agents along the northern border in the winter of 1822–23, it raised the question of whether the US government truly intended to suppress the flow of liquor into Indian country as Congress had long said it would do. Americans who were engaged in the Indian trade west of Lake Superior worried that the new customs agents might, in fact, work to the disadvantage of their own countrymen if they tried to enforce the prohibition against liquor trafficking. So the traders went on the offensive, claiming that the Hudson's Bay Company continued to supply ardent spirits to the Indians; therefore, they must be permitted to do the same or else abandon the field to the British. Governor Cass of Michigan heard the traders' pleas and came to their defense. In spite of his compunctions about the liquor trafficking, he had to weigh the Indians' welfare against the national interest in securing the Indian trade along the northern frontier with Britain. In June 1823, he wrote to the US Indian agent at Sault Ste. Marie, "You are therefore authorized to permit the introduction of whiskey in such limited quantities as you may think circumstances will justify, into the Indian [country] on our boundary west of Lake Superior, and adjoining the trading posts of the Hudson's Bay Company."[9]

The liquor trade may have been the main point of friction between Tanner and Côté, but it was not the only one. The two men formed such a mutual dislike that Tanner spent little time at the trading post all that winter and spring. If he was not running *en dérouine*, then Côté usually sent him off to fish or hunt for several days at a time. In eight months, he spent barely a dozen nights under the same roof with his superior.[10]

At last the day came when Côté and his men loaded their many packs of furs into canoes and started for Mackinac, leaving Tanner to his own resources. Under the terms of his contract, he was now free to make his way to Red River. First, however, he needed to construct a small canoe and replenish his stock of moccasins. Côté had been such a hard taskmaster that Tanner had had no time for those preparations. When he was finally ready to go, the trees were leafing out and the days were turning warm.[11]

Children of the Fur Trade

❋ 40 ❋ In the years since his divorce from Red Sky of the Morning, Tanner had had little contact with his three older children. He and his first wife had separated into different bands, and the children had gone with their mother. His son and two daughters were about eighteen, sixteen, and fourteen years of age in 1823. Over the years Tanner had maintained some slight connection with them, but that was all. To obtain custody over these three children after his long separation from them posed an altogether different challenge from the one he had faced with Therezia and his younger set of children.

He had two alternatives. He could go straight to his estranged wife and children and the chiefs of their band and present himself as an Indian, submitting his claim to tribal law. Or he could go to the Hudson's Bay fort and appeal to the whites, thereby elevating his case to the level of a dispute between nations. By taking the latter course, he would be identifying himself as a white man and clearly repositioning himself outside the Ojibwa nation. The break with the Indians would be irrevocable. Nevertheless, that is what he chose to do. Perhaps the choice meant nothing more than his doing whatever was necessary or expedient to reclaim his children. But that seems unlikely. He was not naïve about the consequences. Rather, it seems his choice had a harder edge to it.

As Tanner well knew, the Hudson's Bay men were no strangers to the problem of reclaiming mixed-blood children from the Indians. Most company officers had mixed-blood children of their own. Like Tanner himself, many of them had children by more than one native wife, or had been through long periods of separation from their country-born children, or had allowed their sons and daughters to be absorbed into Indian bands. The crucial difference between his situation and that of so many Hudson's Bay fathers was that he had lived among the Indians as an Indian, not at the posts. He no doubt knew that the Hudson's Bay men had their own concerns about the rights and responsibilities of paternity in Indian country. What he could not have known, however, was that the ground for fur-trader fathers was shifting right beneath his feet.

By the early 1820s, fur traders' mixed-blood offspring were numerous. So numerous, historian Jennifer S. H. Brown has written, that they "could no longer be assimilated into the scattered Indian population, absorbed within company employ, or simply shipped *en masse* to Britain or Canada." Fur traders had long wrestled with the problem of "placing" their offspring. Their private struggles ranged from the basic question of who had guardianship over the children, to the largely financial matter of how to give them a formal education, to the more philosophical issue of whether these children should ultimately be directed toward the culture of their native mothers or their European fathers. As Brown revealed in her seminal work, *Strangers in Blood: Fur Trade Company Families in Indian Country*, fur traders and their country-born wives formed several different family patterns to cope with these dilemmas. The patterns varied according to whether the father worked for the Hudson's Bay or the North West, whether he was an officer or servant (or, in the case of the North West, bourgeois or engagé), whether the mother was native or mixed blood, and whether the child was male or female. Family patterns changed over time, too. The merger of the companies in 1821 formed a watershed, according to Brown, because the reorganized Hudson's Bay Company acquired the status of a de facto colonial government and began to address these issues more fulsomely. Nowhere was this more the case than at Red River, where many interracial families went to retire.[1]

There were now two distinct populations of interracial families inhabiting the Red River valley. One was the Métis, who were predominantly French-speaking, Roman Catholic, and committed to a hunting and fishing way of life. The other group was primarily composed of retired Hudson's Bay men and their Indian wives and children. These families were predominantly English-speaking, Protestant, and oriented toward a farming way of life. The Métis lived to the south and west of the Forks; the English-speaking families lived to the north. The progeny of the latter group were termed "country-born" to distinguish them from Métis.[2]

With its large number of mixed-blood children, Red River provided an attractive setting for missionary work. The Jesuits arrived in 1818 and naturally gravitated to the Métis. An Anglican mission was established under Hudson's Bay Company auspices two years later for the benefit of the English speakers. The first Anglican missionary, John West, was fundamentally interested in converting Indians as well as providing Christian services to the faithful. But he soon recognized that he could not bring Christianity to the Indians without first raising them from a state of savagery. Therefore, his program centered on taking Indian children from their parents and educating them in a boarding school. It was a strategy that would soon underpin missionary work among the Indians all across North America.[3]

The Reverend West opened a boarding school for Indian children at the same time that he started a day school for the settlers' children. As winter set in, he persuaded Be-gwais, the chief of the Red River Ojibwas, to enroll his nephew in the boarding school, with the expectation that the boy would remain there until the family returned for him in the spring. After just a week, however, the boy's mother missed her son and came back. West allowed the boy to go to his mother each night and return to school each day. But after a week of this arrangement, his star pupil ran away for good. West made the mother give back the suit of clothes he had provided to the boy, lest other Indians get the idea that they could enroll their children temporarily merely to have them clothed. A rather small incident by itself, it pointed to the conflict between school and home that would plague thousands of Indian families over the coming century.[4]

There were other harbingers of change in the Red River valley. From uncertain beginnings, the colony was taking root as a permanent agricultural settlement. The Nor' Westers and their allies had opposed the colony mainly on the grounds that agricultural settlement would displace the Indians and Métis, wipe out the game, and destroy the fur trade. After the merger, the Hudson's Bay Company had the paradoxical task of governing the Red River valley so as to support both the fur trade and the colonization program that would eventually lead to its undoing. To protect the former, it revoked the Selkirk land grant and reinstated the company's monopoly on trade, making it illegal for settlers to hunt, trap, and barter furs. At the same time, it kept faith with Selkirk's vision of establishing a community where Hudson's Bay men could retire with their families. Each new family would receive twenty to twenty-five acres of land, plus an allotment of seed, tools, and ammunition upon arrival. Besides being afforded religious instruction and education for their children, the settlers would have police protection, a magistrate, and a new governor. The company directors also envisioned founding a children's home at Red River to accommodate the many "orphans" at the posts who had been abandoned by their fathers.[5]

Tanner returned to Red River knowing nothing about these budding institutions. As he paddled up the river he could see there were many more settlers' homes built since the time he had left, but Fort Douglas, now Fort Garry, still rose on the grassy bluff below the Forks and several buffalo-hide tepees stood nearby as before. Making his way to the fort, he introduced himself to the chief factor, explaining his errand and presenting his letters of reference from Governor Clark and the late Lord Selkirk. But the factor, after perusing these documents, stated flatly that he was not interested in helping him. He did not offer a reason, but Tanner surmised that he simply could not be bothered, as he would soon be departing for Hudson Bay. After their meeting Tanner was standing outside the fort, somewhat at a loss over where to turn next, when a man hailed him from the Métis encampment. The man turned out to be Charles Brousse, the Métis interpreter who had befriended him several years before. Brousse invited him into his lodge, where Tanner learned that the colony had a new governor. Governor and factor hated each other, Brousse shrewdly observed. If the factor refused to help him, the governor likely would.[6]

Tanner went the next day to the governor's house, which, like the factor's, stood inside the walls of the fort. The governor, whose name was Andrew Bulger, gave him a friendly reception, particularly upon hearing how the factor had turned him out of the fort the previous night. Despite his cordial manner, he had a stiff, military bearing. Some ten years younger than Tanner, he introduced himself using his former army rank of captain rather than his present title of governor. He invited Tanner to come into his house and dine with him, and he offered him a room for the duration of his visit. As Tanner explained his business, he got a feeling that this man already knew much about him and had learned of his arrival at Red River and his purpose there even before he came to his door. Tanner explained that he intended to go by himself to find his children, but he hoped that Captain Bulger would support his effort to reclaim them if it became necessary. The governor indicated that he would.

Next, Tanner inquired with some Indians at the fort about his children's whereabouts. They told him that his children were with a band of Ojibwas encamped at Prairie Portage. But they also warned him that the Ojibwas were aware of his arrival and his purpose. They said that some of the men in the band had threatened to kill him if he tried to take away the children. Undeterred, he left for Prairie Portage without further delay.[7]

As he came into the encampment he tried to show the men that he was not afraid of them and that he meant no harm. He only wanted to see his children. He experienced no hostility at first; the chief of this band invited him into his lodge and told him where he could find his former wife and daughters.[8]

Tanner's *Narrative* gives only a vague impression of how it went when he was reunited with his children. The two teenage girls *appeared pleased.* Most likely they were reserved. At least two years had passed since their last encounter with their father, maybe more. The girls were now of an age to be changing fast, both physically and emotionally. No doubt they were aware, as others in the band were aware, that their white father had returned from afar to see them, and probably they were privy to the rumor that he wanted to take them away. So their feelings at seeing their father must have been mixed.

The son, his firstborn child, was almost a man now. As Tanner considered the three children's future, he saw that this one was so grown up and accustomed to an Indian's life it would be folly to take him to Mackinac. The boy was too old to register in school, and he would surely detest the white man's system of working for wages. So the father had to admit that the son must take his own path, and it seems that they now kept aloof from each other.

And how did it go between him and Red Sky of the Morning? On their reunion the *Narrative* is brief to the point of obfuscation. *The mother of these children was now an old woman.* When Tanner related these more recent events in his life, he would not even utter his ex-wife's name, much less describe any feelings he had for her, or she for him. One imagines Red Sky of the Morning as being very much on guard, knowing that her ex-husband had come for the children. Tanner was as coy with her as he was with the rest of the band, determined not to reveal his intentions until the opportune time. And yet, as he took up his former place in his children's lodge, he must have made some sort of effort to reengage with his former wife. There must have been at least a tentative beating in his heart, for he had come all this way to get his children by her, and he longed so desperately for the bonds of family.

After a few days, Tanner learned who it was in this band who was threatening to kill him. He discovered his old rival, Gi-ah-ge-wa-go-mo, lived in the village. Though Gi-ah-ge-wa-go-mo and Red Sky of the Morning had long since parted company, the fellow still had it in for him. At length when the two came face to face, Gi-ah-ge-wa-go-mo warned him he must leave the village or he would be killed. Tanner was defiant, recalling their past confrontation and taunting him. "If you had been a man, you would have killed me long ago, instead of now threatening me. I have no fear of you." Tanner's warrior pose kept his old rival at bay. Gi-ah-ge-wa-go-mo tried to provoke him into declaring what he wanted to do with his children, but Tanner refused to answer him, for he could see that until he verbalized his intentions the chief would make no move against him.[9]

Tanner waited until the band moved camp from Prairie Portage to Fort Garry. Only then, in the protection of the fort, did he announce that he wanted to have his children back. As he had suspected might happen, the chief and all the principal hunters rejected his demand. So Tanner went to Captain Bulger, who, true to his word, came to his aid. Bulger sent his interpreter, Brousse, with a message that the Indians bring the children into the fort.

The children entered the fort accompanied by a dozen other members of the band, and everyone stood in a group outside the governor's house, three or four adults surrounding each child. Bulger asked Tanner to identify his son and two daughters; then he sent one of his guards into the house to get the children a bite to eat. The guard returned with a half-eaten loaf of bread from Bulger's own table, which he attempted to hand directly to one of Tanner's children. As Tanner could plainly see, Bulger's gesture was a breach of protocol and an insult to the Indians, for it suggested that the Hudson's Bay men thought of the adult Indians as no better than children. A man angrily snatched the bread away, tore it into pieces, and pointedly distributed the morsels to all of the other adults, leaving none for Tanner's children. Bulger then had the storehouse unlocked, telling Tanner to go inside and get something else for them. Tanner went in and found some bags of pemmican, opened one, and brought out several pounds of it. Following native protocol this time, he invited all the Ojibwa to sit down and offered a piece of pemmican to each person. When everyone had eaten, Bulger appealed to them to hand the children to their father, but the Indians still refused.[10]

The next day, the governor called the principal men of the band as well as Tanner to a council. They all sat on the floor of the council room, and Bulger took out a peace pipe and ceremoniously lit the bowl and passed it around. He called on his guards to bring presents into the room and deposit them on the floor. He told the principal men that he was honoring them with these gifts and that he was asking them, as on the previous day, to return the children to their father. He went on to explain that Tanner came before them not as an Indian but as a white man under the protection of the Great Father beyond the waters. He did not need to remind them that the Great Father recognized the right of all white fathers to reclaim their children. Furthermore, Bulger continued, Tanner made his request with the blessing of the Great Spirit, for the Great Spirit created all people, red and white, and clearly the Great Spirit had created these children to be Tanner's. Bulger urged the Indians to accept the presents as a sign of his people's goodwill toward them. Then he ordered his guards to open the door of the council room so they could see his armed militia parading back and forth in front of the house.[11]

Not to be intimidated, the Indians insisted on caucusing among themselves for a good while. At length, their chief made a counterproposal. They would allow Tanner to take his two daughters but not his son. The boy wished to remain with them, and he was old enough to choose for himself. Moreover, they would only give up the girls under one condition: Tanner must take Red Sky of the Morning as well. If Tanner wanted to provide for his daughters again, then he must provide for their mother, too. Tanner saw the justice in this arrangement and gave his consent. The Indians then added a stipulation: several of their people would follow Tanner for the first few days of the journey to ensure that he did not turn the woman out of his canoe. Tanner agreed to their stipulation as well.[12]

By using the power of the Hudson's Bay Company to secure custody of his daughters, Tanner severed what little remained of his bond with the Ojibwas. Though he spoke their language, ate and dressed as they did, knew their rituals and beliefs, and had long ago mingled his blood with theirs, those things gave him no more standing than most other fur traders had. Allegiances mattered to the Ojibwas most of all, and gradually Tanner had transferred those to the white traders. His appeal to Captain Bulger repre-sented a culmination of that process.

There was a dramatic arc to Tanner's thirty years among the Indians, an arc that encompassed the waxing and waning of his Indianness. Almost from the start of his captivity at the age of nine, he had striven to adopt the Indians' ways and to bring himself higher in their esteem. His efforts had begun with learning their language and customs and becoming a camp helper. After a few years, he had learned to hunt and trap. Under the nur-turing care of Net-no-kwa, he had become a good Indian son and provider. Then, taking Red Sky of the Morning as his wife, he had entered further into Ojibwa life as a husband and father. And finally, through his induction as a warrior, he had made himself almost completely Indian. But there re-mained the matter of his race.

Until around the time of the Lewis and Clark expedition, the Indians of the northern prairies practically ignored the fact that he came from the white race. However, that changed under the rising influence of the Shawnee Prophet, the growing pressure on Indian tribes from the advancing frontier of American settlement, and the ruinous strife between the rival fur compa-nies north of the border. Tanner's skin color increasingly made him a person of suspicion and undermined his Indianness. And as he himself formed new relationships with the whites who were outside the usual bounds of the fur trade—first as a hunter for the Red River colony, then as a scout for Selkirk's mercenaries, and finally as a wage-earning employee of the American Fur Company—little by little he moved out of the Indians' camp back into the camp of the white men. It was Tanner's misfortune to become Indian during a time when the two peoples grew increasingly polarized and race conscious.

Whites would come to think of Tanner as so completely Indian that he was hopelessly alienated from the white man's world. What they failed to see was that Tanner had lost his Indianness as well as his whiteness. Attempting to straddle two cultures, he found himself rejected by both.[13]

Tanner's heavy-handed reliance on Captain Bulger to reclaim his children finally alienated him from the Ojibwas for good. Tanner must have understood the gravity of what he had done, for he now decided on a route back to Mackinac that would entail minimal contact with other Indians. Tanner set out down the Red River with his two daughters and their mother and the mandated escort. After four days' journey, the escort turned back and Tanner picked a seldom-used route that would avoid the Ojibwas living around Lake of the Woods. He was not exactly in flight from Indian country, but he no longer called it his home, either.

The Ambush

❋ 41 ❋ That year of 1823, a new medicine man arose among the Rainy Lake Ojibwas. An elder by the name of Two Hearts, he created a stir among his people when he began raising the dead from their graves. On one occasion, he promised the relatives of a girl who had died in the autumn to make her appear in the following spring. When the traders heard reports from the Indians that Two Hearts was raising the dead, they assumed he must be digging up the recently deceased and employing some kind of ruse to hold the corpses erect so that the relatives, when they looked on through the thick forest, were deceived into thinking that the spirits had risen from the dead and were moving about by their own will. The traders noted that the medicine man always kept the viewers at a distance and that he never performed his magic when any white men were around.[1]

That summer, Two Hearts grew wary of the Americans. Members of the US Boundary Commission entered the Rainy Lake country to survey the international boundary, and Two Hearts stealthily followed their movements. On numerous occasions he espied the American surveyors holding their shiny metal instruments up to the sun as if to pray. He speculated as to their intentions and their relationship to the American traders who had come into the area the previous year.[2]

The Rainy Lake country was already a land too poor to sustain the 300 to 400 Ojibwas living there, and the advent of the American traders only made the Ojibwas' problems worse. Competition over hunting territories between family subsistence groups stiffened, and the upstart Americans used whatever low means they could to relieve the Ojibwas of their furs. Two Hearts declined to trade with the Americans at all. He and his two grown sons hunted on the north side of the international boundary, trading their skins to the British at Rainy Lake House. Because so many Ojibwa suffered from hunger and low spirits, Two Hearts's influence as a medicine man was felt all around the Rainy Lake country.[3]

Not far from where Two Hearts made his camp that summer, six or seven other family subsistence groups came together to fish by the inlet to Rainy Lake at Kettle Falls. Their chief, Waw-wish-e-gah-bo, had accumulated an inordinately large debt at the Rainy Lake House over the previous few years. His younger brother, Ome-zhuh-gwut-oons, or Little Clear Sky, took debt from both the British and the American traders and hunted on both sides of the line. Little Clear Sky was not the only Rainy Lake Ojibwa who ignored the traders' admonitions to respect the international border, but he was among the most fiercely independent about that. When McLoughlin made a list of all the Ojibwa hunters in his district that spring, he noted the fact that Little Clear Sky hunted both north and south of the line, describing him as "a lazy fellow and a rogue."[4] Côté, the American Fur Company clerk, was more direct with him. Upon learning that Little Clear Sky took debt from him in the fall only to trade most of his skins to the opposition in the spring, he briefly incarcerated the young man and gave him a whipping for it.

Little Clear Sky was still smarting from the American trader's offense when he was informed one day that Tanner—the man his people called the Long Knife—had just passed by the encampment in his canoe with his former Ojibwa wife and two daughters. On an impulse, he jumped in his own canoe and went after him.[5]

Tanner had seen few people on their journey thus far. They had bypassed Lake of the Woods altogether, and they had glided past Rainy Lake House with barely a wave to the people on shore. When Little Clear Sky caught up with them and brought his canoe abreast of theirs, Tanner instantly felt on guard. He did not recognize the young man as someone he knew, though the young man insisted they were in some way related. Little Clear Sky shadowed them as they continued paddling, and though Tanner gave him no encouragement, he seemed eager to strike up a conversation. After a while, he told Tanner about his recent ill treatment by the American trader, Côté.[6]

When Tanner and his family stopped to camp at the end of the day, Little Clear Sky stopped as well, making his camp with them. In the morning, as Tanner and his family prepared to embark, Little Clear Sky watched them so as to be ready to push off when they did. Where he was going he would not say. He only seemed interested in tagging along and talking to Tanner.

Around midday they landed the canoes to take a shore break. Tanner was reclining on the riverbank in the summer sunshine, his guard temporarily lowered, when he turned on his elbow and saw that the young man and his older daughter had both disappeared from view. In the next moment his daughter emerged from the underbrush, looking agitated. Little Clear Sky came sauntering out of the bushes a little way behind her. As the girl went to her mother, Tanner let the incident pass. When they took another shore break later in the day, he saw this daughter whisper something to Red Sky of the Morning and begin to cry.[7]

Little Clear Sky camped with them again that night. His constant presence had become oppressive, and yet when he stood up and wandered off into the woods by himself, Tanner was at once on edge over letting him out of his sight. After everything else that had occurred that day, he felt vaguely menaced and went to see what the young man was doing. He found him sitting on the ground with his medicine bag open, carefully inserting a long piece of deer gut into a musket ball. Supposing that he might be short of powder or balls or flint, Tanner offered to give him whatever he needed from his own supply. A little too quickly, Little Clear Sky responded that he had plenty.

Tanner found him very odd. The young man had chirped like a little bird when they first met; he had continued to be friendly through the last day and a half; and now he was surly. Growing more and more suspicious of him, Tanner returned to camp, watching for the young man to follow behind. When Little Clear Sky finally appeared, he was wearing all his ornaments as if dressed for war. He strode into their camp, grandly settled himself by the fire, and sat there silent and erect, observing Tanner. But in time he spoke up, and soon he was talking in his friendly way again. By and by, he asked Tanner for his knife so he could cut a piece of tobacco.

Asked for his *knife*. That raised the hair on Tanner's neck. Yet, determined to conceal his rising suspicions, he decided to give it to him. Slowly easing the knife out of his belt, he set it on the ground between them. He was curious to see what the young man would do next. Little Clear Sky took his time using it and then, feigning absentmindedness, slipped it into his own belt. Now Tanner felt certain that this man was his enemy, though what his motive or plan might be was still a blank. Rather than challenge him right then, he decided to give his adversary more time. *Perhaps he will return it to me in the morning,* he thought.

As night fell, the woman and girls retired to their shelter, but Little Clear Sky made no move to prepare his own camp bed. Tanner finally lay down by the fire with a blanket, making his bed where he could keep an eye on his enemy. In the glow of the fire, he could tell that the young man remained wide awake, his eyes watchful. As the mosquitoes were bothersome, Little Clear Sky continued to stoke their smudge fire, using its smoke to get relief from the mosquitoes. Occasionally he took a pine bough and waved it over the embers like a fan, pushing the smoke in Tanner's direction, an incongruous act of kindness for an enemy, it seemed to Tanner, as if Little Clear Sky were doing him an honor before moving to attack him. After a while it began to rain. Tanner suggested that Little Clear Sky might lie down next to him and share his blanket. Little Clear Sky declined, even as thunder sounded in the distance and the drub of raindrops began to quicken. Gathering more wood, Little Clear Sky kept feeding the fire as the thunderstorm broke. Once, after an especially loud thunderclap made him jump, he threw a pinch of tobacco into the fire for an offering. All through the downpour Little Clear Sky kept his vigil, while Tanner lay with the blanket pulled over his head save for a little fold through which he watched his adversary's every move. Neither one slept all night.

In the morning, Little Clear Sky ate with the family and then abruptly pushed off in his canoe while the others were still packing up. Tanner did not get his knife back. When Tanner's family was ready to go, the older daughter refused to get in the canoe. She seemed afraid but would not say why. Red Sky of the Morning soothed her and, as Tanner later thought, tried to keep him from paying much attention to her. At last she got into the canoe, and they set out.

Little Clear Sky was not far ahead of them on the river. They saw him at a distance each time they rounded a bend. But about midmorning they came upon a set of rapids where Tanner was surprised not to see him anywhere in view, for he would have had to paddle very hard to get through the rapids and around the next bend so quickly. The river being about eighty yards wide at that point, the only way through the rapids was to steer to one side within about ten yards of the riverbank. Before starting up this channel, Tanner took off his leather frock and put it between his knees.[8]

Halfway through the rapids, he heard the discharge of a gun and the whistle of a ball passing his head. He felt a ping on his right shoulder, and in the next instant realized that the paddle had slipped from his hand. His right arm hung limp at his side. A cloud of smoke rose, and there at the river's edge was Little Clear Sky scurrying through the brush. Glancing down, Tanner saw blood splattered all over the frock balled between his knees. His daughters were screaming as they and their mother clambered out of the canoe. The canoe turned sideways in the rapids and was thrown against a rock outcrop in the middle of the stream. Alone in the canoe now, Tanner clung to the gunwale with his good left hand then tumbled out into the rushing water. He tried to pull the canoe with him onto the slanting rock, but the current was too strong. Grabbing his gun instead, he let the canoe slip from his grasp and crawled onto the slab of rock. Lying on his back next to the rushing current, he attempted to load his gun one-handed but quickly fainted from the effort. When he came to a minute or two later, his daughters and Red Sky of the Morning were back in the canoe, only now a considerable distance downstream from where he lay. He cried out to them, but his cry was drowned in the din of the rapids. They drifted with the current around the bend and were gone from view.[9]

Tanner took stock of his situation. His enemy was probably hiding in the dense brush somewhere along the riverbank, watching him, waiting to see if he would die. Probing his wounds, Tanner found that the ball had smashed clear through his arm and entered his breast just below the armpit, lodging somewhere very near his lung. Believing the wound to be mortal, he called out to Little Clear Sky to spare him further agony and finish what he had begun. "Come, if you are a man, and shoot me again!" he cried. As there was no answer, and as he was too weak to move from his rock in the middle of the river, he could only lie on his back in the hot sun and await death. Soon the blood-sucking flies swarmed around him, buzzing and biting.[10]

Late in the afternoon his strength began to return. He slipped into the river and swam across the channel, paddling with his gun and one good arm. Reaching the shore, he stood and let out a war whoop in defiance of his enemy, then he found a spot in the woods where he could see across the river and watch for him. After a while he saw his foe dragging his canoe down to the riverbank. Evidently, Little Clear Sky had lost sight of him and did not know he was now himself being watched. It was surprising, considering the care he had taken to prepare the ambush. Tanner watched Little Clear Sky put his canoe in the water and begin descending the river, aiming to pass right by Tanner's hiding place. At this point, Tanner sorely regretted having allowed his enemy to keep his knife the night before. He could not shoot him, because in crossing the river he had failed to keep his powder dry. And though he longed to leap out and club him with his gun, he knew he was too weak. So Little Clear Sky got away.[11]

As evening came on, Tanner resolved to treat his wounds. He tore what clothing he had into strips. Then, using his teeth and left hand, he wrapped this makeshift bandaging loosely around his right arm. He then set the broken bones in his arm as best he could and cinched up the bandage to hold them in place. Next, he broke off small tree branches with which to fashion a splint and used a bit of cord to make a sling for his arm. Finally, he peeled bark from a chokecherry bush, chewed it into a wad, and used that to plug the hole in his side. His exertions had opened the wounds again and now, as he lay down to rest, he could see his blood all over the bushes and ground. *I must lie still*, he thought.[12]

He had begun to think he might survive his wounds after all. In the fading light, he prayed to the Great Spirit to pity him and ease his pain. As if in answer to his prayers, the swarming mosquitoes lifted and disappeared.

Comforted by the thought that he was not alone, that the Great Spirit watched over him on his bed of moss, he drifted in and out of consciousness. But each time he fell asleep, he was awakened by the same dream: a trader's canoe was approaching and he must call it to shore. Then, several hours into the night, he was roused not by this dream but by actual human voices. It seemed that his two daughters were crying in distress, though their calls were barely audible over the sound of the rapids. He imagined that they had escaped from their mother and returned to him in the night and that Little Clear Sky had pursued them and was just now discovering their hiding place. In his delirium he thought they were crying for help, as Little Clear Sky was about to butcher them. Yet he was too weak to call out or move. Their cries soon faded away.

In fact, the girls and their mother did come back that night but not for the reason he imagined. Moments after the ambush, when Tanner was briefly unconscious and seemingly about to die, Red Sky of the Morning had steered the canoe to the edge of the river and thrown all of his clothes and possessions into the bushes. Later, worried that his blood-soaked frock might catch the eye of a trader or voyageur in a passing canoe, she had reconsidered and paddled back upstream to dispose of the incriminating articles better. When she and her daughters arrived back at the place, the girls began to keen for their father, imagining that he was dead. Though they were a few hundred yards below where Tanner lay, that was the commotion he heard.[13]

In the morning Tanner heard male voices and spotted a party of Hudson's Bay men on the riverbank above the rapids. They had just finished breakfast and were pushing off again. He recognized the canoe as that of Alexander Stewart, the chief factor at Fort William. This time of year, Tanner remembered, he would be traveling to York Factory, taking the voyageurs' route to Rainy Lake and Lake of the Woods. If he could ride in their canoe, they might overtake Red Sky of the Morning. Tanner waded out into the river to wave them down. As the voyageurs caught sight of him, they ceased paddling and gazed in astonishment at this naked and bloodied white man shouting to them in Ojibwa. As they made no move to turn his way, Tanner thought for a moment that they were going to pass by and leave him there. Finally, his tongue found a few words of English, and he called to Mr. Stewart by name. Instantly, the voyageurs plied their paddles and brought the canoe over to where he stood. Making a bed for him in the canoe, they took him onboard.

Tanner insisted that before they proceeded they must examine the riverbank a little downstream, as he feared that his daughters had been murdered there. After this search turned up nothing, they were left to conclude that the girls had escaped with Red Sky of the Morning. As for Little Clear Sky, they decided to look for him in the Ojibwa encampment at Kettle Falls. Should they find him there, they would demand revenge to put this matter swiftly to rest. And since Tanner would not be able to avenge himself, they would attempt to put the man to death themselves.

Approaching the encampment, Stewart directed Tanner to lie hidden in the canoe while he and his interpreter made inquiries. Stewart then went to the chief, Waw-wish-e-gah-bo, and asked him if he had any recent news of the man they knew as the Long Knife. Waw-wish-e-gah-bo claimed to know nothing. Stewart called every man in the encampment forward and gave them some tobacco. Then he directed Tanner to stand up in the canoe and reveal himself. They all knew, declared Stewart, that the chief's own brother, Ome-zhuh-gwut-oons, had attempted to kill the Long Knife. Stewart wanted the men in this band to see for themselves how gravely Tanner was wounded. His point was that if Tanner should die, then this band would be held responsible. And then the traders would be back, demanding blood for blood.[14]

At the next stop on their journey, Tanner asked Stewart to examine his wounds. Looking him over, Stewart confirmed that all the damage had been caused by a single ball. (Tanner was sure he had heard another ball zing past his head, so Little Clear Sky must have packed a double charge in his gun.) That single ball had passed all the way through Tanner's breast muscle and lodged next to the breastbone, coming to rest perhaps six inches from its point of entry in his side. Realizing that the ball must be removed or he would die, Tanner pleaded with Stewart to cut him open and get it out. Stewart, however, would not do it, so Tanner asked for a razor and proceeded to operate on himself with his one good hand. Making an incision just to the right of his breastbone, then feeling with finger and thumb, he pried loose the flattened ball and was relieved to find no fragments of rib bone with it. But he could not find the deer gut he had seen Little Clear Sky pack into the musket ball. He had to presume that this long piece of sinew, which he knew must be laced with medicines, now lay coiled in his breast. That meant he would have to wait for the wound to push it out as it healed. There was nothing to do but trust to luck that Little Clear Sky's medicines would not kill him in the meantime. Still, despite that danger, he thought he had improved his chances considerably by getting the musket ball out.[15]

The Pardon

{ 42 } While Tanner waited for rescue, Red Sky of the Morning was in flight with her daughters. She had nothing to fear from Little Clear Sky, as Tanner had first imagined; nor did she fear revenge from her former husband, for she presumed he was dead. Rather, she feared what the traders might do to her when they found his body. Surely the traders would suspect her involvement in the murder. By returning up the Maligne River to dispose of the blood-soaked clothing better, she had lost a whole night. And as most of their journey below the Maligne was on slack water through a chain of large lakes, she knew that her canoe was no match in speed against the many strong paddles of the traders' canoes. When at last they entered the Rainy River, she and her daughters were physically and emotionally spent, and they still had the problem of how to slip past the trading house unseen. As they came into view of some Hudson's Bay men on the riverbank, Red Sky of the Morning and her daughters broke down and practically surrendered themselves.

The men took them to the fort, where they were placed under guard. Some of the men recognized them as Tanner's wife and daughters, for they had seen them pass in the other direction with Tanner in his canoe only a week earlier. As the woman was now quite agitated and the girls were terrified, and as not one of them would give a satisfactory explanation for what had become of Tanner, the men suspected there had been a murder. So they insisted that the three remain at the fort until the next traders' canoe arrived from the east, bringing news.

A few hours later, when the Hudson's Bay canoe carrying Tanner arrived at the landing, everyone was surprised to see the missing man himself on-board. Red Sky of the Morning was shocked to see that her husband was still alive. She panicked and tried to run into the woods with her daughters. She and the girls did not get far, however, before the men of the fort chased them down and hauled them back.[1]

Once everyone was gathered inside the fort, Tanner and Red Sky of the Morning were made to face one another as though in a court of law. Tanner found he could barely bring himself to look at her. Almost numb standing there, he understood Stewart to say that the Hudson's Bay people would leave it to him to say how the woman should be punished. He did not know how to respond to this. What came to mind was how he had called out to her after being shot and how she had left him there to expire on that rock in the middle of the rapids, to bleed and bleed under his attacker's watchful eye. She must have helped to lay the ambush, he thought. He had no doubt she had wanted him to die.

Besides Stewart, there was another Hudson's Bay officer present at the proceeding, the fort trader, Simon McGillivray. Tanner did not know him; this was their first encounter. McLoughlin, the chief factor at Rainy Lake House, was away at Hudson Bay for the summer, so Stewart, as chief factor at Fort William, was the senior officer present. When Tanner did not respond to Stewart's invitation to decide the woman's punishment, the Hudson's Bay officers began to discuss her fate among themselves. They said she was as guilty of the attempted murder as the young man, Little Clear Sky, for she had clearly put him up to it. Under English law, attempted murder normally drew the death penalty. As the woman was accessory to a capital crime, and they were far from a proper court of law, they suggested that everyone present agree that she was guilty of attempted murder and that they put her to death without further ado. The simplest and fastest way, which they proposed to Tanner, was that the fort's servants take her outside and beat her to death.[2]

Tanner finally spoke. No, he did not want her put to death. She was the mother of his children. What he wished was that she should be sent away from the fort, without provisions, and with the injunction never to return. She would never again see her daughters, for now they were his. Stewart stuck to his word and did as Tanner said. He told his men to escort the old woman out of the fort and run her off into the woods.[3]

As far as the girls were concerned, no one wanted to press the issue of what they might have known about the murder plot beforehand. As they were Tanner's dependents, the Hudson's Bay men had no interest in punishing them. In any case, Tanner would need their help while he recovered from his wounds.

Stewart left Tanner in the care of the chief trader, McGillivray. McGillivray gave Tanner and his daughters a room in the fort and a supply of food. The girls stayed with their father, cooked for him, and dressed his wounds. After a month went by, Major Joseph Delafield of the US Boundary Commission stopped at Rainy Lake House and left him additional supplies, including tea, sugar, clothes, and a tent. The American official found him recovering from his wounds with "no danger to apprehend but the mortification of the limb." Tanner wanted to accompany the American commission back to the United States, but Delafield insisted that he was still too weak to travel.

A few days after Delafield's visit, Tanner reached a milestone on his long road to recovery. The deer gut had begun to waggle out of the purple hole in his arm where the musket ball had entered. In one determined stroke he pulled the whole nasty thing out. It was about five inches long, as thick as his finger, and greenish-black in color. He hoped that with the removal of this object his arm would finally start to heal. McGillivray was less sanguine; he thought Tanner's wounds already looked and smelled gangrenous.[4]

One day, without any explanation or notice, McGillivray ordered Tanner to vacate the fort. As soon as Tanner and his daughters were settled in their tent outside the stockade, the trader sent for the girls to come back into the fort. His ostensible reason was that they needed to be fed and cared for. Tanner firmly rejected this. He had received enough food from Delafield to feed himself and his daughters for several weeks, and he saw right through the trader's ploy. He knew that his daughters would be required to sleep with the men. But McGillivray persisted, threatening to confiscate Tanner's provisions unless he ordered his daughters to submit. At one point McGillivray even sent some men to take the girls by force. But Tanner was prepared for this, and on his cue the girls fled to a nearby farm. This farm, the only one in the area, belonged to a free man by the name of Vincent Roy. Over the preceding weeks the girls had befriended Old Roy's granddaughters. With Old Roy vouching for their safety, they were finally persuaded to return to Rainy Lake House to care for their father. Fortunately, the God-fearing old Frenchman had some influence over McGillivray, because McGillivray had recently married his daughter.[5]

For four and a half weeks, Tanner lay in his tent outside the fort. For part of that time he lay alone, deprived of his daughters' comfort while they took refuge with Old Roy. He may well have wondered if he truly had his daughters' affections or not. Though he had saved their mother from execution, they still had much to fear by staying with him near the fort. Even when his daughters returned and sat stoically at his bedside, he must have wondered if he had any friends at all outside the little shelter of their canvas-walled tent. He was in some such bleak reverie one morning when a man suddenly appeared at the door. It was his friend Charles Brousse, humbly asking him in the Ojibwa manner for permission to enter his lodge.

Brousse explained that he had just arrived with a party of American soldier-explorers. He had brought a doctor with him who was waiting outside. This doctor wanted to inspect Tanner's wounds and ask him some questions. Then, brimming with advice for his friend, Brousse crouched by the head of the cot and spoke to him confidentially. He must talk to the leader of this party, a man by the name of Major Long. Perhaps Major Long would make a place for Tanner and his daughters in his canoes and take them all to Mackinac.[6]

"We Met with an American"

{ 43 } Stephen Long's expedition arrived at Rainy Lake House early in the morning on August 31, 1823. Long would later write in his journal: "At the H. Bay Co.'s Fort we met with an American by the name of Tanner." William Keating, who eventually prepared the official report from all of the expedition's journals, reworked this entry into the sentence, "At Rainy Lake we met with a man, whose interesting adventures deserve to be made known to the public." Keating's elaboration of Long's sentence is ironic, because at first the explorer did not want to have much to do with Tanner.

Long thought whatever time they spent with Tanner should mainly fall to other members of the expedition. Shortly after their arrival, he went to visit the wounded American in his tent, taking along the expedition surgeon, Say, and his interpreter. After a brief introduction Long departed, leaving Say to examine Tanner's wounds and to interview him about his unusual personal history and circumstances. Say made a clinical report to Long later that day. As for his history and character, Say shared what he had learned when they dined with the trader, Simon McGillivray, that evening. On the following day, September 1, the expedition's Keating and Seymour visited Tanner and asked him more questions about his unusual life experience. Long, meanwhile, took measurements of the Koochiching Falls and inspected the fort's wheatfield and vegetable garden. Of course, this was consistent with the expedition members' usual division of labor: Long was the mapmaker, not an ethnographer.

Around midday, the rain stopped and the canoemen went to work repairing the canoes. Long ordered the canoemen to break up the most badly damaged canoe and use it for material for patching the other two. As always, he was anxious to keep the expedition moving with a minimum of delay. Then he went to his tent to write in his journal.[1]

Long was surprised when Tanner shuffled into his camp later that day, holding his lame arm against his chest. The wounded American was said to have lain flat on his back for most of the time since the shooting, and though Say had reported that he was now able to stand and walk, his tent was a considerable walk from their camp. Long was even more surprised by Tanner's request. Despite his shaky condition, he wanted the expedition to give him and his daughters passage to Mackinac. *Impossible,* Long probably said to him at first. Having just decided to reduce the number of expedition canoes from three to two, he had to inform Tanner that they would not be able to accommodate three more people.

Tanner went back to his tent, but after a while he returned. Apparently in their first meeting the two men were unable to communicate satisfactorily, and Tanner was determined to try again. This time, Long pressed Tanner for more information. If he were to grant his request and take him onboard at the risk of overloading the expedition canoes, possibly exposing his own men to danger, then he needed to know more about him. What kind of relationship did he have with his daughters? And the girls' mother? And what about his other Indian family, whom he had left in Mackinac?

Seeming to grow tired of all these questions, Tanner withdrew. But in a short while he appeared yet again, this time presenting Long with a leather pouch. Long found three folded letters inside it. None bore a seal; evidently they were letters of reference that had been given directly to Tanner. Carefully unfolding each one on top of his desk, he began to read. The first one was penned by the late Lord Selkirk. Dating from the time when Tanner had been in search of his white family, the letter was addressed to American newspaper publishers, and it outlined Tanner's history as Selkirk had gotten it from him when the two were at Red River. The second letter was signed by a fur trader in Montreal. Long did not recognize the name, but he found it to be a moving testament to Tanner's loyalty and courage. The third one impressed him most of all. It bore the signature of his very own mentor, Governor William Clark of Missouri. It was an authentic testimonial, written in the hand of the venerable old explorer himself, and dated St. Louis, 1820. After reading it over a second time, Long gave Tanner a gruff apology. *You were a fool not to have shown this to me before.* With that, he promised him a place in the canoes.[2]

After Tanner had gone, Long pondered the situation some more. Should the expedition be treating him as an American citizen? He was a former captive of the Indians, and now he had been wounded by an Indian and was trying to return to the States. Those were all circumstances which would indicate he had a claim to be rescued.[3] But Tanner was hardly a U.S. citizen. *Half-savage, half-civilized,* was how he struck Long. Who were his people? To whom did he have allegiance? Where would he live? Long could not get a bead on it. Was he an Indian or a white man? In Long's America, it had to be one or the other.

❄

Then the girls went missing. Tanner stood at the door of Long's tent, so upset he could hardly speak. Charles Brousse, the interpreter, explained that their father had given them leave to say good-bye to an Indian woman in the fort and the girls had failed to return. Long assumed they had run away to avoid going in the expedition canoes. But he could not completely discount Tanner's suspicion that they had been taken by the Hudson's Bay men and were under threat of being raped. So, with Dr. Say, Tanner, and Brousse, Long went to Simon McGillivray, the master of the fort, to investigate the very serious charge that Tanner had laid against the Hudson's Bay men.

Long and his entourage met with the trader in the officer's house. Ironically, it was the same room where McGillivray had entertained them the evening before, where the conversation—in Tanner's absence—had turned to a discussion of Tanner's misfortunes, the girls' mother's plot to get him murdered, and the single-minded way in which Tanner vowed to get revenge on his assailant. What a savage mind, everyone had agreed then. Now this same man stood face to face with the trader, accusing the trader's men of doing savage things to his daughters.

McGillivray was indignant. He swore that none of his men could have laid a hand on the girls. The girls were nowhere in the fort. Probably they had stolen one of the canoes and fled downriver to Lake of the Woods to join their mother. Long pressed McGillivray to initiate a search. Perhaps they would find evidence of which way the girls had run, he suggested. Or, perhaps someone had seen the girls take off. McGillivray refused. The men argued. McGillivray's defensiveness made Long push harder. Even though he guessed the trader was probably right that the girls were runaways, not captives, he had a shadow of doubt.

Then the door burst open and McLoughlin stood there, his hulking frame filling the doorway. Ten weeks he had been away, and this fracas in the officer's house was his welcome home. But the doctor held his temper. He immediately took charge of the meeting, providing assurances all around. No, he affirmed, it was not possible the girls had come to any harm inside the fort. Yes, he agreed, they must be found and returned to this place posthaste, so that Tanner could leave with the American expedition. No, the search would not be undertaken till morning—it was pitch dark and pissing rain outside. Long found that he trusted McLoughlin more than he trusted

McGillivray. "The deportment of this gentleman," Long later wrote in his journal, "was calculated to leave on our minds the most favourable impressions as to his humanity and hospitality."[4]

In the morning, the men searched all around for the girls' tracks in the wet earth. However, no evidence was found of their departure either by canoe or foot. McLoughlin offered a reward to anyone who could find their trail, catch them, and bring them back safely. Two Indians volunteered. While Tanner waited anxiously, the rain lifted and Long's canoemen went to work repairing the canoes. The search for the girls notwithstanding, Long was eager to get underway. Toward dusk, the two Indian searchers returned, empty-handed. With the repairs on the canoes completed, Long announced that the expedition would wait until 10:00 a.m. the next morning to make its departure in the hope that the girls would come back by their own volition before then.[5]

That night and the next morning there was still no sign of them. As the hour advanced, everyone tried to console Tanner and persuade him to leave with the expedition anyway, without his daughters. The Americans urged him to put his own safety first and not forfeit this chance to get back to Mackinac and proper medical care before winter. McLoughlin promised to make every effort to learn where the girls had gone. As soon as he discovered who they were with, he said, he would rescue them and keep them with him at Rainy Lake House until Tanner was healthy enough to return for them in the spring. McGillivray went on arguing—brutally, it seemed to Keating—that the girls had surely decided to forsake their father and join their mother at Lake of the Woods. Tanner would not even admit that possibility, for he believed the girls felt a stronger attachment to him and were sincere when they told him they would accompany him to Mackinac. He still feared they were captive. What if the girls' captors were in collusion with some of the mixed-blood dependents living around the fort? Maybe the girls were hidden in one of their wigwams? If that should be the case, McLoughlin responded, then he would find them soon enough and keep them safe in his custody.[6]

At last Long's men persuaded the anguished father to leave without his daughters. The canoes were loaded with fresh provisions purchased from the Hudson's Bay Company. McLoughlin presented Long two pounds of tea as a parting gift. Tanner sat in Long's canoe wedged among the packs with his right arm immobilized. The canoes pushed off. The strong and stout voyageurs sitting fore and aft of Long and Tanner dug their paddles into the water with their customary gusto. From the bank above the canoe landing, McLoughlin waved farewell.

It was to be a short parting between the doctor and the wounded American, however. At the first portage, Tanner debarked and walked onshore with the expedition without complaint, but on the next stretch of water his arm began to swell and ache unbearably. Just before they reached a small rapid at the outlet of Rainy Lake, Tanner suddenly announced that he could proceed no farther. The pain was too much. Pointing to the guardhouse at the outlet of the lake where employees of the trading post stood watch for Indians, he requested to be put ashore there. From that point, he could easily return to Rainy Lake House. Long directed the voyageurs to land the canoes.[7]

Tanner's relief was clearly visible as he parted from the expedition—so much so that Long, Say, and Keating each remarked upon it and described the moment in their journals. Long focused on Tanner's medical condition: the "considerable inflammation" of his arm, the sweat beading all over his face and hands, revealing a breaking fever. Say saw the sheen on Tanner's cheeks and thought he was crying. It startled him, since until that moment Tanner had shown relatively little emotion through all his pain and torment. In fact, others had told Say that no one had ever seen the man shed a tear. "But it was evident that the conflict of emotions in his mind, at the time that he was compelled to land from our canoes, overpowered him, and his eyes glistened with a tear which he attempted in vain to shake off." Keating, for his part, thought the flash in Tanner's eyes was something else, a gleam of hope as his thoughts turned to renewing the search for his daughters. Although Keating believed along with the others that the girls had run off to find their mother, he also recognized that Tanner was utterly convinced of their loyalty to him. That could mean but one thing: that they were being held captive until he left the area. When Keating considered the girls—about sixteen and fourteen years of age, physically attractive, socially engaging—he well understood Tanner's apprehension about their chances at the trading post.[8]

As there was a fair wind, Long's pilot ordered the voyageurs to hoist sail for the all-day journey across the big waters of Rainy Lake. With the wind filling their square sails, the two canoes raced out into the sparkling cold waters. When the members of the expedition looked back, they saw Tanner's solitary figure slowly diminish to a dark speck on the shoreline and finally disappear into the featureless forest-covered horizon that rimmed the whole, vast lake.

"At the H. Bay Co.'s Fort we met with an American by the name of Tanner," Long had tersely written in his journal on the previous day. The words fail to satisfy. Unfortunately, he did not elaborate on them much,

though it is clear from the official narrative of the expedition that he rumi-
nated over Tanner's unusual history and character afterwards and tried to
put the man in some kind of context. Was he a lost American citizen? A
tragic outcast? Or a useless vagabond and misanthrope? Was he, in a sense,
still a captive of the Indians? Or had he turned quite Indian himself?

Long was a man of many strong loyalties—to God and country, to the
army, to his men, to his Christian marriage. Personally, he did not care for
this man who had broken so many bonds of his own. Tanner had forsaken
the white man's world for what end? That he might live among a race of
savages? For Long, that was Tanner's own errant choice, as it was the shame
of all white Indians.

The Onus of Revenge

❋{ 44 }❋ John McLoughlin first learned that John Tanner had been shot and seriously wounded in midsummer of 1823, when he was away at York Factory. He also received the intelligence that the shooter was the good-for-nothing Little Clear Sky. Probably the news reached him by way of Alexander Stewart, the chief factor at Fort William who had rescued Tanner after the shooting.[1]

Tanner's situation was the first thing to command McLoughlin's attention when the chief factor arrived back at Rainy Lake House with his brigade late in the evening on September 1, 1823. Besides Tanner, he found Major Long and his party camped at the fort, and when he entered the officer's house he walked into the middle of an argument between Long and the chief trader, Simon McGillivray, over the whereabouts of Tanner's daughters. Obviously there was no hope of finding the girls that night in pitch darkness. But as soon as he got control of the meeting, McLoughlin promised Long that he would organize a search in the morning.[2]

McLoughlin's thoughts turned from Tanner to the assailant, Little Clear Sky, when he sat down to record the events in the post journal later that night. What could have motivated this young man to shoot Tanner? McLoughlin considered Little Clear Sky to be a poor, useless hunter and a rogue—utterly untrustworthy—and he also knew that this same Ojibwa had taken credit from the American traders across the river. But he had heard of nothing between Little Clear Sky and Tanner that would precipitate a murder attempt. He put no stock in the theory that Tanner's former wife was behind it. "Mere suppositions," was his brusque comment on that.[3]

McLoughlin had to decide whether to send his men to Little Clear Sky's village to mete out punishment. Between traders and Indians, blood for blood was the law. When Indians killed traders, the fur companies usually responded with lethal force, either finding the responsible Indians and summarily executing them or, if the perpetrators could not be found, killing other Indians in their stead. There were no procedures for the gathering and weighing of evidence, no trials by jury, or jail sentences. The traders gave no quarter, believing that the least show of clemency would be construed as weakness. And they could not afford to appear weak, because the Indians greatly outnumbered them. The traders' rule was that they would always come to one another's defense—even traders of different companies or nationalities would unite in case of Indian troubles—and when it became necessary, they would exact revenge. They believed that if a killing went unpunished it would invite more killings, whereas if they retaliated in kind Indian violence against them would be minimized.[4]

McLoughlin subscribed to this general view.[5] He was an authoritarian as well as a humanitarian. But he was also a practical businessman. If anything moderated his approach to the Indians, it was his strong sense that they must be dealt with as trading partners first. The Hudson's Bay Company utterly depended on the Indians as hunters, for it had no other way of obtaining furs so cheaply. "It is therefore clearly our interest, as it is unquestionably our duty, to be on good terms with them," he would later write.[6] Demanding blood for blood made sense only insofar as it would further the company's interest in maintaining proper relations.

McLoughlin and his fellow traders thought retaliation worked because it dovetailed with the Indians' own custom of blood revenge. In his previous observations on the Ojibwa, McLoughlin had marveled at how the revenge principle tended to check violence within tribal society. As he wrote in his "Description of the Indians from Fort William to Lake of the Woods," the Ojibwa lived in a state of complete freedom with virtually no tribal government and no judicial system. And yet, the revenge principle was so clearly expressed that it functioned as a powerful restraint. "The fear of retaliation operates as strongly on their minds as punishment by law in the civilized world."[7]

But the "justice" which the fur traders recognized in the revenge principle was not simply a borrowing from Indian law; it also resonated with their own Christian beliefs and English common law. Some years later, when McLoughlin was in charge of the entire Columbia District and Simon McGillivray was chief trader at Fort Walla Walla, he advised McGillivray regarding a situation similar to the one he confronted at Rainy Lake in 1823. A prominent Indian killed one of McGillivray's men and the culprit's tribesmen would not give him up—how was McGillivray to approach those Indians? "If I was addressed on the subject by any of them," McLoughlin intoned, "I would say the Almighty has forbid the shedding of innocent blood, and commanded that he who shed man's blood by man shall his blood be shed, and in obedience to this command, if a Chief among us was to Kill a slave that Chief would be killed."[8] All men were equal when they committed a capital offense. Under English law in that day, murder and attempted murder were both punishable by death.

McLoughlin finally decided against trying to capture and punish Little Clear Sky. That may have been because he knew the Indians drew a sharp distinction between murder and attempted murder. In Indian law, the motivation behind a bad deed mattered little compared to the actual result. No one would dispute that Little Clear Sky's attack was premeditated with intent to kill. But the act of "attempted murder" had no standing in Indian law. If the Hudson's Bay men killed Tanner's young assailant in retaliation, it was doubtful that Little Clear Sky's people would see the justice in it.

Other circumstances weighed against the operation of the revenge principle in this case as well. Since Tanner was disabled and incapable of taking his own revenge, it was unclear who should take revenge on his behalf. Where did the onus lie? Tanner was not an employee of the Hudson's Bay Company. It was not even clear that he was a fur trader. True, he had been engaged by the American Fur Company the previous fall. But his contract had expired in the spring, and he was acting on his own at the time of the shooting. And though he was a white man who had come under the care of the Hudson's Bay Company after the shooting, he had lived so long among the Indians that his case might be considered an Ojibwa matter. McLoughlin, like many traders, made it a policy not to meddle in the internal affairs of the Indians. Or, as another Hudson's Bay officer once said about Indian-on Indian murders, "The practice of the company in such cases was to outlaw the murderer and kill him when caught—it might be years afterwards."[9]

As there was to be no retaliation against Little Clear Sky, the problem boiled down to what should be done for Tanner. McLoughlin organized a search for Tanner's missing daughters as promised, but at the end of the day he called it off. In all likelihood, he thought, the girls had gone back to their mother in their home village. With Long, he persuaded Tanner to take passage with the American expedition back to the United States while he had the chance. The next morning, as the Americans made ready to go in their two canoes, McLoughlin sold them fresh produce from the garden. Then he watched them paddle away, relieved to have Tanner off his hands.

The next morning, however, one of McLoughlin's men reported that the American expedition had landed Tanner at the guardhouse at the outlet of Rainy Lake. From there, he had taken passage in a Hudson's Bay canoe back downriver. Now he was at the American trading post across the river. After the hubbub over his runaway daughters, Tanner had gone back to Côté, of all people.

For McLoughlin the news smarted a bit. It was surprising after everything the doctor had done for him. Once, years ago, when McLoughlin served at the former North West post, he had taken Tanner under his care after

Tanner fell from a tree and broke his ribs. A year or two later, the doctor had taken him into that same house again after Tanner spilled his canoe in the Rainy River. On that occasion Tanner had been accompanied by two wee daughters—a younger pair than the two teenage girls who were now missing. And McLoughlin could recall a third time, when he lived at Fort William, that Tanner came to him for help. Tanner was on his way back to the States looking for passage to Mackinac. The doctor had arranged for him to board the company's sloop for its run across Lake Superior. Three times McLoughlin had shown Tanner his friendship. And yet, instead of returning to Rainy Lake House and placing himself under the doctor's care for a fourth time, now he sought help on the American side of the river. "I cannot imagine the reason of his going there except that perhaps Major Long advised him to go there," McLoughlin confided to the post journal.[10]

But Long had given Tanner no such advice, as McLoughlin soon discovered. Four days later, the doctor received a letter from Long recommending Tanner to his care and promising that the Hudson's Bay Company would be reimbursed for expenses. McLoughlin found Long's promise of reimbursement by the US government so naïve as to be insulting. "Does he take us for such fools?" he wrote in the post journal. "Does the Major think we will not do our utmost to assist a fellow being in distress when he can get no provisions from any one Else and is laying in the Bed of Sickness?" Better if Long had simply asked him to take care of the wounded American on humanitarian grounds, the proud doctor felt. Long's message was doubly irritating because it arrived just hours after he received a note from across the river, purportedly from Tanner, though it looked suspiciously like a forgery penned by the American outfit's summer caretaker, a Mr. Davenport. Saying he had nothing to eat, Tanner (or was it Davenport?) asked for a bushel of corn, fifty pounds of flour, twenty pounds of grease, and a bag of potatoes. Thinking that the communication was likely a ruse by Davenport to fill the American post's larder at Hudson's Bay Company expense, McLoughlin sent over just a small fraction of the amount of food requested, with a note stating that more would be provided from day to day. (McLoughlin was correct in his suspicion: Tanner later stated that the daily rations McLoughlin sent across were mostly consumed by the young Davenport and his wife, with Tanner receiving hardly any.) Still, the scanty daily rations that McLoughlin sent to Tanner were not calculated to fetch the invalid back to Rainy Lake House. Tanner stayed at the American fort, while McLoughlin sent food across the river each day.[11]

On October 2, Côté arrived with the American Fur Company's winter contingent. The sight of the flotilla coming up the river dashed McLoughlin's hopes that his competitor would pull out of the area. In fact, Côté was much better supplied than in the previous year: his flotilla of five canoes included two large canoes filled with a dozen bales of trade goods and several kegs of rum. That evening, Côté paid a visit to the chief factor. The competitors discussed prices: McLoughlin wanted to trade with the Indians at one fathom of cloth for five made beaver, Côté wanted to put the price at one for four. McLoughlin explained his object in setting a higher price and told him to think it over. The subject of Tanner's lingering convalescence did not arise.[12]

As McLoughlin soon discovered, Côté took a sterner view of Tanner's situation than he. The attempted murder, in Côté's judgment, unquestionably invoked the rule of revenge, and Côté wanted no part of it. As Tanner was Côté's former employee as well as his fellow countryman, he saw Tanner's right of revenge as nothing but a liability for his own interests. If Tanner were to remain under his care, it would send a damaging signal, conveying to the Rainy Lake Indians that the Americans were Tanner's people and that they would seek revenge on the wounded American's behalf. In which case, the Indians would fear going to the Americans and would trade with the British instead. When Côté saw Tanner lying on a bed inside the house, his only remark to him was, "Well, you have been making a war by yourself." The next morning he evicted him. To distance himself and his outfit from Tanner and his troubles, Côté would not even allow the former employee to pitch his tent on the US side of the river.[13]

Tanner ferried across the Rainy River and knocked at McLoughlin's door. The wounded American proposed to embark with a company of Hudson's Bay men who were set to leave for the Red River valley. The doctor inspected his wound and advised against it; although a month had passed since Tanner's aborted trip with Major Long, the arm was still not in shape for travel. McLoughlin told him to go back to the American clerk and tell him that if he could lodge over there then he, the Hudson's Bay doctor, would provide medicine and advice. Tanner went away but soon came back. This time he had a message from Côté stating that the Americans definitely could not lodge him, for their house was too small. McLoughlin recognized full well the real reason for the Americans evicting him. "The fact is," he wrote in his journal, "they are afraid if he remains with them it will be the cause of quarrels with the Indians." He then told Tanner to go back and tell Côté if his people would help Tanner put up his tent on the American side of the portage then he would assign a man to bring him water and firewood and change his dressings every day. Back went Tanner a third time. Returning to McLoughlin yet again, he explained that Côté was adamant: he could not stay there. For McLoughlin, this was proof of what Côté and his men were thinking. "They are afraid that the man's relations who shot him would not go to their House," he wrote in the journal. In other words, Côté was trying to see it like the Ojibwas: whichever house took in Tanner, the onus of revenge would affix to that house. And so the Ojibwas would avoid Tanner's house and trade with the other. McLoughlin found the whole business deplorable. "This conduct in a manner forcing him out of this house is very inhumane and unfeeling," he fumed.

McLoughlin yielded. Tanner could stay in the men's quarters at Rainy Lake House until such time as he was able to make his camp on the American side. The chief factor knew that he was handing the heartless Côté a tactical victory in their little battle over Tanner's care. But he was a doctor and a humanitarian as well as a trader, and he would do the right thing whatever it might cost him in trade with the Indians.[14]

Journeys Home

{ 45 } In just eleven days, Stephen Long and his men traveled from Rainy Lake to Fort William, making upwards of forty portages along the way that ranged in length from a few hundred yards to three miles. Long would later describe the country as "rugged, wild and romantic . . . composed of a ceaseless alternation of lakes, islands, rivers, waterfalls, abrupt precipices, rugged hills and mountains everywhere clad with forests." At Fort William, the Hudson's Bay traders advised him that the weather was too stormy and the season too far advanced to embark on Lake Superior in their frail canoes. However, as the explorer was determined to get home before winter, the Hudson's Bay traders led him to an old Mackinaw boat that the US Boundary Commission had used three months earlier, scuttled, and sunk in the river. The boat was raised and repaired, and in that shaky vessel the expedition set sail. Hugging the shore, and being repeatedly forced to beach their craft to wait out squalls, the expedition took some two weeks to reach Sault Ste. Marie.[1]

From Sault Ste. Marie, they proceeded to Mackinac, where Long officially disbanded the expedition in early October. While the soldier escort headed for Prairie du Chien, Long and the scientists boarded a revenue cutter bound for Detroit. From Detroit, Long and his companions traveled via steamer on Lake Erie to Buffalo, by stage from Buffalo to Rochester, then by canal boat on the partially constructed Erie Canal to Albany, and finally by steamer and stage from Albany to Philadelphia. Long reported back to the War Department in November. True to form, he had rushed his men over a distance of some 4,500 miles in six months, covering an average of twenty-five miles per day.[2]

The explorer returned with new, broad observations about the fur trade and Indians. As an army officer, Long had always taken the military view that the fur trade was the surest means for the United States to pacify and subjugate the Indian tribes on the western frontier. The fur trade tethered the roaming Indians to the white man's trading posts; it established a dependent relationship between Indians and traders that slowly destroyed the tribes' ability to resist American control. The army's chief concern about the fur trade was the need to Americanize it—replace British traders operating on US soil with American traders—in order to break the British-Indian alliance of the Revolutionary War era once and for all.

On his last expedition, Long found that the fur trade existed on the northern frontier as part of a natural buffer against foreign invasion. The territory along the US border west of Lake Superior was inhospitable to agricultural settlement and practically all a wilderness. It formed a natural barrier to an invader in the same way that the Great American Desert, or Great Plains, gave assurance that the nation would never face a significant foe to the west. The United States was fortunate that the whole extent of British territory lying west of the Great Lakes was now vested in the reorganized Hudson's Bay Company. Since it was the policy of the Hudson's Bay Company to restrain agricultural settlement so as to protect its interests in the fur trade, there seemed to be little prospect of a foreign population building up in that region. The United States would have no need to maintain military defenses along its northwest frontier except as might be necessary to deal with Indian uprisings.[3]

As for the Indian tribes, Long had come to appreciate even more fully than on his past expeditions why they bore such animosity toward the United States. Nothing could be more devastating to their hunting way of life than the encroachment of American settlements on their territory. White settlement led to depletion of the game supply, robbing the Indians of their subsistence and turning them into a race of paupers. When his expedition passed through Ohio, Indiana, and Illinois, Long saw the shattered remnants of the once powerful nations of the Shawnee, Delaware, Miami, Potawatomi, and Kickapoo. As the party continued its journey through the upper Mississippi country, it was evident to him that the Menominee, Winnebago, Sac, Fox, and Ioway tribes, already feeling the pinch of a diminishing game supply, awaited a similar fate in the not-too-distant future. As they proceeded farther west and north, Long assumed that the various Sioux tribes and the many small bands of Ojibwas were declining in numbers as well. Although the Sioux and Ojibwas faced no imminent threat of invasion by white settlers, he believed they were steadily being reduced through their constant wars against each other. (Long was mistaken about that, but he was no different from other whites of his era in perceiving intertribal warfare to be a cause as well as a symptom of the Indians' inexorable demise.)

What struck the explorer most forcefully in his observations of the Indian frontier was that white-Indian contact tended to bring out the worst in both races. For the Indians, contact with the whites was such a defeating prospect that it only deepened their innate distrust of outsiders and their animosity toward Americans. For the civilized whites, meanwhile, contact with savage Indians too often led to the whites' own moral degeneracy. The hard, fraught, often brutal white-Indian relations that Long witnessed around trading posts reinforced his Puritan notion that human beings, no matter how civilized, were intrinsically prone to individual and cultural degeneracy. The official report of the expedition did not mince words on this point, saying that the intercourse between US citizens and Indians was "of a nature calculated to vitiate and deprave the former."[4]

For Long, the encounter with John Tanner gave proof that the Indian and white races must be kept apart. In Long's mind, the hapless Tanner personified the problem of degeneracy. Tanner's many years of living among the Indians had shaped him to such an extent that he was probably irretrievably lost to the civilized world. When Long and his men discussed with one another the potential, suggested by some including Tanner's brother Edward, that he might find his way back to the white man's ways by embracing Christianity and serving as a missionary to the Indians, they finally concluded that it did not seem possible. While his "strong mind" appeared to have "rejected the superstitions of Indians," nevertheless, he seemed too hard-headed and instinctual in his mental processes ever to accept the abstract teachings of the Bible and the Christian faith in God. His thirty years among the savages had dulled the sensibilities common to civilized men.[5]

They talked about Tanner for days after leaving him behind at Rainy Lake. Thomas Say wrote the most extensive notes on him of any of the expedition members. Keating incorporated them verbatim into the official report. "What will be the future destiny of Tanner appears to us very uncertain," Say wrote, in a passage that reflected Long's thinking as much as his own. "We much question whether he can ever be satisfied with sharing in the occupations and comforts of civilized life. We think it more probable that the wandering and irregular habits which he seems to have imbibed from the Indians will soon drive him back from the settlements to his usual haunts in the woods."[6]

Two days into their eleven-day trek from Rainy Lake House to Fort William, Long and his men came to the place where Tanner had been ambushed six weeks earlier. It was on a small stream called the Maligne, or Bad River, so named because the many rocks and rapids made it an especially treacherous and arduous passage for canoes. They stopped for dinner just below the first set of rapids and recalled Tanner's chilling vow of revenge against his attacker. While the others ate, Seymour got out his drawing materials and made a sketch of the scene. As the rapids made a considerable fall, Long decided to name them Tanner Falls in honor of the man whose strange and adventurous life was so entwined with this wilderness.[7] Today, the falls are known still as Tanner Rapids, while the small lake at the head of the Maligne River is called Tanner Lake.

❄

At Rainy Lake House, Dr. McLoughlin finally took charge of Tanner's medical case, allowing him to convalesce there through the winter of 1823–24. By the end of October he directed the patient to perform light chores, and by the second week in November he encouraged him to do a little hunting. On one such hunting excursion, Tanner fell ill and returned to the fort so exhausted that he was laid up for several days afterwards. On November 27, McLoughlin noted in the post journal: "Opened the Wound in Tanner's Arm—it seems there is some fragment of Bone yet to come."[8]

It was customary in the posts to celebrate Christmas and New Year's with feasting, dancing, and a week-long respite from winter chores. On Christmas Day, McLoughlin gave the twenty men under his charge twenty-five pounds of flour, four pounds of sturgeon, and a gallon of spirits to have a Christmas feast. McLoughlin joined with them in the week-long holiday, as evidenced by his perfunctory entries in the post journal over that time: on December 27, "fair but Cold—all hands idle"; on the 28th, "fair but very cold—"; on the 29th, "The men bought a little liquor and are Keeping up the Holidays"; and on the 30th, "the men unwell or rather too much spent to work after their frolic." (The usually abstemious Tanner may have sat some of this out.) On New Year's Day, McLoughlin gave the men another twenty-five pounds of flour, three pounds of sturgeon, and another helping of spirits. He also invited the American trader Côté to come join in their festivities. He took care to extend this invitation to all of the women at the American establishment and none of the men, except for Côté. "I do this to prevent any misunderstanding arising in consequence of men going with Stories from one house to the other." After a late night of drinking, fiddling, dancing, and flirting, one more day was given over to rest and recuperation.[9]

Gradually, McLoughlin integrated Tanner into workaday life in the fort. One evening shortly after New Year's, he sent Tanner to get water—no easy task when the water lay beneath several inches of ice. Tanner slipped and fell on the ice, breaking his humerus where it had been shattered previously as well as fracturing his collar bone. McLoughlin put him on bed rest again for several weeks while the bones mended. Finally, when spring came, he ordered the patient onto his feet. He assigned Tanner to snare rabbits near the fort, a task normally given to women. He paid Tanner in cash for the rabbit skins, knowing that he would need a little money as soon as he was fit to leave his care.[10]

Little Clear Sky remained at large. Not surprisingly, his name vanished from McLoughlin's roll of Indian hunters for the winter of 1823–24. Perhaps he left the area, knowing the fur traders were after him. Or perhaps he went over to the American side and simply managed to elude the Hudson's Bay traders. Whatever his fate may have been, McLoughlin did not dwell on it. Discussion of the offense faded away. The young man's motive for trying to kill Tanner was never discovered.

If the bad blood existing between Tanner and Little Clear Sky did cause any of Little Clear Sky's people to avoid Rainy Lake House and trade with the Americans instead, as McLoughlin feared, the effect turned out to be negligible. By January, the chief factor felt confident he was outdoing the opposition for a second winter in a row. By June, Rainy Lake House had acquired a total of thirty-three packs, the Americans just sixteen.[11]

McLoughlin fulfilled George Simpson's expectations during his two years as chief factor of the Rainy Lake District. In the first season he succeeded in eliminating the petty American traders by intercepting their trade and starving them out. If he was unable to do the same with the American Fur Company, then at least he was able to divide the Indian trade peaceably with the Americans along the US border.

In the spring, word came to McLoughlin that he would be reassigned to another post when the Council of the Northern Department met at York Factory in July. George Simpson wanted him to take over administration of the enormous Columbia District in the Far West. Many years earlier, the North West Company had made the same request of him and he had refused to go. This time he accepted. The circumstances had changed. The "troublous times" between the rival fur companies had passed, and the Hudson's Bay Company held unchallenged dominion over the Indian trade in British territory. As chief factor of the Columbia District, he would be in charge of a huge territory stretching from the heights of the Rocky Mountains westward to the Pacific Coast and from the mouth of the Columbia River northward to Russian Alaska and southward to California. Remote as it was vast, and still rich in furs, the Columbia District was an important post. At last he had obtained the high position in the fur trade that he had long felt to be his due.[12]

On June 10, 1824, the McLoughlins embarked for Hudson Bay with twenty-five voyageurs in four fully laden canoes. Besides the doctor and his wife, the other family members on board were seven-year-old Eloisa and three-year-old David. The rest of their children were widely dispersed and well provided for. Marguerite's third daughter, Mary McKay, had married a chief trader the previous summer. McLoughlin's son Joseph, age sixteen, was employed by the Hudson's Bay Company at Sault Ste. Marie. Their son John, twelve, was now in his third year of studies at a school in Terrebonne, in the care of his great uncle Simon. And their daughter Eliza, ten, was a pupil in the Ursuline convent in Quebec.[13] So, with their two youngest children at their sides, John and Marguerite McLoughlin bid farewell to the Rainy Lake country, their home for a majority of the past twelve winters, and to Rainy Lake House, their residence for the past two years.

❄

At the approach of summer, Tanner asked McLoughlin's help in finding him passage to Mackinac. By then he had reconciled himself to leaving the country without his daughters. He had discovered that they had returned safely to their former band at Lake of the Woods. Maybe, someday, he would come back for them.

He dropped his vow of revenge against Little Clear Sky. In presenting his story a few years later, he just let the matter slip. Perhaps he saw the futility in it when he decided to leave the Rainy Lake country for good. As an ex-patriot of the Ojibwa nation, to mete out punishment for Little Clear Sky's bad deed lost all meaning for him. It is worth recording the fact, as Tanner did not, that in all his years among the Indians he never killed a man. He was tomahawked in the head twice, shot once, robbed a number of times, assaulted with a hoe by his mother-in-law, and condemned to death by a medicine man, and through it all he inflicted little physical pain upon others. He did not have a taste for hurting people.

As the Hudson's Bay Company no longer had canoes going all the way to Mackinac, Tanner made arrangements through McLoughlin to go with the American trader, Côté. In spite of their troubled personal history, Côté agreed to it. But as the date of departure drew near, Côté discovered an alternative; he sent Tanner with some voyageurs in a small canoe to the American Fur Company's trading post at Fond du Lac. When Tanner reached Fond du Lac, he was able to transfer to a large canoe for the journey around the north shore of Lake Superior. At Sault Ste. Marie, he found passage with still another canoe for the remaining distance to Mackinac.[14]

After more than thirty years in Indian country, a part of him, at least, clung to the belief that he was home at last.

Mackinac, 1824–and After

Nineteenth-century travelers found Mackinac Island an exotic, even enchanting, place. Three miles long and a mile wide, it rises precipitously out of the clear, blue waters of Lake Huron. Henry Rowe Schoolcraft, a geologist and ethnographer who served for many years as Indian agent in the Michigan Territory, said that the Ottawas named the island Mish-i-nim-auk-in-ong for its resemblance to a great turtle rising from the lake. In Ottawa legend its original inhabitants were a race of little men, or "turtle spirits," who had dropped from the sky. On moonlit, wind-still, summer nights, it was said, fishermen could see the turtle people's lodge shining atop the white cliffs and hear them singing and dancing on the island's summit. Schoolcraft walked the whole circumference of Mackinac Island in one day and found its rugged interior a "labyrinth of curious little glens and valleys." Most of it was covered by cedar, juniper, and pine, but there were grassy openings where the Indians had once cultivated the soil, gathering up the rocks in stone circles that had long since grown over with moss.[1]

Elizabeth Thérèse Baird, the granddaughter of Thérèse Schindler, to whom Tanner had entrusted his infant daughter, Lucy, remembered the village on the south end of the island the way it appeared around 1814. "How vividly I still see the clear, shining broad beach of white pebbles and stones, and clear blue water of the 'Basin.' The houses were of one story, roofed with cedar bark. . . . True, the houses were quaint and old; however, they were but few, not enough to mar the beauty, but rather to add to the charms of the little crescent-shaped village."[2]

In a less nostalgic vein, an American Fur Company clerk by the name of Gurdon S. Hubbard recorded his first visit to Mackinac in the summer of 1818. "This island was then in its gayest season. All the traders attached to the American Fur Company were assembled there, having brought in their furs, and were preparing to receive their outfits to depart again to their several trading-posts." Hubbard thought the island had about 500 inhabitants excluding the fort's garrison of three companies. Most of the villagers were Métis and French Canadians who lived by fishing and trading with the Indians. "With few exceptions," he wrote, "they were poor and improvident."[3]

An American woman named Myra Peters Mason who spent the summer of 1824 on the island found little in the village to admire. She informed her sister that the Métis were "a grade below any other species of the human race I have ever seen." Mackinac, she proclaimed, was a "half-way place in every sense of the phrase between civilization & barbarism."[4]

Although Tanner did not record his feelings about Mackinac, he probably looked to it as a haven. Perhaps the placement of a fort, a trading house, an Indian agency, and a largely Métis village all in such close proximity gave him hope of blending into the polyglot community. Possibly, too, the pleasant island setting rekindled old memories of the springtime idyll on Isle Royale he had once enjoyed in his early youth. In any case the strong Métis presence, with its proud embrace of mixed-race families and dual Indian-European heritage, must have appealed to him. He would not have used the terms "civilization" and "barbarism" to describe the juxtaposition of Anglo-American and Métis elements in the community, but he would have agreed with the American woman's assessment that Mackinac was a "half-way place."

Yet this unique social environment was not to last. With the United States consolidating its hold on the fur trade in US territory and the Hudson's Bay Company coming to serve as the instrument of colonial rule in British territory, frontier communities like Mackinac, Sault Ste. Marie, Prairie du Chien, and Red River were being forcibly restructured. In Mackinac the process of Americanization began with the opening of boys' and girls' boarding schools around 1814 and intensified with the establishment of a Presbyterian mission in 1823. A new Anglo-American elite was born, which spearheaded the transformation. The elite included Indian agent George Boyd, the American Fur Company's Robert Stuart, missionary William Ferry, leading businessmen and fort officers, and the wives of these men—altogether some twelve to fifteen families, all of whom hailed from the eastern United States or Britain. They introduced American law, pushed American forms of local government and commerce, made English the dominant language, preached evangelical Protestantism, and expected the Métis to accept American customs.[5] All of which made it impossible for Tanner to adjust and fit in with the community even though that was his hope.

Tanner's first experience with the new regime was also perhaps his most devastating. Returning to Mackinac in the early summer of 1824 after an absence of almost two years, he discovered that his three children by Therezia had been bound out to American families. In a practice dating back to colonial times, local authorities bound out needy children to prevent their being a burden on the county's taxpayers. Binding out was a pauper apprentice system whereby the child's labor was given to the master in return for the child's keep and the promise that the child would be taught a craft. Usually the system was restricted to orphans and illegitimate children. When the local authorities bound out Tanner's children, it showed that they had decided Therezia could not care for them and, furthermore, that they regarded the children as fatherless, since they considered Tanner and Therezia to be unmarried. The oldest child, Martha, was bound out to the fort commander's family. The youngest, James, just two years old, was placed with the Indian agency's blacksmith. The middle child, Mary, was put in yet another household. When Tanner learned of their situation, he was furious. He felt betrayed.[6]

Before leaving Mackinac in the fall of 1822, he had arranged for Martha and Mary to attend the new boarding school for girls. The first of its kind in the territory, the school was intended for the daughters of American Fur Company employees. Robert Stuart had seen to its establishment a few years earlier, employing Schindler's daughter, Marienne, as headmistress. The girls were taught to read and write, keep house, and make their own clothes. Although Tanner's *Narrative* says nothing of his children being bound out, it does disclose that while he was away for two years the authorities seized what little property he had in Mackinac to pay for the girls' board. It appears that the authorities hounded Therezia for the debt, and when she had nothing else to give them they made her surrender the children.[7]

Tanner's mistake was that he had entrusted the children to the company's care even though his personal affairs might detain him in Indian country longer than the one-year term of his employment contract. Of course, had he not been attacked by Little Clear Sky he would likely have gotten back within twelve months. Returning to Mackinac fully a year later than planned, he finally collected the pay the company owed him for the previous year. Ironically, he had to use every last penny of his income to get his children back. Afterwards he had nothing. "I have no money, no clothing, & nothing to eat," he informed the Indian agent. "I am in such a situation that I am unable to go anywhere." All he had left, he claimed, was "one old Blanket."[8]

A month later Tanner found employment as an interpreter for Indian agent Boyd. As an employee of the field service of the US Office of Indian Affairs, he became part of a far-flung bureaucracy within the War Department. The Indian field service had seventeen agencies and twenty-three subagencies in operation that year. Mackinac Agency had a staff of five when Tanner came on board: besides Boyd, there was another interpreter, an assistant interpreter, a blacksmith, and a striker.[9] Interpreters were typically paid a dollar per day, making it one of the best-paid positions within the laboring class in fur-trade society. So, the outlook for Tanner would seem to have brightened: he had secured a steady government job in one of the two occupations, interpreter and missionary, most often taken up by repatriated white Indians like himself.

Yet a good job could not save Tanner from sinking further into disillusionment and loneliness. His adversities were not economic but cultural and psychological. His strange manners, his emotional intensity, his "quick and piercing blue eyes"—character traits that bespoke not just his Indian upbringing but the markings of trauma—put white people off. He could not form lasting relationships. One perceptive observer said that he lacked the submissive and compliant manner that would have helped him get along in his new station as a government interpreter.[10] Governor Cass met with him a dozen years after their first acquaintance and found him "a forlorn, heart broken man."[11] Unable to find acceptance, Tanner grew increasingly hard and mean toward his own wife and children, losing their affections one by one. Whites who wrote about him in his lifetime almost invariably cited the disintegration of his family as proof that he was either insane or hopelessly maladjusted after his return to white society. What they failed to see was that their own society was deeply implicated in the family's undoing.

On July 30, 1830, Michigan's territorial legislature enacted a bizarre little law aimed specifically at taking Tanner's eighteen-year-old daughter Martha away from him. Entitled "An act authorizing the sheriff of Chippewa county to perform certain duties therein mentioned," the first section authorized the sheriff to remove Martha from her father's custody and place her in a missionary establishment; the second section provided that if Tanner should threaten Martha or her new custodians, it would constitute a misdemeanor punishable by fine and imprisonment. One Michigan jurist later commented that the act was "probably the only law ever passed in America attaching criminal consequences to injuries to a single private person."[12]

The background to that law is naturally somewhat complicated. Two years before the law was passed, Tanner had taken a job as interpreter for Indian agent Henry Schoolcraft at the Sault Ste. Marie Agency, moving his children to Sault Ste. Marie. The following year Schoolcraft had had to reduce Tanner's hours and pay; consequently, Tanner had taken a second job as interpreter for the Baptist mission there. He began to assist his second employer, the Reverend Abel Bingham, in translating the Gospels. Schoolcraft and Bingham soon entered into a bitter feud in which Tanner's shared employment was at first just one irritant among several. However, when Tanner took Bingham's side in a vicious controversy surrounding one Sophia Cadotte, a pupil at the mission school who was also a servant legally bound to Schoolcraft, it led to a falling out between him and the Indian agent. Schoolcraft was a thug who used the power of his office to settle scores. Besides heading the Indian agency, he also served as a member of the territorial legislature. When he went to Detroit to attend the summer session of the legislature, he not only influenced Governor Cass to remove Tanner from his post, he vindictively pushed that law through the chamber as well.[13]

Even before Tanner was betrayed by his employer, other pressures came to bear on his marriage to Therezia. In the mid- to late 1820s, the Presbyterian missionaries in Mackinac entered into a "religious war" with the Roman Catholic laity. Both sides began to measure their strength by how many converts they could make each year, and both sides took their proselytizing to nasty extremes. When the local authorities caught Catholic Métis inducing Indian children to run away from the Presbyterian mission school, they had them stripped and flogged on the public street. In that charged atmosphere, Therezia converted to Catholicism.[14]

According to Elizabeth Thérèse Baird's recollection, when Tanner moved from Mackinac to Sault Ste. Marie he asked Therezia to join him there, but she refused to go unless he would marry her in the Catholic Church. Denying her request, he insisted (once again) that they were already married in the Indian way and she was fully his wife. One wonders if Therezia's desire to be legally married had less to do with religious conviction than it did with preventing the local authorities from seizing her "illegitimate" children again. In any case, when Tanner would not consent to be married in the Catholic Church she remained in Mackinac, and that was the end of their relationship.[15]

A few years later, Tanner himself converted to the Protestant faith at Sault Ste. Marie. The Baptist missionary Bingham performed his baptism in the St. Mary's River on August 21, 1831. Unfortunately, there is no explicit record of what Tanner thought or felt about his conversion to Christianity. One could imagine that it was in some way an act of desperation, a last bid for acceptance by the white community. When Tanner gave his story to Edwin James, he told him a pertinent anecdote. It was a tale about a baptized Indian, a man who had followed the beseechings of a missionary, renouncing his own people's religion and adopting that of the whites. After death, the spirit of this man journeyed to the gates of the white man's heaven and demanded admittance, but the gatekeeper would not let him in, for he was an Indian. "Go," the gatekeeper said to him, "for to the west there are the villages and the hunting grounds of those of your own people who have been on the earth before you." So the dead man's spirit journeyed some more and came to the villages where the dead of his own people resided, only to be met by the chief, who barred him from entering there as well. "You have been ashamed of us while you lived," the chief told him. "You have chosen to worship the white man's God. Go now to his village, and let him provide for you." The Indian having lived by two creeds, his spirit had nowhere to rest. Now Tanner was that Indian.[16]

In the year of his religious conversion, Tanner went to Detroit to search for his daughter Martha. Though he did not find her, he met a white woman there whom he married, brought back to Sault Ste. Marie, and introduced to the Baptist church fellowship. Schoolcraft wrote disparagingly in his diary that the bride was formerly "a chamber-maid at old Ben Woodworth's hotel."[17] Bingham's daughter, Angie Bingham Gilbert, a more sympathetic source on Tanner, recollected years later that Tanner's new wife was a widow by the name of Mrs. Duncan. People in Detroit, Gilbert said, became interested in Tanner and recommended the widow to him. "He probably did not give any exhibition of temper while there, and she finally consented to marry him."[18] The marriage lasted less than a year. By the following summer it was rumored that Tanner abused her and threatened to kill her and that when he was away she entertained soldiers from nearby Fort Brady in their home. In the midst of these domestic problems, Tanner's son James ran away from home. One day, Tanner encountered his ten-year-old son in the village and gave him a severe beating, for which he was arrested and put in jail. When his wife heard that he was incarcerated, she took the opportunity to make her escape. Her church friends took up a collection and bought her passage on the next vessel bound for Detroit. When Tanner was released from jail and learned what had happened, he felt betrayed yet again; his fellow parishioners had spirited away his wife while he was locked behind bars.[19]

After that episode, Tanner's relations with the community rapidly deteriorated. People feared that in retaliation for the removal of his wife he would harm somebody. In Gilbert's words, he became "a source of worry to nearly every one." Although the Reverend Bingham still valued Tanner's skill as an interpreter and translator, he could no longer pay his salary. In October 1833 Bingham reluctantly dismissed him from employment. At the same time, acceding to the wishes of his parishioners, Bingham banished Tanner from the church fellowship.[20]

Ostracized by the community, robbed of his daughter Martha, and deserted by his son James and his wife from Detroit, Tanner had no one. His daughter Mary had left him sometime before, though the circumstances of her departure are not known. Around this time, word came to him that she had been shot dead by an Ojibwa man somewhere up north. She was twenty years old.[21]

Tanner lived out the rest of his years in Sault Ste. Marie as a semirecluse. He mostly withdrew to his house, which stood on the bank of the St. Mary's River near the Indian agency. Increasingly given to fits of rage, he was jailed from time to time for making a public disturbance. The children of the village came to regard him as the "bogeyman."[22]

As he approached old age he still craved friendship. It seems he found a small measure of what he was looking for in the Reverend Bingham's two young daughters. They were of a size and manner to remind him of his own two daughters by Red Sky of the Morning. The girls often passed by his house while he sat in the door gazing toward the sunset. Sometimes they came to visit him. On other occasions, just as they came into view, they would suddenly join hands and scurry past his house. Maybe they saw something in his look that made them take fright. The younger of the two, Angie, would later remember, "When he was pleasant we were interested in seeing him but when angry, we were very much afraid of him."[23]

Nearly seventy years later, Angie Bingham Gilbert presented her recollections of Tanner to the Michigan Pioneer and Historical Society. Notwithstanding her childhood fear of him, it was a surprisingly sympathetic, admiring portrait. He was a "remarkable man," very intelligent, with "many beautiful ideas." Her father had informed her that Tanner had once been an excellent interpreter and missionary. When Tanner was not in a rage, she remembered, he could be pleasant, interesting, and even "gentlemanly."

She recalled his striking appearance. "He was a very strange and in some ways a noble looking man. He was tall and spare, with long white hair which he wore parted in the middle and drawn back behind his ears like a woman's. He had a fierce eye, and his countenance was most forbidding."[24]

Gilbert was not alone in forming a strong impression of Tanner's "fierce eye." One Dr. Charles A. Lee of New York met Tanner late in life when he tried to interview him about Indian medicine. He found in his eyes "the most savage, vindictive, suspicious and I may add demoniac, expression I ever saw." He was too frightened to go through with the interview.[25]

Henry Schoolcraft dwelt on Tanner's eyes, too, when he wrote about him in his diary following a tense confrontation the two men had several years after Tanner lost his job at the Indian agency. Going into a canoe-house on the agency grounds, Schoolcraft turned around to find Tanner had followed him in. They stood facing each other in the confined space between the raised canoes. "He began to talk after his manner," Schoolcraft wrote. Then, looking him in the eyes, Schoolcraft "saw mischief . . . in their cold, malicious, bandit air." Schoolcraft shook his cane at him. Tanner backed out.[26]

On the evening of July 4, 1846, Tanner's house was engulfed in flames.

People assembled to try to put out the fire, but they kept their distance after someone discovered gunpowder had been placed around the perimeter of the property as if to ignite an even bigger conflagration. As the crowd stood back and watched the house burn to the ground, people speculated that "Old Tanner" would be found dead inside. Picking through the charred ruin the next day, however, they found no human remains.

Two days after the fire, on July 6, another village alarm was raised when James Schoolcraft, the Indian agent's younger brother and the sutler for Fort Brady, was found dead on his property with a bullet through his heart. Witnesses heard the gunshot but did not see the shooter. Dressed in a robe and house slippers, James Schoolcraft had been walking down a garden path that led away from the house and was evidently taken by surprise by someone hiding in the bushes. The killing occurred in the afternoon; it seemed he had risen late after sleeping off the effects of a hard night of drinking with army officers on July Fourth, one and a half days earlier.[27]

Suspicion fell immediately on Tanner. To most of the excited townspeople, it now seemed that Tanner had burned down his own house, committed the murder, and fled. His resentment of Henry Schoolcraft was well known. Presumably upon discovering that the Indian agent was out of town he had waited a day for him to return and had then killed the brother instead. The townspeople imagined that he was now lurking nearby, crazed and homeless and potentially still murderous. They promptly organized a manhunt. The men did not venture too far into the woods, however, as they knew Tanner was a good marksman. After a few days, they gave up the search.[28]

Cooler heads suggested another theory about the murder of James Schoolcraft. A one-ounce ball and three buckshot found in the victim's body matched the contents of a government cartridge fired from an army musket. A young officer at Fort Brady by the name of Lieutenant Bryant Tilden was said to have a motive for the killing: he and James Schoolcraft had been vying for the attention of a young lady. At the officers' party on the evening of July Fourth the two men had quarreled. Tilden was overheard to say "cold lead would fix it." However, before he could be formally charged with murder the army whisked him away to fight in the Mexican-American War.[29]

Not long afterwards, Tilden was charged with another crime, court-martialed, convicted on counts of murder and burglary, and sentenced to be hanged. The sentence was commuted, and he resigned from the army. Though he was never formally charged in the Schoolcraft case, he felt the need to proclaim his innocence. He died in New York in 1859. After he died, rumors surfaced that on his deathbed he confessed to killing Schoolcraft. The most compelling story of the deathbed confession was offered by Gilbert, who recalled a conversation she had with Martha Tanner in Mackinac some forty years after the murder. Martha Tanner told her that she had had a letter from Tilden's wife stating that her husband had confessed to shooting James Schoolcraft. Martha stated further that being a Roman Catholic she had shown Mrs. Tilden's letter to her bishop, who had taken it from her saying that it must be destroyed.

Although the suspicion of Tilden lingered, the prevailing view was that Tanner killed Schoolcraft. Many worried that he might be hovering about, waiting to kill again. One Indian woman claimed she had seen him darting through the forest with dead grass and pine boughs tied to his arms and legs, dressed for hunting. Other Indians who came down the St. Mary's River reported seeing his campfire through the trees and hearing him singing Indian songs. When, after a few weeks had passed, smoke was observed rising in a dozen places around the surrounding country, it was said he was setting fire to the woods. Nervous parents kept their children in at night. A guard was posted around Henry Schoolcraft's house as well as around the Reverend Bingham's house. The local authorities offered a reward for Tanner's capture, while the governor of Michigan announced he would do all in his power to bring him to trial. The fear that he would return and commit more murders went on for weeks. The excitement would long be remembered as the "Tanner summer."[30]

He was never heard from again.

❋

In the spacious Far West, Dr. John McLoughlin had full rein to exercise his ambition and skill as an administrator. There he built an empire on a scale few nineteenth-century traders could have imagined. For twenty years he served as chief factor of the Hudson's Bay Company's sprawling Columbia District. From his headquarters at Fort Vancouver on the lower Columbia River, he oversaw a vast trade network that stretched up and down the Pacific Coast from Alaska to California, penetrated inland to the Great Salt Lake, and followed sea lanes to Hawaii, Tahiti, and the Far East. He managed a complex infrastructure of trading posts, trapper brigades, company ships, sawmills, and farms. He advised his superiors on how the company could best compete with its American and Russian rivals. He conducted diplomacy with Indian tribes. He forged his own policy for dealing with the arrival of American settlers. He was patriarch over the whole unorganized territory.

McLoughlin developed a reputation among the Pacific Northwest Indians as a just and powerful white chief. He was proud of the name that

Indians gave him: "The White-headed Eagle." He supposed the name alluded to his impressive authority over his men as much as it did to his
giant physique and white mane of hair, or the eagle-like glower he wore
when addressing a council. He delivered a stern message to his own people
on how they must treat Indians. As Hudson's Bay Company servants, they
were obliged to cultivate good relations with their trading partners. Anyone
under his charge who maliciously harmed an Indian would be punished the
same as if the attack was made on a white person. Anyone who murdered
an Indian would be subject "to the penalties of a capital indictment in the
criminal courts of Canada." He hoped for similar vigilance and restraint by
the tribes. He expected them to punish their own bad men, and he wanted
to leave them to their own affairs as much as possible. "In dealing with the
Indians we ought to make allowance for their way of thinking," he said.[31]

While McLoughlin talked of respecting natives' way of thinking, he did
so with the tribes' political rather than cultural autonomy in view. When
missionaries came to the Oregon country with the hope of converting Indians to Christianity, he applauded their efforts. Always a humanitarian, he
believed the missionaries could benefit Indians most by introducing them
to agriculture. He argued that teaching them how to read and write and
instructing them in Scripture ought to be secondary concerns at best. In his
view, if a few Indians gathered around the missions, learned how to farm,
and took their new knowledge back to their people, then it would free them all
from dependence on the hunt. "Teach them first to cultivate the ground and
live more comfortably than they do by hunting, and as they do this, teach them
religion," he advised the missionaries. McLoughlin believed the Indians'
customary way of life could not last in Oregon any more than the fur trade
could long endure there. Both would disappear under the approaching tide
of white settlement.[32]

A man once asked the doctor if he thought Oregon would become a settled country. His response was that wherever men could raise wheat the land
would become settled. As McLoughlin found Oregon's fertile soil and mild
climate to be much more favorable for farming than any other place he had
known, he expected the land to fill with farms relatively quickly. As early as
1829, he started a claim at the falls of the Willamette River twenty-five miles
south of Fort Vancouver. He erected mills next to the falls. Eventually he
moved to his valuable claim after retiring from the company. He always anticipated that Oregon would grow and prosper. He naïvely expected to have
more influence on the new state than the way it played out. While he was
chief factor he encouraged freemen (retired company servants) and Métis
to immigrate to the Willamette valley from Red River and elsewhere in the

Hudson's Bay Company's territories. He told them that Oregon would be a good place to raise their mixed-blood children "as white and Christians." Furthermore, he thought that a strong Métis presence would tend to promote peace between settlers and Indians. In looking to Oregon's future, he vainly hoped that Indians would be well treated by whites when the latter came to outnumber them.[33]

Two of McLoughlin's own Métis children were among the few hundred Canadians who answered his call and took up farms in the Willamette valley. His oldest son, Joseph, served as a trapper on expeditions to California for a number of years and then retired from the company and established a farm about forty miles south of Fort Vancouver. His stepson, Thomas McKay, also settled in the valley, where he married a woman of the Chinook tribe, made a farm, and continued to serve the company as an occasional guide and trapper. McLoughlin's younger daughter, Eloisa, grew up in the "big house" at Fort Vancouver, married a company clerk, and eventually settled in the area as well.[34]

McLoughlin urged his younger two sons, John Jr. and David, to get an education and make a life for themselves outside of farming and the fur trade. Both sons did a turn at medical school in Paris under the watchful eye of his brother David, while from the other side of the world McLoughlin paid their expenses. Both young men circled back to farming and the fur trade in the Pacific Northwest in spite of their education and their father's wishes. McLoughlin's son David later left Oregon for the California gold fields, then went to the mines in British Columbia, and finally settled on a farm in northern Idaho, where he married a Kutenai woman and lived on into old age in obscurity. John Jr. was less fortunate. After a troubled youth in Terrebonne living with his great uncle, followed by a restless passage through early manhood in Paris and Montreal, he started to show some promise as a Hudson's Bay Company clerk in the Far West. Tragically, while superintending a remote post in coastal Alaska in 1842, his life was cut short when he was shot and killed by one of his own men in a drunken brawl.[35]

There was a curious parallel between McLoughlin's older son's unhappy life and John Tanner's. Both were separated from their parents' home and thrust into an alien culture while in the same early stage of life. McLoughlin took his son John Jr. from Fort William to Terrebonne to live with his uncle Simon when the boy was eight years old. Although McLoughlin's aim was to get his son a formal education, he was at a tender age to be deposited so far from home. McLoughlin saw little more of him after that, and Marguerite had even less contact. John Jr. seems to have been psychologically damaged by the separation in much the same way Tanner was traumatized by his captivity. There is a chilling hint of it in a missive Simon Fraser wrote to his great nephew in 1836, when John Jr. was a troubled young man of twenty-three. "I have so bad an opinion of you that I think you equal to any species of meanness," the letter began, and then it made oblique reference to John Jr.'s childhood uprooting:

> When a boy of about eight years of age I was obliged to take you from the Reverend Mr Glen on account of the habit you had of soiling your breeches and remaining in that condition for days.... I blamed your mother for the filthy habit—I am now convinced I was wrong—the blame lay solely on your innate perversity at school in Terrebonne—Messrs Glen Walker and Gill repeatedly urged me to take you away alleging that you corrupted the morals of the other boys.... You appear to me born to disgrace every being who has the misfortune to be connected with you.... If you have any the least affection for your father mother or brothers you will retire to some distant far country that you may never more be heard of.... You have nothing left besides being a day labourer in civilized society or an hunter among savages.[36]

Dr. McLoughlin never learned of the circumstances of his boy's early failing at school, nor did he know how his uncle abused the boy's feelings toward his mother and Métis heritage. Though John Jr. begged to join his parents in Oregon, McLoughlin insisted that he stay in the East to get an education. Years later, when John Jr. was a young man adrift in Montreal running up debts, he joined with other disaffected Métis sons of the fur trade on an escapade to the Red River country to start a rebellion among the Métis and Indians. The adventure turned into a debacle, bringing John Jr. to one of the low points in his short, turbulent life. Clearly John Jr.'s psychological problems stemmed from feelings of abandonment as well as ambivalence over his Métis heritage. Yet father and son never discussed those matters between them in all of their pained correspondence over the years. Though McLoughlin was a doctor, he did not have the insight of modern psychology for comprehending his son's problems. Indeed, McLoughlin never expressed doubts about having parted with his son at such a young age; he only admitted to regrets that he himself did not live "close to the Civilized World" so as to "superintendent the Education" of his children.[37]

McLoughlin came from a proud family in which heritage and higher education were esteemed above all else. As a fur trader and leader in the Hudson's Bay Company, he held fast to the value of a good education while insisting that respect for heritage had to be liberalized to include the Métis culture that he had married into. He envisioned a future for his empire on the Columbia, as well as for his family, that would be inclusive of whites, Indians, and Métis. Historical forces far beyond his control overwhelmed his efforts both in the public arena and in what he attempted to do for his sons.

Until the early 1840s, Oregon's small settler population of under a thousand people was composed of roughly equal numbers of Americans and British subjects. The United States and Britain jointly occupied the Oregon country under an international convention. In the early 1840s, American immigration increased and the settlers' numbers began to tip heavily in favor of the United States. When the new settlers arrived in the Willamette valley, they looked askance at the polyglot population of French Canadians, Scots, Métis, Hawaiians, and eastern Indians (mostly Iroquois and Delawares) who made up the British portion of the resident settler population. The Americans harbored racial attitudes that were not at all inclusive; most of them were anti-Indian, antiblack, and opposed to marriage between whites and Indians or blacks. They looked upon the many cross-cultural marriages and Métis offspring as a degenerate population.[38]

Far from becoming an inclusive society, Oregon trended the other way in the 1840s. Willamette valley residents met in the summer of 1843 to organize a provisional government. Some put forward a proposal to push out all settlers who had taken an Indian wife, and others suggested a constitutional provision to prohibit "half-breeds" from owning land. The constitution as adopted did not include either of those provisions, but it did come to exclude blacks from the territory. An unusual, racially integrated party of white and black Missourians on its way to the Willamette valley halted in dismay when it received the news and then made course for the future Washington Territory instead.[39]

McLoughlin refused to recognize the provisional government. Some of the American settlers countered him by threatening to confiscate the Hudson's Bay Company's property or deny certain British subjects rights of US citizenship when Oregon became American soil, which they presumed it would. Despite those tensions in the community, McLoughlin extended a helping hand to hundreds of American immigrants later that same year as they arrived in Oregon at the end of their exhausting overland journeys. By opening his stores and giving the Americans generous terms of credit (much of it never repaid) he was "simply converting necessity into virtue"— keeping the needy immigrants from starving so they would not resort to storming the fort and seizing the supplies for themselves. Those calculated moves earned him a huge debt of gratitude among the new populace and were long remembered as acts of humanity.[40]

As the settler population in Oregon swelled, Americans called for expanding the nation's borders to the Pacific with the annexation of the Oregon country. Events rapidly moved beyond McLoughlin's control and influence. By the Oregon Treaty of 1846, the United States and Britain agreed to partition the Oregon country along the forty-ninth parallel. The Hudson's Bay Company vacated Fort Vancouver and moved its headquarters north to Vancouver Island in today's British Columbia; meanwhile, McLoughlin left the company and moved from Fort Vancouver to his claim at the Willamette Falls. By an act of Congress in 1848, Oregon became an organized territory. Two years later, Congress enacted the Donation Land Claim Act, an early homestead law promoted by and for the white settlers of Oregon. The law authorized the survey of Oregon lands without regard to Indian title, and it provided for the distribution of land claims to eligible settlers. Eligibility requirements under the law affirmed white privilege over other racial groups. Thus, Indians were pushed out of the way, Métis thrust into the shadows, Hawaiians persuaded to return to Hawaii, and blacks excluded. It was not the inclusive society McLoughlin had desired.

The Donation Land Claim Act also targeted McLoughlin's valuable claim at the Willamette Falls, conveying what it called the "Oregon City claim" to the Oregon Territory for use as an educational endowment. This narrow provision in the law preempted McLoughlin's just claim and was nothing but a vindictive blow against the former British patriarch now that his twenty-year reign over the Oregon country was ended. It did not dispossess him of his house, but it did deprive him of a considerable part of his rightful estate. Moreover, his foes did not stop with passing the law but also challenged his application for US citizenship, since US citizenship was a necessary condition for obtaining a land grant under the law. Although he did eventually achieve US citizenship, the holdup in his application kept him from pressing his claim before much of the land was parceled out to others. Ironically, McLoughlin's declaration of intention to become a US citizen took away whatever recourse for protection of property he might have had as a British subject under the Oregon Treaty of 1846.

McLoughlin did not see the political knives come out against him until it was too late. Embittered by this perceived treachery on the part of a few bigoted politicians, he found it was not enough for the Americans to take the Indians' land and establish a government of white men for the white man, they had to work out their anti-British fervor as well, and he was their victim. In an open letter to the citizens of Oregon, he protested that he was not even an Englishman. "I am a Canadian by birth, and an Irishman by descent," he wrote. Their shady politics had left him "in the decline of life, and in the decrepitude of old age, to the companionship of adders."[41]

McLoughlin died of natural causes at the age of seventy-two on September 3, 1857, at his home in Oregon City, his Marguerite and daughter Eloisa nearby. At the time of his death, the Oregon Constitutional Convention was in session in nearby Salem, preparing the territory for statehood. While McLoughlin lay dying, he summoned one of the convention delegates, a young man by the name of LaFayette Grover, a future governor of Oregon, to come into his chamber so he could make a last request: he wanted Grover to promise him that after he was gone the state of Oregon would return the land to its rightful owners, his family. The old trader had fire in his belly to the end. "You are a young man and will live many years in this country," he rasped to his visitor. "As for me, I might have been better shot like a bull"— and he spit out the words, according to Grover's account—"I might better have been shot forty years ago!" McLoughlin paused, looking for an acknowledgment that he had been wronged. Getting none, he went on, "than to have lived here and tried to build up a family and an estate in this government." Then he concluded, almost in a whisper, "I planted all I had here."[42]

After his death, McLoughlin's historical reputation rose as anti-British sentiment receded. By the late nineteenth century, old pioneers hailed the memory of the Hudson's Bay Company chief factor, recalling his humanitarian aid to arriving settlers and insisting that he was the early friend of the American cause. Many years after he was gone, he became known as the "Father of Oregon."

❄

Retiring from western exploration after his 1823 expedition, Stephen H. Long turned to various nation-building endeavors in the settled part of the United States for the remainder of his career with the US Topographical Engineers. His latter activities, which came to span the whole antebellum period, included surveying for a national road, building railroads in Maryland and Georgia, and improving navigation on the Ohio and Mississippi rivers. He headed the Office of Improvements of Western Rivers for a decade and a half. He supervised dredging of sandbars and removal of snags on the Mississippi and its tributaries and oversaw construction of a small fleet of steam-powered snagboats, each vessel operated by a crew of thirty to forty men. Late in life he was promoted to the rank of colonel and was appointed chief of the Corps of Topographical Engineers.

Long's nearly half century of military service spanned the years 1814 to 1863, coinciding almost exactly with the life of the Topographical Engineers as an elite unit in the army. During Long's early career as an explorer, nationalists pressed for a federal role not only in safeguarding the nation's frontiers but also in strengthening the nation's transportation system. Nationalists wanted army engineers to deploy not only to build fortifications but also to survey major roads and improve waterways, the nation's arteries for communication and commerce. The General Survey Act of 1824 authorized federal assistance for those so-called internal improvements. A further act of Congress in 1838 elevated the Topographical Engineers from a branch of the Corps of Engineers to a corps by itself. For the next quarter century, the Corps of Topographical Engineers flourished as the work of the "topogs" came to span an even wider array of nation-building projects, from dredging harbors and charting coastlines to surveying routes for transcontinental railroads. During and after the Mexican-American War, the topogs devoted more and more of their time to the trans-Mississippi West.[43]

Long was immensely gratified to see the topogs take on the work of internal improvements. Although his own assignments after 1824 did not take him west of the Mississippi River ever again, he remained a westward expansionist at heart. His political hero was Henry Clay of Kentucky, the longtime US congressman and speaker of the house. An ardent nationalist, Clay championed internal improvements as one of three major components of his "American System" for growing the national economy (along with protective tariffs and a national bank). Improving the nation's roads and waterways would stimulate commerce between the North, South, and West and bind the three sections together.[44]

American nationalism turned inward in the 1820s as efforts toward nation building focused less on territorial expansion and more on internal improvements and economic growth. US Indian policy reflected the trend. Around the time that Long completed his western expeditions, the frontier of American settlement stood on a ragged north-south line down the length of the Mississippi valley. A few fingers of white settlement reached across the Mississippi and up the major tributaries draining from the west. East of the line of settlement, there were several large pockets of Indian-held lands where whites were discouraged from settling. The American populace fixated on getting access to those remaining Indian lands in the east. It demanded that the US government force all eastern tribes to cede their lands and move westward. The dispossessed tribes were to "remove" to unorganized territory lying beyond the Mississippi. Since the Great Plains constituted a Great American Desert unsuitable for white settlement, proponents of "Indian removal" claimed the tribes would find those lands to be a safe haven from further white encroachment, a "permanent Indian frontier," an agreeable place for the tribes' subsistence. In 1830, Congress enacted the Indian Removal Bill and President Andrew Jackson signed it into law.

Although the federal policy of Indian relocation was not new, but rather a continuation of forced relocations that had already occurred in the states of Ohio, Indiana, and Illinois over the preceding decades, it nonetheless took on a more draconian cast under the Jackson administration. A series of forced emigrations ensued for tribes still residing east of the Mississippi. The major tribes who were targeted for relocation were the Choctaw, Chickasaw, Cherokee, Creek, and Seminole tribes, known collectively as the "Five Civilized Tribes" for their decades-old effort to adopt the white man's forms of land tenure, government, and religion in order to avoid this very outcome.

Although Stephen Long was not consulted during the final debate over the Indian Removal Bill, his legacy of western exploration from 1816 to 1823 helped prepare the ground for Indian relocation. In particular, his description of the Great Plains as a wasteland for white settlement, which would serve as a haven for nomadic tribes and a buffer against foreign invasion, provided intellectual cover for the US government's big lie in the 1830s that the central and southern plains would be set aside as a *permanent* Indian territory.[45]

Americans in Long's day were of two minds about Indian peoples. Some thought they should be absorbed into the American nation through a process of acculturation, that is, they had to be raised from "savagery" to "civilization" as nineteenth-century Americans understood those terms. Others thought the goal of assimilating Indian peoples into the nation was unachievable; therefore, tribes had to be removed from the nation or else face destruction by the overwhelming numbers of white settlers pressing on their lands. "Removal," according to the latter view, was the tribes' only alternative to extinction. Concepts of nation and culture in Long's day did not admit other possibilities. Outside of the fur trade, the idea of cultural mixing was generally abhorred. The further notion that Indian peoples might retain part of their own traditions within a culturally diverse nation was scarcely imaginable then. Long's often dark and pessimistic pronouncements about western tribes were, unfortunately, consistent with mainstream opinion in his time.

By the time Long reached old age in the mid-nineteenth century, the fur trade in the United States had faded into obscurity. Americans mostly went west in search of other riches: gold in California, free land in Oregon, freedom from religious persecution in Brigham Young's Mormon West, and boundless timberlands in the Ojibwas' homeland in northern Wisconsin and Minnesota. In the Illinois country, where Long's western explorations began and where he planned to retire, the white population grew to over a million by the mid-1850s. Long marveled over the transformation. "The region so wild, solitary and dreary in 1816," he told an interviewer in 1854, "is now occupied by a numerous and widespread population, and checkered with counties, towns, villages, and cities scattered in every direction over its broad and fertile surface." Chicago had been the site of a minor frontier military post when he had visited the place in 1816; now in 1854 it was a booming western city of 80,000 residents. Practically his whole route through Illinois in 1816, he recalled, had been through "a trackless wilderness, known and frequented almost exclusively by savages." He neglected to add that in the 1820s and '30s the US government forced all those "savages" to leave the state. The small number of Illinois Indians who were still surviving in the mid-1850s lived in exile and degradation in the western territories. Yet so pleased was Long that the Illinois country had become settled by white people, he seems to have been callous to the fate of the Indians.[46]

The old western explorer probably gave no more consideration to the legacy of Indian dispossession when, a few years later, he decided to speculate in Chicago real estate. He bought a five-acre lot in a subdivision at the western edge of the growing city. The land speculation was strictly a money-making proposition, and it succeeded for him splendidly. Long made a killing on a small piece of the tribes' ceded lands. His wife, Martha, who outlived him by several years, eventually sold the property for many times the investment price, clearing nearly $40,000. That sum was equal to about $700,000 in today's dollars, and it lifted Stephen and Martha Long into the top 1 percent of American households by property wealth. Although Long would never have admitted it, in truth the estate he bequeathed to his heirs rested in large part on the nation's gobbling up of the Indian estate.[47]

When one considers Stephen H. Long's accomplished life next to the hard life of John McLoughlin and the tragic fate of John Tanner, Long easily appears to have been the most fortunate, the most personally fulfilled of the three. As each man came from a different background and identified with a different people, Long comes across as the one who got to play with the winning team. The comparison tends to put Long in an unflattering light by today's standards, and that is not quite fair to him. The lessons to be taken from looking at Long in this context are less about him than they are about the place of privilege he occupied. If Long was blind to the huge advantages that race and nationality gave him, he was no more blind than millions of his countrymen.

In one respect Long was the least fortunate of the three men. He lived to see his nation descend into bloody civil war under the curse of slavery.

In 1858, Stephen Long moved his western headquarters to Alton, Illinois, opposite St. Louis on the Mississippi River. At age seventy-three, he wanted to join his four younger brothers who had settled in Alton over the preceding decades, gather his family around him, and ease into a comfortable retirement from the army. Stephen and Martha were accompanied to Alton by their oldest son, William, who was mentally handicapped and had remained in their care since birth, and their second son, Henry Clay Long, who was an engineer like his father. Taking up residence in a stately and commodious house on a quarter section of land, they were soon joined by their daughter Lucy and son-in-law Marcus P. Breckenridge and four Breckenridge grandchildren. The four adults and four grandchildren all lived with Stephen and Martha in the big house.[10]

Moving to Alton brought Stephen Long full circle, back to the confluence of the Mississippi and Missouri rivers, the very place where all of his explorations of the Illinois country, the upper Mississippi, the Arkansas, and the Great Plains had started. Yet the great river rolling past his new home in southern Illinois was not the same river of his younger days. It was not the river he had imagined when he wrote "Voyage in a Six-Oared Skiff." Nor was it the same stream he had referenced in his letters to President Monroe and Secretary of War Calhoun when he proposed an ambitious program of army exploration. The Mississippi River no longer lay at the threshold of the Great West, its western tributaries pointing off propitiously in the direction of unknown lands and national destiny. Now the Mississippi River thrummed with steamboats laden with southern cotton and northern manufactures. Its broad, gray waters separated the free state of Illinois from the slave state of Missouri, forming part of the line between North and South. Its muscular current pulled irresistibly at the riverbanks, hissing of another national fate in the offing.

Years before Stephen and Martha moved to Alton, Stephen's younger brother Enoch took part in that town's first bloodletting of the sectional strife that culminated in the American Civil War. In 1837, Enoch rallied to the defense of Alton's abolitionist newspaper editor Elijah P. Lovejoy when his printing press—his fourth since taking up the antislavery cause—was attacked by a proslavery mob. Lovejoy's few dozen defenders exchanged gunfire with the mob, and Lovejoy was shot and killed in the hail of lead, becoming a martyr to the abolitionist cause. When Stephen and Martha took up residence in Alton more than twenty years later, memories of that night were still intense. Alton remained a hotbed for abolitionist agitation and southern angst. Runaway slaves from neighboring Missouri were spirited through the town on the underground railroad, and slavecatchers from Missouri occasionally raided and clashed with the townspeople. A number of houses in Alton contained hideaways for fugitive blacks transiting through the community.[49]

The year Stephen and Martha moved to Alton was also the year of the Lincoln-Douglas debates. The two statesmen met in Alton for their seventh and final debate. Proslavery Missourians flocked to the event from across the river to support Stephen Douglas, while Free-soil Republicans came down from northern Illinois by steamboat to cheer for Abe Lincoln. It is doubtful that Long was in the audience that day, as he did not complete his move to Alton until the following month; but he would have received a first-person account of the event from Enoch or another brother shortly afterwards. Douglas went first and held forth for an hour, wooing the proslavery members of the crowd with his insistence that the Founding Fathers had never intended that the rights of US citizenship would apply to people of all races. For this, the Missourians gave the senator from Illinois a big hand of applause. Lincoln thundered back that the Founders' ringing phrase "all men are created equal" admitted no other interpretation. Then, elaborating on his declaration in an earlier debate that "a house divided against itself cannot stand," he went on to make one of his strongest denunciations of slavery yet. American democracy would not endure, Lincoln said, without accomplishing slavery's "ultimate extinction." At the end of his ninety-minute speech there were shouts from the crowd, "Hurrah for Abe Lincoln as next president!"[50]

Stephen Long's position on slavery by this time is not known, but he was certainly a staunch unionist and probably a supporter of the insurgent Republican Party. As a new arrival in Illinois, Long would not have been able to cast a ballot, for in those pre–Civil War days the state laws did not provide for soldier absentee voting. During the early months of 1859, as the election results slowly came in, Long saw the Republican Party win control of the US House of Representatives, while Lincoln lost in his contest with Douglas. In that era before popular election of US senators, voters of each state elected their US representatives, while state legislators elected the US senators. Illinois voters elected four Republicans and five Democrats to the 36th Congress, while the Democratically controlled state legislature reelected Douglas to the US Senate by a vote of 54 to 46.

It is a reasonable guess that Stephen Long cast a ballot for Lincoln two years later in the presidential election of 1860. As an ardent supporter of the late Henry Clay, Long would have admired Lincoln's high praise of Clay and likely would have followed Lincoln's example in transferring his allegiance from the defunct Whig Party to the young Republican Party. During the winter of 1860–61, when southerners were in an uproar over the election, Long took the precaution of withdrawing federal funds from the US Assay

Office in St. Louis and holding them in his home in Alton to prevent their falling into the hands of secessionist Missourians.

Long was overseeing snag removal on the Lower Mississippi around New Orleans when the southern states seceded from the Union one by one in the early months of 1861. After Louisiana seceded (in January), Long ordered his men to remain in the state long enough to complete a series of soundings near the mouth of the Mississippi before they pulled out. He knew the information that they obtained would be important for producing navigational charts for US naval commanders in the coming conflict.

In June 1861, he wrote to his superiors that in spite of his "advanced age and infirmities" he wanted to continue in public service. He applied for a promotion to colonel and was granted the higher rank, along with elevation to chief of the Corps of Topographical Engineers. Long took up his new duties in the nation's capital in December 1861.

In war, the Topographical Engineers reverted to their original role of producing military maps for the army. As the topogs were no longer needed for nation-building surveys and civil engineering works, Congress abolished the Corps of Topographical Engineers in 1863 and Long at last retired. The old soldier was back home in Alton when Union forces took Vicksburg, the last Confederate stronghold on the Mississippi River. He died on September 4, 1864, at the age of seventy-nine, while the war still raged.[51]

John Tanner as a Source

When John Tanner told his story to Dr. Edwin James, he did more than record his remarkable experiences for the reading public. He also made himself a valuable source for future ethnographers and historians. His autobiography provides a rare firsthand account of Indian life by a man who was, for a time, nearly Indian himself in every way except race. No less an authority than Native American writer Louise Erdrich has testified to the authenticity of Tanner as an Indian voice: "John Tanner was culturally an Ojibwa, and as such he is claimed by many to this day, for he lived as an Ojibwa, married an Ojibwa woman, cared devotedly for his mixed-blood children, and was never able to accommodate himself to a non-Indian life."[1] Since no actual Indians who lived in the same time and place as Tanner ever recorded their experiences in writing, his *Narrative* stands as a unique description of their world. It is remarkable in the richness of its details about western Ottawa and Ojibwa culture on everything from the waxing political power of medicine men in the time of the Shawnee Prophet to the manufacture and use of skin boats early in the spring, when it was still too cold to make birchbark canoes. Tanner belonged to that generation of Ottawas and Ojibwas who moved west with the fur trade and adapted their ancient woodland culture to the northern prairie environment. As part of that process, Tanner acquired horses and learned how to hunt bison both with gun and bow and arrow. Sometimes in preparing his *Narrative*, Tanner spoke directly as a historian of his people's cultural adaptations, as when he stated that his friend, Sha-gwaw-koo-sink, an Ottawa, introduced the cultivation of corn among the western Ojibwas.

Since Tanner's *Narrative* is unique and valuable, it bears asking whether the book is truly trustworthy. How could this man in his forty-eighth year of life be able to recall events in such sharp detail going back to when he was just nine years old? How was he able to tell his story so chronologically without the aid of written records to jog his memory? How could his halting English, which he had had to relearn when he was in his late thirties, have been transcribed into such eloquent prose?

Part of the answer lies in the fact that Tanner was absorbed into an oral culture that used storytelling as a means for bringing people together, articulating their shared cultural identity, and recording their past. Preliterate peoples developed the arts of memory to a degree our modern minds find difficult to grasp. Tanner recounted events with almost fantastic specificity, giving the number of beaver taken in a particular winter or the type of food eaten in a particular meal. "When we first arrived," Tanner recounts in a characteristic passage, "the wife of Po-ko-taw-ga-maw happened to be cooking a moose's tongue for her husband, who had not yet returned from hunting." Lest we think such an ability to recall details is not humanly possible, compare Tanner's memory of an event in August 1805 with Alexander Henry's journal entry of the same date. Tanner: "Mr. H., the trader at Pembinah gave the Ojibbeways a ten gallon keg of powder, and 100 pounds of balls, to pursue after the party that had killed the chief." Henry: "I gave them a 9 Gallon Keg of Gun Powder and 100 lbs of Balls to encourage them to revenge the death of my *Beau-Pere* and family."

Elliott Coues was the first historian to recognize the value of Tanner's *Narrative* as a historical source. Coues, an army surgeon and naturalist as well as a historian, is best known for editing the Lewis and Clark journals in the 1890s. Coues also edited the journals of North West Company fur trader Alexander Henry, who lived in the Red River country during the same period as Tanner. He identified numerous instances in which Henry's journal and Tanner's *Narrative* corroborate and complement one another. Of course, Tanner's editor did not have access to Henry's journal, nor did Henry have access to Tanner's account, so their corroboration is totally authentic.[2]

Besides Henry's journal, other corroborating sources are found in the records of the Hudson's Bay Company, the voluminous witness testimony that flowed from the Red River strife in the years 1814 to 1818, and Ojibwa oral traditions recorded by the tribal historian William W. Warren in his *History of the Ojibway Nation*, written in 1852. And for the events at Rainy Lake House in 1823, Tanner is corroborated not only by the journals of the Long expedition but also by those of the British-US Boundary Commission that passed through the area soon after his attempted murder.

Tanner had an outstanding ability to recall the names of individuals (especially considering the fact that many of the names were not in his own tongue). His *Narrative* is almost unfailing in its accurate associations of people, places, and years. For example, his *Narrative* correctly places "Shabboyer" (Charles Jean Baptiste Chaboillez) at Grand Portage in 1798, "M'Glees" (Hugh McGillis) at Fort Alexandria in 1802, "M'Kee (John McKay) at Brandon House in 1805, and "Mr. Tace" (John Warren Dease) at Rainy Lake in 1814. Many similar instances could be cited. Tanner's *Narrative* simply does not read like a fake.

Additional proof of Tanner's veracity comes from internal evidence in his *Narrative*. There are no inconsistencies or patent untruths marring Tanner's account. Tanner's editor, Dr. Edwin James, commented that Tanner's tribulations with his wives and in-laws were the only things he talked about "with some want of distinctness."[3] Yet even in this sensitive area, Tanner did not dissemble the truth so much as brush over the details. A jumble of passing mentions of his first and second wives and fleeting references to the number of children in his care and their approximate ages at given points in time can be marshaled to reconstruct an entirely plausible and consistent picture of his Indian families. Altogether, Tanner had twelve children, two of whom died within a few years of birth and three more of whom were born after 1823, the year he concluded his story.[4]

Tanner's story would be much harder to verify if he had not told it in straightforward chronological order. From the time of his capture at the age of nine until his first return to the United States at the age of thirty-seven, Tanner did not supply his editor with a single date. Yet his entire story is structured according to its own internal timetable spanning twenty-eight winters. Tanner accounted for every single year in his own way, laying down such definite markers for the passage of time as the changing seasons, the Indians' seasonal rounds (such as making sugar in the spring or harvesting wild rice in the fall) and the number of days or months spent at certain camps or hunting grounds. Without necessarily intending to do so, Tanner included a few datable events in his story. For example, he was at Pembina when Alexander Henry supplied the Ojibwas with ammunition to retaliate against the Sioux after the attack outside Henry's fort. Henry's journal confirms that this event occurred in August 1805.[5] A sprinkling of such datable events throughout Tanner's *Narrative* gives added assurance that Tanner's memory was accurate.

Tanner did include two references to contemporary events in the United States: the Lewis and Clark expedition and the War of 1812. These references appear to be a deliberate effort to orient American readers to his Indian-oriented chronology. Ironically, in each instance he got the date a bit wrong. In the first instance, Tanner recalled being informed when he visited the Hudson's Bay Company's Brandon House that Lewis and Clark were encamped at the Mandan village. For any historian combing the *Narrative* for datable events, this one jumps out—it seems that Tanner's internal chronology has come to the year 1804. In fact, Tanner was still speaking of 1803; he inserted the detail one year too soon—a minor lapse of memory considering that he visited this same trader at Brandon House two years in a row in the fall of 1803 and the fall of 1804.

It may be as a result of this error that Noel Loomis, in writing the introduction to the 1956 reprint edition of Tanner's *Narrative,* counted back the years in Tanner's internal chronology and gave the date of Tanner's capture as 1789 rather than 1790. Loomis's wrong year for Tanner's capture was repeated on the back cover of the 1994 Penguin Books edition, and it has been carried into numerous other descriptions of Tanner's experience by other modern writers. Yet there can be no mistaking the actual year in which Tanner's captivity began. Just two weeks after the Indian raid, one John Garnett swore under oath to Robert Johnson, Woodford County magistrate, that the nine-year-old boy was taken from a field on the Tanner farm and carried off across the Ohio River on or about the last day of April 1790. Garnett's deposition is printed in *American State Papers,* providing positive proof that Tanner was taken captive in 1790, not 1789.[6]

Tanner's second historical error is more perplexing. Twice while relating his story, he referred to conversations he had had with traders about the war between the United States and Britain. In the first instance he recalled being informed specifically of the capture of Mackinac. These recollections obviously allude to the War of 1812. But when calendar years are put to Tanner's internal chronology of passing winters, it appears that the first time traders informed him about the war was in the spring of 1808 and the second time was in the spring of 1809. The historian must wonder, what is going on here? Did Tanner misremember when the conversations with the traders took place? Or did he depart from a strictly chronological telling at this point in his story? Certainly his *Narrative* becomes more complex when it covers this phase of his life, reflecting the greater complexity of his adult relationships as he juggled the roles of husband, father, son, warrior, and sometimes principal hunter for his group. Yet the pulse of the passing winters never falters, and if one is inclined to count them, the years do add up—1808, 1809, 1810, 1811—until Tanner's story begins to entwine with the emergence of the Red River colony with its many datable events, at which point the chronological structure and actual dates of Tanner's *Narrative* once more become indisputably clear.

It turns out there is a simpler explanation for the discrepancy between Tanner's chronology and his references to the War of 1812. When Tanner recalled traders telling him about the war between the United States and Britain, the point he was making in his story was that he was then considering going to the United States in search of his American kin but was dissuaded from doing so by the knowledge that there was a war on. In the words of his *Narrative,* "I now heard of the war between the United States and Great Britain, and of the capture of Mackinac, and this intelligence deterred me from any attempt to pass through the frontier of the United States territory which were [*sic*] then the scenes of warlike operations."[7] Probably what occurred on these two occasions was that the traders exaggerated rumors of impending war in order to keep Tanner, whom they considered to be a productive hunter, from leaving their territory. British traders were known to employ that tactic. As with Tanner's reference to Lewis and Clark, the purported reference to the War of 1812 is misleading. When Tanner related his story in 1828, he was no doubt aware that the United States and Britain had fought a war in the general time period that he lived among the western Ojibwa, but he may have never realized (or particularly cared) that the war actually broke out some years after the traders began talking it up.

The question remains: to what degree do the words in the *Narrative* belong to Tanner and to what degree do they come from his editor, Dr. Edwin James? As with all such collaborative efforts between people from oral and written traditions, the question cannot be answered with precision. The original manuscript would likely provide vital clues, but it has been lost. James professed to have taken down Tanner's story with as light an editorial touch as he could muster. "It ought to be distinctly understood," James wrote in his introduction to the 1830 book, "that his whole story was given as it stands, without hints, suggestions, leading questions, or advice of any kind, other than 'to conceal nothing.'"[8] But even if this statement is accepted at face value, James still had to turn Tanner's spoken narrative into words for print.

Whatever credence we give the *Narrative* must in part depend on the reputation of the editor. When the two men began their collaboration, Edwin James already possessed a solid reputation as a humanist, scientist, and scholar. Born in 1797, he was raised on a farm outside Middlebury, Vermont, attended Middlebury College, and afterwards studied medicine in Albany, New York. He joined Major Long's scientific expedition to the Rocky Mountains in 1820 as botanist and geologist, which gave him his first opportunity to observe Indian cultures. With Long's steadfast support, James devoted much of the following year to writing the official history of the expedition, *Account of an Expedition from Pittsburgh to the Rocky Mountains.* The volume was widely read and roundly praised in both the United States and Britain. In 1823, James was supposed to join Major Long's northern expedition, but, through a miscommunication, the young doctor did not make his way to the right rendezvous point on the Ohio River and had to be left behind, which bitterly disappointed him. Had he accompanied Long on his second scientific expedition, he would have met Tanner convalescing

at Rainy Lake House. In 1825, James became an army surgeon and was assigned to Fort Crawford at Prairie du Chien, Wisconsin, where he began his
study of the Ojibwa language.[9] He also started a Sunday school for Ojibwa
children, his first effort to bring Christianity to the Indians. Transferring to
Fort Mackinac in May 1827, he soon became acquainted with Tanner, and
the two men talked over the possibility of putting Tanner's story into writing. Before embarking on the project, James prudently consulted Peter S.
Duponceau, a well-known linguist and president of the American Philosophical Society. It is likely that James wanted assurances that the book
would not be received as a fake.[10]

Tanner and James worked on the book that summer. It is not known
whether Tanner narrated in Ojibwa or English; it may have been some of
each. James described Tanner's command of the English language in 1827 as
"imperfect." Yet it may have been superior to James's knowledge of Ojibwa.
(Four years later, Tanner would assist James in translating the New Testament into Ojibwa, and the translation would eventually be ridiculed as
being quite wide of the mark.) James must have interpreted Tanner's dicta-
tion extensively, for the *Narrative* contains a great deal of erudite vocabulary
and formal syntax that could not possibly be Tanner's own words in English.
Yet the editor's claim that he strove to present Tanner's narrative "as nearly
as possible, in his own words, and with his own manner" still rings true.[11] As
bibliographer John T. Fierst has pointed out, Tanner's attention to omens,
animal spirits, and the power of dreams in the *Narrative,* and his frequent
use of foreshadowing in telling his story, shows that he had absorbed much
of the Ottawa and Ojibwa consciousness, and James, as Tanner's editor, "did
not, in any large degree, have access to this reality, this web of meaning
behind Tanner's words." So, on the whole, James can be given high marks
for his editorial skill in bringing forth Tanner's distinctive voice and point
of view.[12]

The historical authenticity of the *Narrative* ultimately depended on the
integrity of the publisher, too. It is significant that Tanner, not James, took
the initiative to get the manuscript in print. Unfortunately, little is known
about Tanner's relationship with the publisher. The story must be pieced
together from a few clues, beginning with a statement in the penultimate
paragraph of the *Narrative* that Tanner left Mackinac in the summer of
1828 "and proceeded to New-York for the purpose of making arrangements
for the publication of my narrative."[13] En route to New York, he probably
paid a visit to Messrs. Carey and Lea in Philadelphia, proprietors of what
was then the largest publishing house in the United States. It would seem
that Tanner tried to interest the Philadelphia publishers in the manuscript

first, because two years later Carey and Lea printed a lengthy article about Tanner's *Narrative* in their literary magazine, *American Quarterly Review*, in which they stated that they knew Tanner personally, had had the opportunity to judge for themselves that he was an honest man, and had anxiously awaited the publication of the book since their meeting. The reason why Carey and Lea did not choose to accept Tanner's manuscript is not known, but it may have been that they were put off by a recent controversy over another book, *Manners and Customs of Several Indian Tribes Located West of the Mississippi . . . to Which is Prefixed the History of the Author's Life during a Residence of Several Years among Them*, by John Dunn Hunter. Like Tanner, Hunter was captured by Indians as a small child and lived among them until he was an adult. Unlike Tanner, Hunter sought a formal education after returning to white society and then wrote his book himself. Embraced as a wonder by the American literati for the first few years after his book appeared, Hunter was subsequently denounced as an imposter. (Even after his reputation unraveled in the United States, Hunter found continued support in England, and the modern view of him is that he was probably legitimate.) The controversy surrounding the strange case of John Dunn Hunter gave the nascent American publishing industry a black eye. When Carey and Lea later praised Tanner's book in the *American Quarterly Review* they took great pains to insist that it was not another fake like Hunter's book.[14]

If Tanner did in fact meet with rejection from Carey and Lea, he had better luck with G. & C. & H. Carvill, located at 108 Broadway in New York. This publishing house was among the top half-dozen houses in New York's newly ascendant book trade. It produced scientific and religious tracts, collections of poetry, government documents, and artists' engravings, among its varied works.[15] It is not known what terms Tanner received for the publication of his book. It appears that the publisher commissioned a painting to be made of Tanner by the well-known portrait painter, Henry Inman, with the intention of having an engraving made from it to be used in the book. Inman's partner, Cephas G. Childs, produced a mezzotint from the portrait, which appeared as a frontispiece in the 1830 edition.[16]

The artists' portraiture of John Tanner was the last piece in the collaboration that went into making Tanner's autobiography both a valuable historical document and a literary achievement. The portrait is the only likeness of Tanner known. In Inman's color painting, Tanner's reddish hair and blue eyes stand out. He is dressed in a dark green greatcoat with gold buttons, a white stock and high white collar, a white tie, and tie pin. He wears the dignified attire of a bourgeois gentleman.[17] The portrait presented Tanner to his contemporary readers as a full-fledged member of American society, redeemed from savagery, restored to civilization. It was clearly the image that the publisher wanted in order to make the author a credible source and the book a standout in the popular genre of the captivity narrative.

But there is something timeless about this portrait, too. One can only imagine the thoughts running through Tanner's mind when he sat for his portrait in the artist's studio, completing what was to be the last step in bringing his story to the American public. And yet, one might say that his inner thoughts are all there in the captured image. Above the greatcoat and high collar, Tanner's deeply lined face and tousled hair give a sense of the hard, fractured life that lay behind him—from his youthful days with the Ottawa, through his coming into manhood on the northern prairies, to his subsequent struggle to reclaim a place in the white man's world. His Indian braids are long gone, but his memories are as hard as steel. The set of his jaw and the expression around his mouth hold a measure of contempt. The furrows in his brow carry a trace of malice. His eyes accuse.

ACKNOWLEDGMENTS

This book is dedicated to the memory of my old friend Bob Bassett, whose commitment to the writer's art was a great inspiration to me, and who played an important role in the making of this book.

My friendship with Bob began thirty-six years ago when I was in my junior year at the University of Montana and I moved into a basement apartment with a common kitchen that I shared with Bob and two other men. Bob was then a forty-year-old bachelor, already turning a bit gray in the whiskers. I remember he wore workingman's shirts and pants and a pair of scuffed-up oxfords. He was writing a novel; I think it was his third or fourth by that point in his life. He did not have much else in his basement room besides books, a desk, a bed, a dresser, and probably a typewriter. In spite of our big age difference, we soon formed a strong friendship around good conversation and chess.

Bob was a true writer, a rare individual who wrote and wrote for the sheer satisfaction of creating fictional characters, crafting good prose, and finding new things to say about the world. He wanted to get published, but when it didn't happen he kept right on going. Like all true writers, he was a voracious reader. We shared an interest in Russian history. About a decade after we met, he completed a degree in Russian and moved to Moscow with his young bride, another Russian language student. They went shortly after the collapse of the Soviet Union and were there through the rise of Putin. As time passed, we lost touch. Bob returned to Montana when he reached retirement age, and our friendship resumed. I read his last big opus, *The Song of Isaac*, a novel based loosely on the story of Isaac and Abraham. He kept on writing to the very end of his life.

Bob was not only a great friend and inspiration; he also did me an enormous good turn when he agreed to read and edit my first draft of this book. I was astonished by how well he got to know Tanner, Long, and McLoughlin from his careful reading of the manuscript. I benefited hugely from his editing. He had a fine, intuitive grasp of what I was trying to do, and he helped me move the writing in the direction that I wanted it to go.

There are many others in addition to Bob Bassett who I want to thank for their generous help and support. My first debt is to the National Park Service, and five individuals in the agency in particular. Way back in 1999, I was given the task to research and write a short study of fur traders and the environment in the area now encompassed by Voyageurs National Park, Minnesota. Historians Mary Graves and Don Stevens oriented me to historical materials held at the park, while ethnographer Tom Thiessen and archeologist Jeff Richner made their research files available to me at the Midwest Archeological Center in Lincoln, Nebraska. Thiessen's painstaking transcriptions of dozens of handwritten Hudson's Bay Company post journals were a gold mine of source material. The following year I took part in a small fur trade history conference held at Grand Portage National Monument, Minnesota, put on by Don Stevens and the monument superintendent, Tim Cochrane. The Voyageur project and the Grand Portage conference gave me the inspiration for *Rainy Lake House,* and I have benefited from subsequent professional contact with Stevens, Graves, Thiessen, Richner, and Cochrane over the years since then.

Four academic historians who took part in the conference at Grand Portage offered guidance and a cordial welcome as I waded deeper into fur trade history. They were: Ted Karamanski, Laura Peers, Jennifer S. H. Brown, and Bruce M. White.

More than a decade on from the Voyageurs project, in 2011, the National Endowment for the Humanities provided me with the critical financial support I needed to write the book. I am indebted to Richard White and Dan Flores for writing such effective letters in support of my grant application, as well as three anonymous reviewers who evaluated my proposal, and the NEH staff for favoring me with a grant. This book would not have been possible without the NEH.

Ann Emmons and Christopher Preston read portions of the first draft and gave valuable feedback. My son Ben read the whole first draft, and parts of the second draft as well, and gave me some very perceptive and useful pointers.

Bobby Ferenstein, who I met through her daughter Jennifer, did me the kindness to edit the manuscript with her professional hand before the manuscript had yet found a publisher.

Patrick Thomas, another pro who I met through our mutual friend Caleb Kasper, generously gave the manuscript a critical read and offered valuable advice.

My mother and late father, Nancy and Bill Catton, read the whole manuscript in 2013. In characteristic form, they did not shy from applying their pen and giving their son critical comments. Their strong intellectual and emotional support has been a boon to me all of my life. Mom, as a bibliophile and volunteer at the public library, scouted for used books about the fur trade and steadily added them to my bookshelves over the past decade and a half.

Sally Thompson, whose fascination with Jesuit missionaries in the Pacific Northwest parallels my interest, read the near final draft and helped me improve it. Fur trade scholar and friend Bill Swagerty also gave me helpful support.

My literary agent Roger Williams saw the potential for this book where untold numbers of others declined to take a chance with it. He has been a fabulous advocate and guide. Elizabeth Demers, senior acquisitions editor at Johns Hopkins University Press, got behind it and brought it to fruition. Her perceptive reading of it provided me the pointers I needed to tighten parts of it and elaborate a few others, and she gave me the time to accomplish it.

My wonderful sons, Wally, Ben, and Eli, have been an inspiration to me throughout the project. They were my companions in this study for innumerable conversations and outings over the years.

Diane Krahe, my wife and partner in history, has been more indulgent and nurturing of my project than anyone. She was instrumental at an early stage, helping me frame and write my proposal to the NEH. She listened and responded as I read chapters out loud to her. She gave the manuscript the last thorough editing and suggested the addition of one crucial paragraph near the end. To her I owe my biggest thanks.

NOTES

CHAPTER 1. THE EXPLORER

1. John Livingston, *Portraits of Eminent Americans Now Living: With Biographical and Historical Memoirs of Their Lives and Actions* 4 (New York: 107 Broadway, 1854), 488–89.

2. Stephen H. Long, *The Northern Expeditions of Stephen H. Long: The Journals of 1817 and 1823 and Related Documents,* Lucile M. Kane, June D. Holmquist, and Carolyn Gilman, eds. (St. Paul: Minnesota Historical Society, 1978), 213; William H. Keating, *Narrative of an Expedition to the Source of the St. Peter's, Lake Winnepeek, Lake of the Woods, etc.,* 2 vols. (London: Geo. B. Whittaker, Ave-Marie Lane, 1825), 2:113.

3. Keating, *Narrative,* 2:114, 124; John Tanner, *A Narrative of the Captivity and Adventures of John Tanner (U.S. Interpreter at the Saut De Ste. Marie) during Thirty Years Residence among the Indians in the Interior of North America,* Edwin James, ed. (1830; reprint, Minneapolis: Ross & Haines, Inc., 1956), 276, 279.

4. John J. Bigsby, *The Shoe and the Canoe, or Pictures of Travel in the Canadas* (1850; reprint, New York, Paladin Press, 1969), 2: 272; George Simpson, "Character Book," in *Hudson's Bay Miscellany 1670–1870,* Glyndwr Williams, ed. (Winnipeg: Hudson's Bay Records Society, 1975), 190; Joseph Delafield, *The Unfortified Boundary: A Diary of the first survey of the Canadian Boundary Line from St. Regis to the Lake of the Woods,* Robert McElroy and Thomas Riggs, eds. (New York: privately printed, 1943), 410.

5. Delafield, *The Unfortified Boundary,* 423; Long, *The Northern Expeditions of Stephen H. Long,* 214–16; John Phillip Reid, *Patterns of Vengeance: Crosscultural Homicide in the North American Fur Trade* (San Francisco: Ninth Judicial Circuit Historical Society, 1999), 45, 82–83.

6. Say quoted in Keating, *Narrative,* 2:125. Long referred to Say's piece in his own journal entry of September 2.

7. Long, *The Northern Expeditions of Stephen H. Long,* 214.

8. James Axtell, *The Invasion Within: The Contest of Cultures in Colonial North America* (New York: Oxford University Press, 1985), 303–4.

9. Keating, *Narrative,* 2:114; Long, *The Northern Expeditions of Stephen H. Long,* 214; "A Captive Found," *The Weekly Recorder* 5, no. 5 (September 11, 1818), 39; "Indian Captive Reclaimed," *The Weekly Recorder* 5, no. 27 (February 12, 1819), 215.

10. Phillips D. Carleton, "The Indian Captivity," *American Literature* 15 (May 1943), 169; Roy Harvey Pearce, "The Significance of the Captivity Narrative," *American Literature* 19 (March 1947), 13; Annette Kolodny, "Review Essay of *Narratives of North American Indian Captivities* and *The North American Indian Captivity,* in *Early American Literature* 14 (1979), 232.

11. Kathryn Zabelle Derounian-Stodola and James Arthur Levernier, *The Indian Captivity Narrative, 1550–1900* (New York: Twayne Publishers, 1993), 2. The authors give a "conservative" estimate of "tens of thousands," but this includes the whole nineteenth century.

12. C. C. Lord, *Life and Times in Hopkinton, N. H.* (Concord, NH: Republican Press Association, 1890), 30–32.

13. Ibid., 30–32, 414, 428.

14. Ibid., 396–97.

15. Richard G. Wood, *Stephen Harriman Long, 1784–1864: Army Engineer, Explorer, Inventor* (Glendale, CA: Arthur H. Clark Company, 1966), 22–24.

16. Reginald Horsman, *The Frontier in the Formative Years, 1783–1815* (New York: Holt, Rinehart and Winston, Inc., 1970), 21–24; Wood, *Stephen Harriman Long*, 28–29.

17. Lord, *Life and Times in Hopkinton, N. H.*, 92, 96.

18. Ibid., 80–90.

19. John R. Bell, *The Journal of Captain John R. Bell, Official Journalist for the Stephen H. Long Expedition to the Rocky Mountains, 1820*, Harlin M. Fuller and LeRoy R. Hafen, eds. (Glendale, CA: Arthur H. Clark Company, 1957), 134.

20. Wood, *Stephen Harriman Long*, 28.

21. Livingston, *Portraits of Eminent Americans*, 477; Wood, *Stephen Harriman Long*, 30–34; Long, *The Northern Expeditions of Stephen H. Long*, 210.

22. Ne-Do-Ba, "The Abenaki of Moor's Charity School & Dartmouth College, Chronological List of Students—With Notes" (August 2000), at www.nedoba.org/ne-do-ba/odn_ed02.html <June 4, 2010>.

23. Derounian-Stodola and Levernier, *The Indian Captivity Narrative, 1550–1900*, 160–61.

24. Wisconsin Historical Society, "Mohawk Indian or French Prince?" (March 2009), at www.wisconsinhistory.org/odd/archives/001202.asp <June 4, 2010>; Colin W. Calloway, *Indian History of an American Institution: Native Americans and Dartmouth* (Lebanon, NH: University Press of New England, 2010), 80.

25. Roger L. Nichols and Patrick L. Halley, *Stephen Long and American Frontier Exploration* (Newark: University of Delaware Press, 1980), 21–26.

Chapter 2. The Hunter

1. Richard White, *The Middle Ground: Indians, Empires, and Republics in the Great Lakes Region, 1650–1815* (New York: Cambridge University Press, 1991), 413–53; Colin G. Calloway, *The Shawnees and the War for America* (New York: Penguin Group, 2007), 89; Colin G. Calloway, *The Victory with No Name: The Native American Defeat of the First American Army* (New York: Oxford University Press, 2015), 26–33.

2. John A. M'Clung, *Sketches of Western Adventure* (1832; reprint, New York: Arno Press & The New York Times, 1969), 222.

3. Tanner, *Narrative*, 2.

4. Ibid., 2–3.

5. Ibid., 3; "The Northwestern Indians, Communicated to Congress on the 9th of December, 1790," *American State Papers: Indian Affairs*, 1:89.

6. James M. Volo and Dorothy Denneen, *Family Life in Native America* (Westport, CT: Greenwood Press, 2007), 216–17; Nancy Shoemaker, *A Strange Likeness: Becoming Red and White in Eighteenth-Century North America* (New York: Oxford University Press, 2004), 134–37; Christina Snyder, *Slavery in Indian Country: The Changing Face of Captivity in Early America* (Cambridge, MA: Harvard University Press, 2010), 109–12.

7. Tanner, *Narrative*, 3–4. Tanner states that his knowledge of this event was abetted by information he later extracted from Kish-kau-ko when he found him in Detroit in 1818, as well as his brother's recollections. Some of the details are also found in two articles in *The Weekly Recorder* 5, no. 5 (September 11, 1818) and 5, no. 27 (February 12, 1819), which are based on interviews with Tanner when he was in Detroit. It is worth noting that Tanner retained a strong memory of the event through his many years among the Indians, as evidenced by details in the first article—details that could not have come either from Kish-kau-ko or from his brother Edward, with whom he had not yet reconnected in the month this article was written.

8. Tanner, *Narrative*, 5.

9. Ibid., 5–6.

10. Ibid., 7–8; Helen Hornbeck Tanner, "The Glaize in 1792: A Composite Indian Community," in *Rethinking the Fur Trade: Cultures of Exchange in an Atlantic World*, Susan Sleeper-Smith, ed. (Lincoln: University of Nebraska Press, 2009), 362–63.

11. Tanner, *Narrative*, 8.

12. Ibid., 8–9.

13. Ibid., 9; Volo and Denneen, *Family Life in Native America*, 216.

14. Tanner, *Narrative*, 10–12; Snyder, *Slavery in Indian Country*, 102–5.

15. Tanner, *Narrative*, 13–14.

16. Ibid., 15.

17. Ibid., 15–16; J. Maurice Hodgson, "Captors and Their Captives," *The Beaver* 301 (Spring 1970), 29–30.

18. Tanner, *Narrative*, 16, 18–20, 22, 34, 36.

19. Priscilla K. Buffalohead, "Farmers Warriors Traders: A Fresh Look at Ojibway Women," *Minnesota History* 48, no. 6 (Summer 1983), 238, 244.

20. Tanner, *Narrative*, 16; Laura Peers, *The Ojibwa of Western Canada, 1780 to 1870* (Winnipeg: University of Manitoba Press, 1994), 22.

21. Tanner, *Narrative*, 19; Carolyn Podruchny, *Making the Voyageur World: Travelers and Traders in the North American Fur Trade* (Lincoln: University of Nebraska Press, 2006), 258.

22. Tanner, *Narrative*, 17–18.

Chapter 3. The Trader

1. T. C. Elliott, "John McLoughlin, M.D.," *Oregon Historical Quarterly* 36, no. 2 (June 1935), 182–86; Jean Morrison, *Superior Rendezvous-Places: Fort William in the Canadian Fur Trade* (Toronto: Natural Heritage Books, 2001), 53; Tanner, *Narrative*, 204–5.

2. Jane Lewis Chapin, ed., "Letters of John McLoughlin, 1805–26," *Oregon Historical Quarterly* 36, no. 4 (December 1935), 320–37; Burt Brown Barker, *The McLoughlin*

Empire and its Rulers: Doctor John McLoughlin, Doctor David McLoughlin, Marie Louise (Sister St. Henry) (Glendale, CA: Arthur H. Clark Company, 1959), 166.

3. Dorothy Nafus Morrison, *Outpost: John McLoughlin and the Far Northwest* (Portland: Oregon Historical Society Press, 1999), 8–14.

4. George A. Wrong, *A Canadian Manor and Its Seigneurs: The Story of a Hundred Years, 1761–1861* (Toronto: Bryant Press Limited, 1908), 132; Morrison, *Outpost*, 3–12.

5. Barker, *The McLoughlin Empire and its Rulers*, 61; W. Stewart Wallace, ed., *Documents Relating to the North-West Co.* (Toronto: Champlain Society, 1934), 19; W. Stewart Wallace, "Notes on the Family of Malcolm Fraser," *Bulletin des recherches historique* 39 (May 1933): 269.

6. Morrison, *Outpost*, 15. Additional details on Simon Fraser were gleaned from the following online sources: Philippe Dubé, *Charlevoix: Two Centuries at Murray Bay* (Montreal: McGill-Queens University Press, 1990), 27; "L'Histoire Complète de la Seigneurie des Mille-Îles en 10 Points," at www.shgim.ca/html/histshmi9.html <January 20, 2011>; Alexander Hislop, ed., *The Book of Scottish Anecdote: Humorous, Social, Legendary, and Historical* (Edinburgh: Edinburgh Publishing Co., 1874), 619. McLoughlin's uncle Simon should not be confused with another Simon Fraser who was a wintering partner in the North West Company and who gave his name to the Fraser River in British Columbia. This uncle never belonged to the North West Company.

7. Morrison, *Outpost*, 16.

8. Dorothy Morrison and Jean Morrison, "John McLoughlin, Reluctant Fur Trader," *Oregon Historical Quarterly* 81 (Winter 1980), 377–86.

9. Ibid. The petition for medical license and endorsements are reproduced in Elliott, "John McLoughlin, M.D.," 182–83. The reference to the West Indies is found in Chapin, ed., "Letters of John McLoughlin, 1805–26," 323.

10. The contract with the North West Company is reproduced in Morrison and Morrison, "John McLoughlin, Reluctant Fur Trader," 387–89.

11. Ibid.

12. Chapin, ed., "Letters of John McLoughlin, 1805–26," 323, 327.

13. Ibid., 327.

14. Jane Lewis Chapin, ed., "Letters of Dr. John McLoughlin," *Oregon Historical Quarterly* 37, no. 4 (December 1936), 294–95. Emphasis in the original.

15. McLoughlin's relations with his employers are well analyzed by W. Kaye Lamb in the introduction to his edited volume, *McLoughlin's Fort Vancouver Letters, First Series, 1825–1838* (Toronto: Hudson's Bay Record Society, 1941), xxxi–xxxvi.

CHAPTER 4. "THE ENGLISH MAKE THEM MORE PRESENTS"

1. William Crawford to S. H. Long, June 18, 1816, and July 2, 1816, National Archives (hereafter cited as NA), Record Group 107—Records of the Office of Secretary of War (hereafter cited as RG 107), Letters Sent, M6, Roll 9.

2. Livingston, *Portraits of Eminent Americans*, 478–79.

3. Stephen H. Long to John Harris, June 10, 1811, Harris Papers, Dartmouth College Archives. See also Simon Baatz, "Philadelphia Patronage: Institutional Structure

of Natural History in the New Republic, 1800–1833," *Journal of the Early Republic* 8 (Summer 1988), 111–38.

4. S. H. Long to Isaac Roberdeau, August 27, 1822, NA, Record Group 77—Records of the U.S. Corps of Engineers (hereafter cited as RG 77), Entry 306, Box 1.

5. General Joseph Swift quoted in Wood, *Stephen Harriman Long*, 38.

6. *The Port-Folio* 2, no. 6 (December 1822), 496.

7. Livingston, *Portraits of Eminent Americans*, 477; *National Register* 3, no. 13 (March 29, 1817), 196.

8. *National Register* 3, no. 13 (March 29, 1817), 197–98.

9. Ibid.

10. Leo E. Oliva, "The Army and the Fur Trade," *Journal of the West* 26, no. 4 (October 1987), 21–22; Edgar B. Wesley, "Some Official Aspects of the Fur Trade in the Northwest, 1815–1825," *North Dakota Historical Quarterly* 6 (April 1932), 201–9; R. S. Cotterill, "Federal Indian Management in the South, 1789–1825," *Mississippi Valley Historical Review* 20 (December 1933), 337–40.

11. Chase C. Mooney, *William H. Crawford, 1772–1834* (Lexington: University Press of Kentucky, 1974), 85–89.

12. William Crawford to the Senate, March 13, 1816, *American State Papers: Indian Affairs*, 2:27.

13. Ibid.; Cotterill, "Federal Indian Management in the South, 1789–1825," 333–46; Herman J. Viola, *Thomas L. McKenney: Architect of America's Early Indian Policy, 1816–1830* (Chicago: The Swallow Press, Inc., 1974), 6–9; Edgar B. Wesley, "The Government Factory System Among the Indians, 1795–1822," *Journal of Economic and Business History* 4 (1931–32), 487–511; Michael Witgen, *An Infinity of Nations: How the Native New World Shaped Early North America* (Philadelphia: University of Pennsylvania Press, 2012), 332–37.

14. William Crawford to the Senate, March 13, 1816, *American State Papers: Indian Affairs*, 2:28; Mooney, *William H. Crawford*, 87.

15. William Crawford to the Senate, March 13, 1816, *American State Papers: Indian Affairs*, 2:65–66; Mooney, *William H. Crawford*, 88.

16. William Crawford to the Senate, March 13, 1816, *American State Papers: Indian Affairs*, 2:28.

17. Mooney, *William H. Crawford*, 13–14, 89, 189.

18. *National Register* 3, no. 13 (March 29, 1817), 193.

CHAPTER 5. ENCOUNTERS WITH THE SIOUX

1. Nichols and Halley, *Stephen Long*, 43.

2. Stephen H. Long, "Voyage in a Six-Oared Skiff to the Falls of Saint Anthony in 1817," 2nd ed., *Collections of the Minnesota Historical Society* 2 (1889), 9; Livingston, *Portraits of Eminent Americans*, 479; Nichols and Halley, *Stephen Long*, 44.

3. Reuben Gold Thwaites, ed., "The Fur Trade in Wisconsin, 1812–1825," *Wisconsin Historical Collections* 20 (1911), 62; Henry Putney Beers, *The Western Military Frontier, 1815–1846* (Philadelphia: Times and News Publishing Co., 1935), 20, 25; Long, "Voyage in a Six-Oared Skiff," 9; Johnson quoted in Viola, *Thomas L. McKenney*, 17.

4. Long, "Voyage in a Six-Oared Skiff," 60–62; W. Eugene Hollon, *The Lost Pathfinder: Zebulon Montgomery Pike* (Norman: University of Oklahoma Press, 1949), 63.

5. Long, "Voyage in a Six-Oared Skiff," 62.

6. Ibid., 9–10.

7. Ibid., 11–13.

8. Ibid., 18–20.

9. Ibid., 26–27, 30, 40–44, 47.

10. Ibid., 42–43, 82.

Chapter 6. Race and History

1. Nichols and Halley, *Stephen Long,* 47. Long submitted the earlier report to the American Philosophical Society, but the society declined to publish it. Whatever steps he took to get this one published have not come to light. Late in his life the manuscript finally did get into print under the title *Voyage in a Six-Oared Skiff to the Falls of Saint Anthony in 1817,* though by then it was no more than a historical artifact.

2. Long, "Voyage in a Six-Oared Skiff," 45.

3. A. Hallam, *Great Geological Controversies,* 2nd ed. (New York: Oxford University Press, 1989), 1–26.

4. Long, "Voyage in a Six-Oared Skiff," 44, 52–53.

5. Ibid., 63–64.

6. Thomas S. Garlinghouse, "Revisiting the Mound Builder Controversy," *History Today* 51, no. 9 (September 2001), 39–40.

7. Robert F. Berkhofer, Jr., *The White Man's Indian: Images of the American Indian from Columbus to the Present* (New York: Vintage Books, 1978), 34–38.

8. William Stanton, *The Leopard's Spots: Scientific Attitudes Toward Race in America, 1815–59* (Chicago: University of Chicago Press, 1960), 3–14.

9. Berkhofer, *The White Man's Indian,* 48–49.

10. Ibid., 113.

11. James H. McCulloh, *Researches on America: Being an Attempt to Settle Some Points Relative to the Aborigines of America, &c.* (Baltimore: Joseph Robinson, 1817), 35, 213–17; Stanton, *The Leopard's Spots,* 10.

12. *The Portico, A Repository of Science & Literature* 2, no. 2 (August 1, 1816), 103.

Chapter 7. To Civilize the Osages

1. Livingston, *Portraits of Eminent Americans,* 481.

2. Richard G. Wood, "Stephen Harriman Long at Belle Point," *Arkansas Historical Quarterly* 13 (Winter 1954), 338–40.

3. Livingston, *Portraits of Eminent Americans,* 481; Stephen H. Long, "Hot Springs of the Washitaw," *American Monthly Magazine and Critical Review* 3 (1818), 85–87.

4. Stephen H. Long to Thomas Smith, January 30, 1818, NA, RG 107, Letters Received, M271, Roll 2.

5. L. Bringier, "Notices of the Geology, Mineralogy, Topography, Productions, and Aboriginal Inhabitants of the Regions around the Mississippi and its confluent wa-

ters," *American Journal of Science and Arts* 3 (1821), 41; Thomas Nuttall, "A Journal of Travels into the Arkansas Territory," in Reuben Gold Thwaites, ed., *Early Western Travels, 1748–1846* 13 (1821; reprint, Cleveland, 1904–8), 191–92.

6. Stephen H. Long to Thomas Smith, January 30, 1818, NA, RG 107, Letters Received, M271, Roll 2.

7. Ibid.

8. Ibid.

9. Lovely quoted in Grant Foreman, *Indians and Pioneers: The Story of the American Southwest before 1830* (New Haven: Yale University Press, 1930), 39–40. The two travelers were Thomas Nuttall (Foreman, p. 164) and Henry Schoolcraft (Foreman, p. 53).

10. Stephen H. Long to Thomas Smith, January 30, 1818, NA, RG 107, Letters Received, M271, Roll 2.

11. Ibid.

CHAPTER 8. WESTWARD MIGRATION

1. Tanner, *Narrative,* 19–20.

2. Peers, *The Ojibwa of Western Canada,* 14–18.

3. Jeanne Kay, "Native Americans in the Fur Trade and Wildlife Depletion," *Environmental Review* 9, no. 2 (Summer 1985), 120–22.

4. Peers, *The Ojibwa of Western Canada,* 15.

5. Tanner, *Narrative,* 12–13, 27.

6. Tanner, *Narrative,* 19–20; Christopher Vecsey, *Traditional Ojibwa Religion and Its Historical Changes* (Philadelphia: The American Philosophical Society, 1983), 60–61.

7. Tanner, *Narrative,* 19–22.

8. Ibid., 20–22.

9. Ibid., 22–23.

10. Ibid., 23–24.

11. There is no surviving record of the Grand Portage trading post for the winter of 1794–95. However, the journal of Charles Jean Baptiste Chaboillez does record the frequent comings and goings of Indians at this post in 1797–98. Harold Hickerson, ed., "Journal of Charles Jean Baptiste Chaboillez, 1797–98," *Ethnohistory* 6, no. 3 (Summer 1959), 265–313, and no. 4 (Autumn 1959), 363–427.

12. Tanner, *Narrative,* 24; Bruce M. White, "A Skilled Game of Exchange: Ojibway Fur Trade Protocol," *Minnesota History* 50 (Summer 1987), 229–30.

13. Tanner, *Narrative,* 24–25.

14. Ibid., 15, 25. In Tanner's first interview on his return to the United States in 1818, he gave his American name as John Taylor. See "A Captive Found," *The Weekly Recorder* 5, no. 5 (September 11, 1818), 39. Tanner's Ottawa name was translated as "The Falcon" by Edwin James. Recent scholarship finds the true translation to be "The Swallow." See John T. Fierst, "'A 'Succession of Little Occurrences': Scholarly Editing and the Organization of Time in John Tanner's Narrative," *The Annals of the Association for Documentary Editing* 33 (2012), 4.

15. Tanner, *Narrative,* 26.

16. Ibid., 27.

17. Ibid., 27–28.

18. Peers, *The Ojibwa of Western Canada,* 31–32.

19. Tanner, *Narrative,* 26, 30.

20. Ibid., 31.

21. Ibid., 32–33.

22. Ibid., 34.

Chapter 9. Six Beaver Skins for a Quart of Mixed Rum

1. Tanner, *Narrative,* 27, 37–38, 44, 50–53.

2. Peers, *The Ojibwa of Western Canada,* 29.

3. Tanner, *Narrative,* 34–35, 44.

4. Ibid., 35–37, 76.

5. Ibid., 35–36; Peers, *The Ojibwa of Western Canada,* 96.

6. Tanner, *Narrative,* 36–37. A similar description of these vessels is found in Elliott Coues, *New Light on the Early History of the Greater Northwest: The Manuscript Journal of Alexander Henry, Fur Trader of the North West Company, and of David Thompson, Official Explorer of the Same Company, 1799–1814, Exploration and Adventure Among the Indians of the Red, Saskatchewan, Missouri, and Columbia Rivers* (New York: F. P. Harper, 1897), 181. Canoe making was one activity in which Ojibwa men and women combined efforts. Buffalohead, "Farmers Warriors Traders: A Fresh Look at Ojibway Women," 238.

7. Tanner, *Narrative,* 31, 37–39; David H. Stewart, "Early Assiniboine Trading Posts of the Souris Mouth Group, 1785–1832: Amplification of a Paper Read Before the Society, November 1928," *Manitoba Historical Society Transactions* Series 2, no. 5 (1930); Robert Goodwin, Brandon House Post Journal, Hudson's Bay Company Archives (hereafter cited as HBCA), B.22/a/8 (entries for September 13 and December 11, 1800, and March 10 and April 30, 1801). The identification of Mouse River Fort as Brandon House is based on Tanner's later reference to this place as the Hudson's Bay Company establishment and to its proprietor as M'Kie, or John McKay (120).

8. Tanner, *Narrative,* 38.

9. Hickerson, ed., "Journal of Charles Jean Baptiste Chaboillez, 1797–98," 277.

10. Tanner, *Narrative,* 38–39.

11. Ibid., 39.

12. Ibid., 39–40; John McKay, Brandon House Post Journal, HBCA, B.22/a/10 (May 29, 1803); Charles M. Gates, ed., *Five Fur Traders of the Northwest* (St. Paul: Minnesota Historical Society, 1965), 108.

13. Tanner, *Narrative,* 41–44.

14. Ibid., 44–46. The matter of Sag-git-to's paternity is conjectural. Tanner notes there was now a third small child in the group, but he does not state that Sag-git-to was the father. Considering how the group divided up at this point, it would seem to be a safe deduction. Tanner states later in the narrative (52) that all three children belonged to Net-no-kwa's daughter, though one was given to the young widow of Taw-ga-we-ninne.

15. Ibid., 44–50. Alexander Henry (the Younger) is known for his excellent journal,

which has been edited and published. Henry's career in the fur trade started in 1791, but the journal unfortunately only begins in 1799, more than a year after this encounter.

16. Ibid., 51. There is no mention of this incident in Hickerson, ed., "Journal of Charles Jean Baptiste Chaboillez, 1797–98," as the journal ends in May 1798, probably a few months before this incident occurred. However, the journal makes it evident that twenty-one packs was a very sizeable quantity to find in the possession of one group of Indians. Probably it was this that led the traders to take such coercive measures. The journal notes three instances of Indian women trading at the post, and in each case the traders' conduct was apparently no different than with Indian men. See also Bruce M. White, "The Woman Who Married a Beaver: Trade Patterns and Gender Roles in the Ojibwa Fur Trade," *Ethnohistory* 46, no. 1 (Winter 1999), 126–27.

17. Tanner, *Narrative,* 51–52.

CHAPTER 10. THE TEST OF WINTER

1. Calvin Martin, *Keepers of the Game: Indian-Animal Relationships and the Fur Trade* (Berkeley: University of California Press, 1978), 3.

2. Arthur J. Ray, "Periodic Shortages, Native Welfare, and the Hudson's Bay Company 1670–1930," in *The Subarctic Fur Trade: Native Social and Economic Adaptations,* Shepard Krech III, ed. (Vancouver: University of British Columbia Press, 1984), 1–10; Charles A. Bishop, "The First Century: Adaptive Changes among the Western James Bay Cree between the Early Seventeenth and Early Eighteenth Centuries," in ibid., 22–24, 45–46; Arthur J. Ray and Donald B. Freeman, *"Give Us Good Measure": An Economic Analysis of Relations between the Indians and the Hudson's Bay Company before 1763* (Toronto: University of Toronto Press, 1978), 241–44.

3. Tanner, *Narrative,* 52–53.

4. Ibid., 54–58.

5. Ibid., 58–59.

6. Ibid., 60.

7. Ibid., 61.

8. Ibid., 52, 61, 66–67; Bruce M. White, *Grand Portage as a Trading Post: Patterns of Trade at "the Great Carrying Place"* (Grand Marais, MN: Grand Portage National Monument, National Park Service, 2005), 82. See also Carolyn Gilman, *The Grand Portage Story* (St. Paul: Minnesota Historical Society Press, 1992), 87.

9. Tanner, *Narrative,* 64–67; Robert Goodwin, Brandon House Post Journal, HBCA, B.22/a/7 (entry for April 23) and B.22/a/8 (entry for September 13); Podruchny, *Making the Voyageur World,* 217–20. The Hudson's Bay Company employed Indians as "Fort hunters" in the Far North, too. See Shepard Krech III, "The Trade of the Slavey and Dogrib at Fort Simpson in the Early Nineteenth Century," in *The Subarctic Fur Trade,* 114.

10. Tanner, *Narrative,* 64–65.

11. Ibid., 65–66.

12. Ibid., 67.

13. Ibid., 68.

CHAPTER 11. RED SKY OF THE MORNING

1. Tanner, *Narrative*, 48.

2. Ibid., 66, 69.

3. Peers, *The Ojibwa of Western Canada*, 47; Harold Hickerson, "The Genesis of a Trading Post Band: The Pembina Chippewa," *Ethnohistory* 3, no. 4 (Fall 1956), 308.

4. Frank Raymond Secoy, *Changing Military Patterns on the Great Plains (17th Century through Early 19th Century)* (Seattle: University of Washington Press, 1953), 1–5, 104–6.

5. Tanner, *Narrative*, 70, 76–77.

6. Net-no-kwa may have felt differently. The following year, Tanner put all six horses in fetters and left them in his mother's charge with instructions to remove the fetters at the first snow. She did not do it, and the horses all died. Tanner, *Narrative*, 80.

7. Daniel W. Harmon, *A Journal of Voyages and Travels in the Interior of North America* (1922; reprint, New York: AMS Press, Inc., 1973), 51–52. The Gros Ventre were allied with the Blackfeet nation against the Assiniboine, Cree, and western Ojibwa. For a discussion of the intertribal alliance systems on the northern Great Plains, see John C. Ewers, "Intertribal Warfare as the Precursor of Indian-White Warfare on the Northern Great Plains," *Western Historical Quarterly* 6, no. 4 (October 1975), 397–410.

8. Harmon, *A Journal of Voyages and Travels*, 51–53.

9. Ibid.

10. Tanner, *Narrative*, 76. The trader was probably the proprietor of Swan Lake House. Unfortunately, the post journal for Swan Lake House for 1801–2 has not survived.

11. Ibid., 80; on Hugh McGillis, see Coues, *New Light on the Early History of the Greater Northwest*, 215.

12. Tanner, *Narrative*, 84–85, 101.

13. Ibid., 84–85.

14. Ibid., 89–90; Roger M. Carpenter, "Womanish Men and Manlike Women: The Native American Two-spirit as Warrior," in *Gender and Sexuality in Indigenous North America 1400–1850*, Sandra Slater and Fay A. Yarbrough, eds. (Columbia: University of South Carolina Press, 2011), 146–64; Walter L. Williams, *The Spirit and the Flesh: Sexual Diversity in American Indian Culture* (Boston: Beacon Press, 1986), 1–3, 21–22, 31, 41–42; Edward D. Neill, "History of the Ojibways, and their Connection with Fur Traders, based upon Official and other Records," *Collections of the Minnesota Historical Society* 5 (St. Paul: Minnesota Historical Society, 1885), 452–53.

15. Tanner, *Narrative*, 90–91; Williams, *The Spirit and the Flesh*, 93–94.

16. Tanner, *Narrative*, 100–102.

17. Ibid., 101–3.

CHAPTER 12. WARRIOR

1. On the causes of intertribal warfare on the northern Great Plains, see W. W. Newcomb, Jr., "A Re-examination of the Causes of Plains Warfare," *American Anthropologist* 52, no. 3 (July–September 1950), 317–30; Secoy, *Changing Military Patterns on the*

Great Plains; Ewers, "Intertribal Warfare as a Precursor of Indian-White Warfare on the Northern Great Plains," 397–410; Richard White, "The Winning of the West: The Expansion of the Western Sioux in the Eighteenth and Nineteenth Centuries," *Journal of American History* 65, no. 2 (September 1978), 319–43; Gary Clayton Anderson, "Early Dakota Migration and Intertribal War: A Revision," *Western Historical Quarterly* 11, no. 1 (January 1980), 17–36; and Tim E. Holzkamm, "Eastern Dakota Population Movements and the European Fur Trade: One More Time," *Plains Anthropologist* 28, no. 101 (1983), 225–33.

2. Harold Hickerson, *The Chippewa and Their Neighbors: A Study in Ethnohistory* (New York: Holt, Rinehart and Winston, Inc., 1970), 64–88.

3. Peers, *The Ojibwa of Western Canada,* 6–7; William W. Warren, *History of the Ojibway Nation* (1885; reprint, Minneapolis: Ross and Haines, 1957), 163–65, 187, 231, 235, 257, 355–56.

4. Tanner, *Narrative,* 108–9.

5. Ibid., 111–14.

6. Alexander Henry, *The Journal of Alexander Henry the Younger, 1799–1814,* Barry M. Gough, ed. (Toronto: Champlain Society, 1988), 2:173–74; Tanner, *Narrative,* 124–25.

7. Henry, *The Journal of Alexander Henry the Younger,* 2:174.

8. Tanner, *Narrative,* 125; Warren, *History of the Ojibway Nation,* 264.

9. Henry, *The Journal of Alexander Henry the Younger,* 2:175; Tanner, *Narrative,* 125.

10. Tanner, *Narrative,* 125–27.

11. Ibid., 127–28.

12. Ibid., 126–31.

13. Ibid., 129–31; Ernest Alexander Cruikshank, "Robert Dickson, The Indian Trader," *Wisconsin State Historical Society Collections* 12 (1892), 138; Louis Arthur Tohill, "Robert Dickson, British Fur Trader on the Upper Mississippi," *North Dakota Historical Quarterly* 3, no. 1 (October 1928), 21–24.

14. Tanner, *Narrative,* 132–41.

CHAPTER 13. FORT WILLIAM

1. Henry, *The Journal of Alexander Henry the Younger,* 2:144.

2. White, *Grand Portage as a Trading Post,* 113.

3. Victor P. Lytwyn, "The Anishinabeg and the Fur Trade," in Jean Morrison, ed., *Lake Superior to Rainy Lake: Three Centuries of Fur Trade History* (Thunder Bay, ON: Thunder Bay Historical Museum Society, 2003), 34.

4. The earliest physical descriptions of McLoughlin by his contemporaries appear somewhat later in his career, so his appearance at this time must be somewhat conjectural. See, for example, Frederick Merk, ed., *Fur Trade and Empire: George Simpson's Journal* (Cambridge: Harvard University Press, 1931), 23.

5. Chapin, "Letters of Dr. John McLoughlin," 293–94.

6. Grace Lee Nute, "Border Chieftain," *The Beaver* 282 (March 1952), 35–39.

7. Podruchny, *Making the Voyageur World,* 203–5.

8. Harmon, *A Journal of Voyages and Travels,* 126, 130–31.

9. Ibid., 118–19, 130. Harmon's wife eventually did accompany him back to Vermont, but that was not his expectation when he married her, nor was it the typical pattern. See Sylvia Van Kirk, *"Many Tender Ties": Women in Fur-Trade Society in Western Canada, 1670–1870* (Winnipeg, MB: Watson & Dwyer Publishing Ltd., 1980), 138–39.

10. Van Kirk, *"Many Tender Ties,"* 93–94.

11. Wallace, ed., *Documents Relating to the North West Company,* 211.

12. Podruchny, *Making the Voyageur World,* 247–49, 252–57.

13. The most reliable source on McLoughlin's first wife is the fragmentary information provided by his son David as cited in Morrison, *Outpost,* 51. Her connection to Fort William is suggested by the biographical sketch of McLoughlin in US House, *Report of Lieut. Neil M. Howison, United States Navy to the Commander of the Pacific Squadron,* House Misc. Rept. 29, 30th Cong., 1st sess., 1848, 12–13.

CHAPTER 14. MARRIAGE *À LA FAÇON DU PAYS*

1. T. C. Elliott, "Marguerite Wadin McKay McLoughlin," *Oregon Historical Quarterly* 36, no. 4 (December 1935), 344–45; Marjorie Wilkins Campbell, *The North West Company* (Toronto: Douglas & McIntyre, 1957), 19, 28.

2. Van Kirk, *"Many Tender Ties,"* 36–37; Sylvia Van Kirk, "The Role of Native Women in the Creation of Fur Trade Society in Western Canada, 1670–1830," in *The Women's West,* Susan Armitage and Elizabeth Jameson, eds. (Norman: University of Oklahoma Press, 1987), 53–62.

3. Ibid., 51, 54–59; Podruchny, *Making the Voyageur World,* 248–49.

4. Morrison, *Outpost,* 58–59; Jean Morrison, "McKay, Alexander," in *Dictionary of Canadian Biography Online* at www.biographi.ca <January 30, 2011>; Jennifer S. H. Brown, *Strangers in Blood: Fur Trade Company Families in Indian Country* (Vancouver: University of British Columbia Press, 1980), 157. Thomas McKay was born in 1796 at Sault Ste. Marie, according to Reuben Thwaites, ed., *Early Western Travels,* Vol. 21 (Cleveland: A. H. Clark, 1907), 201; or he was born in 1797 at Ile á la Crosse according to John C. Jackson, *Children of the Fur Trade: Forgotten Métis of the Pacific Northwest* (Missoula, MT: Mountain Press Publishing Company, 1995), 70.

5. Morrison, *Outpost,* 58. See also Fred Lockley, *Oregon Trail Blazers* (New York: Knickerbocker Press, 1929), 162–63. Lockley based his chapter on McLoughlin on an interview with Mrs. M. L. Myrick, a granddaughter of McLoughlin who served as his private secretary when she was a girl. Myrick stated that McLoughlin met Marguerite at Fort William.

6. Mother and son finally met again in 1824, and Thomas eventually settled in Oregon near his mother and stepfather. Morrison, *Outpost,* 117–18, 128; Elliott, "Marguerite Wadin McKay McLoughlin," 344; Jackson, *Children of the Fur Trade,* 69–72.

7. Brown, *Strangers in Blood,* 96–98, 158, 170–76; Podruchny, *Making the Voyageur World,* 206–11.

8. Morrison, *Outpost,* 58; James Douglas quoted in Adele Perry, " 'Is your Garden in England, Sir': James Douglas's Archive and the Politics of Home," *History Workshop Journal* 70 (August 2010), 75; Col. James K. Kelly, "Dr. John McLoughlin," undated

manuscript, Box 2, Oregon Historical Society Collections, McLoughlin-Fraser Family Papers, MSS 927 (hereafter OHSC, MSS 927), Box 2, Folder 2. Speaking to the couple's relationship later in life, one Elizabeth Wilson said that the doctor treated his wife "like a princess" and assigned her a place of honor when "handing her out to dinner." See Theressa Gay, *Life and Letters of Mrs. Jason Lee: First Wife of Rev. Jason Lee of the Oregon Mission* (Portland: Metropolitan Press, 1936), 155.

9. Nute, "Border Chieftain," 35–39.

10. Jean Morrison, "Fur Trade Families in the Lake Superior–Rainy Lake Region," in Morrison, ed., *Lake Superior to Rainy Lake,* 95.

11. Jean Morrison, ed., *The North West Company in Rebellion: Simon McGillivray's Fort William Notebook, 1815* (Thunder Bay, ON: Thunder Bay Historical Museum Society, 1988), 28–31.

CHAPTER 15. BAD BIRDS

1. John McLoughlin, "Description of the Indians from Fort William to Lake of the Woods," Richard H. Dillon, ed., *Amphora* 8 (Spring–Summer 1971), 11.

2. Ibid., 12. McLoughlin referred to a prophet in the direction of Fond du Lac. This was probably Le Maigouis, the Trout, who was active among the Ojibwa in 1807 and 1808. He was a disciple of Tenskwatawa, the Open Door, the younger brother of Tecumseh, otherwise known as the Shawnee Prophet. See R. David Edmunds, *The Shawnee Prophet* (Lincoln: University of Nebraska Press, 1983), 51–53.

3. Harold A. Innis, *The Fur Trade in Canada: An Introduction to Canadian Economic History* (New Haven: Yale University Press, 1930), 258–59. Innis gives year-by-year returns for the North West Company for 1804 through 1818 and comments, "The tendency toward decline was persistent. Declining returns were of serious consequence to the organization of a concern which required a heavy capital outlay for its operations."

4. Chapin, ed., "Letters of John McLoughlin, 1805–26," 328.

5. "Some Account of the Trade Carried on by the North West Company," in *Report of the Public Archives of Canada for the year 1928,* Arthur G. Doughty, ed. (Ottawa: F. A. Ackland, 1929), 63–65.

6. Innis, *The Fur Trade in Canada,* 261–68.

7. John McLoughlin, Lac La Pluie Post Journal for 1822–1823, HBCA, B. 105/a/9 (entry for September 14, 1823).

8. Innis, *The Fur Trade in Canada,* 269; Walter O'Meara, *The Last Portage* (Boston: Houghton Mifflin Co., 1962), 133.

9. Gordon Charles Davidson, *The North West Company* (New York: Russell & Russell, 1967), 224. The volume of liquor reached another high in an earlier period of competition between the North West Company and the XY Company during the years 1798–1803. The Montreal merchants claimed that imports of liquor then soared to 50,000 gallons annually. See Samuel Hull Wilcocke, Simon McGillivray, and Edward Ellice, *A Narrative of Occurrences in the Indian Countries of North America, since the Connection of the Right Hon. The Earl of Selkirk with the Hudson's Bay Company . . .* (London: B. McMillan, 1817), viii–x.

10. Wallace, ed., *Documents Relating to the North West Company,* 268–69.

11. Daniel Francis, "Traders and Indians," in *The Prairie West: Historical Readings,* R. Douglas Francis and Howard Palmer, eds. (Edmonton: Pica Pica Press, 1985), 64.

12. Henry, *The Journal of Alexander Henry the Younger,* 2:405.

13. McLoughlin, "Description of the Indians from Fort William to Lake of the Woods," 13.

14. Colin G. Calloway, *Crown and Calumet: British-Indian Relations, 1783–1815* (Norman: University of Oklahoma Press, 1987), 152–54.

Chapter 16. The Restive Partnership

1. Douglas MacKay, *The Honourable Company: A History of the Hudson's Bay Company* (Indianapolis: The Bobbs-Merrill Company, 1936), 47–48; Eric W. Morse, *Canoe Routes of the Voyageurs: The Geography and Logistics of the Canadian Fur Trade* (Ottawa: Royal Canadian Geographical Society, 1962), 9.

2. Innis, *The Fur Trade in Canada,* 237–38.

3. Campbell, *The North West Company,* 35–36, 112–14; David Thompson, *Travels in Western North America, 1784–1812,* Victor G. Hopwood, ed. (Toronto: MacMillan of Canada, 1971), 120.

4. Gregg A. Young, "The Organization of the Transfer of Furs at Fort William: A Study of Historical Geography," *Thunder Bay Historical Museum Society Papers and Records* 2 (1974), 30–32; Joseph D. Winterburn, "Lac La Pluie Bills Lading, 1806–1809," in Morrison, ed., *Lake Superior to Rainy Lake,* 59.

5. Theodore Catton, *The Environment and the Fur Trade Experience in Voyageurs National Park, 1730–1870,* Special History Report prepared for the National Park Service (Missoula, MT: Historical Research Associates, Inc., 2000), 74–75.

6. Francis, "Traders and Indians," 51.

7. Louise Phelps Kellogg, *The British Regime in Wisconsin and the Northwest* (Madison: State Historical Society of Wisconsin, 1935), 103; Wallace, ed., *Documents Relating to the North-West Co.,* passim.

8. Francis, "Traders and Indians," 51.

9. Innis, *The Fur Trade in Canada,* 258.

Chapter 17. The Pemmican War

1. John A. Alwin, "Pelts, Provisions and Perceptions: The Hudson's Bay Company Mandan Indian Trade, 1795–1812," *Montana: The Magazine of Western History* 29, no. 3 (July 1979), 17–27; Catton, *The Environment and the Fur Trade Experience in Voyageurs National Park, 1730–1870,* 7–9.

2. Thompson, *Travels in Western North America,* 89.

3. George Colpitts, *Pemmican Empire: Food, Trade, and the Last Bison Hunts in the North American Plains, 1780–1882* (New York: Cambridge University Press, 2015), 94–97.

4. John Morgan Gray, *Lord Selkirk of Red River* (London: MacMillan & Co., Ltd.), 16–20, 56–66; Alexander Ross, *The Red River Settlement: Its Rise, Progress, and Present State* (1856, reprint, Minneapolis: Ross and Haines, Inc., 1957), 16–18.

5. Campbell, *The North West Company*, 202–3.

6. John Perry Pritchett, *The Red River Valley, 1811–1849: A Regional Study* (New Haven: Yale University Press, 1942), 56–87.

7. Ibid., 79, 128–39.

8. MacKay, *The Honourable Company*, 135–38; Campbell, *The North West Company*, 205–08.

9. Wilcocke, McGillivray, and Ellice, *A Narrative of Occurrences in the Indian Countries of North America*, 24–28, and Appendix, 28; Pritchett, *The Red River Valley*, 141.

10. J. M. Bumsted, *Lord Selkirk, A Life* (East Lansing: Michigan State University Press, 2009), 245.

11. Quoted in Gray, *Lord Selkirk of Red River*, 104.

12. Wallace, ed., *Documents Relating to the North West Company*, 290; Morrison, ed., *The North West Company in Rebellion*, 36; Burt Brown Barker, "McLoughlin's Proprietory Account with North West Company," *Oregon Historical Quarterly* 45, no. 3 (September 1944), 39–40.

13. Quoted in Morrison, *Outpost*, 74–75. Emphasis in the original.

14. Wallace, ed., *Documents Relating to the North West Company*, 291.

15. Quoted in Pritchett, *The Red River Valley*, 148.

16. Gray, *Lord Selkirk of Red River*, 106; Morrison, ed., *The North West Company in Rebellion*, 12.

17. Chapin, ed., "Letters of John McLoughlin," 330–31.

18. Campbell, *The North West Company*, 212–13; Pritchett, *The Red River Valley*, 150–54.

19. Tanner, *Narrative*, 205.

20. John McLoughlin, Lac La Pluie Post Journal for 1823–1824, HBCA, B.105/a/9 (entry for September 1, 1823).

21. Tanner, *Narrative*, 205.

Chapter 18. The Battle of Seven Oaks

1. Morrison, ed., *The North West Company in Rebellion*, 27–29.

2. Ibid., 24.

3. Ibid., 28.

4. Ibid., 30.

5. Quoted in Gray, *Lord Selkirk of Red River*, 135.

6. Pritchett, *The Red River Valley*, 172.

7. John Halkett, *Statement Respecting the Earl of Selkirk's Settlement upon the Red River* (1817; reprint, Toronto: Coles Publishing Co., 1970), 101.

8. Quoted in B. C. Payette, *The Northwest* (Montreal: Printed privately for Payette Radio Limited, 1964), 442.

9. Quoted in Gray, *Lord Selkirk of Red River*, 148.

10. Halkett, *Statement*, xxxi, xlviii, lxvi; Morrison, *Outpost*, 84; Pritchett, *The Red River Valley*, 178–79.

11. Pritchett, *The Red River Valley*, 179.

12. Ibid., 180; "Summary of Evidence in the Controversy between the Hudson's Bay Company and the North-West Company. Reprinted from Papers relating to the Red River Settlement, 1815–19. Ordered by House of Commons to be printed July 19, 1819." In *Collections of the State Historical Society of North Dakota*, Vol. 4 (Fargo, ND: Knight Printing Co., 1913), 553.

CHAPTER 19. THE SURRENDER OF FORT WILLIAM

1. Campbell, *The North West Company*, 223–24; Gray, *Lord Selkirk of Red River*, 153–54.

2. Halkett, *Statement*, 60, lxxxv; Wilcocke, McGillivray, and Ellice, *A Narrative of Occurrences in the Indian Countries of North America*, 63–67; Gray, *Lord Selkirk of Red River*, 129, 137; Pritchett, *The Red River Valley*, 181–85.

3. Gray, *Lord Selkirk of Red River*, 155.

4. Halkett, *Statement*, xcii.

5. "Summary of Evidence in the Controversy between the Hudson's Bay Company and the North-West Company," 556–62.

6. Halkett, *Statement*, xcii–xciii; Gray, *Lord Selkirk of Red River*, 156–57.

7. Halkett, *Statement*, xciii.

8. Ibid., 67.

9. Ibid., xciv; Gray, *Lord Selkirk of Red River*, 163.

10. Campbell, *The North West Company*, 230–31.

11. Wilcocke, McGillivray, and Ellice, *A Narrative of Occurrences in the Indian Countries of North America*, 82.

CHAPTER 20. LORD SELKIRK'S PRISONER

1. Halkett, *Statement*, 179–83, lxxxvii–lxxxviii; Nicholas Garry, "Diary of Nicholas Garry," in *Transactions of the Royal Society of Canada*, 2nd Series, Vol. 6 (Ottawa: James Hope & Son, 1900), 113; Wilcocke, McGillivray, and Ellice, *A Narrative of Occurrences in the Indian Countries of North America*, 102–3; Morrison, *Outpost*, 89–90.

2. S. Marinozzi, G. Bertazzoni, and V. Gazzaniga, "Rescuing the Drowned: Cardiopulmonary Resuscitation and the Origins of Emergency Medicine in the Eighteenth Century," *Internal Emergency Medicine* 6, no. 4 (August 2011), 353–56.

3. T. C. Elliott, "Documentary Letters of Dr. John McLoughlin," *Oregon Historical Quarterly* 22, no. 3 (September 1922), 366, 370; Morrison, *Outpost*, 95, 97, 99, 103.

4. Halkett, *Statement*, lxxxix.

5. Ibid.

6. Ibid., lxxxviii–lxxxix; Payette, *The Northwest*, 414; Morrison, *Outpost*, 92.

7. Gray, *Lord Selkirk of Red River*, 240–77; Bumsted, *Lord Selkirk*, 331–58.

8. Morrison, *Outpost*, 93.

9. Barker, *The McLoughlin Empire and its Rulers*, 169.

10. *Report of the Proceedings connected with the disputes between the Earl of Selkirk and the North West Company at the Assizes Held at York in Upper Canada, October 1818* (Montreal: Printed by James Lane and Narum Howes, 1819), passim.

11. *Report of the Proceedings*, 215.

Chapter 21. Time of Reckoning

1. Brown, *Strangers in Blood*, 107–10.

2. Halkett, *Statement*, cv–xcvi.

3. Barker, *The McLoughlin Empire and its Rulers*, 171.

4. Barker, "McLoughlin Proprietory Account with North West Company," 44. The page from the ledger, which is reproduced in the *Oregon Historical Quarterly*, leaves room for various interpretations. Furthermore, McLoughlin's letters refer to other accounts besides this one, so it would seem that the North West Company ledger book presents at best an incomplete picture of McLoughlin's finances. For example, McLoughlin stated to his Uncle Simon in 1820 that he had sent a total of £500 to his family since 1816. But this does not necessarily contradict Barker's assessment, and as Barker also points out, after the North West Company and the Hudson's Bay Company amalgamated in 1821, McLoughlin remained in debt to his new employer until 1829.

5. Colin Robertson, *Colin Robertson's Correspondence Book, September 1817 to September 1822*, edited by E. E. Rich, assisted by R. Harvey Fleming (Toronto: Champlain Society, 1939), 82.

6. Statement by David McLoughlin, June 20, 1901, OHSC, MSS 927, Box 1.

7. Campbell, *The North West Company*, 248–49; MacKay, *The Honourable Company*, 151–52.

8. Quoted in Lamb, ed., *McLoughlin's Fort Vancouver Letters*, xlii; W. Kaye Lamb, "Dr. John McLoughlin," in *Dictionary of Canadian Biography Online* at www.biographi.ca <May 15, 2016>.

9. Quoted in ibid.

10. Ibid., xliii.

11. Campbell, *The North West Company*, 255–56.

12. Lamb, ed., *McLoughlin's Fort Vancouver Letters*, xliv; Campbell, *The North West Company*, 256; Davidson, *The North West Company*, 175; Morrison, *Outpost*, 99.

13. Barker, *The McLoughlin Empire and its Rulers*, 170–71.

14. Lamb, ed., *McLoughlin's Fort Vancouver Letters*, xlv; Robertson, *Colin Robertson's Correspondence Book*, cv.

Chapter 22. London

1. Robertson quoted in Peter C. Newman, *Caesars of the Wilderness: Company of Adventurers*, Vol. 2 (New York: Viking, 1987), 184.

2. Ibid., 184–86; Campbell, *The North West Company*, 244–45; MacKay, *The Honourable Company*, 150–51.

3. Robertson, *Colin Robertson's Correspondence Book*, 139.

4. Ibid., 138–39.

5. Ibid., 139.

6. "Now and Then, London," *The Beaver: Magazine of the North* Outfit 300 (Spring 1970), 24; *Diary of Woodfall's Register* (London), January 26, 1790.

7. Stella Margetson, *Regency London* (New York: Praeger Publishers, 1971), 12–13.

8. G. E. Mingay, *Georgian London* (London: B. T. Batsford, Ltd., 1975), 86–88.

9. Margetson, *Regency London,* 62–65; Paul Johnson, *The Birth of the Modern: World Society, 1815–1830* (New York: HarperCollins Publishers, 1991), 458–62.

10. Robertson, *Colin Robertson's Correspondence Book,* 142; MacKay, *The Honourable Company,* 158–62; Newman, *Caesars of the Wilderness,* 206–7.

11. Newman, *Caesars of the Wilderness,* 204–5.

12. Robertson, *Colin Robertson's Correspondence Book,* 142–43.

13. Ibid., 145.

14. Lamb, ed., *McLoughlin's Fort Vancouver Letters,* xlvii; MacKay, *The Honourable Company,* 158.

15. John S. Galbraith, *The Hudson's Bay Company as an Imperial Factor, 1821–1869* (Berkeley: University of California Press, 1957), 14.

16. Robertson, *Colin Robertson's Correspondence Book,* cvi.

17. Harold A. Innis, "Interrelations Between the Fur Trade of Canada and the United States," *Mississippi Valley Historical Review* 20, no. 3 (December 1933), 329.

18. Richard G. Montgomery, *The White-Headed Eagle: John McLoughlin, Builder of an Empire* (New York: The MacMillan Company, 1934), 46; Brown, *Strangers in Blood,* 111–12; E. E. Rich, *The History of the Hudson's Bay Company, 1670–1870,* Vol. 2, *1763–1870* (London: The Hudson's Bay Record Society, 1959), 406–7.

19. MacKay, *The Honourable Company,* 160.

20. Ibid., 161–62.

21. Ibid., 158–59.

22. Morrison, *Outpost,* 107.

23. Barker, *The McLoughlin Empire and its Rulers,* 84–85.

24. Quoted in Morrison, *Outpost,* 100.

25. Barker, *The McLoughlin Empire and its Rulers,* 88–94.

26. Simpson letter reproduced in Lamb, ed., *McLoughlin's Fort Vancouver Letters,* xliv.

27. John S. Galbraith, "British-American Competition in the Border Fur Trade of the 1820s," *Minnesota History* 36 (September 1959), 241–42; Simpson letter quoted in Lamb, ed., *McLoughlin's Fort Vancouver Letters,* xliv.

CHAPTER 23. THE WONDER OF THE STEAMBOAT

1. Stephen H. Long to James Monroe, March 13, 1817, NA, RG 107, Letters Received, M221, Roll 74.

2. After the War of 1812, the army was organized into northern and southern divisions; Jackson commanded the southern division and Major General Jacob Brown commanded the northern division. When Long explored the Illinois River, he passed out of the southern division and technically transferred from Jackson's to Brown's command, though he was acting under the secretary's special orders and reported to General Smith at Fort Belle Fontaine again the next year. Jackson was also aggrieved that he only learned of Long's expedition when he read about it in the *National Register.* See Andrew Jackson to George Graham, January 14, 1817, Graham to Jackson, Feb-

ruary 1, 1817, Jackson to James Monroe, March 4, 1817, and Monroe to Jackson, December 2, 1817, *The Papers of Andrew Jackson,* 7 vols., Harold D. Moser, David R. Hoth, and George H. Hoemann, eds. (Knoxville: University of Tennessee Press), 4:85–87, 97–98, 155; John Spencer Bassett, *Correspondence of Andrew Jackson,* 2 vols. (Washington: Carnegie Institution, 1927), 2:xi–xii; Livingston, *Portraits of Eminent Americans,* 479; Nichols and Halley, *Stephen Long,* 38; Wood, *Stephen Harriman Long,* 45.

3. Smith quoted in Nichols and Halley, *Stephen Long,* 64.

4. John C. Calhoun to Thomas A. Smith, March 18, 1818, in US House, *Annual Report of the American Historical Association for the Year 1899,* Vol. 2, *Calhoun Correspondence,* 56th Cong., 1st sess., 1900, Serial 4012, 134–35.

5. Long quoted in Wood, *Stephen Harriman Long,* 54; Nichols and Halley, *Stephen Long,* 65; George Rogers Taylor, *The Transportation Revolution, 1815–1860* (New York: Rinehart & Company, Inc., 1951), 63–64.

6. Nichols and Halley, *Stephen Long,* 64; Wood, *Stephen Harriman Long,* 60–61.

7. Wood, *Stephen Harriman Long,* 60–61; Nichols and Halley, *Stephen Long,* 64–67.

CHAPTER 24. A CHRISTIAN MARRIAGE

1. The deaths of Martha's father and two siblings were recorded at Christ Church, Philadelphia (Beverly Bode Howard personal communication, August 31, 2010). The adopted sister married John Norvell, publisher of *The Gazette,* and later moved to Michigan, where John Norvell was elected to the US Senate. Her obituary in the *Detroit Free Press* (reproduced at www.findgrave.com <August 31, 2010>) gives her name as Isabella H. Norvell. Genealogist B. B. Howard established her family origins, adoption, and marriage to Norvell (which occurred in 1822). The date of marriage of Sarah Dewees Hodgkis and her second husband, Caleb Foulke, is available in "genealogy search" at www.christchurchphila.org. Martha's stepfather's occupation and residences were recorded in Philadelphia city directories (1805–19) at www.archive.org and in John Thomas Scharf, *History of Philadelphia, 1609–1884* Vol. 3 (Philadelphia: L. H. Everts and Co., 1884), p. 2300, also at www.archive.org.

2. William B. Skelton, *An American Profession of Arms: The Army Officer Corps, 1784–1861* (Lawrence: University Press of Kansas, 1992), 190, 403.

3. "Topographical Engineers," no date, NA, RG 77, Entry 306, Box 1; Rev. William Travis, comp., *History of the Germantown Academy: Compiled from Minutes of the Trustees from 1760 to 1877,* Horace Wemyss Smith, ed. (Philadelphia: Ferguson Bros. & Co., 1882), 48; Skelton, *An American Profession of Arms,* 190–92.

4. Samuel J. Watson, "Flexible Gender Roles during the Market Revolution: Family, Friendship, Marriage, and Masculinity among U.S. Army Officers, 1815–1846," *Journal of Social History* 29, no. 1 (Fall 1995), 83.

5. Ibid., 91.

6. Skelton, *An American Profession of Arms,* 206–7.

7. Roger L. Nichols, ed., *The Missouri Expedition, 1818–1820: The Journal of Surgeon John Gale with Related Documents* (Norman: University of Oklahoma Press, 1969), 61.

8. *Democratic Free Press* (Philadelphia), March 5, 1819. The marriage of Stephen

Long and Martha Hodgkis, together with other Hodgkis and Dewees marriages and baptisms performed in the church, are found in "genealogical search" at www .christchurchphila.org.

9. Carl N. Degler, *At Odds: Women and the Family in America from the Revolution to the Present* (New York: Oxford University Press, 1980), 10–14.

10. Anya Jabour, *Marriage in the Early Republic: Elizabeth and William Wirt and the Companionate Ideal* (Baltimore: Johns Hopkins University Press, 1998), 9; Degler, *At Odds,* 26–29. Stephen and Martha Long named their four sons after distinguished men whose association with the family alternately reflected well on one or the other marriage partner. They named their firstborn son William Dewees after Martha's uncle, the prominent Philadelphia physician. The next son they named Henry Clay after the Kentucky statesman and presidential hopeful—obviously an expression of Long's own political convictions at the time. The third son was named Richard Harlan after another Philadelphia physician and friend of the Dewees family. The fourth son was named Edwin James after the young physician and naturalist who accompanied Long on his expedition to the Rockies. (This man was the same Edwin James who helped John Tanner write his autobiography.) They did not follow this pattern in naming their two daughters, the fourth and sixth children in birth order, whom they named Mary and Lucy. Thus, they placed their sons and daughters in separate spheres as soon as they christened them. The sons' names showed a public face; the daughters' names did not. "Long Family Genealogy" lists the children as follows: William Dewees Long b. Philadelphia, October 11, 1820, Henry Clay Long b. February 18, 1822, Richard Harlan Long b. Philadelphia, October 3, 1824, Mary Long b. Philadelphia, 1828, Edwin James Long b. Baltimore, June 11, 1829, d. 1830, Lucy Leonis Long b. Philadelphia, October 13, 1832.

11. Tanner, *Narrative,* 277. The characterization of Stephen Long in Tanner's *Narrative* is complicated by the fact that Tanner's translator and editor, Edwin James, knew Long himself very well from the expedition to the Rocky Mountains and their subsequent collaboration in writing and publishing *Account of an Expedition from Pittsburgh to the Rocky Mountains.* Letters that Edwin James sent to his family before and after the expedition were quite negative about Long; however, James was admiring of Long in his public writings and the two remained lifelong friends. Stephen and Martha named one of their children after Edwin James. See Carlo Rotella, "Travels in a Subjective West: The Letters of Edwin James and Major Stephen Long's Scientific Expedition of 1819–1820," *Montana: The Magazine of Western History* 41, no. 4 (Autumn 1991), 20–35.

12. Volo and Denneen, *Family Life in Native America,* 43–47. For an example of whites' selective perception, see the description of marriage among the Omaha in James, *Account of an Expedition from Pittsburgh to the Rocky Mountains,* 240–44.

13. Nancy F. Cott, *Public Vows: A History of Marriage and the Nation* (Cambridge, MA: Harvard University Press, 2000), 26.

14. William R. Swagerty, "Marriage and Settlement Patterns of Rocky Mountain Trappers and Traders," *Western Historical Quarterly* 11, no. 2 (April 1980), 164–68, 176–

77. See also White, "The Woman Who Married a Beaver: Trade Patterns and Gender Roles in the Ojibwa Fur Trade," 109–47.

15. Quotations from J. H. Johnston, "Documentary Evidence of the Relations of Negroes and Indians," *Journal of Negro History* 14, no. 1 (January 1929), 25.

16. Jedediah Morse, *A Report to the Secretary of War of the United States on Indian Affairs* (New Haven, 1822), 64, 73–74, 78–79.

17. Stephen H. Long, "Report of the Western River Expedition," February 20, 1821, NA, RG 77, Entry 292A, Bulky File 107, p. 101.

CHAPTER 25. UP THE MISSOURI

1. Philip Drennen Thomas, "The United States Army as the Early Patron of Naturalists in the Trans-Mississippi West, 1803–1820," *Chronicles of Oklahoma* 56, no. 2 (Summer 1978), 187.

2. Nichols and Halley, *Stephen Long*, 67–70.

3. Stephen H. Long to John C. Calhoun, April 20, 1819, *The Papers of John C. Calhoun* Vol. 4, W. Edwin Hemphill, ed. (Columbia: University of South Carolina Press, 1967), 33; Nichols and Halley, *Stephen Long*, 71–75.

4. Stephen H. Long to John C. Calhoun, April 20, 1819, *The Papers of John C. Calhoun* 4:33–32.

5. Wood, *Stephen Harriman Long*, 71–72; Nichols and Halley, *Stephen Long*, 78.

6. Wood, *Stephen Harriman Long*, 72–73; William Darlington, comp., *Reliquiae Baldwinianae: Selections from the Correspondence of the Late William Baldwin, M.D.* (New York: Hafner Publishing Co., 1969), 306.

7. Nichols and Halley, *Stephen Long*, 66; Louis C. Hunter, "The Invention of the Western Steamboat," *Journal of Economic History* 3, no. 2 (November 1943), 217.

8. *Niles Weekly Register* 16, no. 412 (July 24, 1819), 368.

9. Nichols and Halley, *Stephen Long*, 81.

10. Ibid., 82–87.

11. *American State Papers: Military Affairs*, 2:324; Wood, *Stephen Harriman Long*, 85–86; Cardinal Goodwin, "A Larger View of the Yellowstone Expedition, 1819–1820," *Mississippi Valley Historical Review* 4, no. 3 (December 1917), 307; Charles M. Wiltse, *John C. Calhoun: Nationalist, 1782–1828* (Indianapolis: The Bobbs-Merrill Company, 1944), 182–85.

12. Stephen H. Long to R. M. Johnson, January 20, 1820, in US House, *Documents in relation to the claim of James Johnson for transportation on the Missouri and Mississippi Rivers*, 16th Cong., 2d sess., H.Doc. 110, March 1, 1821, 73–75; Livingston, *Portraits of Eminent Americans*, 483; A. O. Weese, ed., "The Journal of Titian Ramsay Peale, Pioneer Naturalist," *Missouri Historical Review* 41 (January 1947), 162–63.

13. Roger L. Nichols, "Stephen H. Long," in *Soldier's West: Biographies from the Military Frontier*, Paul Andrew Hutton, ed. (Lincoln: University of Nebraska Press, 1987), 31.

14. Nichols and Halley, *Stephen Long*, 95.

15. Ibid., 102.

16. Stephen H. Long to John C. Calhoun, October 28, 1819, *The Papers of John C. Calhoun* 4:388–89.

17. Stephen H. Long to John C. Calhoun, January 3, 1820, *The Papers of John C. Calhoun* 4:542–47.

18. Goodwin, "A Larger View of the Yellowstone Expedition, 1819–1820," 309; Nichols, "Stephen H. Long," 32.

19. Nichols and Halley, *Stephen Long,* 111.

20. John C. Calhoun to Stephen H. Long, February 29, 1820, NA, RG 107, Letters Sent, M6, Ro11 11.

21. Nichols, "Stephen H. Long," 32–33.

Chapter 26. To the Rocky Mountains

1. Robert J. Miller, *Native America, Discovered and Conquered: Thomas Jefferson, Lewis & Clark, and Manifest Destiny* (Westport, CT: Praeger Publishers, 2006), 1–8, passim.

2. Stephen H. Long to Isaac Roberdeau, December 24, 1821, NA, RG 77, Entry 306, Box 1.

3. James P. Ronda, "'To Acquire What Knolege You Can': Thomas Jefferson as Exploration Patron and Planner," *Proceedings of the American Philosophical Society* 150, no. 3 (September 2006), 409–13.

4. Stephen E. Ambrose, *Undaunted Courage: Meriwether Lewis, Thomas Jefferson, and the Opening of the American West* (New York: Simon & Schuster, 1996), 76–77, 93–95, quotation on 81.

5. Jerome O. Steffen, "William Clark," in *Soldiers West: Biographies from the Military Frontier,* Paul Andrew Hutton, ed. (Lincoln: University of Nebraska Press, 1987), 16.

6. Ibid., 15.

7. Ambrose, *Undaunted Courage,* 95.

8. Nichols and Halley, *Stephen Long,* 15. See also Thomas, "The United States Army as the Early Patron of Naturalists in the Trans-Mississippi West, 1803–1820," 171–93.

9. Bell, *The Journal of Captain John R. Bell,* 58.

10. Nichols and Halley, *Stephen Long,* 166–70, 176–78. See also Richard H. Dillon, "Stephen Long's Great American Desert," *Montana: The Magazine of Western History* 18, no. 3 (July 1968), 58–74.

11. Nichols, "Stephen H. Long," 34–35; Thomas, "The United States Army as the Early Patron of Naturalists in the Trans-Mississippi West, 1803–1820," 191.

12. Nichols, "Stephen H. Long," 33–35; Wood, *Stephen Harriman Long,* 106–8; Bell, *The Journal of Captain John R. Bell,* 103; Livingston, *Portraits of Eminent Americans,* 485.

13. Maxine Benson, ed., *From Pittsburgh to the Rocky Mountains: Major Stephen Long's Expedition, 1819–1820* (Golden, CO: Fulcrum, Inc., 1988), 152, 187–88.

14. Ibid., 237–38, 273.

15. Ibid., 283.

16. Thomas, "The United States Army as the Early Patron of Naturalists in the Trans-Mississippi West, 1803–1820," 191.

17. Stephen H. Long, "Report of the Western River Expedition," February 20, 1821, NA, RG 77, Entry 292A, Bulky File 107, pp. 87, 90–91.

18. Ibid.

19. William B. Skelton, "Army Officers' Attitudes Toward Indians, 1830–1860," *The Pacific Northwest Quarterly* 67, no. 3 (July 1976), 115–16.

20. Stephen H. Long, "Report of the Western River Expedition," February 20, 1821, NA, RG 77, Entry 292A, Bulky File 107, p. 92.

21. Ibid., 101.

22. Skelton, "Army Officers' Attitudes Toward Indians, 1830–1860," 113–24.

Chapter 27. Mapmaker

1. Stephen H. Long to John C. Calhoun, December 12, 1820, *The Papers of John C. Calhoun* 5:478–80.

2. Wiltse, *John C. Calhoun: Nationalist, 1782–1828*, 198–224.

3. Stephen H. Long to Alexander Macomb, June 22, 1822, NA, RG 77, Entry 14, Box 7; Stephen H. Long to Isaac Roberdeau, September 13, 1822, September 15, 1822, and October 26, 1822, NA, RG 77, Entry 306, Box 1.

4. Livingston, *Portraits of Eminent Americans*, 485; Bell, *The Journal of Captain John R. Bell*, 281–82, 306.

5. Stephen H. Long to John C. Calhoun, July 18, 1821, Long to Isaac Roberdeau, August 24, 1821, October 7, 1821, and December 24, 1821, NA, RG 77, Entry 306, Box 1.

6. Stephen H. Long to John C. Calhoun, June 15, 1821, James Duncan Graham to Calhoun, July 24, 1821, and Calhoun to Long, July 31, 1821, *The Papers of John C. Calhoun* 6:192, 278, 306; Long to Calhoun, July 18, 1821, NA, RG 77, Entry 306, Box 1.

7. Livingston, *Portraits of Eminent Americans*, 485.

8. Wood, *Stephen Harriman Long*, 112–13.

9. Stephen H. Long to Isaac Roberdeau, August 24, 1821, NA, RG 77, Entry 306, Box 1.

10. Stephen H. Long to Christopher Van Deventer, February 8, 1821, NA, RG 107, Letters Received, M221, Roll 90.

11. Stephen H. Long to Isaac Roberdeau, October 7, 1821, NA, RG 77, Entry 306, Box 1; John C. Calhoun to Long, November 8, 1821, NA, RG 107, Letters Sent, M6, Roll 11; *The Philadelphia Index or Directory for 1823* (Philadelphia: Robert Desilver, 1823), 230.

12. Nichols and Halley, *Stephen Long*, 161–63; Edwin James, compiler, *Account of an Expedition from Pittsburgh to the Rocky Mountains, performed in the years 1819 and '20*, 2 vols. (Philadelphia: H. C. Carey and I. Lea, 1823).

13. Stephen H. Long to Isaac Roberdeau, October 7, 1821, NA, RG 77, Entry 306, Box 1.

14. Stephen H. Long to Isaac Roberdeau, May 3, 1822, and June 10, 1822, NA, RG 77, Entry 306, Box 1; Long to Alexander Macomb, March 2, 1823, and April 2, 1823, NA, RG 77, Entry 264, Box 2. See also Herman R. Friis, "Stephen H. Long's Unpublished Manuscript Map of the United States Compiled in 1820–1822(?)," *The California Geographer* 8 (1967), 75–87, especially 85–87.

15. Stephen H. Long to Isaac Roberdeau, December 24, 1821, January 29, 1822, and January 30, 1822, NA, RG 77, Entry 306, Box 1.

16. Stephen H. Long to Isaac Roberdeau, December 24, 1821, NA, RG 77, Entry 306, Box 1.

17. *American State Papers: Military Affairs,* 3:502; Stephen H. Long to Isaac Roberdeau, June 10, 1822, September 15, 1822, and October 26, 1822, NA, RG 77, Entry 306, Box 1.

18. Under Pennsylvania's "Act for the gradual Abolition of Slavery" (1780), all persons born of slave mothers were free; however, young slaves could be brought into the state and manumitted in exchange for an indenture, which bound their labor until they were twenty-eight years old. Whites, on the other hand, were indentured in the state for a maximum of four years. The loophole in Pennsylvania's antislavery law encouraged many Philadelphians to acquire young black servants who had been born into slavery in nearby Delaware, Maryland, or Virginia. These persons could be bought and sold and compelled to work on the master's terms just like a slave. They were entitled to leave the master's premises or marry only with the master's permission. Sometimes the master paid for the servants to obtain a certain amount of schooling or instruction to prepare them for their eventual freedom. At a minimum the master was expected to provide "freedom dues" on the servant's twenty-eighth birthday amounting to two suits of clothes. See Edward Raymond Turner, *The Negro in Pennsylvania: Slavery—Servitude—Freedom, 1639-1861* (1911; reprint, New York: Negro Universities Press, 1969), 78, 93, 96–99.

19. Stephen H. Long to Alexander Macomb, March 11, 1823, NA, RG 77, Entry 14, Box 9.

20. Ibid.

21. Wyndham D. Miles, "A Versatile Explorer: A Sketch of William H. Keating," *Minnesota History* 36 (December 1959), 297–98.

22. Keating, *Narrative,* 1:143, 327.

23. Ibid., 1:2.

24. Innis, "Interrelations between the Fur Trade of Canada and the United States," 329–32.

25. Keating, *Narrative,* 1:2.

26. Stephen H. Long to Alexander Macomb, May 23, 1823, NA, RG 77, Entry 14, Box 10; Keating, *Narrative,* 2:56–57.

27. Keating, *Narrative,* 1:5.

Chapter 28. The Northern Expedition

1. Keating, *Narrative,* 1:76.

2. Ibid., 149–52, and 2:242–43.

3. Ibid., 123–25, 228–29, and 2:39.

4. Ibid., 442–45.

5. Nichols and Halley, *Stephen Long,* 191–97; Wood, *Stephen Harriman Long,* 125–27; Keating, *Narrative,* 1:350, 445.

6. Keating, *Narrative,* 1:445–47.

7. Clair Jacobson, "A History of the Yanktonai and Hunkpatina Sioux," *North Dakota History* 47, no. 1 (1980), 6, 10.

8. Keating, *Narrative*, 2:5–8. The sketch of Wanatan is reproduced as the frontispiece. See also Gwen Westerman and Bruce White, *Mna Sota Makoce: The Land of the Dakota* (St. Paul: Minnesota Historical Society Press, 2012), 120.

9. Keating, *Narrative*, 2:5–8.

10. Ibid., 12–14.

11. Ibid., 14–15.

12. Ibid., 16–17.

13. Ibid., 19–20, 32.

14. Ibid., 37, 39, 42, 44.

15. Ibid., 42–43.

16. Gerhard J. Ens, *Homeland to Hinterland: The Changing Worlds of the Red River Metis in the Nineteenth Century* (Toronto: University of Toronto Press, 1996), 20.

17. Keating, *Narrative*, 2:39–40.

18. Ibid., 40–41. The origin of Métis culture is complicated and lies somewhere in the late seventeenth to mid-eighteenth centuries in the Great Lakes region of Canada, when mixed-blood offspring of French fur traders began to carve out a distinct role for themselves as middlemen in the trade relations between Europeans and Indians. The development of a large and distinct Métis community in the Red River valley commenced in the early 1800s and stemmed mainly from the policies and practices of the North West Company. Ens, *Homeland to Hinterland*, 14–17.

19. Keating, *Narrative*, 2:54–55.

20. Ibid., 55, 72.

21. Ibid., 72–74.

22. Long, *The Northern Expeditions of Stephen H. Long*, 191–207.

Chapter 29. The Coming of the Prophet

1. Tanner, *Narrative*, 98; Alwin, "Pelts, Provisions and Perceptions," 22.

2. Edmunds, *The Shawnee Prophet*, 33–41.

3. Ibid., 38. For analysis of evolving Indian ideas about race, and Indian cultural responses to white Americans in particular, see Snyder, *Slavery in Indian Country*, especially 158–62.

4. Ibid., 70–71; John Sugden, *Tecumseh: A Life* (New York: Henry Holt and Company, 1997), 166, 170–73.

5. Edmunds, *The Shawnee Prophet*, 40; Sugden, *Tecumseh*, 146–47; John T. Fierst, "Strange Eloquence: Another Look at *The Captivity and Adventures of John Tanner*," in *Reading Beyond Words: Contexts in Native History*, Jennifer Brown and Elizabeth Vibert, eds. (Peterborough, ON: Broadview Press, 1996), 226–27.

6. Tanner, *Narrative*, 144–45.

7. Ibid., 145–47.

8. Ibid., 146.

9. Ibid., 146–47. For another, similar account of the Ojibwa response to the Shawnee Prophet, see Warren, *History of the Ojibway Nation*, 320–23.

10. On the orphans, see Tanner, *Narrative*, 121, 148. On being denied due respect for his hunting prowess, see pages 120–23.

11. Henry, *The Journal of Alexander Henry the Younger*, 1:182–84; Tanner, *Narrative*, 147, 157.

12. Tanner, *Narrative*, 147.

13. Peers, *The Ojibwa of Western Canada*, 63–64; Hickerson, "The Genesis of a Trading Post Band," 232–24; Henry, *The Journal of Alexander Henry the Younger*, 1:195, 294.

14. Dan Flores, "Bison Ecology and Bison Diplomacy: The Southern Plains from 1800 to 1850," *Journal of American History* 78, no. 2 (September 1991), 475–76; Charles R. Watrall, "Virginia Deer and the Buffer Zone in the Late Prehistoric–Early Protohistoric Periods in Minnesota," *Plains Anthropologist* 13, no. 40 (May 1968), 81–86.

15. Hickerson, *The Chippewa and Their Neighbors*, 106–119.

16. Tanner, *Narrative*, 74–75, 146, 158–61, 168; Warren, *History of the Ojibway Nation*, 354; Henry, *The Journal of Alexander Henry the Younger*, 1:300.

17. Tanner, *Narrative*, 161–62; Snyder, *Slavery in Indian Country*, 172–75.

18. Tanner, *Narrative*, 151–52.

19. Ibid., 157, 166–67.

20. Reginald Horsman, *The Causes of the War of 1812* (Philadelphia: University of Pennsylvania, 1962), 158–71; Calloway, *Crown and Calumet*, 228.

21. Edmunds, *The Shawnee Prophet*, 50–53, 76; Warren, *History of the Ojibway Nation*, 323–24; Sugden, *Tecumseh*, 174.

22. Warren, *History of the Ojibway Nation*, 324; Tanner, *Narrative*, 168–69, 185–90.

23. Tanner, *Narrative*, 168–69, 184–85, 252; Vecsey, *Traditional Ojibwa Religion and Its Historical Changes*, 76, 88–91.

CHAPTER 30. A LOATHSOME MAN

1. Tanner, *Narrative*, 172; Pritchett, *The Red River Valley*, 89; George Bryce, "The Five Forts of Winnipeg," in *Proceedings and Transactions of the Royal Society of Canada for the year 1885*, Vol. 3 (Montreal: Dawson Brothers Publishers, 1886), 138.

2. Tanner, *Narrative*, 172.

3. Ibid., 172–73.

4. Ibid., 173.

5. Ibid., 174.

6. Ibid., 174–75.

7. Ibid., 120, 176–77. This entire incident was described in brief in a letter of John Allan of Montreal dated November 1818, as reproduced in Keating, *Narrative*, 2:121–22. The document was among the reference letters Tanner carried with him in 1823 and was written as an attest to his honorable relations with the traders.

CHAPTER 31. SORCERY AND SICKNESS

1. Tanner, *Narrative*, 203–4.

2. Ibid., 167, 171, 187; D. Wayne Moodie and Barry Kaye, "Indian Agriculture in the Fur Trade Northwest," *Prairie Forum* 11, no. 2 (Fall 1986), 173–74.

3. Tanner, *Narrative*, 206–7, 252; Elizabeth T. Baird, "Reminiscences of Early Days on Mackinac Island," *Wisconsin Historical Collections* 14 (1898), 47–55.

4. Tanner, *Narrative*, 185–86; John West, *The Substance of a Journal During a Residence at the Red River Colony and Frequent Excursions Among the North-West American Indians, in the Years 1820, 1821, 1822, 1823* (1824; reprint, Project Gutenberg eBook, 2007), 27; Shawn Smallman, "Spirit Beings, Mental Illness, and Murder: Fur Traders and the Windigo in Canada's Boreal Forest, 1774–1935," *Ethnohistory* 57, no. 4 (Fall 2010), 574, 578.

5. Tanner, *Narrative*, 186–87.

6. Ibid., 188–90.

7. Ibid., 191–92; Anastasia M. Shkilnyk, *A Poison Stronger Than Love: The Destruction of an Ojibwa Community* (New Haven: Yale University Press, 1985), 95–99.

8. Tanner, *Narrative*, 190–91.

9. Moodie and Kaye, "Indian Agriculture in the Fur Trade Northwest," 175; Tanner, *Narrative*, 190–92.

10. Tanner, *Narrative*, 192; Pritchett, *The Red River Valley*, 77–79, 93–103.

11. Tanner, *Narrative*, 192–93; Pritchett, *The Red River Valley*, 103.

12. Tanner, *Narrative*, 192–93.

13. Ibid., 193–94; Paul Hackett, *A Very Remarkable Sickness: Epidemics in the Petit Nord, 1670–1846* (Winnipeg: University of Manitoba Press, 2002), 41, 129–36.

14. A. Irving Hallowell, *The Ojibwa of Berens River, Manitoba: Ethnography into History*, edited with preface and afterword by Jennifer S. H. Brown (Fort Worth, TX: Harcourt Brace Jovanovich College Publishers, 1991), 68–71; Tanner, *Narrative*, 193–94.

15. Tanner, *Narrative*, 194.

16. Ibid., 154–55, 157, 162–66, 195, 201.

17. Ibid., 200–201.

18. Ibid., 201–3.

19. Ibid., 204–5.

20. Ibid., 205–6.

21. Ibid., 207–8.

Chapter 32. Taking Fort Douglas

1. Tanner, *Narrative*, 204, 211, 213; Moodie and Kaye, "Indian Agriculture in the Fur Trade Northwest," 178.

2. D. W. Moodie, "Agriculture and the Fur Trade," in *Rethinking the Fur Trade*, 89–90, 102.

3. Halkett, *Statement*, xviii, xlviii; Tanner, *Narrative*, 209.

4. Tanner, *Narrative*, 209–11.

5. Ibid., 209–12; Halkett, *Statement*, xlvii–xlix.

6. Tanner, *Narrative*, 212–13.

7. Ibid., 213.

8. Ibid., 213–14; M.S. by Lord Selkirk Relating to Red River, National Archives of Canada (hereafter NAC), Selkirk Papers, Roll C-12, pp. 12769–70.

9. Tanner, *Narrative;* M.S. by Lord Selkirk Relating to Red River, NAC, Selkirk Papers, Roll C-12, pp. 12770–74; Pritchett, *The Red River Valley,* 194.

10. Tanner, *Narrative,* 214–16.

11. Ibid., 201; John McLoughlin, Lac La Pluie Post Journal for 1823–1824, HBCA, B.105/a/9 (entry for September 1, 1823).

12. Tanner, *Narrative,* 214; Pritchett, *The Red River Valley,* 194. On Be-gwais, see Hugh A. Dempsey, "Peguis," in *Dictionary of Canadian Biography Online* at www.bio graphi.ca <September 30, 2011>.

13. Tanner, *Narrative,* 214; George Bryce, "Sketch of the Life of John Tanner, A Famous Manitoba Scout," *Historical and Scientific Society of Manitoba* 30 (1888), 3.

14. Tanner, *Narrative,* 214–15.

15. Ibid., 215; M.S. by Lord Selkirk Relating to Red River, NAC, Selkirk Papers, Roll C-12, pp. 12778–12780; Pritchett, *The Red River Valley,* 194.

16. Tanner, *Narrative,* 216.

17. Ibid., 221; Bryce, "Sketch of the Life of John Tanner," 3.

18. Tanner, *Narrative,* 221–22. Selkirk's description of Tanner is quoted in Bryce, "Sketch of the Life of John Tanner," 3–4.

19. Tanner, *Narrative,* 221. Probably another factor influencing Tanner was that Therezia gave birth to another child around this time. This child, their fourth, died of measles in the fall of 1819 (Tanner, p. 252).

20. Ibid., 221–22.

21. Bryce, "Sketch of the Life of John Tanner," 3–4.

22. "Indian Captive Reclaimed," *The Weekly Recorder* 5, no. 27 (February 12, 1819), 215. See also the note on Edward Tanner in *Wisconsin Historical Collections* 8 (1879; reprint, 1908), 475.

CHAPTER 33. ROUGH JUSTICE

1. Tanner, *Narrative,* 226.
2. Ibid., 229–30; Hallowell, *The Ojibwa of Berens River, Manitoba,* 87–91.
3. Tanner, *Narrative,* 225–29.
4. Ibid., 230–31.
5. Ibid., 231–32.
6. Ibid., 232–33.
7. Ibid., 233.
8. Ibid., 233–34.
9. Ibid., 234.

CHAPTER 34. IN SEARCH OF KIN

1. Tanner, *Narrative,* 234–35; Myron Momvyk, "Charles Oakes Ermatinger," in *Dictionary of Canadian Biography Online* at www.biographi.ca <October 8, 2011>.
2. Tanner, *Narrative,* 235–36; Frank B. Woodford, *Lewis Cass: The Last Jeffersonian* (New Brunswick, NJ: Rutgers University Press, 1950), 116.

3. Tanner, *Narrative,* 236; "A Captive Found," *The Weekly Recorder* 5, no. 5 (August 2, 1818), 39.

4. William Carl Klunder, *Lewis Cass & the Politics of Moderation* (Kent, OH: Kent State University Press, 1996), 31–33; Francis Paul Prucha and Donald F. Carmony, "A Memorandum of Lewis Cass: Concerning A System for the Regulation of Indian Affairs," *Wisconsin Magazine of History* 52, no. 1 (Fall 1968), 35–50; Jay H. Buckley, *William Clark: Indian Diplomat* (Norman: University of Oklahoma Press, 2008), 116–23; Witgen, *An Infinity of Nations,* 338–44. Illinois gained statehood in December 1818 and was its own territory prior to statehood. Illinois governor Ninian Edwards was also involved in Indian policy, though not as much as Cass and Clark.

5. Tanner, *Narrative,* 236; "Abstract of expenditures by William Clark, Governor of Missouri Territory, as Superintendent of Indian Affairs, from 1st January to 31st December, 1820," *American State Papers: Indian Affairs,* 2:290. Emphasis added.

6. "Indian Captive Reclaimed," *The Weekly Recorder* 5, no. 27 (February 12, 1819), 215.

7. Tanner, *Narrative,* 241–43.

8. Ibid., 243–44.

9. Ibid., 247–48; "The Indian Captive Reclaimed," *The Philadelphia Register and National Recorder* 1, no. 7 (February 13, 1819), 127.

10. Tanner, *Narrative,* 248; "The Indian Captive Reclaimed," *The Philadelphia Register and National Recorder* 1, no. 7 (February 12, 1819), 127.

11. Tanner, *Narrative,* 248–49; "The Devil Worshipped," *The Latter Day Luminary* 1, no. 7 (May 1, 1819), 362; "Substance of the Minutes of the Board," *The Latter Day Luminary* 1, no. 8 (May 2, 1819), 379.

12. Tanner, *Narrative,* 248, 250; "The Indian Captive Reclaimed," *The Philadelphia Register and National Recorder* 1, no. 7 (February 12, 1819), 127.

13. Tanner, *Narrative,* 250.

14. Margaret Jacobs, *White Mother to a Dark Race: Settler Colonialism, Maternalism, and the Removal of Indigenous Children in the American West and Australia, 1880–1940* (Lincoln: University of Nebraska Press, 2009), 52–53. Also pertinent for Clark was the fact that he himself had adopted two mixed-blood children, the daughter and son of Sakakewea and Toussaint Charbonneau, following their mother's death in 1812.

15. Tanner, *Narrative,* 250.

CHAPTER 35. BETWEEN TWO WORLDS

1. Tanner, *Narrative,* 252.

2. Baird, "Reminiscences of Early Days on Mackinac Island," 50–51.

3. Susan Sleeper-Smith, "Women, Kin, and Catholicism: New Perspectives on the Fur Trade," in *Rethinking the Fur Trade,* 462–65.

4. Baird, "Reminiscences of Early Days on Mackinac Island," 51–52.

5. John Tanner to Martin Van Buren, November 10, 1837, reprinted in John T. Fierst, "Return to 'Civilization,' John Tanner's Troubled Years at Sault Ste. Marie," *Minnesota History* 50, no. 1 (Spring 1986), 25. Another record of Lucy Tanner, of her formal

baptism performed in Detroit on August 4, 1821, is printed in *Wisconsin Historical Collections* 19 (1910), 134.

6. Tanner, *Narrative,* 253.

7. Ibid., 253–54.

8. Ibid., 254–55.

9. Buckley, *William Clark,* 120.

10. Tanner, *Narrative,* 256–57; "Abstract of expenditures by William Clark," 2:290.

11. Tanner, *Narrative,* 257.

12. Carl O. Sauer, "Homestead and Community on the Middle Border," in *Land and Life: A Selection from the Writings of Carl Ortwin Sauer,* John Leighly, ed. (Berkeley: University of California Press, 1963), 33–34; Cardinal L. Goodwin, "Early Exploration and Settlement of Missouri and Arkansas," *Missouri Historical Review* 14 (April–July 1920), 400–401.

13. Tanner, *Narrative,* 257.

14. Ibid., 257–58. The scenario described here is an educated guess as to what actually happened. Tanner's *Narrative* states: "On the ensuing spring an attempt was made to recover something for my benefit from the estate of my father; but my stepmother sent several of the negroes, which it was thought might fall to me, to the island of Cuba, where they were sold. This business is yet unsettled, and remains in the hands of the lawyers."

15. Ibid., 259–61.

16. Baird, "Reminiscences of Early Days on Mackinac Island," 53.

17. Tanner, *Narrative,* 261–64.

CHAPTER 36. CHIEF FACTOR

1. Interview with Eloisa Harvey, June 20, 1878, OSHC, MSS 927, Box 2. Eloisa's mention of separate spheres is reinforced by a later description of Dr. and Mrs. McLoughlin in US House, *Report of Lieut. Neil M. Howison, United States Navy to the Commander of the Pacific Squadron,* House Misc. Rept. 29, 30th Cong., 1st sess., 1848, 12–13.

2. Morrison, *Outpost,* 343.

3. Simpson, "Character Book," 190. The character sketch was written in 1832.

4. John Nicks, "Orkneymen in the Hudson's Bay Company 1780–1821," in *Old Trails and New Directions: Papers of the Third North American Fur Trade Conference,* Carol M. Judd and Arthur J. Ray, eds. (Toronto: University of Toronto Press, 1980), 102–3; John McLoughlin, Lac La Pluie District Report for 1822–1823, HBCA B.105/e/2.

5. John McLoughlin, Lac La Pluie Post Journals for 1822–1823 and 1823–1824, HBCA, B.105/a/8 and 9; Lac La Pluie Account Books for 1821–1822, 1822–1823, and 1823–1824, HBCA, B.105/d/4–6.

6. John McLoughlin, Lac La Pluie District Report for 1822–1823, HBCA, B.105/e/2.

7. Harold Hickerson, "Land Tenure of the Rainy Lake Chippewa at the Beginning of the 19th Century," *Smithsonian Contributions to Anthropology* 2 (1967), 54; John Cameron, Lac La Pluie Post Journal for 1825–1826, HBCA, B.105/a/11 (entry for May 15, 1826); John McLoughlin, Lac La Pluie District Report for 1822–1823, HBCA, B.105/e/2.

8. John McLoughlin, Lac La Pluie Post Journal for 1822–1823, HBCA, B.105/a/8 (entry for October 7, 1822).

9. John McLoughlin, Lac La Pluie Post Journal for 1822–1823, HBCA, B.105/a/8 (entry for November 2, 1822).

10. White, "A Skilled Game of Exchange," 231; Peers, *The Ojibwa of Western Canada,* 34.

11. Ray and Freeman, *"Give Us Good Measure,"* 231–45.

12. John McLoughlin, Lac La Pluie Post Journal for 1822–1823, HBCA, B.105/a/8 (entry for November 2, 1822).

Chapter 37. Providence

1. Podruchny, *Making the Voyageur World,* 211–17.

2. Hickerson, "Land Tenure of the Rainy Lake Chippewa at the Beginning of the 19th Century," 50; John McLoughlin, Lac La Pluie District Report for 1822–1823, HBCA, B.105/e/2; John McLoughlin, Lac La Pluie Post Journal for 1822–1823, HBCA, B.105/a/8 (entries for September 23 and 30, 1822).

3. John McLoughlin, Lac La Pluie Post Journal for 1822–1823, HBCA, B.105/a/8.

4. John McLoughlin, Lac La Pluie Post Journal, HBCA, B.105/a/8 (entries for December 28, 1822, and January 4, 1823).

5. Mary Black-Rogers, "Varieties of 'Starving': Semantics and Survival in the Subarctic Fur Trade, 1750–1850," *Ethnohistory* 33, no. 4 (Fall 1986), 353–70.

6. John Cameron, Lac La Pluie Post Journal for 1825–1826, HBCA, B.105/a/11 (entry for May 13, 1826).

7. Calloway, *Crown and Calumet,* 167–68.

8. John McLoughlin, Lac La Pluie Post Journal for 1822–1823, HBCA, B105/a/8 (entry for September 15, 1822).

9. McLoughlin, "Description of the Indians from Fort William to Lake of the Woods," 10.

10. John McLoughlin, Lac La Pluie Post Journal for 1823–1824, HBCA, B.105/a/9 (entry for January 23, 1824); John McLoughlin, Lac La Pluie Post Journal for 1822–1823, HBCA, B.105/a/8 (entries for March 17, April 12, May 10, May 17, May 26, 1823).

Chapter 38. Opposing the Americans

1. Galbraith, "British-American Competition in the Border Fur Trade of the 1820s," 241–42; Simpson letter quoted in Lamb, ed., *McLoughlin's Fort Vancouver Letters,* xliv.

2. John McLoughlin, Lac La Pluie Post Journal for 1822–1823, HBCA, B.105/a/8 (entry for September 26, 1822).

3. John McLoughlin, Lac La Pluie District Report for 1822–1823, HBCA, B.105/e/2.

4. David Lavender, "Some American Characteristics of the American Fur Company," in *Aspects of the Fur Trade: Selected Papers of the 1965 North American Fur Trade Conference* (St. Paul: Minnesota Historical Society, 1967), 36–37.

5. Astor quoted in Galbraith, *The Hudson's Bay Company,* 53.

6. Arthur J. Ray, "Some Conservation Schemes of the Hudson's Bay Company,

1821–1850: An Examination of the Problems of Resource Management in the Fur Trade," *Journal of Historical Geography* 1 (1975), 50; R. Harvey Fleming, ed., *Minutes of Council Northern Department of Rupert Land, 1821–31* (Toronto: Champlain Society, 1940), 314–15; Galbraith, *The Hudson's Bay Company*, 54.

7. Galbraith, "British-American Competition in the Border Fur Trade of the 1820s," 245.

8. Quoted in Galbraith, "British-American Competition in the Border Fur Trade of the 1820s," 244.

9. John McLoughlin, Lac La Pluie District Report for 1822–1823, HBCA, B.105/e/2; John McLoughlin, Lac La Pluie Post Journal for 1822–1823, HBCA, B.105/a/8.

10. John McLoughlin, Lac La Pluie Post Journal for 1822–1823, HBCA, B.105/a/8 (entry for April 17, 1823).

11. John McLoughlin, Lac La Pluie District Report for 1822–1823, HBCA, B.105/e/3; John McLoughlin, Lac La Pluie Post Journal for 1823–1824, HBCA, B.105/a/9 (entry for September 15, 1823).

CHAPTER 39. WORKING FOR WAGES

1. John McLoughlin, Lac La Pluie Post Journal for 1822–1823, HBCA, B.105/a/8 (entry for October 5, 1822).

2. Tanner, *Narrative*, 261; Frederick Jackson Turner, *Character and Influence of the Indian Trade in Wisconsin: A Study of the Trading Post as an Institution* (Baltimore: Johns Hopkins Press, 1891), 64–65. Employing French Canadians was a touchy matter, because American traders had long sought legislation to bar the British from trading with Indians on US soil. Congress finally passed such a law in 1816, prohibiting all foreigners from engaging in the Indian trade. But traders in the Great Lakes region, particularly John Jacob Astor, found the measure too stringent, for it deprived them of the French Canadian labor pool. Largely at Astor's urging, the policy was relaxed to allow American companies to hire French Canadians as voyageurs and interpreters.

3. Tanner, *Narrative*, 261–62; Donald MacPherson, Lac La Pluie Post Journal for 1817–1818, HBCA, B.105/a/5 (entry for October 10, 1817); Roderick McKenzie, Lac La Pluie Post Journal for 1819–1820, HBCA, B.105/a/7 (entry for October 8, 1819); Podruchny, *Making the Voyageur World*, 238–39.

4. Tanner, *Narrative*, 262; Podruchny, *Making the Voyageur World*, 201–3, 220–25; *American State Papers: Indian Affairs*, 2:67; Gates, ed., *Five Fur Traders of the Northwest*, 144.

5. Tanner, *Narrative*, 262.

6. Ibid., 262–63.

7. Ibid., 263.

8. Ibid., 263–64. The quantity of furs may be off the mark. According to Tanner's account, he was directly involved in trading for 600 pounds of furs the first time and more than 1,200 pounds the second time, and these figures do not include furs traded at the post. John McLoughlin reported that Côté's outfit departed at the end of the season with just twelve packs weighing a little more than 1,000 pounds. John McLoughlin, Lac La Pluie District Report for 1822–1823, HBCA, B.105/e/2. How

McLoughlin came by his figure is not clear. The return for Rainy Lake House that year was closer to what Tanner indicated for his outfit.

9. Lewis Cass to Henry R. Schoolcraft, June 10, 1823, printed in *Wisconsin Historical Collections* 20 (1911), 306–7. Also see Cass's speeches and letters at 248–53.

10. Tanner, *Narrative,* 264.

11. Ibid., 264–65.

CHAPTER 40. CHILDREN OF THE FUR TRADE

1. Brown, *Strangers in Blood,* 177, 199–204; quotation on 200. See also Tina Loo, *Making Law, Order, and Authority in British Columbia, 1821–1871* (Toronto: University of Toronto Press, 1994).

2. John E. Foster, "Program for the Red River Mission: The Anglican Clergy 1820–1826," *Histoire Social/Social History* 2, no. 4 (November 1969), 49–50.

3. Foster, "Program for the Red River Mission," 62–68; J. R. Miller, *Skyscrapers Hide the Heavens: A History of Indian-White Relations in Canada* (Toronto: University of Toronto Press, 1989), 130–31.

4. West, *The Substance of a Journal,* 118–19.

5. Fleming, ed., *Minutes of Council Northern Department of Rupert Land, 1821–31,* 314–15.

6. Tanner, *Narrative,* 265. The quarrel between the factor and the governor was over the right of the settlers to trade furs. The colonists supplemented their meager farm produce by trading furs south of the border with the Americans. The factor insisted this was illegal and wanted the governor's assistance in stopping it. On the quarrel, see Robert S. Allen and Carol M. Judd, "Bulger, Andrew H.," in *Dictionary of Canadian Biography Online* at www.biographi.ca <October 25, 2011>. On the smuggling, see Pritchett, *The Red River Valley,* 250–71.

7. Tanner, *Narrative,* 265.

8. Keating, *Narrative,* 2:116; Tanner, *Narrative,* 265..

9. Tanner, *Narrative,* 203–4, 265–66.

10. Ibid., 266–67.

11. Ibid., 267.

12. Ibid., 267–68.

13. For a generalized depiction of Indians' changing racial attitudes in the late eighteenth and early nineteenth centuries, see Snyder, *Slavery in Indian Country,* 158–62.

CHAPTER 41. THE AMBUSH

1. John McLoughlin, Lac La Pluie Post Journal for 1823–1824, HBCA, B.105/a/9 (entry for April 26, 1824); John D. Cameron, Lac La Pluie Journal for 1825–1826, HBCA, B.105/a/11 (entry for October 2, 1825).

2. Bigsby, *The Shoe and the Canoe,* 2:266.

3. John McLoughlin, Lac La Pluie District Report for 1822–1823, HBCA, B.105/e/2; Hickerson, "Land Tenure of the Rainy Lake Chippewa at the Beginning of the 19th Century," 53–54.

4. John McLoughlin, Lac La Pluie District Report for 1822–1823, HBCA, B.105/e/2. For Wah-wish-e-gah-bo's debt, see Robert Logan, Lac La Pluie Account Book for 1818–1819, HBCA, B.105/d/1.

5. Tanner, *Narrative*, 268.

6. Ibid.; Delafield, *The Unfortified Boundary*, 421.

7. Tanner, *Narrative*, 268.

8. Ibid., 268–70.

9. Ibid., 270; Delafield, *The Unfortified Boundary*, 423.

10. Tanner, *Narrative*, 270–71.

11. Ibid., 271; Delafield, *The Unfortified Boundary*, 423.

12. Tanner, *Narrative*, 271–72.

13. Ibid., 272–74.

14. Ibid., 275; Reid, *Patterns of Vengeance*, 42–45.

15. Tanner, *Narrative*, 275.

CHAPTER 42. THE PARDON

1. Tanner, *Narrative*, 276.

2. Ibid., 275–76; Delafield, *The Unfortified Boundary*, 423.

3. Tanner, *Narrative*, 276.

4. Ibid.

5. Tanner, *Narrative*, 276–77; Delafield, *The Unfortified Boundary*, 424; Tom Thiessen research notes on Vincent Roy, Sr. shared with author, 1999; Christi Corbin, personal communication with author, August 15, 2004; Wayne A. Jones, personal communication with author, August 16, 2004; Wayne A. Jones, "Keeping Up with the Joneses" (2011) at http://wc.rootsweb.ancestry.com/cgi-bin/igm.cgi?op=AHN& <November 3, 2011>.

6. Tanner, *Narrative*, 277.

CHAPTER 43. "WE MET WITH AN AMERICAN"

1. Long, *The Northern Expeditions of Stephen H. Long*, 213–14.

2. Tanner, *Narrative*, 277.

3. The relationship between captivity and rights of citizenship were hotly debated in two other important contexts in Long's day: impressment by the British navy and hostage-taking by the Barbary pirates. See Lawrence A. Peskin, *Captives and Countrymen: Barbary Slavery and the American Public, 1785–1816* (Baltimore: Johns Hopkins University Press, 2009).

4. Long, *The Northern Expeditions of Stephen H. Long*, 215; Keating, *Narrative*, 2:115; Tanner, *Narrative*, 277; John McLoughlin, Lac La Pluie Post Journal, September 1, 1823, HBCA, B. 105/a/9, 1. For additional perspective on sexual relations between voyageurs and native women in the trading posts, see Podruchny, *Making the Voyageur World*, 260–67.

5. Long, *The Northern Expeditions of Stephen H. Long*, 215.

6. Ibid., 216; Keating, *Narrative*, 2:115–16. As the chief factor was willing to make

this offer without ever having met the teenage girls for himself, it would seem almost certain that Marguerite McLoughlin was behind it, and that she was the kindly mixed-blood woman in the fort whom the girls had gotten their father's permission to go see shortly before they ran away.

7. Long, *The Northern Expeditions of Stephen H. Long,* 216–17; Keating, *Narrative,* 2:117.

8. Long, *The Northern Expeditions of Stephen H. Long,* 217; Keating, *Narrative,* 2:116, 123.

Chapter 44. The Onus of Revenge

1. John McLoughlin, Lac La Pluie Post Journal for 1823–1824, HBCA, B.105/a/9 (entry for September 1, 1823); Tanner, *Narrative,* 204–5, 245.

2. Long, *The Northern Expeditions of Stephen H. Long,* 215.

3. John McLoughlin, Lac La Pluie Post Journal for 1823–1824, HBCA, B.105/a/9 (entry for September 1, 1823).

4. John Phillip Reid, "Restraints on Vengeance: Retaliation-in-Kind and the Use of Indian Law in the Old Oregon Country," *Oregon Historical Quarterly* 95, no. 1 (Spring 1994), 49–52.

5. The best evidence of this is found in McLoughlin's response to the slaying of one company officer and four employees in Oregon in 1825. McLoughlin sent an expedition to retaliate, and the result was one Indian killed and two villages burned. Justifying the expedition beforehand, he wrote, "To pass over such an outrage would lower us in the opinion of the Indians, induce them to act in the same way, and when the opportunity offered kill any of our people, & when it is considered the Natives are at least an hundred Men to one of us it will be conceived how absolutely necessary it is for our personal security that we should be respected by them, & nothing could make us more contemptible in their eyes than allowing such a cold blooded assassination of our People to pass unpunished." Justifying it after the fact, he wrote, "It is certainly most unfortunate to be obliged to have recourse to hostile measures against our fellow beings but it is a duty we owed our murdered Countrymen & I may say we were forced by necessity, as had we passed over the atrocious conduct of their murderers, others by seeing them unpunished would have imitated their example." John McLoughlin, *The Letters of John McLoughlin from Fort Vancouver to the Governor and Committee,* E. E. Rich, ed. (London: The Champlain Society for the Hudson's Bay Record Society, 1941), 57–58, 65.

6. Quoted in Morrison, *Outpost,* 174–75.

7. McLoughlin, "Description of the Indians from Fort William to Lake of the Woods," 15.

8. Jane Lewis Chapin, ed., "Letters of Dr. John McLoughlin," *Oregon Historical Quarterly* 37, no. 1 (March 1936), 255.

9. Reid, "Restraints on Vengeance," 50.

10. Keating, *Narrative,* 2:115–16; Tanner, *Narrative,* 278; John McLoughlin, Lac La Pluie Post Journal for 1823–1824, HBCA, B.105/a/9 (entries for September 4 and 8, 1823).

11. John McLoughlin, Lac La Pluie Post Journal for 1823–1824, HBCA, B.105/a/9 (entry for September 4, 1823); Tanner, *Narrative,* 278.

12. John McLoughlin, Lac La Pluie Post Journal for 1823–1824, HBCA, B.105/a/9 (entry for October 2, 1823).

13. Tanner, *Narrative,* 279.

14. John McLoughlin, Lac La Pluie Post Journal for 1823–1824, HBCA, B.105/a/9 (entry for October 5, 1823); Tanner, *Narrative,* 279.

CHAPTER 45. JOURNEYS HOME

1. Livingston, *Portraits of Eminent Americans,* 487–88; Long, *The Northern Expeditions of Stephen H. Long,* 229.

2. Livingston, *Portraits of Eminent Americans,* 487–88; "Major Long's Expedition," *Daily National Intelligencer,* November 3, 1823.

3. Keating, *Narrative,* 2:238–39.

4. Ibid., 240–41.

5. Ibid., 123.

6. Ibid., 122–23.

7. Long, *The Northern Expeditions of Stephen H. Long,* 219.

8. Tanner, *Narrative,* 279; John McLoughlin, Lac La Pluie Post Journal for 1823–1824, HBCA, B.105/a/9 (entries for November 8, 10, 22, and 27).

9. John McLoughlin, Lac La Pluie Post Journal for 1823–1824, HBCA, B.105/a/9.

10. Tanner, *Narrative,* 279.

11. John McLoughlin, Lac La Pluie District Report for 1823–1824, HBCA B.105/e/3.

12. Interview with Eloisa Harvey, June 20, 1878, OSHC, MSS 927, Box 2.

13. Elliott, "Marguerite Wadin McKay McLoughlin," 339; Morrison, *Outpost,* 121–22.

14. Tanner, *Narrative,* 279–80.

EPILOGUE

1. Edwin O. Wood, ed., *Historic Mackinac: The Historical, Picturesque and Legendary Features of the Mackinac Country* (New York: The MacMillan Company, 1918), 2:59, 67, 137, 142, 144.

2. Elizabeth Thérèse Baird, "Indian Customs and Early Recollections," *Wisconsin Historical Collections* 9 (1882; reprint, 1909), 316–17.

3. Gurdon S. Hubbard, "Journey of Gurdon S. Hubbard," *Michigan Pioneer Historical Collections* 3 (1881), 125.

4. Quoted in Keith R. Widder, *Battle for the Soul: Métis Children Encounter Evangelical Protestants at Mackinaw Mission, 1823–1837* (East Lansing: Michigan State University Press, 1999), 49, 54.

5. Widder, *Battle for the Soul,* 56.

6. Baird, "Reminiscences of Early Days on Mackinac Island," 53; Jean B. Russo and J. Elliott Russo, "Responsive Justices: Court Treatment of Orphans and Illegitimate Children in Colonial Maryland," in Ruth Wallis Herndon and John E. Murray, eds.,

Children Bound to Labor: The Pauper Apprentice System in Early America (Ithaca, NY: Cornell University Press, 2009), 154–58.

7. Tanner, *Narrative*, 280; John E. McDowell, "Therese Schindler of Mackinac: Upward Mobility in the Great Lakes Fur Trade," *Wisconsin Magazine of History* 61, no. 2 (Winter 1977–78), 137. Possibly the French Canadians in Mackinac had some influence in this case. In Quebec, single mothers who were too poor to care for their children would take it upon themselves to bind them to another family, employing a notary public to draw up an indenture. Gillian Hamilton, "The Stateless and the Orphaned among Montreal's Apprentices, 1791–1842," in Herndon and Murray, eds., *Children Bound to Labor*, 166.

8. John Tanner to Henry Rowe Schoolcraft, July 21, 1824, quoted in Maxine Benson, "Schoolcraft, James, and the 'White Indian,'" *Michigan History* 54, no. 4 (1970), 314. See also Maxine Benson, "Edwin James: Scientist, Linguist, Humanitarian" (Phd dissertation, University of Colorado, 1968), 245.

9. George Boyd to Lewis Cass, August 23, 1824, in "Fur-Trade in Wisconsin," *Wisconsin Historical Collections* 20 (1911), 345; Richard B. Bremer, *Indian Agent and Wilderness Scholar: The Life of Henry Rowe Schoolcraft* (Mount Pleasant, MI: Clarke Historical Library, Central Michigan University, 1987), 55–56; Widder, *Battle for the Soul*, 59.

10. Edwin James, "Introductory Chapter," in Tanner, *Narrative*, xvii.

11. Governor Cass to Henry R. Schoolcraft, October 18, 1830, in *Territorial Papers of the United States* 12, *Territory of Michigan 1829–1837*, Clarence Edward Carter, comp. and ed. (Washington: Government Printing Office, 1945), 210.

12. Judge Joseph H. Steere, "Sketch of John Tanner, Known as the 'White Indian,'" *Michigan Pioneer and Historical Collections* 22 (1894), 247; James V. Campbell, *Outlines of the Political History of Michigan* (Detroit: Schober & Co., 1876), 415.

13. Fierst, "Return to 'Civilization': John Tanner's Troubled Years at Sault Ste. Marie," 26–30.

14. Keith R. Widder, "The Persistence of French-Canadian Ways at Mackinac after 1760," *Proceedings of the Meeting of the French Colonial Historical Society* 16 (1990), 52; Baird, "Reminiscences of Early Days on Mackinac Island," 46; "Sketch of the Life of Hon. Robert Stuart," *Michigan Pioneer and Historical Collections* 3 (1881), 58–59.

15. Baird, "Reminiscences of Early Days on Mackinac Island," 53.

16. Benson, "Schoolcraft, James, and the 'White Indian,'" 324; Tanner, *Narrative*, 161–62.

17. Henry R. Schoolcraft, "Sketches from Schoolcraft's Diary at Mackinac— 1835–1841," in Wood, *Historic Mackinac*, 2:235.

18. Angie Bingham Gilbert, "The Story of John Tanner," *Michigan Pioneer and Historical Collections* 38 (1912), 198.

19. Fierst, "Return to 'Civilization': John Tanner's Troubled Years at Sault Ste. Marie," 34–35.

20. Gilbert, "The Story of John Tanner," 197; "Sketch of the Life of the Rev. Abel

Bingham," *Michigan Pioneer and Historical Collections* 2 (1880), 155; Fierst, "Return to 'Civilization': John Tanner's Troubled Years at Sault Ste. Marie," 34–35.

21. John Tanner to Martin Van Buren, November 10, 1837, reprinted in Fierst, "Return to 'Civilization': John Tanner's Troubled Years at Sault Ste. Marie," 25.

22. P. G. Downes, "John Tanner: Captive of the Wilderness," *Naturalist* 9 (Fall 1958), 32.

23. Gilbert, "The Story of John Tanner," 197–99.

24. Ibid.

25. Quoted in Benson, "Schoolcraft, James, and the 'White Indian,'" 324.

26. Schoolcraft, "Sketches from Schoolcraft's Diary," 234.

27. Gilbert, "The Story of John Tanner," 200.

28. Ibid. Fierst explores another possible motive for Tanner to kill James Schoolcraft. During his years of declining employment with the Sault Ste. Marie Agency, Tanner faced financial problems and incurred debts to James Schoolcraft. Tanner tried to recover back pay from the federal government and was finally denied. The paper trail may exaggerate Tanner's attention to his financial woes. The breakup of his family mattered most to him, and those he thought responsible for it were his worst enemies. Local tradition held that he was often heard to say "as Henry R. was beyond his reach, James, the next of kin, must die in his stead." If he did not actually make that threat, it would seem likely that that was his sentiment. "Sketch of the Life of the Rev. Abel Bingham," 155.

29. Steere, "Sketch of John Tanner," 248–50; Gilbert, "The Story of John Tanner," 200; Benson, "Schoolcraft, James, and the 'White Indian,'" 326.

30. Steere, "Sketch of John Tanner," 250; William Cullen Bryant, "Letters of a Traveller," in Edwin O. Wood, ed., *Historic Mackinac,* 2:395; Benson, "Schoolcraft, James, and the 'White Indian,'" 325. Steere relates that a skeleton was discovered near the village many years later that some thought was Tanner's remains. Fierst notes that Tanner was in poor health in 1846 and would have been hard put to return to the north country. Benson speculates that if Tilden shot Schoolcraft and wanted Tanner to be blamed for the murder, then he may have found and killed Tanner during the manhunt. Some sources say Tilden eagerly volunteered to lead the manhunt. All sources agree that there is no conclusive evidence who killed Schoolcraft or what finally happened to Tanner.

31. John McLoughlin, "Autobiography," in S. A. Clarke, *Pioneer Days of Oregon Country* (Portland: J. K. Gill Company, 1905), 215–17; Morrison, *Outpost,* 174–75.

32. John McLoughlin to Edward Ermatinger, February 1, 1836, in T. C. Elliott, ed., "Letters of Dr. John McLoughlin," *Oregon Historical Quarterly* 23, no. 4 (December 1922), 368; Gay, *Life and Letters of Mrs. Jason Lee,* 16; McLoughlin, "Autobiography," 220.

33. John McLoughlin to Alexander H. H. Stuart, July 15, 1851, in Barker, *The McLoughlin Empire and its Rulers,* 330–33; McLoughlin, "Autobiography," 217.

34. Jackson, *Children of the Fur Trade,* 62–63, 183; Barker, *The McLoughlin Empire and its Rulers,* 329; Morrison, *Outpost,* 278, 465.

35. Jackson, *Children of the Fur Trade,* 230; Barker, *The McLoughlin Empire and its Rulers,* 107–25; Morrison, *Outpost,* 221–27, 278–83, 339–49, 435, 465.

36. Simon Fraser to John McLoughlin, January 12, 1836, in Barker, *The McLoughlin Empire and its Rulers,* 218–20.

37. Barker, *The McLoughlin Empire and its Rulers,* 178, 190–91; Morrison, *Outpost,* 221–27, 279–83, 339–49; John McLoughlin to John McLeod, March 1, 1833, in Mrs. Eva Emery Dye, ed., "Documents," *Washington Historical Quarterly* 2, no. 2 (January 1908), 166–68; John McLoughlin to Edward Ermatinger, February 1, 1836, in T. C. Elliott, ed., "Letters of Dr. McLoughlin to Edward Ermatinger," *Oregon Historical Quarterly* 23 (December 1922), 365–71.

38. Carlos Arnaldo Schwantes, *The Pacific Northwest: An Interpretive History* (rev. ed., Lincoln: University of Nebraska Press, 1996), 144.

39. Jackson, *Children of the Fur Trade,* 222–23; Schwantes, *The Pacific Northwest,* 114, 153.

40. Galbraith, *The Hudson's Bay Company,* 226–27.

41. Morrison, *Outpost,* 460–61.

42. Hubert Howe Bancroft, *History of Oregon,* Vol. 2 (San Francisco: History Company, Publishers, 1888), 130–31. In 1862, the state sold the land to the heirs for a nominal sum.

43. Frank N. Schubert, ed., *The Nation Builders: A Sesquicentennial History of the Corps of Topographical Engineers, 1838–1863* (Fort Belvoir, VA: Office of History, United States Army Corps of Engineers, 1988), 9–18, 23–26; Forest G. Hill, *Roads, Rails and Waterways. The Army Engineers and Early Transportation* (Norman: University of Oklahoma Press, 1957), 220.

44. Long's keen interest in the changing mission of the Topographical Engineers is evidenced in his correspondence with Isaac Roberdeau, April 16, 1822, September 9, 1822, and March 28, 1823, NA, RG 77, Entry 306, Box 1. See also Schubert, ed., *The Nation Builders,* 8–9. Long's support of Clay for president is disclosed in his September 9, 1822, letter to Roberdeau, as well as his naming of his second son, Henry Clay Long.

45. Long had little to say about Indian relocation in the 1830s. The governor of the state of Georgia once asked his opinion about possible resistance by the Cherokees to forced relocation. Long replied that he thought the Cherokees would submit without a struggle but if any should resist then resistance must be met with "firmness and severity tempered as much as possible with humanity, otherwise a spirit of desperation will likely be engendered in the minds of the Indians and they will be stimulated to sell their lives as dearly as possible." Quoted in Wood, *Stephen Harriman Long,* 197.

46. Livingston, *Portraits of Eminent Americans,* 478–79.

47. The five-acre lot is described in Long's will, a copy of which is filed with Military Bounty Land Warrant 276 120/55, NA, RG 49—Records of the General Land Office. The sale price is reported in Norman L. Freeman, reporter, *Reports of Cases at Law and in Chancery Argued and Determined in the Supreme Court of Illinois,* vol. 117 (Springfield, IL: Printed for the Reporter, 1887), 309, and it is consistent with Chicago land values at the time of sale as described in Homer Hoyt, *One Hundred Years of Land*

Values in Chicago: The Relationship of the Growth of Chicago to the Rise of its Land Values, 1830–1933 (Washington: Beard Books, 1933), 108. Long's estate included $40,000 for the Chicago property and about $48,000 for his home and property in Alton, Illinois. The top 1 percent in Illinois in 1870 had property wealth of $50,000 or greater, according to Frank Manzo IV, "The History of Economic Inequality in Illinois, 1850–2014," March 2016, at Illinois.epi.org/countrysideonprofit/wp-content/uploads/2013/10/ The-History-of-Economic-Inequality-in-Illinois-FINAL.pdf <October 11, 2016>.

48. The circumstances of Long's children and grandchildren living with him in Alton are explained in relation to a suit brought by his heirs over his estate, as reported in Freeman, *Reports of Cases at Law*, vol. 117, 306–9.

49. Harvey Reid, *Biographical Sketch of Enoch Long, an Illinois Pioneer* (Chicago: Historical Society's Collection, 1884), 87–105; Wood, *Stephen Harriman Long*, 251.

50. "Seventh Debate: Alton, Illinois," at www.nps.gov/liho/learn/historyculture/ debate7.htm <June 14, 2016>; "Alton, Madison County, October 15, 1858," at www.mr lincolnandfreedom.org <June 14, 2016>.

51. Wood, *Stephen Harriman Long*, 250–63; Schubert, ed., *The Nation Builders*, 75–76.

Postscript

1. Louise Erdrich, "Introduction," in *The Falcon: A Narrative of the Captivity and Adventures of John Tanner* (New York: Penguin Group, 1994), xi.

2. Amplifying Coues, ethnohistorian Harold Hickerson included a short chapter on the "Tanner-Henry data" in his book, *The Chippewa and Their Neighbors*.

3. Tanner, *Narrative*, 252.

4. The most important source on Tanner's family besides Tanner himself is Baird, "Reminiscences of Early Days on Mackinac Island," 17–55. Although some of Baird's statements about Tanner's family are in error, she is a reliable source on one point: on August 4, 1820, Tanner placed his wife and their newborn daughter, Lucy, in the temporary care of Baird's grandmother at Mackinac after which Tanner proceeded on his journey with his other three small children from this marriage. I have estimated the years of Tanner's two marriages and ten children's births as follows (references in parentheses): first marriage in 1804 (Tanner, *Narrative*, 103); first child, boy, in 1805 (Tanner, 203, 267, 280); second child, girl, in 1807 or 1808 (Tanner, 151, 269, 277, and Keating, *Narrative*, 2:116); third child, girl, in 1809 (Tanner, 277, Keating, 2:116); second marriage in 1809 or 1810 (Tanner, 252); fourth child, Martha, in 1812 (Tanner, 257); fifth child, Mary, in 1813 (Tanner, 207); sixth child in 1814 (Tanner, 207); seventh child in 1817 or 1818 (Tanner, 252); eighth child, Lucy, in 1820 (Baird, 52); ninth child, James, in 1822 or 1823 (Baird, 53); tenth and eleventh children in the mid-1820s (Baird, 53), and twelfth child in 1832. The sixth and seventh children died around 1819–20. Delafield (*The Unfortified Boundary*) confirms that Tanner had six living children when he went to work for the American Fur Company in 1822 (423n). See also John T. Fierst, "Return to 'Civilization': John Tanner's Troubled Years at Sault Ste. Marie," 27.

5. Coues, *New Light on the Early History of the Great Northwest*, 262–63.

6. Noel M. Loomis, "Introduction," in Tanner, *Narrative,* xii; "The Northwestern Indians, Communicated to Congress on the 9th of December, 1790," *American State Papers: Indian Affairs,* 1:89.

7. Tanner, *Narrative,* 157.

8. Loomis, "Introduction," in Tanner, *Narrative,* xix.

9. L. H. Pammel, "Dr. Edwin James," *Annals of Iowa* 8, no. 3 (October 1907), 179–81; Rotella, "Travels in a Subjective West," 25–29.

10. Benson, "Schoolcraft, James, and the 'White Indian,'" 316.

11. Loomis, "Introduction," in Tanner, *Narrative,* xviii.

12. Fierst, "Strange Eloquence," 229. Also see Kyhl Lyndgaard, "Landscapes of Removal and Resistance: Edwin James's Nineteenth-Century Cross-Cultural Collaborations," *Great Plains Quarterly* 30 (Winter 2010), 37–46. Their collaborative translation of the New Testament was published as *Kekitchemanitomenahn Gahbemah-jeinnunk Jesus Christ, Otoashke Wawweendummahgawin* (Albany, NY: Packard & Van Benthuysen, 1833) without attribution to the translators. However, the British and Foreign Bible Society catalogued the work as "The earliest complete N.T. in Chippewa; translated by Edwin James, assisted by John Tanner."

13. See also the report on John Tanner making his way to New York with his manuscript in the *Daily National Journal,* August 14, 1828.

14. "Art. V.—*A Narrative of the Captivity and Adventures of John Tanner,*" *American Quarterly Review,* 8, no. 15 (September 1, 1830), 108. Further evidence that Tanner met with Carey and Lea is found in "John Tanner," *Christian Watchman,* August 22, 1828, which reports that Tanner was passing through Detroit with the manuscript and hoped to find a publisher in Philadelphia or New York. For the modern view of John Dunn Hunter, see Richard Drinnon, *White Savage: The Case of John Dunn Hunter* (New York: Shocken Books, 1972).

15. "The Booksellers' Trade Sales," *American Publishers' Circular and Literary Gazette,* September 26, 1857.

16. Fierst, "Strange Eloquence," 227.

17. Ibid., 227–28.

INDEX